RAPE

Offenders and Their Victims

By the Same Author

The Murderer and His Victim
Homicidal Threats
Psychiatry and the Criminal

RAPE

Offenders and Their Victims

Third Printing

By

JOHN M. MACDONALD, M.D.

Professor of Psychiatry
University of Colorado School of Medicine
Director of Forensic Psychiatry
University of Colorado Medical Center
Psychiatrist to the District Courts of Colorado

CHARLES C THOMAS • PUBLISHER
Springfield • Illinois • U.S.A.

Published and Distributed Throughout the World by
CHARLES C THOMAS • PUBLISHER
Bannerstone House
301-327 East Lawrence Avenue, Springfield, Illinois, U.S.A.

©*1971, by* CHARLES C THOMAS • PUBLISHER
ISBN 0-398-01181-8
Library of Congress Catalog Card Number: 72-143749

First Printing, 1971
Second Printing, 1975
Third Printing, 1979

With THOMAS BOOKS careful attention is given to all details of manufacturing and design. It is the Publisher's desire to present books that are satisfactory as to their physical qualities and artistic possibilities and appropriate for their particular use. THOMAS BOOKS will be true to those laws of quality that assure a good name and good will.

Printed in the United States of America
N-1

PREFACE

T HIS is no armchair theoretical or philosophical study of rape. It was written in police cars, in the detective bureau of a city police department, in the interviewing rooms of a county jail and a state penitentiary, in the maximum security wards of university and state mental hospitals, in the emergency room of a general hospital and in the homes of the victims. Physicians, psychologists, nurses, prison guards, police officers, judges and lawyers have contributed to these pages.

Above all, the rapists and their victims have had their say. Their accounts of the rapes have been quoted extensively, with minimal editing to protect their identity, to avoid undue repetition and to eliminate particularly gruesome details. Rape, like murder, is an unpleasant subject which both fascinates and repels the reader. Unlike murder, it has been curiously neglected by criminologists, psychiatrists and psychologists.

The aim of this book is to throw some light on this crime, the offenders and their victims. A glance at the table of contents will show the range of inquiry. The general reader will pass over the statistics, tiresome yet of interest to the specialist who wishes to know the incidence, location and times of rape as well as the ages, race and criminal records of the participants. If the book arouses greater awareness of the need for preventive action, it will have served a useful purpose.

Denver, Colorado   JOHN M. MACDONALD

ACKNOWLEDGMENTS

Many rapists and their victims, police officers, physicians, judges, lawyers and nurses contributed to this study. The responsibility for the contents of this book is, however, solely my own. The advice of Doctors Bernard W. Murphy, Edgar L. Makowski, Horace Thompson and Thomas L. Canfield; attorneys Rex Scott, James D. Urso, John Bottomly and Joseph R. Quinn, is gratefully acknowledged. Mr. Quinn reviewed the chapter on legal aspects of rape and made useful suggestions.

Denver Police Chief George L. Seaton permitted me to do research in his department. Division Chief Lloyd J. Jamerson, Captain Arthur G. Dill, Leiutenants Paul Montoya and Don Brannan of the Investigative Division, as well as Captain C. Y. Hanson, Lieutenants Donald L. McKelvy and Thomas C. Lahey have been most helpful.

In particular I would like to thank the detectives on the sex detail at the time of this study. Detectives Charles B. Jackson, Henry E. Potter, Robert E. Scherwitz, Louis Shain, Jr. and John E. Moritzsky went out of their way to help me. I have a very high regard for the skill and sensitivity which they showed in talking to offenders, victims and their families. The dedication of this book to Detective Potter is an inadequate expression of my appreciation of his friendship and assistance.

Wayne K. Patterson, Warden of the Colorado State Penitentiary, gave permission for psychiatric examination of convicted rape offenders. Miss Margaret D. Lewis, Executive Director of the Denver Visiting Nurse Service, arranged for me to make home visits to rape victims with members of her staff. Mrs. Berniece Hindmarsh, Mrs. Edith Throckmorton and Miss Alice C. Joyce, as well as Mr. Robert M. Braude of the University of Colorado Medical Center Library provided much useful advice and also help in obtaining rare books from libraries throughout the United States. Mrs. Patricia Ott, Miss Carolyn Miller and Mrs. Kathleen Hunt of the Colorado Psychiatric Hospital assisted in this study.

Many foreign physicians provided information and statistics on rape in their countries. It was not possible to include all their material, but I do appreciate the courtesy of Doctors Laurie K. Gluckman, C. L. Wong, Cecilie Hoigard, Eustace A. Liberakis, T. Asuni, Lidia Uskiewicz, Jordan H. Lackman, L. P. Varma, Raihana R. Beg, Martti Paloheimo; Professors O. Nakata, Orhan M. Ozturk and Nikola Schipowensky.

My thanks are due to many authors and publishers who have permitted reproduction of material. Permission to quote at length is greatly appreciated. For copyright purposes, the source of quotation has been listed, unless otherwise requested, under author, title and publisher in the references at the end of the book.

Preparation of the manuscript has been lightened by the able secretarial assistance of Miss Elaine Steffen to whom I owe a special debt for her patience and skill.

J.M.M.

CONTENTS

RAPE

Offenders and Their Victims

Chapter 1

THE SCOPE OF RAPE

*"A noted defense attorney in the trial of
rape, would twist a coke bottle on the table
and demonstrate to the jury his difficulty in
forcing a pencil into the bottle."*
— Anonymous

*"Any lawyer who says there's no such thing as rape
should be hauled out to a public place by three
large perverts and buggered at high noon, with
all his clients watching."*
— Hunter S. Thompson, *Hell's Angels*

SUFFERING, it has been said, is in the eye of the observer, and not in the heart of the sufferer. Newspaper accounts of rape almost invariably arouse great compassion in the reader, although they seldom convey a full picture of the event. The scope of rape covers a spectrum which, if fully revealed to the reader, would provoke a wide range of responses depending on the facts of the offense. Some women by their reckless behavior tempt fate and the consequences may be bitter or of slight significance and soon forgotten in the rush of life. Other women, innocent of sexual provocation and otherwise circumspect in their behavior, suffer more than the physical burden of venereal disease, pregnancy or serious physical injury.

A dispassionate approach to the problem of rape is not easily obtained; slight acquaintance is not sufficient; prolonged acquaintance breeds a complex mixture of compassion, skepticism and cynicism. The sex detail detective, like the surgeon, should acquire a certain detachment neither experiencing unfeeling indifference nor becoming so emotionally involved that his personal life is affected and his judgment impaired.

For the reader unfamiliar with rape, this chapter provides an introduction which has been written by the victims themselves. All these women have complained to the police of rape, although not all have suffered rape as it is defined in the legal statutes. This is the stuff of police blotters and of those unrevealing notices in the newspapers. "A young woman in Colorado Springs was assaulted and raped last night in her apartment." These accounts were written within a few hours or days of the event. Fictitious names have been substituted and information which might lead to identification has been deleted.

Cases were selected to illustrate some of the many aspects of the hodgepodge of rape. There are no editorial comments and the reader must draw his own conclusions as he reads the lines, and between the lines. It is difficult for a writer to avoid revealing himself, and these women in describing their assailants and the assaults sometimes write their own signatures before reaching the end of their narratives.

WHITE GIRLS IN A NEGRO GHETTO

Two attractive young white college girls following an argument with their roommates visited a nightclub in a Negro neighborhood and then went to a cafe in the early hours of the morning for coffee. The area had a high crime rate particularly for homicide, aggravated assault and rape. Few white people, usually local residents and police, are seen in the area at night. Police officers do not patrol alone in this area but always work in pairs. The girls gave the following account of the rape:

Helen: Joan and I were together that evening having coffee at the Five Points Cafe at approximately 3 A.M. We were having trouble with our roommates and we were both feeling low but not at all like sleeping. We sat together at a booth. A young man had asked if he might have a cup of coffee at our table and we had been discussing our problem with our girl friends with him for close to an hour. A few minutes before we left a young Negro asked if he might also share our booth for a cup of coffee. We said that we were leaving shortly and that he was welcome to sit down.

He introduced himself by name — Johnny something. I don't remember his last name. He seemed very nice. He had a young face and warm smile. We had change on the table and asked what the price of coffee was. At this time Johnny said, "Please let me buy your coffee.' We thanked him, said it had been nice meeting him and started to leave.

At the door the young Negro man who had joined us (Johnny) came up and asked if we might by any chance be going east and if so could we give him a lift to Twenty-ninth and Vine. Although we had only met him briefly, he seemed a nice enough person and it was late. We said yes, and he walked with us the third of a block to my car. As we were climbing into the car, a second Negro man walked up and called to Johnny. He was tall, neat and well dressed.

I think he is the same man who sat next to me at the nightclub when Joan and I stopped there for a drink earlier, but I can't make a positive identification, as I did not pay any attention to the person sitting next to me at that time. At any rate, as he approached he looked vaguely familiar and it appeared that he was a friend of Johnny's. Johnny said, "He needs a ride, too, would you mind dropping him off at the same time?"

We agreed and the second man (whose name was Chester) got in the back seat left side. On the way over to Twenty-ninth and Vine the four of us talked and both men seemed nice and proper. Johnny spoke of his stereo and music, saying both were very good. When we arrived, Johnny asked if we would like to come in for a cup of coffee or some beer and to listen to a little music before we went home.

It now seems such a totally stupid thing that we accepted, but both Joan and I were still upset and the whole thing started because we wanted to divert our attention from thoughts of the argument with our girl friends. We entered the apartment after having locked my car and Joan and I sat together on the left end of the couch. We talked for a while and played music. Joan and I shared a beer, and the two men were drinking wine.

Johnny asked me about my job and I started telling him about it, when he placed his hand on the back of my neck and said that I should be making a lot more money and he could show me how to do it. I became very nervous then and told him I wasn't the least interested in any other job, and I would very much appreciate it if he would forget he ever said such a thing and change the subject. I also moved his hand from the back of my neck and put it on the back of the couch and said that if he had somehow got the impression that I was interested in him in a personal way he was wrong and not to touch me again.

At this time his eyes got mean and he had begun to appear more intoxicated. He frowned at me and got up, walked around to the other end of the couch and sat on its arm next to Joan. I heard him ask her if he could talk to her privately and she said, "What do you want? You can say anything in front of Helen." I had gathered my handbag up off the floor and was just starting to stand up and say that we were leaving when he grabbed Joan by the hand and yanked her to her feet.

I didn't want to start a scene and thought that Joan could handle it verbally, so I waited. The room was large and divided by a drape in the middle. He pulled Joan through this drape and I could hear her say, "What is it? What do you want?" Then I heard more talking but the words were muffled and I couldn't understand. Approximately two minutes passed and then Joan shouted, "Helen, help me!"

I jumped up and parted the curtain. The light was on and he had Joan pinned on her back on the bed. I said, "Leave her alone, we are going to leave now." Just as I said that the other man (Chester) jumped on me from behind and threw me towards the couch. As he was doing this he said to Johnny, "Just do your thing, brother, and I'll take care of this one." Then he jumped on top of me on the couch and said, "Don't fight me, understand? You're not getting out of here until I get what I want, so you might as well accept it and enjoy it."

He said a lot of other things too like "I'm good, baby, you can't get out, don't fight," etc., etc. over and over again. All this while I was saying, "You can't make me, there isn't any way that you can make me, you have no right, no right," etc., etc. Then he told me to sit up and he grabbed my neck and pulled it down and unzipped my dress saying, "I'll get it off one way or another." Then he pushed me down on my back on the couch and grabbed my dress at the shoulders and pulled it, my half-slip and my pants off in one sweep.

I had nothing on except my bra and really panicked then. I started screaming at the top of my lungs and managed to get at least four or five terribly loud screams before he got his hands on my throat. Johnny was shouting from the other room, "Shut her up or I'll knock her around like she'll never forget" etc. Joan begged him to let her talk to me because she knew I was becoming hysterical.

He (Johnny) yanked her off the bed and into the living room all the while holding on to her. She knelt beside me and tried to comfort me saying, "Helen, if you don't stop screaming, we'll never get out of here." Her lip was split and I could see that she was hurt and crying. I felt so terribly trapped and hurt that I began crying and couldn't stop. The more I sobbed the more he shook me and struck me around my head.

Then he must have realized that I might get completely crazy hysterical because he started saying, "Sh sh" and "Stop fighting and let me in and we'll let you go soon." So I put my mind somewhere else and went blank. I just laid there and wouldn't move. He finally entered me and I just closed my eyes and laid perfectly still and cried to myself. He kept shaking me all the while and saying, "Move, damn you, move — kiss me back you bitch — help me, help me," etc.

I shouted at him that I wouldn't do anything and that he was a coward and that he was crazy. I kept begging him to stop. Finally he got fed up with my lack of response and got off of me, yanked me to my feet and threw me on the bed beside Joan and Johnny. She was in the same position that I had been on the couch, flat on the back, not moving and him on top of her banging away. She was just lying there and crying softly.

Chester said, "Let's change and see who has the best." So Johnny grabbed me and climbed on top of me as Chester got on top of Joan. Still we wouldn't move. I could hear Chester saying the same thing to Joan that he said to me like "Move, you bitch," and she told him that she hated everything about him and that he would get no help or satisfaction from her.

After perhaps five minutes Chester said, "Give me my woman back," and again he and Johnny changed places. Chester grabbed me and pulled me into the living room. He threw me down on the couch and forced entry into me again. I was still crying and after perhaps another five minutes Joan came into the living room and said, "He's (Johnny) passed out. Please let Helen and I go now." He got half off of me and shouted at her to go back in the bedroom and wait until he was finished.

She went back and looked for a knife or something to knock him out with, but became afraid that if she missed we would never get out alive. I was in great pain by then and crying loudly again. I begged him to get off of me and told him that I just couldn't take any more. He finally became disgusted and said, "Get the hell out of here" just as Joan walked back in. He got off of me and Joan helped me grab my clothes.

I dressed as fast as I could and was almost into my dress when he said, "Wait and drop me off at Twenty-ninth and Welton." I said, "Why not?" (sarcastically) just as we were opening the door. Joan got to the car first and unlocked it for me. Chester was standing at the door as we sped away and went straight to the police station.

Joan: The other girl described what happened after Johnny came and sat next to her on the arm of the couch: He said, "I want to talk to you." I asked, "What about?" He replied, "I just want to ask you something, come in the next room with me." I said no and started to stand up. He grabbed my arm and took me into the bedroom. (The bedroom and living room were actually one large room divided partially by a small wall and plastic curtain). He sat next to me on the bed and started talking quietly. Things like "I love you. . . I would do anything in the world for you. . . Oh, what's your name again? . . . What is your pay? . . . I always pay my way, I work forty hours a week."

He kept putting his hand on my arm and I kept removing his hand from my arm. I was getting frightened and kept telling him, "Listen, don't touch me. . . I am not a hustler. . . Don't you understand? I don't want anything from you." He then said, "I want some cat tonight and I'm going to get it." He grabbed my shoulders as I tried to leave and pushed me back on the bed. I tried to push him back, scratching his face and arm. He said as he was trying to get on top of me,

"Don't you scream!" I said, "Please let me go." He said, "Stop scratching me."

I called, "Helen, help me!" Helen pulled the curtain back and said, "Listen, let go of her. We're leaving." At that time the other man grabbed Helen from behind and said, "You're not going anywhere." He turned to Johnny and said, "Say, brother, you take care of her and I'll take care of this one." Helen was forced back to the couch and was pleading with him to let her go.

Johnny had unzipped his pants and was trying again to get on top of me. I kicked him four or five times in the crotch as hard as I could, but he didn't even seem to feel it. He was leaning over me and said, "Bitch, you've never had a good ass whippin' before, have you?" He then hit me across the mouth and it started to bleed. He said, "Mother f- - -r, you'd better not kick me again." Helen screamed twice and started to cry. Johnny yelled, "Shut up."

He then stood up, pulling me up by the arm and pushing me into the front room. He told me to tell her to be quiet. Helen was nude except for her bra and the other man was nude except for his shirt. I told Helen to please be quiet, as I was afraid they would kill us. The other man said he would make her shut up and for us to get back to our business. Johnny then forced me into the other room and pushed me onto the bed again. He unzipped his pants, lowered them and fell half on top of me.

He was holding me by the shoulders and told me to take off my pants. I said no and he hit me in the left temple with his fist. He tried to pull off my pants, but I was struggling so he couldn't get them off. He hit me again in the head and said, "Bitch, you'd better make it good. I'm going to have you." I was crying and pleading with him to please let me go. He put his hands beneath my hips and pushed me up to the top of the bed.

He took off my pants and said, "Shut up." I was crying so hard I couldn't and kept saying, "Please let me go." He said, "I don't want to take you crying, so be quiet." I cried louder and he hit me again across the mouth. He forced my legs open and tried to get in me but was having a hard time and I screamed, "No!" He kept trying and just as he entered me the other man and Helen came into the room. . . . After the other man pulled Helen to her feet and pushed her into the living room onto the couch again, Johnny told me to roll over.

He started to roll over and I pushed away from him. He was almost ready to pass out. He placed his right leg over my legs and said, "Give me a hand job." I said no. He pushed me down further, grabbed my wrist and placed and held my hand on his penis moving it. He started to breathe very deeply. So I shook him to see if he was asleep. He was, so I pulled myself away from him and went into the front room. . . . I went into the kitchen, I was looking for a knife or something I could hit him (Chester) with but couldn't find one.

There were men's voices coming through the door and I thought that maybe they were going to come in the apartment, so I went back in the living room. I decided against trying to hit the man with Helen, I thought if I didn't hit him hard enough he might get extremely violent and kill either Helen or I or both of us.

When the police went to arrest the suspects, a man in the next house said that he had heard screams but did not call the police, as he had no telephone. He also said that the music was very loud.

RAPE IN THE STREETS

A twenty-year-old single girl, while walking home from a friend's house shortly after midnight one Saturday, was attacked by a young Negro male. She reports:

I began walking home from a friend's house, crossing into shadows just past the first house on the end of the block. I then heard running footsteps directly behind me, turned to look and was grabbed by a Negro male and thrown to the bank. I screamed before he could get his hand over my mouth. He said he didn't want to hurt me, to be quiet and indicated he wanted me to go back by the side of the house. I sat on the bank for a moment saying, "Just let me get my breath," trying to stall and then he pulled me up and back by the bushes. He had hold of me somehow during that time but didn't force me immediately back, and didn't drag me or use extreme force. He took me back and pushed me down on my back, lowered himself partly over me, began rubbing my body, all the while looking around intently. Coming up the hill I said, "What have I done to you?"

I began talking to him right away saying, "Please don't do this, I love somebody. I love someone so much. Have you ever been in love?" He said, yes, and I said, "Then you should understand what it means to want one man — I don't want to make love to you." He said, "But I'm going to make love to you." I went on asking again that he not do it. He just continued to touch me and look around intently. After a few minutes he got up, drawing me up with him saying he wanted to see something, and drew me after him (holding onto the sleeves of my jacket) to the garage at the back of the house. I held back saying that I didn't want to go in there — to see for himself if he wanted to.

He pushed me into the garage, closing the door almost all the way. He placed me against the wall and undid my Levis and pants pushing them down to the floor, put his arms around me, kissing me and touching me. We continued to talk. I was just kind of avoiding his kisses and not responding. We spoke about choice. I said that I didn't want this because I had to choose the man to make love to and that he wasn't it, etc. He said, "Well, then you've made your choice, and have no choice in this and so have no burden to carry." I asked him what burden he had to carry and he said rather calmly, "I don't know."

At some time I asked him why he had to do this and he said, "I've been fucked over — I just have to make love and then I can live by myself." I asked him why he didn't pick someone who would want him too, and he said he didn't want any of the girls he could get, they all just changed after a while and fucked him over.

I said, "I understand what it is to have cruel things happen, that it's everywhere, that I feel it very strongly and my whole life is directed towards staying away from and out of the reaches of the unthinking cruelty of people." While I was saying I could understand how he felt about what people do to him, he said, "What are you doing — psyching me out?" and I said, "No, I can't do that. I can't get totally inside your head. I'm just trying to explain what you're saying so it's understandable to me." About that time I said, "What else can I do?" and he said, "What do you mean?" I couldn't answer him.

He said, "It's too bad because you seem to be a nice chick (or something to that effect), but you just happened to be the unlucky one walking down the street. You dig?" At all times he seemed calm, yet very alert, didn't swear at me or force me to actively participate. When I moved away from his kisses and kind of tried gently to hold him back, he didn't get angry or violent. We even smoked a cigarette together. He soon decided he couldn't do it in the garage. It was full of bicycles and junk, so he led me outside and down the alley, looking for a suitable place. At one point we hid from an approaching cab. Several times he suggested a place, I said no and he went on.

Once he brought me back next door to the corner house where it started and pushed me down and started to begin and I said, "no – this is too open – you could really get loused up if you got caught." I had begun to think that he was just a person who had been hurt badly and if I just treated him decently and didn't struggle against what there was no question in his mind that he was going to do – that it might make him better.

I had also decided in the garage that I wasn't going to fight him physically because I didn't think I could get away and was afraid if I got violent, he would too and would really hurt me. I was trying to remember what I knew about such people – and also was feeling for his hurt and his disturbance. He was not coarse, seemed intelligent, was able to "reason" with me, respond to my questions and seemed to understand all the things I put to him but had just made up his mind and couldn't be swayed.

We finally ended up about halfway down the block – in some bushes outside of the fences of two yards where he pushed me down, removed my thongs, jeans and underpants – giving me the latter saying, "Put these in your purse, you might have to get back into these (Levis) pretty quick."

He spread my Levis under me, removed his pants about halfway and proceeded to make love to me. Once he got up, telling me to lie flat, then finished the act after reassuring himself it was safe. He was hurting me also during the act and seemed concerned that he was – when he finished, he said, "Okay, that's all" or something. Afterwards he helped me find my shoes and led me out saying, "You go that way and I'll go this way" and "See you," and I replied the same.

A street encounter of a much different character occurred a few months later. The victim was also a twenty-year-old girl who was walking home in the early hours of a Sunday morning. Her assailant was a young Spanish-American male.

I crossed to the other side of the street because I saw someone walking towards me. After walking another block I saw a man walking behind me. Thinking that no one would attempt anything because the street was well lighted, I kept walking. Instead of passing me as I expected when I heard his footsteps behind me, he grabbed me, placing one hand over my mouth, and dragged me to some bushes. I fell and had some difficulty getting my balance. He kept dragging me and telling me to get up.

I screamed – his hand only partially covering my mouth. I was on my knees and he put one arm around my throat and started to choke me as he put his hand firmly over my nose and throat. He took his hand partially away from my mouth as I fell on my stomach. I told him I was sick and had to breathe. He told me to shut up and get up or he would kill me. I got up, his arm still around my neck but not choking me and he pulled me to a gate at a house. The gate must have been locked because he pulled me to some bushes next to the house beside the porch.

I fell in the bushes and he pushed me to the ground. I tried to sit up, but he threatened to pound my head against the brick wall. I kept asking him to let me go. He unbuttoned my shirt, took it off. He stuffed some of it in my mouth, as I had started crying, asking him to let me go. He had to do this several times, as I kept spitting it out. When he finally had enough shirt in my mouth so I couldn't spit it out, he put the rest of the shirt over my face. He pulled my pants off and raped me. He put my arms around his neck and told me to hold him, to pretend he was my boyfriend.

By this time I had the shirt out of my mouth and off my face. I attempted to get away and he grabbed me, holding my head down again. I screamed and he hit me in the mouth with his fist. He asked me what I was going to say if someone came up, and I told him I would say I was with him. He asked me my name and I told him. He asked me where I lived. I told him that I lived with a girl friend and he said he was going to rape my girl friend and he asked for the address. I told him I was new in Denver and didn't know the address.

He was dressed now and ordered me to get dressed. I put on my shirt and my coin purse fell from the breast pocket. He picked it up and said it was insurance that I would come with him so he could rape me all night. I was dressed and he pulled me to my feet. As we got out of the bushes, I saw two men standing on the sidewalk. I jerked away from him and ran to them, asking them to help me because he had just raped me. They said something to him and he said it was just that I didn't want to be with him.

They asked me how he knew my name and I told them and said that he had my coin purse and money. He kept walking away from us and one man said something to him. He turned to the man and said something to the extent do you want to fight about it. We went to find the police, as I looked back I saw him turning to the right. I was hysterical and have difficulty in remembering the sequence of what was said. He told me if I cooperated he would let me go without hurting me.

TWO GIRLS ACCEPT A RIDE TO WORK

Betty: We were standing at the bus stop at 8 P.M., waiting for a bus to go to work. Then this man drove up from behind us in a parking lot and called my name. I didn't pay any attention but then Susan said he was calling me. I turned around and looked at the panel truck to see who it was. I didn't know who it was so I stayed away, then he started naming all these places I had been and who I was with.

We stayed talking about twenty minutes, then he said he would give us a ride to where we were going and I asked Susan and we got in. He drove us to Emerson Street, then he turned into an alley and parked almost at the end. I asked him why he was stopping here and he didn't say anything. He got out, went to Susan's side, opened the door and said get in the back. Susan asked what for and he said, "I got a knife." He told me to get in the back first, then Susan, and then he said to start stripping.

He told Susan to take off her blouse. She refused, he ripped it off of her and then he said, "Everything," so she did, with him forcing her. He ripped my dress off at this time. Then he started kissing Susan's breast and I hit him with a plastic bottle. Him and I started fighting and then I was flat down and he poured some kind of cleaning fluid on our heads. While he was doing this I reached up and grabbed for his glasses and threw them and pushed the fluid away.

He asked for his glasses rather than demanded them. Susan found them and gave them to him. He then started to get in the front, making us lie down flat before getting there. He started the truck, but I got up and grabbed his neck and started fighting somehow. I got in front, opened the door and started running. I don't remember if Susan was behind or not. I ran to this house and started screaming. These people came out and took me in and the police were called. I asked about Susan, the last time I saw her she was getting out of the truck. They told me she had run to another house.

Susan: Well, we had just left Betty's house and it was about eight o'clock and we had to go to work. As we went to go to the bus stop, a stranger appeared. I heard him call Betty's name, so naturally I thought she knew him, and I told her, "I think that man's calling you." So Betty kind of ignored him, but he said, "Gee, I'm not going to bite you." So then Betty said, "Yeah." He said, "I know you, Betty." Betty said, "Where from?" So he started to name the places she started hanging around at. Anyway he started a conversation with both of us.

"Gee," he said, "if you come a little closer maybe you might know me." So Betty and I said, "We can see you from here," and he repeated, "I know you, Betty." So somehow he asked us where we were going and we told him, because he did seem like he knew Betty real good. He said, "I have a little time, why don't I run you over there?" So me and Betty look at each other, and Betty replied, "Can we trust you?" and he said, "Gee, what do you think I am?" and I said nothing.

So we asked him his name and get in the panel truck. . . he turn in this alley and he parked. So Betty asked, "What did you come here for?" and he said, "Nothing." He got out, went around to my side, opened the door and told me to move in. I said, "What for?" and he said, "I got a knife," and pointed to Betty and said, "Get in the back and start stripping. You, too," so I got in the back. He told me to take off my dress, I refused and he pulled it off. He said, "Take off everything," so I was scared and cooperated. I was so scared I didn't quite know what was going on.

So Betty kept struggling and he hit her with a pole. He had me down, there was no way I could move. When he started kissing my breasts, Betty hit him with some kind of plastic bottle. They started fighting again and he picked up some kind of cleaning stuff and threw it all over us and knocked Betty back down. Me and Betty were both screaming for help. Somehow he got up front, Betty grabbed him by his neck. Somehow she got out and as he was ready to take off I flew out of the truck, and started running down the alley — half undressed — for help.

Some hippies heard me and took me in their house and clothed me. The people called the police and I felt safe when they told me my girl friend was next door. The guy had also told us if we try for help and we got out, he would run over us. It was terrible, it happened so fast.

ABDUCTION IN THE STREET

I [a young single girl] was walking down the street about 8:30 P.M. when I realized there was a man walking on the opposite side of the street. He was singing, he crossed the street. By this time he was on the corner. He said, "Excuse me, ma'am" and asked for directions but I wasn't familiar with the area and I told him I couldn't be of any help. When he asked what I was doing, I told him I was walking to a friend's house.

I turned to walk away and he grabbed me around the neck with his arm. I screamed and screamed. He pushed me down, telling me he'd kill me if I didn't shut up, then he put something sharp to my heart. He said it was a knife, that he wasn't going to rape me, he just wanted me to help him out of the neighborhood. He made me get up and told me he just wanted me to walk three blocks with him. I kept talking, he told me to shut up, he'd already killed one person that night.

We walked a block south, where he told me to get into a car. A man had yelled at us from the next block, so we walked a few feet from the car then back to it. He continued to hold the so-called knife at my heart while his other arm was around my neck. I got in the car first on the passenger side then he followed me in, locked the door and climbed over me to the driver's seat. He made me put my arm around him for a block, then he made me lay down. We'd gone west for a while then he allowed me to sit back up.

We were at an intersection, turning north. I noticed the knife was really a screwdriver. I grabbed the steering wheel, honking the horn and he lost control. He began to hit me in the face, I fell back down on the seat, he continued to hit me on the back. I fell back down on the seat, he continued to hit me on the back. I began to fight him again. This time he choked me with his hands. When I opened my eyes we were out by the airport. During our struggle he ripped the buttons off my dress and tore off my gloves.

He kept saying he was going to kill me because I was white. He also kept saying he was going to take off all my clothes and dump me off in Five Points (a Negro area). He asked such questions as "Are you married?" "What time does your husband expect you home?" "What's your husband's name?" "Where does he live?" "What is his name?" "Have you ever gone with a Negro?" "What do you think of the Negroes?"

Then he started on questions like "Have you ever had sex?" "Have you ever screwed a Negro?" "What would you do if you had a black baby?" If I didn't answer, he'd hit me; by this time I wasn't able to sit up. I was more frightened than hurt. He called me a "white bitch" all the time. He parked between two houses in the Stapleton area and told me to get in the back seat. Then he raped me, I had read not to resist, so I didn't.

He hit me a few times during this period because I wasn't responding to him. He then got into the front seat and made me lie down on the back seat. He asked me if I had any money. I said no. He said if I lied to him he would kill me. I didn't have any money, so he went through my I.D. cards. He asked me where I lived, saying he'd kill me if I didn't answer right. He said he had to kill me because I'd call the police. I talked and talked, telling him I wouldn't. He then took me over to Downing and let me out two blocks from Colfax.

It was 9:50 when the man had dropped me off. The man had been drinking. He said two things that implied he'd done this before. When I was struggling he said I fought more than the others had, and when he let me off he said I was the only one he was sorry about.

RAPE IN A VACANT LOT

About 10:15 P.M. Ruth and I decided to go to the Seven-Eleven Store. We left the apartment and started walking on the east side of the street, we heard the bushes move and I looked back but couldn't see anything. I thought it might be a dog. We continued walking, then we heard someone yell, "Come here or I'll shoot you." The voice was just a little bit in back of us. I was walking on the outside next to the street. Ruth grabbed ahold of my arm and we started to run. Just then he was out of the bushes. He grabbed each of us by the hair and jerked us down.

We both fell forward on our faces. This was right next to the street, cars were passing by and we both screamed after he grabbed us. After he knocked us down he said, "Don't look at me." He had on a pair of dark socks and a St. Christopher's medal around his neck. That is all he had on. He still had us by the hair. He said something about having a knife and for us to cooperate with him. He warned us he would hurt us if we didn't shut up. After the cars had gone by, he pulled us up and made us go into the weeds, fifty feet or so from the road. He still had ahold of us by the hair and was kicking us. When he got to where he wanted us, he told both of us to lay down on the ground.

He told us again not to look at him. We both laid down as he told us to. First of all he asked us if we were virgins and Ruth said, no. I think then he said, "Good." He turned me over and started undoing my belt. He was kneeling to the side of me. He was in between Ruth and me. This is when I saw the medal. It had St. Christopher written around the edge. It had a figure of a man on it wearing a belted robe. It was silver colored.

As he was trying to get my jeans off, I was trying to push him away. He told Ruth, "You better tell your friend to cooperate." She didn't say anything. He undid my belt and pulled my jeans down to about my knees. When he got them down that far, he took off both my shoes. Part of the time he would use both hands to undress me and part of the time he used one hand to push Ruth's face down. After he got my shoes off, he took my jeans off. My underpants came off along with my jeans. I was naked from the waist down.

By this time I was kind of sitting up, trying to push him away. He was still on his knees and he was pushing my head down like to make me give him a blow job. His penis was erect, it was hard. I wouldn't get down, and he said, "O.K., chick, if you won't do it this way, then you'll have to take the chance of getting pregnant." Then he pushed me down on my back. He got on top of me and kept reaching down to my knees and finally got my legs separated. After he got my legs apart, he put his dick in my vagina.

Ruth said something like "Wouldn't you rather make love to me, I'm better, I'm more experienced, I'm married." I think she said that to protect me. He hit her on the head and told her to shut up. He continued having intercourse with me, and in the meantime Ruth managed to work off one of her boots, then she reached down and grabbed her boot and hit him over the head with it. Then she started to run.

He jumped off of me really quick and he caught her and dragged her back. He chased her about ten feet. She was struggling with him and trying to pull away from him. He wasn't gone more than thirty seconds before he drug her back. After he brought her back, I told Ruth not to run again because he was going to hurt us.

While he was chasing Ruth, I sat up and my sweater was up, I was trying to pull it down. It's a big sweater, it comes down to my hips and I thought if I could get it down far enough I would run out and try to attract the attention of a car. He had taken one of the arms out of my sweater. When Ruth ran, she ran sort of north toward the Seven-Eleven Store. When he brought her back, he pushed her back down in the weeds and got back on top of me. He put his dick back in my vagina.

Now he was keeping one hand on the back of Ruth's neck so she couldn't move anymore. After he reached his climax, he started crying and said he was sorry, that he wished he could have met me in his other life. I thought he was just going to get up and go, that he wouldn't hurt Ruth. Then Ruth said, "Why do you have to get it this way?" because he wasn't ugly, he was really good looking. He said, "Shut up, bitch," and hit her in the head. He also said his fiance had been raped by some guy and that I was going to have his baby. This was still while he was on top of me.

Then he got up and pushed me on my stomach. Ruth had been saying over and over how cold it was. I guess that while he was raping me, he had his hands behind my back and undid my brassiere, he pushed my bra up above my breasts so that they were exposed. He was sucking on one of my breasts while he was having intercourse with me. I asked him if I could dress and he said no. He took my sweater off and draped it over my back.

Then he went over to Ruth. I couldn't see what he was doing to her because my face was turned down in the weeds, and he told us before not to look at him. Ruth said to him sarcastically, "Do you want me all undressed?" He said, "Yeah." He also said, "I've killed a girl before." Then I don't think he raped her. She told me afterwards that he couldn't get hard again. He told Ruth to turn over after that and he told us to count to two hundred. He said he'd be able to see us for a couple of minutes and if we didn't stay there he'd come back and really fix us. He didn't bother to get dressed, he carried his clothes in his arm. He got his clothes from some weeds and left in the general direction of the Seven-Eleven Store. I could tell from the noise in the weeds. Then both of us got dressed and called the police from the apartment.

RAPE IN THE HOME

I woke up and saw a man standing in my bedroom door. He came into the bedroom and started looking through my jewelry box. Then he went down to the foot of my bed and started to feel my leg. I acted like I was just waking up, stretched a little bit and made like I was looking for my cigarettes. When I stood up he grabbed me. He said, "Be quiet and I won't hurt you." I said, "O.K." He told me to lay back down and he took the pillow and put it over my face.

That made me panic and I started to cry. He told me not to worry, that he was not going to hurt. I told him my baby was due any day and I was having pains. I asked to go to the bathroom and he wanted to know why. I said that I was taking medicine and had to get it. He said, "O.K." but made me undress and held a sheet over my head. Then he helped me into the bathroom. I started groaning and breathing hard and he brought me my clothes and told me to put them on.

He said, "Calm down, I'm not going to hurt you. Just give me some money and I'll leave you alone." I told him that all I had was a dollar and it was in my purse. He asked if my husband kept money anywhere. I told him if he did, it would be in the desk in the living room. I thought I could get away when he went after it but he made me go with him. He looked and said, "You wouldn't lie to me, would you?" I said I wouldn't, that I had been through this once and was beaten up and almost lost my baby. I told him I didn't want this to happen again and I was telling him the truth.

All of this time I was faking the pains and he still made me keep the sheet over my head. He told me to go back to bed and lay down. He asked me if I wanted a drink of water or if I had any medicine I had to take. I told him no but I wanted a cigarette. He took one of his own and lit it for me and told me to hold out my hand and gave it to me. He then backed into the doorway where I wouldn't be able to see his face and told me I could uncover my head, sit up and smoke.

Then he wanted to know if I had any sisters and I told him I had no sisters. He wanted to know how many children I had and I said this would be my first. Then he started to swear and I asked him what was the matter. He said, "I think your husband is a sonofabitch to leave you alone at night. You should leave him." I said that he worked at night, then he asked what time he got home. I told him anytime now and told what kind of job my husband had.

He then told me I was different than the other women and I asked him why. He said because I wasn't trying to fight and scream and I was keeping a calm attitude. I said I didn't want anything to happen to the baby. He asked me if these were labor pains I was having. I said I didn't know if it was that or from being scared. He said, "What are you afraid of? I told you I wasn't going to hurt you, so far have I?" I said "No, but you wake me up in the middle of the night and someone grabs you, don't you think I have a right to be scared?" He said, "I don't know, I've never been scared in my life."

Then I put my cigarette out and he told me to cover my head back up. When I did, he took the cigarette out of the ashtray and said he wasn't going to take any chances. I said my husband should be home anytime and that I had to get to the doctor. He said, "O.K., what is your name?" I told him Rosemarie. He said, "O.K., Rosemarie, I'm going to go, but you stay there and count to one hundred and then call your doctor, but don't call the cops or I will get you."

"You know I do this for a living and there isn't a house I can't get into. If I can't get you, then two guys or two guys and a girl will. You call your doctor and get your ass in the hospital. Now start counting." I started to count and when I reached twenty, he flushed the stool. When I reached fifty, I thought he was gone and he said, "I told you to count to one hundred." By the time I reached one hundred he was gone and my husband was pulling up. I turned on the light and opened the door for my husband. He looked for the guy to see if he was still around. He heard a car start up and ran out the door and saw the car. He tried to follow but lost him and we called the police.

Another young girl describes her experiences when a stranger came to her apartment door.

About 6:15 P.M. I was getting ready for a date. I had just spoken to my boyfriend and he asked if I was ready to go out. I said no and I also had my hair in rollers. So he said he wouldn't come over then. I had just enough time to hang up the phone and put some clothes on when I heard a knock on the front door. I just assumed it was my boyfriend and that he had changed his mind about coming over. So I just opened the door and there was a great big Negro man leaning against the side of the door.

He asked me if I knew someone named Charles. I asked, "Charles who?" Then he started mumbling something. So I started to shut the door. As I shut the door he put his hand in the way and in his right hand was a gun. So I couldn't shut the door, then he pushed his way inside and shut the door. He grabbed me and pointed the gun at my head and said he wanted some money. Well, I didn't have any cash in the house so I said I didn't have any.

He saw the lights on in the back of the apartment and asked who was in here with me. I said my husband. Well, he called my bluff. I couldn't come up with a husband, so he kept hold of me with the gun at my head. I asked him if it was a real gun and he stepped back and flipped the middle out and showed me all the bullets, and put the gun back together. He then grabbed me again and said that if he wasn't going to get any money, he'd take something else.

He started pushing me back to the bedroom. All the time I kept talking but I can't remember what I said. We got back to the bedroom and he said to take off my clothes. I said no. He said if I didn't take them off he would. Right then I screamed as loud as I could and he grabbed me by my throat and started choking me. He picked me up and threw me on the bed, still choking me with one hand so I couldn't even breathe. The other hand was pointing the gun in my stomach.

I finally got his hand off my throat and he said, "Just answer me one question, are you going to take your clothes off or am I?" And I said, "Just answer me one question, Why?" At this point he got up off the bed and stood up, still pointing the gun at me. So I got up, still trying to talk to him and not trying to make him mad. I started moving around the bedroom picking up things, telling him that I had a date real soon and had to get ready.

I noticed then my blouse was ripped in front. So I moved to the kitchen, all the time talking to him. I got to the kitchen. I asked him why he needed the gun. Gee whiz, he was about three times bigger than me and a lot stronger and he sure didn't need a gun. He said he had grown up with one and it was just part of his life. I asked him if he had ever shot anyone. He said yes and that he had just got out of jail.

I asked him if it was someone he knew or hated and he said it was someone he didn't even know. This made me feel real good, so I asked him if he wanted a beer. He did so I got a beer and handed it to him. I still kept talking to him and picking things up in the dining room real casually. He then started talking about himself and his family. He said he had just had a big fight with one of his brothers and got in his car and just started driving and ended up at my apartment.

I asked him why he picked on my apartment. He said he just picked one and if I had been Negro he probably wouldn't have bothered me, but because I was small and white it was different. We kept talking for about twenty minutes while my knees kept knocking together. He asked me if he made me nervous and I told him he scared me to death. I kept joking with him and he finally stopped pointing the gun at me.

He then started saying he was sorry. I said that's okay but next time he decided to break into my apartment and push and choke me to let me know and I'd have my hair dry and the kitchen clean. He then set the beer bottle on the coffee table, said, "Okay, you know, you're all right" and he left. I waited a few minutes after he left and couldn't stand it any longer and ran out the front door over to a friend's place. I completely broke down and when I stopped crying we called the police.

A SADISTIC RAPE

In contrast to the two young women who were successful in avoiding rape in their homes, the following girl was the victim of a very sadistic rape.

I woke up feeling someone stroking my arm. At first I thought I was dreaming but became aware that I wasn't when he started fondling me. He made me turn over on my stomach and put my head in the pillow while he took a dress laying on the bed and blindfolded me with it. He then put a knife at my throat and told me not to attempt to fight or look at him or he would kill me. He said, "I am very dangerous and not afraid to use the knife. If you cooperate, I won't kill you."

He then made me turn on my back and he started kissing me. He demanded that I kiss him back. He proceeded to use his hands to fondle, finally inserting his hand in the vagina and pulling my insides until I started screaming. He stopped because of the noise I was making and asked me to perform unnatural oral sex acts. He then had me turn over on my stomach again and tried to perform rectal intercourse. Again I screamed with pain and he told me to shut up or he would use the knife and really hurt. He told me to turn on my side and as I did, I tried to fight him off.

He was behind me and took his arm and grabbed me around the neck, choking me and putting the knife at my neck. He asked me why I did that. I said, "Because I'm scared and I don't know if you're going to kill me when you're through. I'm just scared." He then told me not to try it again because as long as I was calm he would be, but one more attempt at fighting and he would not think twice about killing me.

He then made me lay on my side and proceeded to use his fingers inserting them in both the rectum and vagina to try and rip me. The pain was unbearable and my groans were loud, so he cupped his hand over my mouth and pushed me on my back, proceeding with intercourse. When he was through, he told me to lay on my stomach and keep my head in the pillow while he dressed. He put the tip of the knife at my back and told me not to move one muscle or he would cut me to pieces. He dressed and I lay there wondering if he would keep his word about not killing me.

He moved the knife slowly up and down my back, and the next few minutes of torment my mind went through was hell. It was as if he was trying to decide whether or not to kill me. I wondered if death would be instant or if he would miss and sever my spine so I would never walk or do anything again but be a vegetable. He then told me to lay there in the same position for about ten minutes until he was gone. I did and then got up and called the police.

A REQUEST FOR A GLASS OF WATER

I [a twenty-year-old single girl] was walking down Fourteenth Street and there was a Mexican about thirty-nine or so and a Negro behind me. I thought the Mexican was following me but thought it also might be my imagination. The Negro stopped me at Fourteenth and Grant as I was turning and told me to be careful because he thought the Mexican was following me. I said, "O.K., thank you." The Mexican saw the Negro point at him so walked a different way.

Two blocks down Grant the Negro crossed over to my side, asked if I'd do him a favor. I said, "What?" He said his '69 green Dodge was stolen and if I saw it would I report it. I said, "O.K." He crossed back on the other side. As I got to Thirteenth and Grant I had to cross to my apartment. He caught up with me and said he wanted a drink of water. I was checking my mailbox and he walked down the hall. I went to my apartment, opened the door and he asked for a glass of water and if he could come in.

I said I didn't think my husband would like it. He asked if I was prejudiced. I said no. He said, "Well, can I have some water and I'll leave?" I said, "O.K., but you have to wait outside." He said, "Why, is your husband home?" I said, "No, just wait." He said, "O.K." I went in, shut the door a little and went in the kitchen to get the water. When I came back, he was in the living room. He sat on the couch and said as I walked in, "You look really good."

I said, "I want you to leave." He asked, "Why?" I said, "Because you scare me and my husband will be home soon. He said, "O.K." He drank the water and started toward the door. I sat down in the chair. He had to go past me to get to the door, and as he was walking by he got on the right side of me and put a knife on the left side of my neck. He said, "Just play it cool, baby."

I glanced at the knife and grabbed it with my right hand. I started toward the door and he grabbed me, shutting the door. I started to scream, so he put his hand over my mouth and said, "Shut up, you bitch." I started stabbing at him. He let go and said, "Why did you cut me? I was just joking." He asked me to get a doctor. I said, "Get out of here before I call the cops." He walked down the hall, then ran.

Thirty minutes later an attendant at a service station almost two miles from the scene of the attempted rape notified the police that there was a man with a severe cut on his hand standing on the street corner. The police approached the man and called an ambulance. At this time a description of a man wanted for attempted rape was broadcast over the police radio. The description was that of the man with the cut hand. At first he said he had cut his hand on a fence, but later he said he had cut it on a metal sign. He also said he had been in the area of Twelfth and Grant, looking for a **furnished apartment.**

COMPLAINT OF RAPE IN A HOTEL

A middle-aged woman who came to Colorado to visit her son-in-law, complained to police that she had been raped by a bellhop in her hotel. She described the event as follows:

I took the limousine to the hotel. The bellhop took my bags to my room. He started to put me in an elevator loaded with men and I refused to get in saying I was scared of all men. So he rode me up alone in another elevator. I locked my room and barred the door with a chair. I slept till around 9 or 10 P.M.

I called room service because my television didn't work. The same bellhop brought another television in. He said if business was slow he might come back for awhile. I had on my robe, I fell asleep. The door was barred with the chair and I woke up to knocking on the door. It didn't stop, so I said wait a minute, got on a robe, took away the chair and it was the same bellhop. He said, "I brought you a sandwich from the kitchen because you're hungry and haven't eaten anything." He brought it in, turned on the television and said he was bushed, that it had been a long day.

He flopped down on the other twin bed. He said there was nothing to worry about, after a little rest he'd leave. He offered a little conversation while I nibbled on the sandwich he brought. The television went off the air. He turned on the radio, he stayed on his twin bed. I stayed on mine. He stayed fully clothed and said he was harmless. He said he was lonely — it was sometimes hard to unwind after a job. He left at 5 A.M.

About 4 A.M. he gave me a couple of kisses and I kept running to the chair or opposite bed to avoid contact, because I told him I wasn't about to bring a baby into this awful world. So he saw a plastic bag in one of my suitcases and said he would use it and nothing would happen. I'm a dumb dame. He swore on a stack of Bibles, he said he'd used it before and it was quite safe.

I said, "Don't bellhops have something else? Don't customers request . . .?" He said he's not that kind of person. He wouldn't leave till he got his way. I couldn't escape it. I said many times that evening that there must be plenty of lonely women in this hotel. I couldn't get him out of my room. He kept saying, "Think of me as your son in the service." He came in at midnight, it happened at 5 A.M.

I called Planned Parenthood today, they're pretty sure I'm pregnant. It happened at a very dangerous time. They referred me to a doctor. He said to wait thirty days and if there was no period, to press rape charges and get a therapeutic abortion. A man like that shouldn't be a bellhop at a place like that. Women should be protected at a good hotel like that.

ANOTHER COMPLAINT OF RAPE IN A HOTEL

A twenty-one-year-old girl telephoned the police department from a hotel lobby to report that she had been raped in room 410 or 411. She said that the man had approached her while she was sitting in the hotel lobby about 10:30 that night. He asked if he could sit on the sofa and she had told him that she did not care as long as he sat on the other end of the sofa. After some conversation he asked her to come up to his room. He said that he had two beds and one was going to be vacant. When she refused, he took her by the arm and she was unable to break away.

He made her stand up and go to the elevator with him. There was no one behind the hotel desk when he forced her into the elevator. The first thing he did after taking her to his room was to call the hotel desk for cigarettes. She resisted him when he tried to kiss her. He then gave her a dollar bill and told her to pay the bellboy when he brought the cigarettes. She replied, "No, you called him, you pay him." The bellboy knocked on the door and the man forced her into the bathroom.

After the bellboy left, she came out of the bathroom and the man asked her to sit beside him on the bed. She refused and he grabbed her by her arm and dragged her to the bed. They both smoked a cigarette and when she got up to leave he told her to take her clothes off. She refused and he unbuttoned her blouse and then tried to pull her pants off. She told him that if he let her go and stood away from her, she would take her pants off. When he turned away, she ran for the bedroom door, but he caught her and forced her back to the bed.

She then took her pants off and he told her to come over to him. She refused and he stood up and said, "I said come over here," so she went over to him. He took his clothing off and started "playing with her." After he raped her, she complained that she was bleeding and went to the bathroom. On leaving the bathroom she walked toward the other bed and he ordered her to come back to him. After he raped her again, she lit a cigarette and started to smoke it. He told her to put it out and raped her a third time.

After going to the bathroom again, she returned to the room and lit a cigarette.

She stayed there until he fell asleep, then she dressed and went to the lobby where she called the police. The suspect admitted having sexual relations with the girl, but he claimed that it was of her own free will. He claimed that after having sexual relations, they heard sirens and the girl jumped out of bed. She said that she did not want to get caught again as she was the night before when she was arrested for being in a hotel room with another man. They looked out the window and saw an ambulance and a fire rescue truck. The girl then quieted down and they both fell asleep. The next thing the suspect knew was being awakened by the police.

Later investigation revealed that the girl did not live at the address she gave the police officers. Court records showed that on the day prior to her complaint of rape she had been charged with vagrancy and illegal occupancy of a hotel room with a member of the opposite sex.

A GROUP RAPE

A young man escorted his girl friend from a fashionable restaurant late one evening to his car, a convertible, in the parking lot. As he was about to drive away, the car door on the driver's side was suddenly opened by a tall Negro who announced, "This is a stickup." Two Negroes pulled the driver from the car and started beating him. The girl locked the car doors and pressed the horn. The man later described to police his night of assault and terror.

I was pulled approximately ten feet from the car. They started beating me, then told me to be quiet and I wouldn't be hurt. I think at this time I was stabbed in the leg. I realized that there were three or four men involved. They started arguing about my friend Anne and decided to take her and myself with them. I was led with my head down and again told to be quiet. I was pushed into the back of a car with my head still down and covered with someone's hand. At this time Anne arrived with one or two of the men.

There was a lot of talk going on between them as to what they were going to do with us. They started the car and started driving around. They started raping Anne, taking turns and asking her if she liked it and told her to answer yes. Also while the rape was taking place one of the men in the front would hit me every so often and say he wanted to kill us both. Then the man holding my head would argue with him and say we hadn't done anything to hurt them. I think during this time the man in front pulled a gun and said he wanted to kill us.

Then I was led to believe the man holding my head also pulled a gun and said if the other man killed us he would kill him. They also started to argue about the money they had taken from me at the restaurant. They started fighting about it and slapping each other and all during this time they continued raping Anne and taking turns while the others would make comments like "How do you like it, white bitch?" and talking to each other about how much she was enjoying it, and during this time they would continue to hit and stab me.

All during this time they would drive around and then stop and park. I think about this time they talked about not having enough gas and what to do with both of us. Someone in front wanted to kill us both, but the man holding my head would say no; then they would argue and call each other crazy. About this time they decided to dump me, they stopped the car and pushed me out. One of the men in front started kicking me, but someone else got out and held the man doing the kicking. He said to me if I wanted to live I better start running and I ran to a house and called the police.

The young woman, who was kept in the car, later reported her account of this kidnapping and rape.

We were about to leave the parking lot when four men approached the car from behind, opened the door and said, "This is a stickup." They took John out of the car and I locked both doors and started blowing the car horn, hoping it would scare them off. Instead two of them ran to the car and tried to break in the driver's window. Then they slashed the convertible top with knives. Two of them got in the car on either side of me and while one held a knife at my throat, the other went through my purse and took my money. They also took a ring which I had on.

The four men involved were Negroes between the ages of twenty and thirty. They threatened me and told me to keep my eyes closed and not look at them. They took me to their car and pushed me in the front seat. They made me lie down as low as I could and started the car. They took off my girdle and panties and unzipped my dress but did not take it off. The one with me in the passenger seat pushed me back and raped me in the front seat. I was then pulled in the back seat with two of them and John.

I was raped in the back seat by the two back there and then they stopped the car and changed drivers so he could rape me. I brushed up against John and could see blood on his shirt. I knew then that he had been cut or stabbed. I did not try to resist in any way because I was afraid they might hurt John and I was hoping we could get out of this alive. They argued among themselves several times trying to persuade one of them not to kill John. They said they did not want a murder rap.

During one of the arguments the man who had threatened to kill John cut one of the others with a knife and this man pulled out a gun. The other man apologized and put his knife in his pocket. I never saw the gun, but I heard the others describe what was going on. They finally decided to let us out. They stopped the car and shoved John out. They shoved me out too and told me to leave, but the two that took John out pushed me back in and they drove around some more.

I was raped again. I don't know who or how many times. I was repeatedly told to keep my eyes closed and my head down and slapped and hit with fists on my face. They finally stopped the car and pushed me out. Two of them pushed me away from the car. They ran to the car and left. I picked up my coat and saw I had a cut on my hand. I ran across the street to a house. Finally a lady let me in and I called the police. I don't think any of them reached a climax while they were having intercourse with me. The other ones would not give them time. They would keep bothering one another.

RAPE OF A FOUR-YEAR-OLD GIRL

In this case the offender's account of the rape is provided. He was alone at home with Mary, the four-year-old daughter of his girl friend, Susan.

I told Mary to take her clothes off and lie on the couch. She started crying when I told her to lay down. She had all her clothes off except her blouse. I have a daughter the same age as Mary. I was hoping someone would come so I wouldn't do it. Something in my mind told me to go ahead and do it. I didn't take off my pants. I just unbuttoned my zipper and put the head of my penis in her. Then I just snapped out of it and I quit. I didn't know what to do. I didn't know what I'd done. I picked her up and said, "It's all over."

I had her in my arms and seen all the blood. I sat her on the toilet in the bathroom. I got the sheet from the couch and put it in cold water. I washed up all the blood on the floor of the living room where I was holding her. I cleaned the blood off her. She was bleeding pretty fast then. I put a lot of toilet paper between her legs. I put it there to stop the bleeding. Then I laid her on the bed and covered her up. I asked her for a kiss. I told her I was sorry. She looked at me and said, "O.K."

Then her mother came home and we started watching television. I went into Mary's room and moved her to the outer side of the bed so she could watch the television. When I lifted up the blanket, I saw a big old splatter of blood. I knew I had to tell Susan something. I told her I hit Mary with a rolling pin. I told Susan to go and look at her. At first Susan didn't want to. Then she went in the bathroom and locked the door. Then she came out. I could see that Mary had thrown up. Susan told me to call the ambulance.

I asked Susan what she was going to tell them. She said she didn't know. I told her I didn't want to go to jail. She then told me to leave and I went down the street. I didn't know what to think. I was thinking of committing suicide. I didn't think I would ever be able to live it down.

Chapter 2

FORCIBLE RAPE

*"For I must talk of murders, rapes and massacres
Acts of black night, abominable deeds."*
— Shakespeare, *Titus Andronicus*

RAPE has long been regarded as one of the most abominable crimes. In some jurisdictions it shares with murder, treason and kidnapping the ultimate penalty of death by execution. Abhorrence of rape is not confined to law-abiding citizens. Within penitentiary walls inmates look down on the rapist and other sex offenders. Yet there is public awareness that some women cry rape falsely, while others by their seductive behavior contribute to their victimization.

Although much has been written on sexual offenses and sex offenders, the rapist has attracted less professional attention than the exhibitionist, the child-molester and the homosexual offender. There are case reports of individual rapists, passing references to the problem of rape and some statistical surveys, but studies specifically directed toward the crime of rape are rare indeed. In 1965 Amir claimed that in the literature available in English there is not even one book dealing exclusively with rape.

Amir has reported the results from a study of 646 cases of forcible rape that occurred in Philadelphia from January 1, 1958, to December 31, 1958, and from January 1, 1960, to December 31, 1960. Information was obtained from the files of the Morals Squad of the Philadelphia Police Department, where all complaints about rape are recorded and centrally filed. The emphasis in this study has not been on the psychological dynamics of the offenders and their victims but on their social characteristics, social relationships and on the act itself, that is, on the *modus operandi* of the crime and the situations in which rape is likely to occur.

The patterns which emerged were derived from information about the 646 victims and 1,292 offenders who were involved in 370 cases of single rape, 105 pair rapes, and 171 group rape events.

"Patterns were sought regarding race, age, marital status, and employment differences, as well as seasonal and other temporal patterns, spatial patterns, the relation between forcible rape and the presence of alcohol and the previous arrest record of victims and offenders. In the analysis of the modus operandi a search for patterns was made regarding the initial interaction and meeting place of offender and victim, the place of the offense, the planning of the crime, the methods used to subdue the victim, the degree of violence in the rape event, the sexual humiliation to which the victim was subjected (other than forced intercourse,) and the degree of the victim's resistance. Further questions were raised regarding rape during the commission of another felony, the interpersonal relationship between victim and offender, victim-precipitated rape, and unsolved cases of rape. Finally, all of these aspects were related to the phenomenon of group rape and to leadership functions in such situations" (Amir).

The author of this book in 1968-69 reviewed the Denver Police Department files on two hundred consecutive victims of forcible rape; 163 women were victims of solitary offenders, seventeen were attacked by a group of two offenders and twenty were victims of a group of three or more men. One woman was raped by the same offender on two separate occasions. Four offenders were each known to have committed more than one of these rapes before their detection and arrest, and one man raped five women. Altogether there were 253 offenders. Statistics derived from the police files will be presented in this and subsequent chapters.

The author was present when many of the victims, as well as others not included in the two hundred cases, were interviewed by detectives or by a nurse from the Denver Visiting Nurse Service. In addition he interviewed some victims privately and also interviewed at length several of the men who raped victims in this study, as well as over one hundred other rape offenders. Information obtained from these interviews, from detectives and police departments, both within and beyond Colorado, and from penitentiary records contributes to the clinical examples provided throughout the book.

RAPE DEFINED

Rape is usually defined as unlawful carnal knowledge of a woman by force and without her consent. Carnal knowledge refers to sexual intercourse. Penetration of the vagina need not be complete (the slightest penetration is sufficient) and sexual emission need not occur. Rape occurs when consent is obtained by threats of violence or deception, as, for example, by impersonating the woman's husband. Women of unsound mind are incapable of giving legal consent. Statutory rape, which is not considered in this chapter, refers to sexual intercourse without force and with the consent of a girl who is under the legal age of consent. The law on rape is reviewed at greater length in Chapter 12.

THE INCIDENCE OF RAPE

The *Uniform Crime Reports* of the Federal Bureau of Investigation give a nationwide view of the incidence of forcible rape based upon police statistics. In the *Crime Reports* forcible rape is defined as rape by force and attempts or assaults to rape. Statutory rape without force is not included. During 1968 there was an estimated total of 31,060 forcible rapes in the United States. Over two thirds of these offenses were actual rapes by force and the remainder were attempts or assaults to rape. In 1968 the number of forcible rapes increased 15 per cent over 1967, and 84 per cent over 1960.

RAPE RATES

Crime rates are usually based upon the number of crimes per unit of population. In 1968 thirty of every 100,000 females in the United States were victims of forcible rape. In 1968 the forcible rape crime rate increased 13 per cent over 1967 and 65 per cent over 1960.

The large core cities recorded a victim risk rate of sixty-two per 100,000 females, while the suburban area rate was twenty-three and the rural area seventeen. The rate was highest in the Western states, forty-eight per 100,000 females. The North Central states recorded a rate of thirty, followed by the Southern and Northeastern states with rates of twenty-eight and twenty-two per 100,000 females respectively.

The Federal Bureau of Investigation has been issuing crime reports only since 1930. Ferdinand, in a study of the annual arrest reports of the Boston police from 1849 to 1951, found that murder, larceny and assault have shown a clear decline in the last one hundred years; burglary and robbery have shown a downward tendency, and manslaughter has declined recently from initial high levels. Only forcible rape has shown a clear tendency to increase over the last one hundred years.

He attributes the increase in rapes reported to the police to the introduction of the automobile, which permits young couples to seclude themselves from the gaze of society, and to the increase in the proportion of the population adhering to a middle-class style of life. A middle-class girl, in his opinion, is much more likely than a lower-class girl to complain to the police when she is molested by her escort.

RAPE RATES IN OTHER COUNTRIES

It is difficult to compare the forcible rape rate in the United States (thirty rapes or attempted rapes per 100,000 females each year) with rape rates elsewhere. Legal definitions of forcible rape, the willingness of victims to report the offense and the efficiency of police in reporting rapes to a central agency vary from one country to another. Attempted rape statistics may be combined with forcible rapes or may not be recorded at all. Available statistics, despite their deficiencies, suggest that the United States has an unusually high rape rate, as well as a high homicide rate.

Rape is a rare crime in some countries. Norway, which has an extremely low rate of crimes of violence, has less than one rape per 100,000 females per year. England, which has a relatively low rate of crimes against the person, has three rapes; Poland, seven rapes, and Japan, twelve rapes per 100,000 females a year. There are fourteen rapes or attempted rapes in Turkey per 100,000 females a year. In Western Nigeria rape is a relatively rare occurrence. Asuni believes that the reasons include early age of marriage, the rather loose nature of the marriage institution in the traditional setting and the lack of the sexual taboos and inhibitions of the Western Culture.

Hong Kong, with a population of about four million (over 95 per cent Chinese), had seven, ten and twenty-two reported cases of rape in the years 1965-66 (April 1965 to March 1966), 1966-67 and 1967-68. The low frequency of rape in Hong Kong may in part be due to lack of opportunity. Wong notes that the city is so densely populated that there are very few places sufficiently deserted at any hour of the day for the crime to be committed. Everywhere is built up and well lit. There are virtually no dimly lit parks, alleys or paths. Many families frequently share one apartment which is only incompletely partitioned into rooms or cubicles. Homosexuality, according to Wong, is also very rare and is virtually never encountered in psychiatric practice. It is rare even among mental hospital and prison inmates. This observation is of interest in view of the relationship between homosexuality and rape.

THE "DARK FIGURES" OF RAPE STATISTICS

The incidence of forcible rape is much higher than that recorded in official statistics. The *Uniform Crime Reports* note that of all the Crime Index offenses, rape is probably the crime most under-reported by victims to police. In 1960 the *Uniform Crime Reports* estimated that slightly over 30 per cent of rapes are reported to the police. The President's Commission on Law Enforcement and Administration of Justice (1967) initiated a national survey to gain an accurate knowledge of the amount of crime. The National Opinion Research Center of the University of Chicago, in a random survey of 10,000 households, asked whether the person questioned, or any member of his or her household, had been a victim of crime during the preceding year. It was found that the forcible rape rate was more than three and one-half times the rate reported in the Uniform Crime Index.

Many women do not report that they have been raped. Indeed the woman's shame may be so great that she does not mention the rape to anyone. Fear of rejection by her husband may seal her lips. On the other hand, ladies of easy virtue may not be greatly excited because some man takes her by force rather than by finesse. Some victims show such a casual attitude toward rape that they do not want to be bothered by the inconvenience of a complaint to the police. One woman came with her husband to a police station to report the theft of a record player. At this time the husband suggested that his wife should also report an attempted rape which had occurred one week earlier.

Fear of newspaper publicity may deter the victim from notifying the police. Editors sometimes show little sensitivity or discretion in their reports of the nature and circumstances of the sexual assault. The account of a well-publicized sexual assault in which the victim's name was reported included reference to discovery of rocks in the vagina of the comatose victim. It is not surprising that some parents of young victims fail to notify the police. The child's experience in the courtroom may be as traumatic as the rape, especially when the victim is unfairly attacked by the defense attorney.

Fear of embarrassment in the courtroom is another factor which may discourage victims from reporting the rape. Defense attorneys often attempt to save their clients from conviction and punishment by insinuating that the victim did not resist the assault or by attempting to discredit the moral character of the victim. It matters not to some attorneys that their accusations may lack any basis in fact.

As many rapists threaten to kill their victims or the children of the victims, fear of retaliation may contribute to the "dark figures." Arrest of the rapist does not preclude danger, since release on bond before trial commonly occurs. Furthermore the offender may be careful to warn the woman that he has friends who will assault her if he is arrested.

Some victims do not report sexual assaults by close relatives or family friends. The young girl who is assaulted by her mother's boyfriend may be discouraged from notifying the police. The mother would rather retain the affections of her lover than protect the welfare of her child. Stepfathers often escape prosecution in this manner.

When the rape is the outcome of some activity forbidden by a parent or husband, no action may be taken; for example, the young girl who continues to associate with a boyfriend of doubtful reputation against the instructions of her parents, and the wife who goes to a drinking party while her husband is on service overseas with the Army may remain silent about the rape. The onset of pregnancy leads to a belated report of the rape to the police.

THE UNDETECTED OFFENDER

The crime of rape poses a serious challenge to law enforcement officers. Clues are often slender. The young woman who is attacked in her dark bedroom late at night may not have a clear view of her assailant's appearance. A towel may be placed over her face or the rapist may wear a mask to avoid identification. Delay in reporting the offense adds to the investigator's task. Other problems in the criminal investigation of rape are reviewed in Chapter 15.

In 1968, 45 per cent of forcible rapes in the United States were not cleared by arrest. Indeed the clearance by arrest rates is lower for forcible rape than for the other Crime Index offenses against the person — aggravated assault, murder and nonnegligent manslaughter. In 1968, 86 per cent of criminal homicides were cleared by arrest. Certain factors aid the homicide investigator; for example, over one fourth of all homicides occur within the family. Homicide offenders and their victims are seldom strangers and suspects are likely to be friends or acquaintances.

In contrast the rapist is more likely to be unknown to his victim. Nevertheless, the higher detection rate in homicide is undoubtedly related to the greater care and thoroughness in the investigation of this offense. Undermanned police departments are unable to assign a sufficient number of detectives to investigate rape and other sexual offenses.

SEASONAL VARIATIONS

"In the spring a young man's fancy lightly
turns to thoughts of love."
— Tennyson, *Locksley Hall*

According to Adolphe Quetelet's "thermic law of delinquency," crimes against the person are more frequent in warm climates and seasons, whereas crimes against property are more prevalent in cold climates and in colder weather. A number of studies over a century ago supported this formula. Guerry showed that the crime of rape occurred in England (1834-56) and France (1829-1860) most often in the hot months. Curcio observed the same thing in Italy (1869). The maximum number of rapes in these countries occurred in June or July and the minimum number in November and December. These authors also found that the maximum number of murders occurred in the hottest months.

Amir (Philadelphia 1958, 1960) found that although the number of forcible rapes tended to increase during the hot summer months, there was no significant association either with the season or with the month of the year. He noted that while Negro intraracial rapes are spread over the year, white intraracial rapes showed a more consistent increase during the summer. Summer was also found to be the season when multiple rapes are most likely to occur.

Recent *Uniform Crime Reports* show a higher incidence of rape in the United States in the warmer spring and summer months. Svalastoga, in his study of rape in Denmark (1946-1956), found confirmation of the so-called thermic law of delinquency, as the lowest monthly incidence of rape occurred in the months of December through March. In a recent survey in

Denver, there were more rapes in July than in November and December combined. The peak months were April and July through September.

Howard Jones has suggested a connection between the increase in sexual crimes which starts in spring and the occurrence of a natural biological tide at this season of the year. He adds that the increased daylight and the warmer months of the summer facilitate social intercourse. Havelock Ellis has reviewed the literature on the phenomenon of sexual periodicity. Throughout the vegetable and animal worlds the sexual functions are periodic. Among most animals heat or estrus usually occurs once or twice a year, in spring and in autumn, sometimes affecting the male as well as the female. Most of the higher animals breed only once or twice a year and at such a period that the young are born when food is most plentiful.

Under the influence of domestication, animals tend to lose the strict periodicity of the wild condition and become apt for breeding at more frequent intervals. Ellis claims that in some primitive human races there is a marked seasonal sexual periodicity. Among the Eskimo, passions are depressed during the long winter nights and a kind of rut affects the young population soon after the sun appears. This periodicity is not confined to the arctic regions. In Cambodia, men seem to experience a "veritable rut" in April and September.

Ellis also draws attention to primitive festivals which are religious and often erotic in character, to herald the change of seasons. Great spring festivals were held in Europe between March and June, frequently culminating in a great orgy on Midsummer's eve. The return of spring was regarded as the period for the return of the reproductive instinct even in man. It is an Irish belief that the girl who jumps thrice over the midsummer bonfire will soon marry and become the mother of many children, and in Flanders women leap over the midsummer fires to ensure an easy delivery (Frazer).

The question whether the increased sexual activity among primitive races during spring and autumn also occurs in civilized population can, in the opinion of Ellis, be most conveniently answered by studying seasonal variations in the birthrate. Quetelet showed that in Belgium and Holland there are a maximum of births in February, and consequently, of conceptions in May. There are a minimum of births about July with consequent minimum of conceptions in October. Villerme's study in France of 17,000,000 births showed that the maximum number of conceptions occurs in April, May and June, while the minimum of births is normally in July. He also showed that in Buenos Aires, where the seasons are reversed, the conception rate follows the reversed seasons.

Mannheim has reviewed the claims that crimes against the person are more frequent in hot climates and in the summer months, whereas crimes against property prevail in cold climates and in winter. He draws the following conclusions: "One gets the impression that the more recent studies, being less prejudiced and using more refined statistical techniques, fail to corroborate the findings of the more enthusiastic and less critical studies of the nineteenth and early twentieth centuries. This does not necessarily force us completely to deny the influence of climatic conditions on criminal behavior. The assumption which lay behind the work of those earlier writers that human emotions, sexual or otherwise, are more intense in hot weather and material human needs more acute in a cold climate may well be true. All we can say for the time being is that the expression of such emotions and material needs in criminal acts has not yet been clearly and unequivocally demonstrated in the available statistics. Nor has that assumption been refuted by this negative fact. The reason for this state of affairs may be, as usual, the complexity of the problem and the corresponding difficulty of establishing trends which are not masked by contrary trends."

THE HOUR AND DAY OF RAPE

> *"The night shows stars and women*
> *in a better light."*
> — Lord Byron, *Don Juan*

> *"Night is a stealthy, evil raven*
> *Wrapt to the eyes in his black wings."*
> — T. B. Aldrich, *Day and Night*

The hours of darkness are most dangerous for women. Fifty-three per cent of the 200 women in the Denver study were raped in the six-hour period between 10 P.M. and 4 A.M. In contrast, less than 6 per cent were raped in the six hours between 7 A.M. and 1 P.M. Rape in daytime is not as rare as is generally believed — almost 20 per cent of the victims were raped between 9 A.M. and 6 P.M. More victims (13%) were raped between 10 P.M. and 11 P.M. than at any other hour of the day or night.

The greater number of rapes occurring between 10 P.M. Saturday and 4 A.M. Sunday than during the same period on other days is highly significant statistically. (Chi square is a measure of the discrepancy between observed and expected frequencies — $p < .001$. See Table I.)

In Denmark, Svalastoga found that exactly two thirds of 141 cases of rape and attempted rape occurred between 10 P.M. and 4 A.M. In Philadelphia, Amir found the highest concentration of rapes (53%) to be on weekends, with Saturday being the peak day. The minimum number of rapes occurred on Tuesday in Denmark and on Wednesday in Denver.

TABLE I

RAPES DURING SIX-HOUR PERIOD 10 P.M. TO 4 A.M.

Day	*Number of Victims*
Sunday to Monday	11
Monday to Tuesday	11
Tuesday to Wednesday	16
Wednesday to Thursday	11
Thursday to Friday	13
Friday to Saturday	12
Saturday to Sunday	32
Total	106

THE INITIAL MEETING PLACE

"In life there are meetings which seem
like a fate."
— Owen Meredith, *Lucile*

Few women are raped in the streets, yet many rape victims encounter their assailants for the first time as they are waiting for a bus, walking home or halted for a traffic light in their cars. Indeed streets are the most dangerous initial meeting place between offender and victim. Among the 143 women in the Denver study who were raped by strangers, seventy (49%) were forcibly seized or enticed while on the street and taken elsewhere prior to the rape.

Twenty-three of these women were attacked as they got in or out of their cars near their homes, stopped for a traffic signal or a punctured tire. One man hid in the car of a well-known nightclub entertainer and attacked her as she was driving home from the nightclub. One woman was helped from her wrecked car following an accident and driven to her rescuer's home, where she was raped. Another woman, after stopping at a hamburger stand, agreed to drive a young man downtown with results which she had not foreseen.

Ten of the forty-seven women who encountered their assailants while walking or waiting in a street willingly agreed to go somewhere with total strangers after brief conversations. The other thirty-seven victims were all forcibly seized and dragged into a yard or driven elsewhere before being raped.

The victim's home is the next most dangerous initial meeting place;

forty-six women were attacked in their homes or apartments by strangers. Only one woman met a stranger-assailant for the first time in the assailant's home. She was going from home to home with a petition favoring the opening of a liquor outlet. The man raped her and the records do not show whether he signed her petition.

The third most frequent initial meeting place was the tavern. Twelve of the thirteen women who first encountered their assailants in a tavern willingly agreed to leave the tavern in the company of a stranger they had met a short time before. Many of them had agreed either to go to another tavern or to accept a ride home.

TABLE II

INITIAL MEETING PLACE OF OFFENDER AND VICTIM*

Place	Denver Percentage	Philadelphia Percentage
Streets	48.9	47.6
Victim's home, apartment	32.2	34.6
Offender's home	0.7	6.7
Taverns	9.0	7.8
Park	1.4	0.7
Elsewhere	7.8	2.6

*Amir lists the initial meeting place for all the 646 victims in his study in Philadelphia. However, the significance of the initial meeting place may be questioned when there was a relationship (relative, employer, friend, etc.) existing prior to the rape. The Denver figures refer only to the 143 cases in which the offender was a stranger to the victim.

THE SCENE OF THE CRIME

Rape Indoors

In U. S. cities more rapes occur in homes and apartments than in any other place. In this respect rape resembles homicide. In the Denver study 33 per cent of the victims were raped in their own homes or apartments, and 21 per cent were raped in the offender's home, or in an abandoned house to which the victim was enticed or taken by force. In Philadelphia 38 per cent of the victims were raped in their homes and 17 per cent were raped in the offender's home. Hotel and motel rooms are more often the scene of statutory rape than of forcible rape.

Other indoor rapes occur in places of employment. The shop or office attended only by a female clerk provides ready opportunity for assault. The presence of an additional clerk does not guarantee safety. The occasional

TABLE III

PLACES OF RAPE

Place	Denver Percentage of 200 Rapes	Philadelphia (Amir) Percentage of 646 Rapes
Indoors, participants' residences	54.5	55.7
Indoors, others	3.5	11.6
Automobiles and trucks	26.0	14.9
Outdoors	16.0	17.8

stickup offender will empty the till, then discourage one female assistant from flight by ordering her to remove her clothes while he rapes the other assistant. There is not always safety in numbers, as in the following case.

A masked gunman entered a shop on a busy street in the noon hour and told the manager, three employees and three customers, "This is a stickup." He had a loose nylon stocking over his face, yellow gloves on his hands and was carrying a revolver with a long barrel. He attached what appeared to be a silencer to the barrel after entering the store. The victims, all women, together with another customer who entered the store during the stickup, were ordered into a back room.

The manager was taken back into the store and instructed to remove her clothes. However, she ran back to join the other women. She was followed by the gunman who ordered the women to give him the money in their purses. Those victims who had only one or two single dollar bills were told to keep their money because of the small amount. After taking over sixty dollars, he told the women to take all their clothes off, so that they could not follow him.

When the women were all lined up against the wall naked, he removed his penis and asked some of the women to feel it. He made comments such as "That's not too bad, now is it?" "Pretty nice, isn't it?" Some of the women were molested, and one was raped while she was standing against the wall. When he started to escort one employee away from the group, the others pleaded with him to leave her alone, as she was four months pregnant.

He then made one of the customers lie down on the floor. While he was raping her, he pointed the revolver at the other women and clicked it three times. Before leaving he warned them not to say anything to the police.

Some rapes occur in women's toilets even in large office buildings where the offender might have good reason to fear detection. One would think that the possibility of interruption by a third party would discourage the would-be rapist, yet many rapes are committed under these circumstances.

A twenty-six-year-old man tried to make the acquaintance of two women in a tavern. He was apparently annoying them and after a brief period both women got up and went into the women's restroom. Immediately thereafter the man forced his way into the restroom and threatened the women with a small knife. He told them he was going to rape them and would cut their stomachs open if they did not cooperate. As he was raping one woman, the other lay beside them praying. Two other women attempted to enter the restroom but the man held the door shut then suddenly ran out past them. Following his arrest he said that he had been drinking all day and did not remember anything until the next morning when his wife woke him up. He was given a ten- to twelve-year sentence.

*   *   *

I [a nineteen-year-old man] went into a tavern. I went into the men's restroom and urinated. I then went into the women's restroom with the intention of rape. The lights were on when I went in. I turned them off. I had been in there about five minutes when this lady came in. I started hitting her with my fists. I hit her in the head. When I hit her, she fell to the floor. While she was on the floor, I tried to get her girdle off. After the woman was knocked down, she didn't fight any more. Another woman came to the restroom. I held the door but I finally opened the door and slugged the other woman. I hit her in the face with my fist. I took off out the back door.

Other offenders select a time at which intervention is unlikely. The manager who keeps his attractive new secretary in the office for extra work in the evening, and the restaurant owner who asks one waitress to help him clean up after the last customer has left may have in mind additional activities not mentioned in the employment contract. Rape in the classroom is not unknown, particularly in some slum areas. Tavern owners who employ cocktail waitresses or "go-go" dancers sometimes force their attentions on these girls.

He asked me how old I was and I told him I was twenty-five. He then asked me when could I start work. I said I could start anytime. That's when he grabbed me; he put both arms around mine, picked me up and laid me on a bench. He had me pinned with his shoulders and right arm. With his left hand he pulled my panties and hose down. I was fighting him and screaming that I'd call the police, and he'd be in trouble if he didn't let me up. He said he always made love to girls before he hired them. I told him I didn't go for that, I didn't need the money that bad. I was screaming and crying. He finally let me up and said he was just teasing me.

Rape in Apartment Houses

Offenders who specialize in apartment house rapes obtain the names of unmarried girls by checking the mailboxes and gain entry to the apartment house by pressing buzzers to a number of the apartments. Invariably some tenant will unlock the front door by remote control without first checking the identity of the person who seeks admission. One man would go to an apartment and ask to speak to one of the single girls listed on the mailbox. If the girl was out, he would ask her roommate for a note pad so that he could leave a message. Once inside the apartment he would show his gun, blindfold the girl and rape her.

Some offenders select apartment houses with a vacancy sign and ask to see the vacant apartment. During the daytime the apartment house manager is often away at other work and leaves his wife in charge. She is a ready victim for these offenders.

A thirty-year-old woman whose husband managed an apartment house was feeding her baby when a man knocked on the door and asked to see an apartment that was for rent. She showed him the apartment and then returned with him to her own apartment. He filled out the necessary papers but gave a fictitious name. Later investigation showed that he had falsely claimed to be an employee of a local truck agency. The man left to get his checkbook from his car. When he returned, he walked behind the woman, who was seated at a breakfast table, put his right hand over her mouth and said, "Get up, don't scream, I have a knife and I'll use it."

He forced her into her bedroom and told her, "I have a knife and I'll use it if you don't cooperate." When she refused to follow his instructions, he threatened to harm her baby. At this time the baby started crying and he allowed her to go into the baby's room. While she was attending to the baby, he took a towel from the baby's crib and masturbated into it. He then tried to undress the victim but desisted when the phone rang. He left the room, and the woman seized the opportunity to escape through the window.

Rape in Hospitals

Rape of patients by hospital staff or by other patients occurs with more frequency than is generally recognized. Hospitals prefer to avoid undesirable newspaper publicity and these cases may not always be drawn to the attention of the police. Young children and unconscious patients in general hospitals and some psychotic mentally retarded or senile patients in mental hospitals are particularly vulnerable to attack. Cohen has reported two cases of sexual molestation in community hospitals and has personal knowledge of three similar instances which had taken place in three major children's hospitals in the United States.

The first patient was an eight-year-old girl who had had early pubescence during the year preceding her admission for a tonsillectomy. At 1 A.M. on the morning following the tonsillectomy, while still hospitalized, she screamed and the nurse who responded noted a man leaving the room by one door as she came in the other door. Physical examination was compatible with sexual attack and motile sperm were found in the vaginal smear. Evidence pointed to an operating room orderly who was quickly apprehended, and after a trial was convicted and sentenced to prison.

*   *   *

The second child was a fairly well developed twelve-year-old-girl ill with bilateral bronchopneumonia in a different hospital. At approximately 4 A.M. during her fifth day of hospitalization, she was assaulted by a foreign exchange resident, who subsequently admitted the attack and was immediately deported.

Rape in Automobiles

Rape in automobiles is more common in the United States than in Europe presumably because of the greater number of cars per unit of population. The higher proportion of compact cars in Europe may also be a factor, although some rapists commit rape in the small Volkswagen, surely not the most convenient place for intercourse. Svalastoga noted that 4 per cent of the rapes in Denmark occurred in autos, and Amir reported a figure of almost 15 per cent in Philadelphia. In Denver 26 per cent of the rapes occurred in automobiles or trucks. Some women were raped in their own cars after the offender forced his way in at a stop sign or parking lot.

> I was driving to the supermarket and I was waiting for a light to change. This man got in my car, he made me turn left on Race Street. Then he told me he wanted sex. I started blowing the horn and he hit me. I jumped out of the car and he caught me and threw me down and started pulling my clothes off. A car came by and he told the man I was his wife. Then he threw me in the back seat and he got in the front seat to drive and I jumped out. He caught me and beat me again and threw me in the front seat.
>
> He sat on my arm while he drove to a church parking lot. I jumped out and ran across to some apartments. He threw me down and choked me and hit me. Another car came down the street and they just stopped and looked. He then drove someplace else and made me pull my clothes off and he raped me. He kept telling me he was going to kill me, that he had a gun and a knife, but I never saw anything.

Rape Outdoors

Relatively few women are raped outdoors in the United States. In Denmark 72 per cent of the victims were raped outdoors in contrast to only 16 per cent in Denver and 18 per cent in Philadelphia. Women may be attacked in parks or as they take shortcuts across vacant lots. Underpasses are more dangerous than open streets. Only eleven of the two hundred Denver victims were raped in a street or alley. The outdoor rapist who encounters his victim in the street usually forces her to accompany him to a backyard or vacant lot.

RESIDENCE OF PARTICIPANTS

In a study of 2,624 sex crimes in Chicago, Erlanson found that 82 per cent of all male sex offenders lived in the immediate neighborhood, that is, within a few miles of the crime scene. Amir found that in 82 per cent of cases of rape in Philadelphia, offender and victim lived in the same neighborhood or vicinity, while in 68 per cent of cases offenders lived in the vicinity of the victims and the scene of the rape. These figures refer only to sex offenses in which the offender is detected.

RAPE AND ECONOMIC CONDITIONS

> *"Rape is definitely an offense of prosperity."*
> — Hans Von Hentig

Nineteenth century statistics from England, Italy, France, Germany and

Australia have been cited by Bonger to show a relationship between sexual criminality and economic conditions. Sex crimes tend to increase in prosperous years and to decrease when economic conditions are unfavorable. Ferri, for example, showed that in France economically bad years brought a diminution of rapes committed upon adults, and favorable years an increase. Annual arrest reports of the Boston police between 1849 and 1951 show sharp rises in the rate of forcible rape during prosperous years (Ferdinand).

Regarding the correlation between the incidence of rape and the business index in New York in the 1930's (see Table IV) Von Hentig comments, "There is a certain, sometimes an astonishing, synchronization. Looking at the years 1930 and 1936, rape and the business index reach about the same height."

TABLE IV*

RAPE AND THE BUSINESS INDEX, 1930-1939

Year	Rape	Business Index
1930	740	98.8
1931	606	71.0
1932	602	48.1
1933	643	56.5
1934	560	61.1
1935	582	69.8
1936	755	90.7
1937	796	98.6
1938	748	61.4
1939	822	85.0

*Taken from Hans von Hentig: *Crime: Causes and Conditions.* McGraw-Hill, New York, 1947.

Bonger comments: "The data upon the relation between the economic situation and these crimes are not as numerous as those upon economic crimes, and there are also many exceptions. With some reservations, however, we can say that an improvement in economic conditions tends to increase the crimes in question. However, this does not teach us much with regard to the etiology of them; the statistics of births have long since shown us that the sexual life is more intense during the periods of economic prosperity, than during those of depression. Better nourishment renders the sexual instincts stronger, without its being necessary that they should manifest themselves in a criminal manner. The proof of this is furnished by those who are sufficiently nourished both in good times and bad and are yet not guilty of these crimes."

ALCOHOL AND RAPE

"Drunkenness does not create vice; it merely
brings it into view."
— Seneca

The role of alcohol in rape is difficult to evaluate. It would be helpful to have the results of breath or blood alcohol tests on one hundred consecutive rapists. As over 50 per cent of forcible rapes in the United States are not cleared by arrest, it is clearly impossible to check, with any degree of confidence, the relationship between rape and alcohol. Shupe found that of forty-two persons arrested during or immediately after the commission of rape in Columbus, Ohio, twenty-one had alcohol in their urine. This finding should be interpreted with caution, as offenders under the influence of alcohol may be less skillful in avoiding detection than sober colleagues in crime.

Bonger provides figures from several studies which date back to the latter part of the nineteenth century. Sullivan claimed that 50 per cent of sexual crimes in England were caused by alcoholism and that acute alcoholism was especially active in the case of rape upon adults. Over 25 per cent of 179 cases of rape and other sex crimes in Austria were committed in a state of drunkenness and over 20 per cent of all sexual offenses in Switzerland were attributed to alcoholism. In contrast, only 6.6 per cent of rapes and indecent assaults in France were committed in a state of intoxication.

Recently Amir (Philadelphia, 1958 and 1960) found that in 24 per cent of 646 rapes alcohol was present in the offender. It was present in 30 per cent of the victims and in both offender and victim in 21 per cent of the rapes. Alcohol was found to be strongly related to violence used in the rape situation, especially when present in the offender only. Radzinowicz in England has also reported that the proportion of more serious or aggravated offenses was highest among offenders who had been drinking. In Philadelphia, alcohol was significantly associated with sexual humiliation forced upon a drinking victim.

Weekend rapes were significantly associated with the presence of alcohol in either the victim, the offender, or both. Amir attributed this association to payday on Friday leading to greater purchase of alcohol and more intense social and leisure activities. Victims under the influence of alcohol may be less alert to situations of danger and less able to defend themselves against assault. Amir also draws attention to the indirect relationship between alcohol in rape in the chronic alcoholic who is not under the influence of alcohol at the time of the crime. His chronic alcoholism may have influenced his general behavior, personality and judgment.

Amir's figures, like those of other research workers, should be regarded with caution. He reports that in the 66 per cent of cases in which alcohol played no role in the commision of the offense, police secured no evidence or did not record that either the victim or the offender had been drinking prior to the crime *(Brit J Addict, 62*:219, 1967). As police officers who make the original report of a rape offense often fail to explore all aspects of the offense, their reports are not a reliable source of information on the use of alcohol.

Amir is careful to acknowledge that if there is any bias in his study, it is in favor of the absence of alcohol. Unfortunately he does not make this clear in all his articles in which he claims to refute the view that rape is associated with drinking. He does not have adequate information to support his rejection of the viewpoint of others as a misconception.

Alcohol impairs judgment and diminishes self-control. Yet many men drink, but relatively few of them rape. Many criminal offenses are assumed to be due to alcohol on insufficient grounds. Excessive use of alcohol and criminal behavior may have the same root cause in psychological conflict. It would be illogical to assume that because a person was drinking prior to the offense, the act was the product of alcohol. Some offenders who rape when they are drunk also rape when they are sober.

THE SEX RATIO AND RAPE

Von Hentig postulated that if there are many more unmarried young men than unmarried young women in a community, social tensions arise which lead to an increase in the number of forcible rapes. It would be of interest to know the rape rate in Gunnison, Colorado, in 1860 during the gold rush. In this year there were 7,557 males in the county but only 678 females, giving a sex ratio of 1,115 males per 100 females. Perhaps the ready availability of prostitutes provided sexual outlet for the miners.

Svalastoga, in support of Hentig's suggestion, cited rape rates in Denmark which showed that the highest rates were in rural areas where girls were in short supply. Direct reference to the extreme sex ratio in rural Denmark is found in one of the rapes. In this case the offender killed the farmer and his wife who tried to help the rape victim. The day before the tragic event the eighteen-year-old future life prisoner was working in the hay fields with his later victim and a married female helper. These two women both asked the young boy what he sought in Western Jutland, because there were no girls. The young man responded that there had to be some, whereupon the younger of the females said, "There is, at most, three."

Although the ratio of women to men was approximately the same in provincial cities as in the capital of Denmark, the rape rate was much lower in the capital. Svalastoga attributed this difference to the higher availability of sexual satisfaction on commercial terms (prostitutes and call girls) in the capital.

RAPE DURING HYPNOSIS

Twenty-two cases of crimes alleged to have been committed under posthypnotic suggestion have been reported by Mayer. The most remarkable case concerns a self-styled nature healer who persuaded a young woman to undergo hypnotic treatment. While she was under hypnosis, he took advantage of her sexually, forced her to commit acts of prostitution, defrauded her out of large sums of money and forced her to make attempts on her husband's life. The crimes came to light when the husband complained to the Heidelberg police that his wife had been made to part with over 3,000 German marks. He did not know the nature healer's name and his wife had "forgotten everything."

Doctor Ludwig Mayer, who was consulted by the police, succeeded in reviving the wife's memory with the aid of hypnosis. She made six attempts on her husband's life and by good fortune none of them was successful. The criminal, presumably to avoid risk of criminal prosecution, instructed her to take her own life. She was told to take Pantopon®, a narcotic drug, but was unable to obtain a prescription for the drug from her doctor. She was told to drown herself but was restrained from doing so by her housekeeper. The so-called nature healer was tried, convicted and sentenced to ten years' imprisonment.

The risk of rape under hypnosis was recognized in France by the Royal Commission appointed by Louis XVI in 1784 to examine animal magnetism or mesmerism. Benjamin Franklin was a member of this commission, which noted the physical proximity of the man who "magnetizes" and his female patient together with the opportunity for sexual abuse. Thoinot describes five alleged cases of rape during hypnosis and concludes that rape is possible although it is extremely rare, as the hypnotic subject obeys only those suggestions that are agreeable to her.

SLEEPWALKING AND ATTEMPTED RAPE

Thoinot in his extensive review of rape during altered states of consciousness reported that he did not know of any case of rape during somnambulism, or sleepwalking.

In this study a young married woman who had been treated by her physician for sleepwalking returned home at 11 P.M. one night, put her children to bed and went to bed with her husband. After falling asleep the next thing she remembered was waking up in her car.

> I woke up looking at the steering wheel of my car, all of a sudden hands went over my eyes and this man said not to scream or he'd kill me. Then I realized I was walking in my sleep. He dragged me out of the car and he kept on telling me not to scream or he'd kill me. I don't know how far he was pulling me but as he

was pulling me I felt something in my back. Then he threw me down.

He let up a little to take his pants off or something and I took the chance and brought my knee up and hit him. I did this twice, then I doubled my fist and hit him as hard as I could, then he fell completely off me. I got up and ran. I heard him kind of screaming and shouting something at me as if he was in pain. But I couldn't hear what he said. I ran into the house and ran into the bedroom screaming to my husband that a man had tried to rape me.

RAPE DURING SLEEP

In 1760 a twenty-year-old girl who had a child swore by all the saints to her parents that she was not conscious of ever having had sexual intercourse with a man. She related that on one occasion, having been vividly impressed by a dream, she had awakened, and had then noticed a great moisture of her genital organs, but without ever having known the cause of it. The faculty of Leipzig declared in its report that it had no doubts concerning the *adventure* [!] and the possibility of coitus during sleep and gave as its opinion that the sleeping woman *could* have been made a mother during her sleep.

An opinion by the faculty of Halle in a similar case, also cited by Thoinot, states that "it is possible that a virgin, being seated on a little chair, may be deflowered during natural sleep if the position of the body permits it." Thoinot does not believe that coitus can be accomplished with a virgin during her sleep. Although he adds that coitus with a sleeping woman who is not a virgin is, strictly speaking, possible, Thoinot warns *"preserve a wise distrust."*

In Dumfries, Scotland, in 1862 a hotel employee was sentenced to ten years' imprisonment for raping the hotel proprietor's wife while she was asleep. The woman stated that owing to great fatigue and want of sleep for some time previous, she had fallen into a more profound sleep than was natural.

> I had been up all night on the previous night and had been much fatigued the week before. My husband was at this time sitting at the fire reading the papers. He was to go to bed after he was done with the papers. I fell asleep and was very sound asleep. I lay down with all my clothes on . . . I felt the pressure of a man and thinking it was my husband, I raised myself up. It was that blackguard – I mean the prisoner. He was lying upon me and when I rose up he drew himself away. My clothes I found folded up and the lower part of my person was exposed. It was his weight that awoke me. He withdrew himself when I awoke . . . In doing so, I felt a discharge from him in my person and all about on my clothes (Cowan).

It is not rare for a man who crawls into bed alongside a sleeping woman to obtain her cooperation in sexual intercourse. Usually the woman, while not fully awake, assumes that her husband has just returned home or that her boyfriend is paying a surprise visit. However, in the cases encountered in this study, the woman very quickly became aware of her mistaken initial impression.

> At approximately 3 A.M. a thirty-seven-year-old woman was aroused from her sleep in her completely dark bedroom when her bedclothes were removed. A nude man got into bed alongside her and started fondling her. In her sleepy state she thought it was her boyfriend who had a key to her apartment. The man had already commenced sexual intercourse when she became aware that he was not her boyfriend. She was extremely frightened and did not say anything. After the man had finished intercourse, she asked him who he was and he replied, "Mr. X." He added that he had seen her before and had wanted her a long time. When asked how he gained entry to the apartment, he replied, "You will know when I leave." He also told her that he had taken two kitchen knives in case he needed to threaten her. The knives were later found in the kitchen sink and a screen was missing from the kitchen window.

RAPE IN WARTIME

> *"War is pusillanimously carried out in this degenerate age;*
> *quarter is given; towns are taken and the people spared;*
> *even in a storm, a woman can hardly hope for*
> *the benefit of a rape."*
> — Lord Chesterfield, *Letters*

The spoils in war have long included the womenfolk of the conquered enemy. In the unsettled conditions following a successful battle, soldiers often take advantage of the lull in fighting by relaxation in wine and sex. Detached writers who deal with this subject relieve the tragedy of the occasion by lighthearted jest. Thus some French women, after their town was captured in World War I, are described as throwing open their windows and calling out to the German soldiers, "When do the atrocities begin?" Byron describes the storming and sack of a city. The smoke was so dense there was no spark,

> *"Of light to save the venerably chaste:*
> *But six old damsels, each of seventy years,*
> *Were all deflowered by different grenadiers.*
> *But on the whole their continence was great;*
> *So that some disappointment there ensued. . .*
> *Some voices of the buxom middle-aged*
> *Were also heard to wonder in the din*
> *(Widows of forty were these birds long caged)*
> *'Wherefore the ravishing did not begin!' "*
> — Lord Byron, *Don Juan, Canto VIII*

A Woman in Berlin translated from the German, gives in diary form the experiences of a German woman when the Russians took Berlin at the end of World War II. The reason why the author prefers to remain anonymous needs no explanation. It is in no way erotic but tells grimly what she suffered at the hands of a succession of Russian soldiers. Ceram, in his introduction, comments that the author was able to rise secretly triumphant from the depths of the maelstrom because, although she had to surrender, she never surrendered herself. After repeated rapes she makes a decision. "It suddenly came to me, I must get hold of a wolf — to protect me from the wolves. An officer. As high a one as possible, Commandant, General — whatever I can get. What's my brain for — and my little knowledge of the enemy's language?"

The Vietnamese conflict is no exception to the rule of rape in wartime. "As an example of minor but deliberate savagery, Daniel Lang's careful account of the *Incident on Hill 192* is a model record. It shows how the thin skin of custom that restrains brutality and lust can be punctured in the conditions of war. First published in the *New Yorker,* the story describes an American Army patrol in Vietnam in November 1966 whose sergeant in command told his four companions as they were setting out on an arduous five-day trip that they would pick up any attractive Vietnamese girl they could find to "raise the morale of the squad" and use her for their own gratification. To avoid discovery they would then kill her and dispose of her body.

"One of the four men under the sergeant's command relished the proposal, two others laughed in weak embarrassment at the suggestion, only one was silently against it. So Phan Thi Mao was taken from her anguished mother and sister, was raped in succession by four of the five men and was killed on the sergeant's orders by one of the team. But it seemed she had not died from the stab wounds he administered and was seen crawling down a hillside into some bushes. Whereupon all but the one objector turned their guns on her. 'You want her gold tooth?' asked the one whose stabbing had been insufficient as he stumbled on the corpse after all movement had ceased in the bushes where the wounded girl had collapsed . . . .

"It is not only a lesson of war but of men's treatment of women primarily as objects of sexual gratification that is exposed so nakedly by what happened on Hill 192. Our culture is slow in rejecting this view of women, and although it is changing, nevertheless it is up against the strong tide of an ad-mass view which founds itself precisely on such treatment of women" (*The Times Literary Supplement,* April 2, 1970).

Kapauku Papuans and Battlefield Rape

Kapauku Papuans have rather unusual laws regarding women on the battlefield. As incessant shooting rapidly exhausts the supply of arrows and, since the warriors find no time to collect stray arrows, this is the task of the women.

Thus they save time and make the war more interesting to the men. Their role as collectors is facilitated by a married woman's immunity from being punished, beaten or shot by anyone except her own husband. It is highly immoral for a man to shoot at a female during a battle and even an accidental injury to one may deprive a brave of all the prestige he possessed before. Even his own relatives would reproach such an unfortunate individual and ridicule him with the taunt "all you can do is shoot a woman." Thus everyone is very careful not to make such a regrettable mistake.

The women exploit this situation to the limit. Not only do they collect arrows behind, on and between the battle lines, as quietly as one would pick flowers or harvest cucumbers, but they even have the courage to climb a hill behind the enemy and shout advice concerning his movements. The only thing left for the poor enemy to do is to dispatch a few warriors to chase the women away from the height . . . . Leaving aside the derogatory and disgusting nature of such an occupation for a warrior, the success of the maneuver is sometimes dubious because of the long sticks wielded by the usually more numerous women. It is the men who sometimes get the pushing and the beating. If it were not for the fact that men actually are killed, the scene would have the character of a farce.

From the description of the behavior of war leaders, one might get an impression of a gallantry similar to that of knighthood in Europe during the Middle Ages. Unfortunately, the reader has to be made familiar with other Kapauku customs which make the war less attractive to the Western observer. Although married women escape any molestation, an unmarried girl is invariably raped if caught by the advancing enemy. Since it is taboo for the enemy to rape girls of the opposite camp, it is the friends and "in-law" relatives of the enemy who rape the girls.

"There is nothing to be sorry for," explained Ijaaj Jokagaibo of Itoda. "These girls like it anyway and some may even get caught willingly. During an attack on Degeipige, I raped a beautiful girl. She screamed and wept all right but this was only a pretence. After the cessation of hostilities, she came after me to Aigii and asked me to marry her. She liked me so much." Even if we take the above statement with reservations and view it as extreme, we have to admit that an attitude toward rape is relative to the cultural milieu in which it happens (Pospisil).

NECROPHILIA

Necrophilia has been variously defined as a morbid fancy for dead bodies, an erotic attraction to corpses and as the desire to possess a dead body for purposes of sexual intercourse. Krafft-Ebing, in his *Psychopathia Sexualis*, describes with equanimity a number of brutal murders in which the victims are disembowelled or otherwise treated unkindly. His dispassionate attitude does not extend to necrophilia, which he refers to as horrible and monstrous. Yet this is a crime without pain or suffering for the victim. He adds that an abnormal and decidedly perverse sensuality is required to overcome the natural repugnance which man has for a corpse and permit a feeling of pleasure to be experienced in sexual congress with a cadaver.

Herodotus referred to this problem in Egypt in the fifth century B. C. "Wives of prominent men and women of great beauty are not delivered at once to the embalmers, but only after they have been dead three or four days. This is done in order to prevent the embalmers from having carnal relations with these corpses. For it was discovered that such an act was committed with a woman newly dead." The practice is obviously not of recent origin yet there are relatively few articles in the literature on this subject.

At the turn of the century, Dubois reported an abominable and revolting custom among the Namburidi caste in India. "The girls of this caste are usually married before the age of puberty; but if the girl has arrived at an age when the signs of puberty are apparent, and happens to die before having had intercourse with a man, caste custom rigorously demands that the inanimate corpse of the deceased shall be subjected to a monstrous connexion. For this purpose the girl's parents are obliged to procure by a present of money some wretched fellow willing to consummate such a disgusting form of marriage; for were the marriage not consummated, the family would consider itself dishonored."

It is not unusual for a rapist to assault a woman and then have sexual intercourse with her as she is dying or shortly after her death. Sexual relationship with the body of a woman who has not died as the result of physical assault in the course of an attempted rape is less common. It may, however, occur more frequently than is generally recognized, as there can be no outcry from the victim. In 1901 Epaulard (cited by Stekel) listed twenty men who had performed sexual intercourse with dead women, but his examples covered a span of five hundred years, as one of them was the infamous Gilles De Rais, Marshall of France.

These men included two medical students, one assistant in anatomy, two grave diggers and a washer of bodies. Funeral home assistants, morgue attendants and grave diggers figure prominently in case reports. Doubtless persons who prefer to embrace the dead seek out such employment. Dalmau reported the case of one patient who was frustrated in an attempt at coitus with a cadaver by the unexpected appearance of the owner of the funeral home where he worked. This man also had sexual intercourse with the living and had informed his physician of between fifteen and twenty rapes including one of a woman in labor.

One grave digger disinterred twenty bodies of children for sexual purposes. He claimed that girls always repulsed his attempts to approach them and that this had driven him to the dead. Another grave digger who dug up the bodies of young girls said:

> "I could find no young girl who would agree to yield to my desires; that is why I have done this. I should have preferred to have relations with living persons. I found it quite natural to do what I did; I saw no harm in it, and I did not think that anyone else could. As living women felt nothing but repulsion for me, it was quite natural I should turn to the dead, who have never repulsed me. I used to say

tender things to them like 'my beautiful, my love, I love you' " (Belletrud and
Mercier, cited by Ellis).

This man who was mentally retarded had no sense of smell, which must
surely be an advantage for necrophiliacs. On the other hand, some authorities
have attached significance to the stench as a psychological factor in the
genesis of this perversion.

A sadistic element is apparent in those men who mutilate the corpse
following sexual relations. The celebrated Sergeant Bertrand, as a youth, had
fantasies while masturbating of raping women, killing them, then defiling the
corpses. As an adult he would dig up bodies of either sex, mutilate them,
then masturbate. He described his first sexual relations with a dead girl:

> I covered it with kisses and pressed it wildly to my heart. All that one could
> enjoy with a living woman is nothing in comparison with the pleasure I
> experienced. After I had enjoyed it for about a quarter of an hour, I cut the body
> up, as usual, and tore out the entrails. Then I buried the cadaver again
> (Krafft-Ebing).

Segal described a man with necrophilic fantasies who extolled the virtues
of a corpse as a sexual object. He described with relish the feeling of power
and security that he could enjoy in making love to a corpse; it is there when
wanted, you put it away when finished with it, it makes no demands, it is
never frustrating, never unfaithful, never reproachful; persecution and guilt,
he said, could be quite done away with. In his sexual relationships with
women he demanded immobility and compliance.

RAPE OF ANIMALS

Although relatively few men are convicted of bestiality in the United
States (Gebhard *et al;* in their study of 1,356 males convicted of sex
offenses, found only five cases of men legally punished for sexual behavior
with animals) farm boys probably indulge in this behavior more often than is
suggested by court statistics. In Austria between 1923 and 1937, 750 men
were convicted of bestiality and between 1951 and 1965, 692 men were
sentenced for this offense. During the first period, two thirds of those
sentenced were between fourteen and twenty-one years of age. Since 1951
the percentage of young offenders has markedly fallen, presumably because
of the improved opportunities for youngsters to take up heterosexual
contacts (Grassberger).

The majority of those sentenced lived in rural areas. Animals preferred
were cows or calves, goats and pigs. Due to their replacement in agriculture,
the number of horses abused dropped from forty-seven to seven during the
two periods. Grassberger found no evidence of the animal's interest in the
act. Zoo directors, however, report that caged animals sometimes learn to
prefer their keepers to their natural mates and that even cases of

victim-precipitated sodomy are not unheard of (Christian Helfer).

A husband who forces his wife to have sexual relations with another man may be convicted of rape. In 1952 in England a twenty-eight-year-old man was sentenced to eight years' imprisonment for forcing his wife to have sexual relations with a dog. The evidence showed that the man on two separate occasions sexually excited the dog and then forced his wife to submit to its having connection with her *per vaginam.* The wife stated in her evidence that she had been terrorized into submission and that the acts were entirely against her will *(R. v. Bourne,* 36 Cr. App. Rep. 125, 1952).

THREATS TO RAPE

> *"Many a one threatens while he quakes for*
> *fear."*
> — W. G. Benham, *Proverbs*

Threats to rape are usually made in writing or over the telephone and the man does not identify himself. Threats are seldom made directly to the woman except in those rapes or attempted rapes where the threat is not so much a menace of some future act but an announcement of an assault already in progress. Threats in writing are sent by mail or are slipped into a mailbox or under the door. A paranoid deaf-mute wrote anonymous letters and tied them to bricks which were thrown through the living room window of the home of a girl he had known at school.

Threats in writing are often dramatic, sadistic, obscene and illiterate. One such note, attached to pictures clipped from a magazine showing a girl tied to a chair with her chest exposed, was placed in a girl's mail slot in an apartment house.

> Listen, I'm going to screw you to do this I will use Chrollform [presumably the writer meant chloroform] when you're asleep. You won't know what happened. See I have raped four girls already. You're my fifth, first unless you give to me willingly I will force my penis into your vigina [sic] and you will now pay double for telling the manager about this last one [a previous note]. Rape now pay later.

A young boy wrote the following letter to a married woman.

> I hate you and your family. I wish somebody would rape you, boy, that would be a laugh! I just might be the man who does it. I have planned to be that guy to do it, but you have never shown up at the place I will attack. One of these nights I will get you and when I do you better watch out because I would hate to hurt that pretty face of yours. This is just a warning you better be careful. Ha, ha, ha, you'll be sorry. Just wait I will get you. Your my next victim, I am going to rape you one of these days. And when I do I'm going to give you a baby, won't that be fun, ha, ha, ha, a baby, a baby. P. S. I see you everyday.

A sixteen-year-old girl received this letter.

> I hope this note finds you in the gutter. Have you been strapped lately? Do you

think I could get into rotation? I'll give you $75 a month for a complete blow job and strap. That's a pretty good deal. Know your schedule is tight cut. I know I won't interfere with your period. Giving you $75 a month leaves me flat busted so you won't mind if I don't use a contraceptive, a rubber. Do you think you could hold fourteen inches of pure muscle, you've had a lot of practice.

Abusive telephone calls are a major problem for telephone companies as well as for the victims. In 1967 Southwestern Bell which serves five states handled more than 58,000 complaints of abusive telephone calls. Often the victim receives only one or two calls but sometimes the calls are continued over several months. Men who make obscene telephone calls may dial their victims at random or select a neighbor or fellow office employee. The caller will sometimes claim that he is working for a modeling agency and offer the girl employment. He will ask the girl personal questions regarding her figure and bust measurement.

One man, who rang a girl in a sorority house, gave a false name and claimed that he had to ask her some questions in order to be accepted as a member of a fraternity at the same university. He asked her, "What are you wearing and describe it?" "Does it have a zipper in front or back?" "What are you wearing underneath?" "What size is your bra?" and others questions of a more indelicate nature. Once the woman, on whatever pretext, is engaged in discussion of intimate personal matters, the conversation moves to suggestions that she pose in the nude for pornographic pictures, have sexual relations with the caller or work as a prostitute.

Some callers do not make any effort to seduce the woman into a sexual discussion but make extremely obscene and sadistic remarks as soon as the woman answers the telephone. One man, in addition to making obscene telephone calls to a woman, ordered lingerie to be sent to her home C.O.D. from a department store. The man who telephones a woman who lives in the next home or apartment house may spy on her with binoculars as she answers the phone. Her appearance of alarm and distress adds to his gratification.

It is not surprising that frequently these telephone callers have a history of acts of indecent exposure. Many of these men are extremely shy and fearful of women. Some claim that they only make calls when they are drunk or under stress. Requests for a date with the woman may lead to the offender's arrest by police who wait in the home. Telephone companies are able to trace calls, but those calls from a public telephone seldom lead to an arrest unless the conversation is prolonged. Victims who do not immediately terminate obscene calls encourage further harrassment. One woman complained to police that a man made the most revolting sexual suggestions to her over the telephone for almost an hour.

Chapter 3

THE OFFENDERS

> *"A man must have his faults"*
> — Petronius, *Satyricon*

PHYSICAL APPEARANCE

> *"It is only shallow people who do not*
> *judge by appearances."*
> — Oscar Wilde, *Picture of Dorian Gray*

LOMBROSO, the Italian criminologist who advanced the concept of the born criminal, believed that there was a direct relationship between physique and crime. In this viewpoint he was preceded by many authors and artists. Kindly Santa Claus is portrayed as a portly gentleman whose rotundity is increased by billowing robes; whereas the devil, the personification of evil, is a thin man whose leanness is accentuated by pointed horns and a long tail. A similar belief in the relationship of physique and character is expressed by Shakespeare in *Julius Caesar.*

> *"Let me have men about me that are fat;*
> *Sleek-headed men, and such as sleep o'nights.*
> *Yond' Cassius has a lean and hungry look;*
> *He thinks too much: such men are dangerous."*

East draws attention to the immortal pictures of William Hogarth, an eighteenth century satirist, illustrating the principles of good and evil in scenes from the lives of the Two Apprentices. The results of Industry and Idleness were forcibly presented by contrasting success and honor in the one with crime and ruin in the other, and the latter in all its ugliness must have impressed those who reflected upon the lessons which the twelve engravings taught. In the nineteenth century the inimitable illustrations of George Cruikshank depicting Fagin, Bill Sikes and other characters in the work of Charles Dickens also emphasized the association of crime and evil-doing with personal ugliness.

Ellis has given a number of examples from literature which relate criminal behavior to physical appearance. When Homer described Thersites as ugly and deformed, with harsh or scanty hair, and a pointed head like a pot that had collapsed to a peak in the baking, he furnished "evidence" as to a criminal type of man. According to the well-known story, a Greek physiognomist who examined Socrates' face judged that the philosopher was brutal, sensuous and inclined to drunkenness; and Socrates declared to his disciples that such, although he had overcome it, was his natural disposition. He was himself a physiognomist; he disliked a certain man who was of pale and dark complexion, such signs, he said, indicating envy and murder. Ellis mentioned the fact that long ago men referred to the organic peculiarities which they believed separated the criminal from the ordinary man and quoted in support among others the proverbs "Salute from afar the beardless man and the bearded woman" and "Distrust the woman with a man's voice."

In the Old Testament (Leviticus 21:18-21) the priest is warned not to allow before the altar "a blind man, or a lame, or he that hath a flat nose, or anything superfluous, or a man that is broken footed or brokenhanded, or crookbacked, or a dwarf, or that hath a blemish in his eye." In contrast there is the New Testament (John 7:24) injunction "Judge not according to the appearance."

Hill found that thirteen of 105 English murderers referred for brain wave examination had physical deformities such as paralysis of face and arms, deafness and lameness. Stanley reported that 12 per cent of prisoners in San Quentin were classified as cripples. No less than twenty of 120 sane homicide offenders studied by Gibbens suffered from a fairly marked physical defect.

Masters and Greaves, utilizing 11,000 police file photographs (front and profile) from Kansas City, St. Louis, Baltimore, Miami and Los Angeles, found that the incidence of surgically correctable facial defects among criminals was almost three times that of the general population. Curiously some common congenital deformities, for example congenital cleft lip, port wine stain and severe facial asymmetries were slightly less common than in the general population. Those men convicted of rape showed an unusually high incidence (26.7%) of acne.

Lombroso, in his later writings, restricted his category of the born criminal with certain physical abnormalities to about 35 per cent of all criminals. Although his theory was discredited in 1913 by Goring in his work *The English Convict,* Earnest Hooton, an American disciple of Lombroso, attempted to refute Goring's work by reporting his anthropological study of the American criminal. The physiques of 13,873 criminals and 3,203 noncriminals were compared.

The 151 Negroid rapists were reported to be remarkably distinct from total Negroid criminals in their bodily measurements. They were reported to be shorter in stature, smaller in head breadth and head circumference and longer in the nose and ear than their fellow convict. The face was described as short and broad. Thick eyebrows occurred more often than in any other group.

Hooton claimed that the 197 white rapists showed an unusual prevalence of blue-grey eye color, deflected nasal septa and facial asymmetries. A deficiency in stature and in sitting height and an excess in chest depth and in relative shoulder breadth were also noted. Hooton concluded: "Sex offenses, and rape in particular, decrease with stature and increase with weight. Thus the short, heavy men are the notable sex offenders and the tall, slender men seem completely uninterested in this type of activity." These conclusions are contained in Hooton's *Crime and the Mind* and *The American Criminal*, published by the Harvard University Press in 1939.

RACE AND RAPE

> *"Rape was an insurrectionary act. It delighted*
> *me that I was defying and trampling upon the*
> *white man's law, upon his system of values,*
> *and that I was defiling his women."*
> — Eldridge Cleaver, *Soul on Ice*

In the United States Negroes have a significantly higher rate of arrest than whites in every offense category except certain offenses against public order and morals. In general, the disparity of rates for offenses of violence is much greater than comparable differences between the races for offenses against property. Thus the President's Commission on Law Enforcement and Administration of Justice noted that the Negro arrest rate for murder is almost ten times the white arrest rate. In contrast, the Negro arrest rate for burglary is only about three and one-half times as high as that for whites. In 1968 approximately 47 per cent of the persons arrested for forcible rape in the United States were Negroes, 51 per cent whites, and all other races comprised the remainder. (In the 1960 census Negroes constituted 10.5 per cent of the population).

In Denver there was over five times the expected number of Negroes among the 253 offenders who raped 200 women. There was over four times the expected number of Spanish-American and only two-fifths the expected number of white offenders. *The Negro rape rate was over twelve times the white rape rate.* The Spanish-American rate was over ten times the white rape rate. In Philadelphia both the male Negro homicide rate and the Negro rape rate are twelve times the white rates for these offenses.

In Denver, Negroes were more likely to attack white women than Negro women. Three in five Negro rapists attacked white women, but only one in twenty-nine white rapists attacked a Negro woman. In contrast Amir reported that rape in Philadelphia in 1958 and 1960 is mainly an intraracial event — white men rape white women, and Negroes rape Negroes.

The 253 offenders in the 13 month (1968-1969) Denver study included 89 whites (35.2%), 86 Spanish-Americans (34%), 76 Negroes (30%) and two men race unknown (0.8%). All offenses were actual rapes and not attempted rapes.

Most of the Negro offenders in Denver operated alone. Only 20 per cent of the Negro offenders were involved in pair or group rapes compared with 39 per cent of the white offenders and 55 per cent of the Spanish-American offenders.

These statistics on rape in Denver and Philadelphia are based upon the victim's identification of the racial and ethnic background of her assailant. These figures are not open to the criticisms usually applied to court and prison statistics which may reflect racial discrimination on the part of judges and jurors. The Denver rape rates per unit of population are based upon 1960 census figures which may not accurately represent the relative proportions of Negroes, Spanish-Americans and other citizens in the community during the period of study (1968 and part of 1969). This criticism cannot be made of the survey in Philadelphia.

Over forty years ago Sellin reviewed the significance of the high rate of Negro criminality:

"The American Negro lacks education and earthly goods. He has had very little political experience and industrial training. His contact with city life has been unfortunate, for it has forced him into the most dilapidated and vicious areas of our great cities. Like a shadow over his whole existence lies the oppressive race prejudice of his white neighbor, restricting his activities and thwarting his ambitions. It would be extraordinary, indeed, if this group were to prove more law-abiding than the white, which enjoys more fully the advantages of a civilization the Negro has helped to create."

"The assumption that the Negro presents the higher rate of real criminality is, therefore, no indictment of the Negro race. The responsibility lies where power, authority and discrimination has its source, the dominant white group. To that group the existence of a high rate of crime among Negroes is a challenge which cannot be brushed aside by platitudes about "race inferiority," "inherited depravity," or similar generalizations. The only way to meet it is by a conscientious and determined search for the causes of crime in general and among Negroes in particular."

In like manner the President's Commission on Law Enforcement recently noted:

"Many studies have been made seeking to account for these differences in arrest rates for Negroes and whites. They have found that the differences become very small when comparisons are made between the rates for whites and Negroes living under similar conditions. However, it has proved difficult to make such comparisons, since Negroes generally encounter more barriers to economic and social advancement than whites do. Even when Negroes and whites live in the same area, the Negroes are likely to have poorer housing, lower incomes, and fewer job prospects. The Commission is of the view that if conditions of equal opportunity prevailed, the large differences now found between the Negro and white arrest rates would disappear."

Eldridge Cleaver, the Black Panther minister of information, while in prison formed an antagonistic, ruthless attitude toward white women. On his release be became a rapist and after practicing on black girls in the ghetto, he deliberately sought out white women as victims. He believed that he was seeking revenge on white men who had raped Negroes. Arrested on charges of assault to kill and rape, he was sentenced in 1958 to a fourteen year term. He describes in *Soul on Ice* his loss of self-respect:

"After I returned to prison, I took a long look at myself and, for the first time in my life, admitted that I was wrong, that I had gone astray — astray not so much from the white man's law as from being human, civilized — for I could not approve the act of rape. Even though I had some insight into my own motivations, I did not feel justified. I lost my self-respect. My pride as a man dissolved and my whole fragile moral structure seemed to collapse, completely shattered."

Ten years after his conviction he was asked whether he was being completely honest when he attributed his sexual attacks solely to ideological motives. He spoke again of his delight in violating what he conceived of as white men's laws and his delight in defiling white women in revenge over the way white men have used black women, adding, "I was in a wild frame of mind and rape was simply one of the weird forms my rebellion took at that stage. So it was probably a combination of business and pleasure."

Both black rage and white guilt contribute to rape. Many Negroes take advantage of the sensitivity of some young white girls to accusations of prejudice, as in the following case.

> A well-dressed young Negro approached a seventeen-year-old white girl while she was standing outside a hippie coffee shop. He introduced himself and they went inside together for coffee. During their conversation he raised the issue of racial prejudice and the girl told him that she was very much opposed to discrimination against Negroes. He invited her to go out with him in his car but she refused. He continued to insist on her joining him in the car and accused her of racial prejudice.
>
> She felt a little foolish telling him she wasn't prejudiced and at the same time refusing to go with him, so she consented to go to the car with him. They sat in the car for a few minutes and he started the engine. She told him she didn't want to go with him but he drove off. She was afraid of him and wanted to jump from the car but was afraid that he would hurt her. She tried to remain calm but started screaming when he stopped the car and tried to kiss her.
>
> The car was parked in an isolated area and she realized that no one would hear her screams. After he had taken off all her clothes, she started screaming again but he held her down and choked her. Following the rape she started talking nicely to him and offered to meet him again at her home the next day. She thought this would give the police an opportunity to arrest him. Although he did not return, she recognized his mug shot on police files. She did not return to aid in prosecution, instead she left for her home in California.

Negroes usually called their white victims "white bitch" and frequently attributed the rape to white exploitation of Negroes and white racial prejudice. One man said he was raping the girl because he was tired of people screwing himself and his parents, and that he got back at society this way. Others asked their victims, "Have you ever gone with a Negro?" "What do you think of Negroes?" and "What would you do if you had a black baby?" A group of Negroes who raped a white girl took pictures of the rape and threatened to publish them in the Black Panther newspaper if she told anyone about the rape.

AGE

Crime is largely a product of youth and masculinity. For as long as crime statistics of any kind have been compiled, they have shown that males between the ages of fifteen and twenty-four are the most crime-prone group in the population. Sixty-four per cent (almost two out of three) of the arrests for forcible rape in the United States during 1968 were of persons under the age of twenty-five. As many rapes are not cleared by arrests, overall figures on the ages of the offenders must be based in part on estimates made by the victim.

A victim is unlikely to mistake the racial background of her assailant, although one elderly victim in this study did so because she based her opinion upon her sense of smell and a faulty hypothesis. The victim is likely to have difficulty in judging the offender's exact age. Even when he volunteers his age, his intention may be to mislead the police rather than to inform his victim. The following statistics must, therefore, be regarded with reserve.

Among the 232 Denver rape offenders on whom age estimates were provided in police files, almost 50 per cent were between fifteen and twenty-five years of age. Almost 75 per cent were below thirty and 8 per cent were forty years or older.

In Philadelphia only 14 per cent were over thirty years compared with 25 per cent in Denver. The median age for offenders was twenty-three in Philadelphia and twenty-five in Denver. Amir reports that for the age group fifty-five to fifty-nine the Negro offender rate is forty-three times the white offender rate. Although few offenders are over sixty years of age, the occasional old-age pensioner stands accused of rape.

MARITAL STATUS

> *"It is not good that man should be alone."*
> Genesis 2:18

A young man charged with rape claimed that the charge was absurd as he was a married man and had ample opportunity for sexual gratification. The man accused by his wife of infidelity would find a skeptical response to such evidence of his fidelity. There is more to rape and to marriage than sexual intercourse. As rapists are predominantly young men, one would expect to find that many of them are unmarried. Many rapists are, however, married.

A survey of seventy-seven rapists in the Colorado State Penitentiary showed that 40 per cent were married, 13 per cent divorced, 5 per cent separated and 43 per cent were single. In his study of thirty Canadian rapists, McCaldon found that 43 per cent were married, 14 per cent divorced, 7 per cent separated and 36 per cent were single. McCaldon noted that considering their relative youth, a high percentage of the rapists were married.

In Holland 43 per cent of all men convicted of rape between 1950 and 1954 were married in contrast to 19 per cent for the period 1931 to 1934 (Grunhut *et al.*). Thus recent studies in three different countries all report that 40 to 43 per cent of rapists were married. In contrast Svalastoga in Denmark found that 24 per cent of the rapists were married.

SOCIAL CLASS

The President's Commission on Law Enforcement and Administration of Justice (1967) noted that study after study in city after city in all regions of the country show that for rape and certain other crimes the offenses, the victims and the offenders are found most frequently in the poorest and most deteriorated and socially disorganized areas of cities. The findings have been remarkably consistent. Serious assaults occur in areas characterized by low income, physical deterioration, racial and ethnic concentrations, low levels of education and vocational skill, high unemployment and other factors.

Svalastoga, in his study of Danish rapists, showed that the rapist is an underprivileged person in several respects. At least 80 per cent had only seven years of schooling and only 3 per cent possessed an intermediate high school diploma. The social and economic status of the parents or foster parents was on the average very low. Only 11 per cent had a middle-class origin, while 85 per cent were working-class people, mostly unskilled. Information was missing for the remaining 4 per cent.

CRIMINAL RECORDS

In his study of rape in Philadelphia, Amir found that 50 per cent of the rapists had previous arrest records. He noted that adults arrested for rape were less likely to be first offenders than adults arrested for other types of offenses. Nine per cent of offenders with criminal records had committed rape in the past, and 4 per cent had been arrested for a sexual offense other than rape. Only 20 per cent of those who had a past arrest record had previously committed a crime against the person with Negro offenders outnumbering the whites in this respect.

Among seventy-seven rapists in the Colorado State Penitentiary 85 per cent had a previous arrest record and 12 per cent had previously been convicted of forcible rape. Altogether 38 per cent had committed previous rapes, been arrested for investigation of rape or had been convicted of other sexual offenses. In Canada, McCaldon found that 95 per cent of thirty rapists in a penitentiary had previous convictions. Nineteen per cent had previously been convicted for sexual offenses and 27 per cent had been convicted for aggressive offenses.

Among the 141 rapists studied by Svalastoga in Denmark, 77 per cent had previous criminal records and 22 per cent had received two or more prison sentences prior to the rape conviction.

MENTAL ILLNESS

There are no satisfactory reports on the incidence of mental illness in rape offenders. McCaldon found that about half of the thirty rapists in a Canadian penitentiary were sociopathic personalities who showed chronic antisocial behavior. Many of the remaining rapists showed hostile, sadistic attitudes toward women. Some were schizoid personalities and others were described as inadequate personalities. Intelligence tests showed an essentially average distribution with the IQ ranging from borderline to superior intelligence.

Clinicians responsible for the treatment of sex offenders with mental and emotional problems have estimated a low incidence of psychosis (less than 1 to no more than 5 per cent) according to Gebhard *et al.* The author shares this clinical impression. The occasional rapist suffers from schizophrenia or posttraumatic personality disorder following a severe head injury. The majority have some form of character disorder. Alcoholism and homosexuality are frequently encountered, but some men convicted of rape do not have any mental disorder.

Weinberg found that in 203 cases of incest three of the offenders had been confined in mental hospitals prior to the offense. Eleven offenders became psychotic during the incarceration. Five were paranoid, one catatonic, two alcoholic, one senile and two had unclassified psychoses.

ANALYSIS OF RAPE

Human behavior is complex and cannot readily be divided into parts and analyzed. Analysis of a rape would require an exploration into the life experiences of the offender, the circumstances on the day of the offense, the role of the victim as well as the contributions of alcohol, drugs, cultural attitudes and many other factors. Reference has already been made to some of these factors, others, particularly the role of the victim and origins of rape, will be reviewed in later chapters. For the moment the focus will be upon the rapist's method and plans of procedure.

There may be no plans and no preparations for rape. This crime, like others, may occur on the impulse of the moment. A young man picks up a girl in a tavern, at a dance hall or at some social gathering. They have several drinks together and the girl raises no objections to remarks of a sexual nature. At closing time he offers to drive her home and she does not object when he parks the car by the roadside in a deserted area or lover's lane. She responds to his embraces but eventually resists his sexual advances. Suddenly he overpowers her, although forcible rape may not have been in his mind until this moment.

> A thirty-two-year-old woman, as she was leaving a tavern in the late afternoon, was asked by a man who had talked to her earlier, if she would like a ride home. He drove her to a vacant lot and after some petting he removed his pants and she removed her pants and panties. Then she "became afraid" and put her pants back on but not her panties. The man said, "You aren't getting away with that," struck her with his fists and raped her.

Other men, who pick up women under similar circumstances, may do so with the deliberate intention of forcible rape in the event of the girl's failure to respond to persuasion. Curiously some of these men, once they have succeeded in picking up their victims, make no effort to seek voluntary compliance with their sexual wishes as in the following case.

> A young woman met a man in a bar about 8 P.M. and drank with him until 10:30 P.M. They then visited two other bars and continued drinking until closing time. She kissed him in the car and he drove her to her apartment. She invited him inside and immediately after entering the apartment he told her to take her clothes off or he would "karate chop her." He went into the bathroom, found a pair of scissors and threatened her with them. "You're going to bed with me or I'll chop you with the scissors." She talked him into putting the scissors back in the bathroom. After raping her, he warned her not to say anything about it or he would get her. The victim later acknowledged that if her assailant had approached her in a polite manner, she would have submitted to sexual intercourse willingly.

Prior planning may be limited to the choice of a suitable location and time for rape, as, for example, a parking lot late at night and the first victim of suitable age to appear is assaulted and raped. More elaborate plans involve choice of disguise, purchase of a gun and careful selection of the intended victim. Amir reports that 71 per cent of the rapes in Philadelphia were planned beforehand.

SELECTION OF VICTIMS

Many offenders select the scene for rape rather than the victim for rape.

The man who breaks into an apartment may know from the apartment mailboxes that there are two women in the apartment, and one or both of these women will be raped regardless of their physical appearance or personality traits. The man who walks the street late at night in search of a victim, or who chooses the hospital parking lot to attack nurses as they come off duty sometimes exercises greater choice in his selection of victims.

Some offenders carefully select women for rape. The attack is postponed for several days or even weeks until their plans meet their needs for perfectionism. One man would pick out a suitable victim on a street and then follow her, perhaps for an hour or more, until she returned to her home. If she returned to an apartment house, he would obtain her name by checking the license number of her car with the motor vehicle bureau. He would claim that he had bumped into a car in a parking lot and needed the owner's name to pay for the damage, or he would use some other subterfuge to obtain the victim's name.

One man waited in his car outside a modelling agency at closing time. A beautiful young girl was selected for rape. He followed the bus which she entered and when she left it, he parked nearby and walked behind her until she reached an alley. After striking her in the head, he dragged her into the alley and raped her. An attractive go-go dancer used to drive home after her performance in a nightclub. Her assailant noted where she parked her car, and one night he hid in the rear seat. When she reached a residential area, he threatened her with a gun and accompanied her to her apartment where he raped her.

The offender may attribute his selection of victims to chance factors beyond his control and claim that he raped any available woman who happened to appear when circumstances were favorable for rape. He may be deceiving himself. One such offender after some years of treatment realized that all his victims resembled his young foster mother who had been both seductive and very domineering. Usually the resemblance was in bodily movements and mannerisms which he had ample opportunity to study in his extensive window-peeping night after night prior to the assault.

Some offenders are very particular in their choice of victims. One man will rape only elderly women, another only women of doubtful reputation, and a third will rape only very young girls. Some rapists show a preference for a certain class of victims, yet do not confine themselves to this one group. The offender-victim relationship will be considered further in the next chapter.

ONE OFFENDER – THREE VICTIMS

Some offenders will attack more than one victim at the same time as in the following case.

Three sisters, Rachael, Mildred and Rosemary, were waiting for a bus when the defendant, driving an automobile, stopped and offered to take them home, which offer they accepted. Mildred sat in the front seat with him while Rosemary and Rachael sat in the back. He drove by a devious course to a comparatively lonely spot on the outskirts of North Sacramento, stopped the car, turned to Mildred and put his arm over the back of the seat.

In response to her question, "What is the big idea?" he replied, "I will tell you what the big idea is. One of you is going to put out, I don't care which," and "Which one is it going to be? Make up your minds." The women then started to get out of the car, but as they did so, defendant stuck a large-sized pocketknife against the side of Mildred, threatening to stick the knife into her stomach if any of them moved. The girls entreated him to let them go, and after some argument he did let Rosemary get out of the car.

Several times defendant repeated his demands, all the while holding the knife against Mildred. Rachael found a hammer in the back seat but before she could strike defendant he grabbed it from her, struck her with his fist, climbed into the back seat and stated, "Since you are so smart, I will just take you." He then tried to put his arms around her. Rosemary, who had returned to the car, grabbed him by the leg while Mildred hit him with her purse, and as a result the three of them were able to get defendant out of the car, where the scuffle continued, during which defendant hit Rachael with his fist.

The defendant finally told the women to walk up the road, which they did. A short distance from the car they began to run. After running about two blocks they heard the car coming behind them, and they turned into a lane leading to a house. Rosemary continued on to the house while Mildred and Rachael climbed through a wire fence into an adjacent field. Defendant drove through the fence, followed them into the field, struck Mildred and ran over her with the car. He then swerved the car quickly toward Rachael but she successfully avoided being hit. Thereupon he turned the car around and drove away *(People v. Bradley* 162 P.2d 38).

DISGUISE

The offender may wear a false moustache or even goatee beard, affect a foreign accent or use some other stratagem to disguise his true identity. One man who attempted to rape two women, wore a blond wig, white print dress and women's shoes. He threatened both victims with a gun, but both of them fled and he did not pursue them. The need for disguise is less when the offender attacks the victim while she is sleeping. A towel or some item of clothing is placed over the woman's face or she is instructed to keep her eyes shut under penalty of death.

The use of ski masks, ski jackets with the hood drawn or a cloth mask across the lower face make it more difficult for the victim to recognize her assailant. False information may be provided to mislead the police. Curiously many offenders include true information which can later aid in their conviction. Presumably this information is provided because the offender's judgment is clouded by alcohol, or his conscious efforts to avoid detection may be thwarted by his unconscious need to confess or to be captured.

THE OFFENDER AS AN IMPOSTER

The sex offender may gain entry into the victim's home by posing as a telephone or public service company employee, building inspector, research worker or magazine salesman. A woman in a hotel room heard a knock on the door. When she asked who was there, she received the reply "Room Service." When she opened the door, two Negroes entered and closed the door before she realized what was happening. She was raped by both of them.

Bogus Telephone Company Employees

About midday a man rang the doorbell of a home and said that he wanted to check on the telephone. He went directly to the phone, picked up the receiver, listened for a minute, then hung up the receiver. He asked me when my husband would be home. I told him about five o'clock. He had a book and pencil which he laid down on the desk. Then he stated, "Let's make love." He grabbed me and we fought. I scratched his face on the left side, drawing blood. His lip was also bleeding.

He said, "If you don't want your kids killed, you'd better send them out in the other room." I told him I had a neighbor coming for lunch. He then said, "Go in your bedroom and shut the door and don't open it." He hollered through the door, "How much money do you have?" I told him about six dollars. I didn't hear anything so I opened the bedroom window and crawled through, taking my children. We ran across the street and called the police. (Similar complaints of attempted rape were reported by two other women in the neighborhood.)

*   *   *

A man carrying a clipboard with some papers on it rang the doorbell of a home and said that he was making a survey for the telephone company. He said that he wanted to make sure that he had the right telephone number for the new telephone directory. Although the names of the woman and her husband were not listed in the current directory, he knew their telephone number. After asking questions about the telephone, he asked what time it was and then requested a glass of water as he had to take a pill.

The woman went to the kitchen to get the water and when she returned the man was in the living room. He locked the screen door and shut the door. When asked to leave, he refused and said, "No, I want you." At this point the victim's baby started crying. The man picked up the baby, put a knife against his chest and ordered the mother to undress. After raping her, he told her not to tell the police or her husband, as he would come back and kill her and her baby.

Bogus Health Officials

A man who claimed that he was from the local health center called at a woman's home and said that he was checking on cancer. He asked the woman to take her clothes off as he had to take a "pap smear." When she threatened to call the police, he left quickly.

*   *   *

A young man called at a girl's apartment and introduced himself as a doctor. When told that he did not look old enough to be a doctor, he said that he had just graduated from medical school. He explained that he was making a survey and that everyone should have a medical examination twice a year. After asking the girl a number of questions about her menstrual cycle and use of birth control pills, he said that he would make an "outer" physical examination. The girl refused and he left her apartment.

Bogus Police Officers

A young man and his girl friend were out driving when they noticed that a driver behind them was blinking his dim and bright lights. When they pulled over to the side of the road, a man came up to their car and said that he was a police officer. He said that the man was speeding and asked to see his driver's license. After checking the license he said that it was a phoney and told the girl to get in his car, as he thought she was a prostitute. He said that he was going to take her to police headquarters and "mug" her. After driving a few blocks, he turned into an alley and told the girl the only way she could prove she was not a prostitute was to take all her clothes off and prove she was a virgin. The girl told him to go to hell, jumped from the car and ran to a gasoline station.

* * *

Two fourteen-year-old youths, a girl and a boy, were attempting to steal a car when they saw a man approaching. They walked to the intersection where the man caught up with them. He told them he worked for the local police department and showed them a yellow card which he said was his identification card. The word "Guard" was printed on the card but he held his hand over the lower part of the card so that the youths could not read it. They later identified a local "Merchant Guard" card as being of similar general appearance. The man advised them that he had helped many children who were in trouble and said he had worked closely with the probation department. He told the youth to go to the girl's home to bring her bicycle. After the boy left, he dragged the victim into an alley and raped her. The victim started screaming but stopped after he struck her on the face.

Bogus Professional Photographers

The offender may claim that he is a professional photographer and entice the victim to his apartment or other location with promises of payment in return for acting as a photographic model. The possibility of a lucrative career as a professional model or screen actress may also be suggested to overcome any reluctance on the part of the victim.

A young man approached a youth outside his home and asked him if he knew any girls of his age and height who would like to model for a magazine with the title *Calling All Girls*. The youth said he knew two girls, Sharon and Joy, who lived nearby and he was asked to get Sharon. This girl was asked several questions about modelling and whether she depended on her parents. About this time Joy, aged thirteen, appeared and was asked the same questions. The youth said he had to leave on his paper route and Sharon went into her home.

The man told Joy to get in his car, as he wanted to take her home to talk to her father about modelling for the magazine. He called at another girl's home, but she was not there. Then he drove Joy into the mountains, and on a back road he asked her to take off her clothes and pose in the nude. She refused, but again he asked her to pose on a rock. After some further discussion, the girl took off her clothes as she feared for her safety. After one picture was taken with a Polaroid® camera, he attempted to rape her but stopped when she started screaming and crying. He drove her home after warning her that if she told her parents her name would be printed in the newspapers.

*   *   *

I [a young woman] met him at the discount house where I work. He said he was a photographer and he wanted me to model for him. I went to his house to look at his photographic equipment. He asked me to pull up my tee shirt and also to pull down my slacks. I did both of these things with a great deal of embarrassment. He said this was necessary to see what kind of a model I would make. When I told him I was interested in voice and singing, he said he would take me to a nightclub and speak to the owner.

At the nightclub he left me at our table while he went and talked to the owner. When he came back, he said the owner was interested but wanted a tape of my voice to study. He said that he would take me back to his apartment to make the tape. Instead he drove me to a location and asked me if I were a virgin. He said people in show business had to do a lot of things they didn't want to do.

He said the owner of the nightclub was a weird one and wanted my yellow panties. I asked him to drive me home. He threw me to the left side of the car and said, "You get out of those underwear right now." I said no twice and he said he would choke me. I was pleading with him, but he raped me. I was too afraid of him to do anything. He slapped my face two or three times and shoved my underwear in my mouth.

The Bogus Family Friend

The man who rapes children often entices his victim into his car by offering the child a ride in his car or by giving her a fictitious message from her parents. He will park his car near a school playground and obtain the name of his intended victim by asking a playmate, "Is that Judy Robinson over by the swings?" The playmate will say, "No, that's so and so." The fact that he knows the girl's name helps to convince her that the stranger does indeed bring a message from her parents.

(A six-year-old girl). The man stopped and said he was a friend of my father's and wanted me to go help find his dog. He said it was a small black one. He told me to come to the car. I had never seen the man before. He opened the door and pulled me in, then he locked the door and drove away fast.

The offender may gain admission to the adult victim's home by posing as a friend of the husband. "Your husband told me to come over here and wait till he gets off work."

THREATS AND FORCE

In order to secure submission and compliance, the rapist will often threaten or physically assault his victim. Even in the absence of threats or blows the offender may convey to his victim by his facial appearance and general behavior the impression that resistance will lead to violence. He may also convey hints of danger by remarks such as "I'm a sexual maniac," "Don't do something, because I'm a little crazy" or "You know I'm not a rational person, so you'd better do as I say." The woman who is caught by surprise may well feel considerable alarm when ordered to comply with her assailant's demands. If she follows instructions without significant resistance, the man may not see any need for violence. Some offenders proceed no further with the rape when the woman cries out, runs away or herself resorts to physical attack.

Homicidal threats were made on the lives of one in four of the two hundred victims in the Denver study. "Come with me or I'll kill you." "Shut up or I'll strangle you with my belt." "Don't move, stand still or I'll shoot you." "I've killed three people and if I have to, I'll kill you even if you are a woman." "If you don't cooperate, we'll kill you right here." "This is a gun, don't scream or I'll kill you." "He kept telling me he would kill me if I didn't stop fighting." The threat to kill may be made on the life of the victim's roommate, husband or child. "He told me to be quiet or he'd kill my baby."

Threats to harm were also made on some victims. "I'll cut you." "You're going to bed with me or I'll chop you with the scissors." "I have a gun in the glove box and will use it on you." "I'll break every bone in your body and I'll leave my mark on you." "Would you like to get hurt? If you shout again, I'll hurt you. If you be good and make love to me, I'll let you go." "He asked me if I could stand to be tortured." "I advise you not to scream or I'll knock your teeth out." "If you scream, I'll punch your teeth out like the one I did in Alaska." One man in addition to threats, pleaded, "Shut up, do you want me to go to the pen?"

Weapons such as a gun, knife or iron bar were shown to one in four of the victims. In other cases the offender claimed that he had a weapon but did not produce it. In some cases the knives used were taken from the victim's kitchen prior to the assault and were left behind after the rape. Thus if arrested on suspicion near the scene of the crime, the offender would not have incriminating evidence in his possession.

Some victims are threatened with rape by friends of the offender. "Cooperate or I'll go get my friend to help." "Either you do it with me or you do it with all the guys here. I've got seven friends out there." "I'm going to let you have a break. There will be three guys out here in a while. So if you don't give it to me now within three minutes, I'll let them do it to you also." The rapist may threaten to call on the victim again and later fulfill this threat.

Among those offenders who use force a few are very careful not to scratch or bruise the victim. "He lifted my coat and dress up and started pulling my underclothes off me. Then he stood up and said he wasn't going to tear my clothes because if he didn't, it would be my word against his. I kicked him as hard as I could but I didn't hurt him. He said he didn't want any marks on me that anyone could see."

Almost half of the two hundred victims in the Denver study were struck with a fist or choked.

An eighty-five-year-old woman who required treatment of her injuries in a hospital reported, "I was asleep and he woke me all of a sudden. He had a black cloth over his face and head. He asked me where my money was. He hit me and he hit me. He tried to rape me and I kept stopping him. He choked me, he tore off my clothes. He tried to kill me and he kept hitting me. The next thing I knew he was ransacking the house and I was next door naked. I knocked on the door and the lady answered. I told her what happened and she called the police. I couldn't talk at first because he had choked me."

The victim may be bound with her stockings or with rope which has been brought for that purpose. She may also be gagged to prevent her from screaming for help. The considerate rapist moistens the gag before leaving.

Extremely sadistic attacks may be made in which the victim's nipples are bitten off; articles such as a bottle, revolver barrel, candle or sticks are inserted into the vagina, sometimes penetrating the abdominal cavity; cigarettes or lighters are used to burn the skin, and blows may rupture internal viscera or cause fractures of bones.

Some offenders do not get the same thrill from the rape when the victim makes no effort to resist. One man used to climax just from holding the woman roughly in his arms as she fought him and he would not then rape her. In talking to him one had the impression that he had no pleasure in raping those who did not resist, that he performed the act almost because he felt this was expected of him.

Masochistic behavior occurs less frequently than assaultive behavior. In the Denver study one man asked his victim to bite him on his shoulder and another asked the girl to beat him.

In Philadelphia, Amir noted that force was used in 85 per cent of the 646 rapes. Of the cases in which force was used, 29 per cent took the form of roughness, 25 per cent were nonbrutal beatings, 20 per cent were brutal beatings and 12 per cent involved choking the victim. Violence, especially in its extreme forms, was found to be significantly associated with rapes by

Negroes. Also, a significant association was found between both group and pair rapes and the use of force. Amir found that excessive degrees of violence were more likely to occur outdoors than indoors.

In Denmark, Svalastoga found that in 141 cases of rape, choking occurred in 20 per cent, beating and kicking in 21 per cent and interference with general body movement in 35 per cent of the cases. Interference with vocalization, presumably a hand across the mouth, occurred in 24 per cent of the cases.

Force may be used not only before the rape, but also during or after the rape. Many offenders become enraged when the victim remains passive and does not respond physically during sexual intercourse (see below). Occasionally the victim is forced to take alcohol or drugs.

THE ACT OF RAPE

The act of rape may take place in a brief time without any attempt at other sexual molestation, with minimal removal of clothing and without conversation. Indeed the offender may stop the assault before he has reached a climax. On the other hand, the victim may be raped only after considerable discussion with the victim who may be taken by car to a distant location. There may be repeated rapes and other forms of sexual assault before the victim is released. Eleven per cent of the rapes in Amir's study involved repeated acts of intercourse.

The victim may be forced to remove all her clothing. Suspects usually just unzip their pants but may also undress completely. Detectives sitting in an unmarked police car late at night in a neighborhood in which several rapes or attempted rapes had been committed by a nude offender, observed a car pull up in front of a house. After a few minutes the dome light in the car went on and a man was seen leaving the car and going between two houses. He looked in a window, crept alongside a fence and appeared to be looking to see if anyone was watching him. He was next seen standing in the nude in front of a window. The detective who tried to arrest him ran into a clothesline; however, the man was arrested later wearing an assortment of men's and women's clothing which he had obtained from clotheslines. His own clothes were found in his car.

The woman may be forced not only to undress herself but also to undress her assailant.

> He said he would drive me home if I got in the back seat. I did as he requested and it looked as though he was trying to start the car. Instead he turned off the engine and got in the back seat. He jumped on me, we were tussling and I scratched his face. He asked me if I saw the creek outside and reminded me I couldn't swim. He said to take my clothes off or he would choke me and throw me in the creek and that he would hold my head under the water until I drowned.

I did as he told me.

He said for me to move closer to him and if I didn't stop trying to resist him he would drown me anyway. So I moved closer. He told me to unzip his pants and leaned back on the side of the car. I told him no. He asked me again if I could swim, so I unzipped his pants. He said to me, "Gee, I didn't make you unzip my pants, you did it yourself." Then he said, "Take out my penis." I said no. He asked me if I wanted to go home tonight. I reached for the door, he pulled me back and said, "You're not going anywhere, you'd never make it home."

USE OF CONTRACEPTIVES

Occasionally the offender will use a contraceptive, usually without stating whether his purpose is to prevent conception or to protect himself from contracting venereal disease. Amir suggests that by using a prophylactic the offender attempts to transform a forced erotic encounter into a regular "affair" or a love relationship. In four per cent of his cases, the offenders used prophylactics. Inquiry may be made whether the victim is taking birth control pills. She may be instructed to take one before the rape or she may be allowed to use birth control cream or insert a diaphragm prior to intercourse. One man said, "I'm stopping because I'm reaching a climax and I don't want to make you pregnant." The offender may reassure the victim, or attempt to do so, by saying that he is sterile and that there is no danger of pregnancy. One man said, "I'll marry you if you have a baby," but he departed without leaving his name or address.

DEMANDS FOR COOPERATION OR AFFECTION

Few victims of rape participate actively in the sexual intercourse and offenders are quick to sense their passive resistance. "He kept trying to get me to respond. He went for the knife again and said he'd use it if he didn't get a little action." Demands for affection take the form of requests for a loving response. The victim is told to act as if she was with her boyfriend. "He kept kissing me and telling me I loved all colored people." "Tell me you love me." "Give me a little sugar." "He said he was going to kiss my mouth and he wanted me to kiss him back. He got on top of me and told me to caress his back, he said to hug him tight and to move my hips."

The offender who is unable to have an erection may ask the victim to fondle his penis. "He was having difficulty in getting an erection, he cursed himself for this. He told me to reach down and play with him so it would get hard." Another man who was unable to have an erection became extremely angry and blamed his victim. He cocked his revolver, placed it against her temple and ordered her to "cooperate properly." "He told me to hold his penis and make it hard again. I refused and he put his knife against my throat and said make it hard."

DIALOGUE

Some men talk at length with their victims. The conversation may center on a detailed discussion with the victim regarding her previous sexual experiences, the frequency of intercourse with her husband, the use of contraceptives and other aspects of sexual intercourse.

> He said that he'd never had sex before, that he wasn't too good at it and would I help him. He asked me my age, if I ever loved anyone and if I had a boyfriend. He said he was thirty-four and he wondered what I'd be doing fourteen years from now when I was his age. He supposed I'd be married and have two darling children. He asked if I was religious and what church I belonged to, and he said he was a Catholic and had sinned.

Discussions of racial problems by Negro offenders, of social injustices by offenders of all races and of the rights and wrongs of rapes are not uncommon. "There was a good and bad in everybody and this was the bad in him. He talked about an hour and a half, then he said, 'Let's try it again.' "

OTHER SEXUAL ACTS

In addition to raping the victim, the offender may indulge in other sexual acts, some of which would not be regarded as abnormal in the absence of coercion. Victims are sometimes so deeply ashamed of perverse sexual acts which have been forced on them that they do not spontaneously report these acts. Tactful questioning may be required to elicit the full account of their humiliation.

Fellatio ("Blow Job")

Fellatio, oral stimulation of the penis, was forced upon 4 per cent of the Denver victims and on 11 per cent of the Philadelphia victims. One man, after ordering his victim to suck his penis, asked her if she had ever done that with her husband who was also present. When she answered in the negative, he forced her at gunpoint to do the same thing to her husband. Another man, who raped his nine-year-old stepdaughter, forced her to suck his penis and swallow the semen telling her that the "white stuff" was good for her. Slang terms may be used, as, for example, "Now, bitch, you're going to blow me." In group rapes the victim may be forced to engage in fellatio with one man while another man is raping her.

Cunnilingus ("Mouth Job")

Cunnilingus, kissing or licking of the female genitals, was noted in 4 per cent of the Denver rapes, and in less than 4 per cent of the Philadelphia rapes. "He started to kiss me on my stomach and he told me to lift up my vagina and he started to kiss and lick it." "He placed his face between my legs, I tried to pull away from him, but whenever I moved he bit my pubic area." One victim said she did not understand when her assailant asked if she had ever been eaten. He replied, "I guess you whites don't do that."

Masturbation ("Hand Job")

Either before or after the rape the victim may be forced to masturbate the offender. "He told me to take it in my hands and squeeze it and then he yelled I wasn't doing it hard enough and he started doing it himself then. Then he made me do it again, making my hand go up and down and he kept saying go faster and I did."

Anal Intercourse

Anal intercourse occurred in 2 per cent of the Denver rapes and in less than 2 per cent of the Philadelphia rapes. Amir noted that white offenders committed anal intercourse and fellatio more often than Negro offenders. These perverse acts were significantly more frequent in indoor rapes and in the presence of alcohol in the offender or in both the offender and the victim.

Voyeurism

Many authorities have stated that the sex offender does not progress from minor to major sex crimes. Yet some offenders commit both minor and major sex offenses. The voyeur, or peeping tom, may also be arrested for rape. Certainly some rapists show strong voyeuristic tendencies in the course of their rapes. One rapist insisted that his victim put on and removed her girdle twice while he watched her. The Polaroid camera provides the photographer with the picture without the need to have the film developed and printed by a commercial agency.

> A married woman was awakened in the early hours of the morning by a man wearing a ski mask, parka and dark glasses. The intruder who held a knife at her throat and a gun at her head told her that no harm would come to her if she did as he said. He ordered her to take him to her daughters' room where he forced the two girls to remove their nightgowns. When the mother objected, she was forced to sit in a closet facing the wall with a pillowcase over her head. He made the older girl pose in the nude while he took several pictures of her in various postures with a Polaroid camera. Several pictures were also taken of the younger girl. After attempting to rape one of the girls, he left with the used flashbulbs and photographic paper in a pillowcase. He repeatedly threatened to kill all three women.

                    *   *   *

I heard a noise at the front window. I went to check my son and he was okay. As I was in the living room I saw this man with a gun in his hand. He asked me for my money and he grabbed my purse from the table. He looked through it. He talked real polite and seemed nervous. He made me take my clothes off and made me pose in different positions with him taking pictures of me with a new Polaroid camera. After he was done taking pictures of me, he raped me. When he first came in, he opened the cylinder of the gun and spinned it. He wore a green ski mask and sunglasses.

ROBBERY AND BURGLARY

Some rapists on first approaching the victim try to set her mind at ease by saying that all they want is her money. As one offender explained, "It's kind of a psychological deal if you get a person off guard. If you're trying to sell something to somebody, get them to say yes to something else, then it's easier to get them to say yes to what you're selling. Kind of a Dale Carnegie thing. I ask them for their money, then I ask them to take their clothes off so I can get away. If you make them feel you're going to do something else, it's easier to rape them."

Many rapists steal from their victims not only money but also other articles of value such as rings and jewelry. One offender told his victim that if she made love to him he would let her have her ring back. Usually the offender does not bargain in this manner. Another man after the rape made several trips between the victim's apartment and his car to remove such items as a television set and clothing. In the Denver study thirty-one of the two hundred victims were robbed as well as raped. In contrast in Philadelphia a felony in the form of burglary or robbery was committed in only 4 per cent of the 646 rape events.

The demand for money may be accompanied by homicidal threats, and failure to provide it may result in a physical assault. One youth told his elderly victim, "If you've got more than twenty dollars I won't kill you." The victim told him he could have all she had which was about forty dollars in her purse. The youth was not satisfied and placing a knife against her head demanded "the rest." Finally she managed to convince him that she had no other money in her apartment.

One man who had taken over ten dollars from two girls returned it before leaving. "He asked for my driver's license and I told him I didn't drive. He remarked that we were very poor people and laughed. He gave us our money back and said ours was the first house that he had ever left money at. This man was very mean. I think that if we would have crossed him he really would have killed someone. I believe that he must have been poor at one time, he seemed to sympathize with the fact that we were poor, as if he knew what it was like."

AFTER THE RAPE

The offender may leave immediately after the rape or series of rapes. Often the offender who has abducted his victim will drive her back to the vicinity of either her home or the initial meeting place. Some offenders remain with their victims for prolonged discussions which in a few cases extend to several hours. Offenders usually leave the victim's home before daybreak but one man stayed for breakfast.

Touching solicitude may be shown for the victim's welfare. "He asked me if I knew anything about crime and I said no. He said, 'Well, you don't have to worry, crime never hits twice in the same place.' " One man was described by the victim as being "terribly concerned for my welfare." She added that he asked her several times if she needed an aspirin or a tranquilizer. On leaving he told her not to call the police, as that would only upset her and make her more nervous. The offender may reassure the victim that he does not have venereal disease.

One man returned to the victim's home some months later and raped her again. On his third visit he again appeared with a gun in hand and asked her if she knew that the front window was still broken. He then fixed the window before leaving without assaulting her. The victim is not out of danger after the rape, as her assailant may beat her savagely without warning or explanation. He may also murder her.

> I was at the Sportsman's Club and I danced a couple of times with this man. He said his name was Henry and then he offered to give me a ride home, but when I got in his car he drove north on the freeway and then he stopped on a side road and made me undress. I argued with him and he made me undress and he hit me and then he raped me. After that he made me get out of his car and he started beating me and kicking me. Then all I remember is that I was hurting something terrible and I tried to get help. By the time two young men stopped to help me I was bleeding so bad and was so dazed that I didn't remember anything else until I was in the hospital. (She lost several teeth and almost seventy sutures were required for ten lacerated wounds of her face.)

AVOIDANCE OF DETECTION

Before the offender leaves the victim, he may bind her or tell her to remain at the scene for a given period of time. "Lay still for five minutes or I'll shoot you through the window and don't think I won't. I'll be out there watching you." He may hide outside the victim's room, then return to make sure that she has not left her bed. Once again he will warn her. The telephone cord is often cut. One man would prevent lights being turned on by switching the electricity off at the circuit breaker on the outside wall of the house. He also unlocked the front and back doors to permit a rapid escape.

Usually the rapist will warn his victim not to tell the police. He may threaten to kill her or members of her family. "If you report this to the police, your daughter will be run over by a car. I know where she goes to school, so it won't be too hard." "Don't call the police or I'll be back. This way all you have lost is a little money and a little pride."

Some men point out the embarrassment likely to result from newspaper publicity or court proceedings. "He said if I called the police and told my boyfriend, it would get into the papers and soon everyone would know it was me that had been raped." "No one will know about this unless you tell. If you tell the police, it will be in the papers and everyone will know what kind of a girl you are. But that's your business, you should just chalk it up to experience."

The victim may be warned of the possible adverse reaction of her husband if she notifies the police. "He told me not to tell my husband because he would always hold it against me and he wouldn't understand. He said that he'd had experience with this before. He said it wasn't my fault, it was his sin and that it was an experience I would have to try to forget." Another man told the woman, "It won't do any good to call the police. I'm from out of town and all the police will do is ask you a lot of stupid questions and your husband will find out."

The victim may be told that rape is difficult to prove and that it is pointless to call the police. He will attempt to convince her that he can show that she participated willingly in sexual intercourse. "I know you're going to tell, but if you do, I'll say you invited me in." One victim warned her assailant that she would get him "sent up for rape." He replied, "No, you can't, I've seven friends out there will say you wanted it, then it will be your word against mine."

A victim asked her assailant, "Is that always the way you have to get a girl, by rape?" He became very angry saying, "Did I rape you?" reaching for his knife and adding, "In that case I'll have to kill you." The girl quickly told him that he did not rape her.

EXPRESSION OF REMORSE

Expression of remorse is not unusual. The offender may apologize profusely for taking the victim's money (but not return it), express remorse for the rape (yet repeat the act a short time later) and make promises (which he may not fulfill) to seek psychiatric treatment.

> He lay over me fully clothed and started sobbing saying what kind of an animal was he, he said a man wouldn't do such things . . . later he started molesting me again.

*   *   *

> He was sorry then and asked if I could forgive him because he was taking this

out on me for what someone had done to him. He told me to comb my hair. Then he took me to a Seven-Eleven Store. He told me right before I got out of the car to turn him into the police because he wanted to serve his time. He sat in the car a minute and then left.

One offender told the victim she was a nice person and apologized for his foul language. Another said he was sorry and asked his victim if she was a Catholic. He kept saying that he wished he had not done it. Yet another gave his victim twenty dollars to replace her blouse which he had torn. One victim asked her assailant to repair her front door which he had kicked open. He replied that he could not do that because he would have to turn on the lights and she would be able to see him. However, he left her five dollars to pay for the damage. A grateful offender paid a florist to send roses to his victim.

Many rapists feel very ashamed of their behavior but may hide their shame behind boastful remarks about their rapes or explanations which blame the victim or society. One man said, "I feel so guilty I sometimes contemplated suicide. If I came out and told you how wrong it is, I'd break down." Another man in the Denver study committed suicide shortly after the rape. One offender before leaving the security ward in which he was confined for psychiatric examination on the order of the court, wrote the following note to the head nurse.

Pat,

Your kindness and your smiles were the high spot of my life. They may not seem like much to other people. But, Pat, when a person has lived a stinking rotten life such as I have, it's a very rare treat.

Thank you so much for your understanding.

Sincerely,

Jim

CONFESSION

In rare cases the offender will go to a police station and confess to rape, as in the following case described by East.

A middle-aged widower attempted to commit incest with his daughter, aged thirteen, on several occasions. Some five weeks later he gave himself up to the police, telling them what had occurred, as he heard voices in the street calling after him referring to what he had done. He vividly described how a voice shouted this out to him in two cinemas, and how he heard voices under his window at night talking about the crime. He had been drinking to excess for some time, and when the daughter, who had made no complaint, was questioned, it was found that the prisoner's self-accusations were true. The hallucinations persisted for some months but no delusions were detected at any time.

REQUESTS TO WITHDRAW CRIMINAL CHARGES

Even after the police have been notified, the offender may continue to threaten his victim. One man, who had dated the girl a few times prior to the rape, telephoned her at work and threatened to throw acid on her. Relatives of the offender may try to persuade the victim to drop the charges. The sister of one offender called on the victim and told her, "I heard about your problem. Don't try to drag my brother into court. Don't you know he's married and your own cousin? If you do, I'll really take care of you with my friends."

One man wrote to his victim's mother from the jail quoting Biblical verses "Avenge not yourselves, but rather give place unto wrath; for it is written, Vengeance is mine; I will repay, saith the Lord. Therefore if thine enemy hunger, feed him; if he thirst, give him drink; for in so doing thou shalt heap coals of fire on his head" (Romans 12:19 and 20). He stated that the Lord had really healed him and advised the victim's mother to go to church, pray and read the Bible — "The Lord is everywhere, look where I have found him." Penitentiary officials have noted that the inmate who arrives at the penitentiary carrying a Bible is almost invariably a sex offender.

The victim of rape may later make threats on her assailant or request her boyfriend to "beat him up." The girl friend of a man who had been jailed for rape received threatening telephone calls. She was told that she would be raped to "make up for what George did."

THE OFFENDER'S WIFE

Many offenders report an unhappy marriage or complain that their wives are not responsive sexually. The rape may occur following an argument with the wife, although some men volunteer that they provoked the argument in order to have an excuse for leaving the home on the night of the rape. Palm and Abrahamsen made a psychological study of eight wives of rapists, using the Rorschach test. Although the number of cases is too small to warrant definite conclusions, the Rorschach records showed a remarkable similarity.

The concept these women had of men and the particular way they related to them was patterned after the relationship they had with their father in early childhood. All the Rorschach records reflected the image and the influence of a threatening and sexually aggressive father figure. Their fear of men was confirmed during interviews after the tests. They conveyed fear of being alone in their apartments lest they be raped, a fear of being followed on the streets, a fear of going out at night, a fear of colored men or other fears of being attacked.

The authors assume that such marked fears represent a defense measure against an underlying wish to be attacked, raped or sexually abused. This assumption that these women unconsciously wished to be handled aggressively was confirmed by Rorschach responses indicating they would relate to threatening figures in a markedly passive, submissive and masochistic way. All these wives had clung to their husbands despite cruel treatment, despite the husband's unfaithfulness, despite social disgrace and often against the advice of parents and friends.

The tests revealed that the overt masochism and submissiveness of these women was a reaction to their strong underlying feelings of hostility against men. The women showed a masculine, aggressive orientation, tended to compete with men and to negate their femininity. Because of their particular personality structure, they unconsciously invited sexual aggression only to encounter it with coldness and rejection. Their husbands complained of their lack of sexual response and frigidity. In some cases a prolonged period of sexual frustration preceded the rape.

The authors, noting that the choice of a marriage partner is largely determined by unconscious needs, ask why all eight men chose this type of wife who frustrated them. On the basis of test data on the mothers of the offenders, they conclude that in the marital relationships the offenders perpetuated certain aspects of the relationships with their mothers. All these rapists had been sexually overstimulated and rejected by their mothers.

"RAPE" BY WOMEN

In some jurisdictions women who seduce young boys or who assist a man in the rape of another woman can be charged with rape. Seduction of young boys by an adult woman probably occurs much more often than crime statistics suggest. Such cases rarely come before the courts. A woman in India, suffering from syphilis, enticed five boys, whose ages ranged from ten to fourteen years, into her house and had sexual relations with them. It was thought that she believed she could rid herself of venereal disease by sexual intercourse with a child.

Occasional cases are encountered in which a woman helps her husband or boyfriend to rape another woman. A thirty-two-year-old laborer was sentenced to a penitentiary for three to six years and his wife was placed on probation for one year for the rape of their thirteen-year-old niece. The girl told police that her aunt took her by force into her uncle's bedroom, where both pulled off her pajamas. Then her aunt held her down while her uncle raped her. Afterwards she was told to go to bed and in the morning not to act as if anything happened. Her uncle threatened to kill her if she told anyone.

> I had my sister's children staying with me. I had first discussed this with my wife as a possibility some time before the kids arrived. I felt at the time that my wife couldn't keep me satisfied. I've since found out that it [sex] isn't as important as I thought. The girl that I am accused of raping is much older looking for her age than most; in fact, she is a matured woman. One thing led to another and I believe that due to my part I had a desire to prove that I was still a man. I

cannot have any more children due to an operation. I believe that this was part of my desire to have intercourse with this girl.

That night I forced by threats my wife to go along with it. She wasn't needed to hold Mary, she just stood by and observed. The day before, however, Nancy fought it off. At that time my wife tried to restrain Nancy but we finally gave up. My wife hated this all the way through. She went along with it, I'm sure, because she loved me, and because I had threatened her with harm to herself. I am ashamed of what I did and know now that I was wrong. In the future I am going to rebuild my life and do right by everyone, not be selfish and give to others what I will be able to and live a good resourceful life.

Reichel-Dolmatoff, in his description of the Kogi, a tribe of the Sierra Nevada de Santa Marta in Columbia, mentions cases of the violation of men by two or three married women who prepare ambushes in the roads or fields. Malinowski in *The Sexual Life of Savages in North-Western Melanesia* describes orgiastic assaults by the women of Vakuta and some other southern villages. Women, when working together in the communal weeding of garden plots, have the curious privilege and customary right to attack strangers from other villages passing within sight.

The man is the fair game of the women for all that sexual violence, obscene cruelty, filthy pollution and rough handling can do to him. Thus first they pull off and tear up his pubic leaf, the protection of his modesty and, to a native, the symbol of his manly dignity. Then, by masturbatory practices and exhibitionism, they try to produce an erection in their victim and, when their manoeuvres have brought about the desired result, one of them squats over him and inserts his penis into her vagina. After the first ejaculation he may be treated in the same manner by another woman. Worse things are to follow. Some of the women will defecate and micturate all over his body, paying special attention to his face, which they pollute as thoroughly as they can. "A man will vomit, and vomit, and vomit," said a sympathetic informant. Sometimes these furies rub their genitals against his nose and mouth, and use his fingers and toes, in fact, any projecting part of his body, for lascivious purposes.

Chapter 4

THE VICTIMS

"Unnatural deeds do breed unnatural problems."
— Shakespeare, *Macbeth*

PHYSICAL APPEARANCE

"Beauty provoketh thieves sooner than gold."
— Shakespeare, *As You Like It*

THOSE who believe that the victim of rape is usually an attractive young girl would be surprised by the procession of the middle aged and elderly as well as the young, the obese and the slim, the neatly dressed and the bedraggled, the sick, the lame and halt to the interviewing rooms of the detective bureau. The appearance of the beautiful, stylishly dressed victim is a matter of comment.

RACE

The two hundred rape victims in the Denver study included 126 whites, forty-two Spanish-Americans, thirty-one Negroes and one Oriental. Although the number of white victims exceeded the number of Spanish-American and Negro victims, the Spanish-American victim rate was three and one-half times, and the Negro victim rate was almost four times the white victim rate. Based upon population figures whites have less than three-quarters the expected number of victims.

In Philadelphia also Negro victim rates exceeded white victim rates. However, the Negro victim rate was almost twelve times higher than that of the white women. In Denver, Negro offenders were more likely to rape white women than in Philadelphia, where rape was found to be mainly an intraracial event.

AGE

"Age . . . is a matter of feeling, not of years."
— George William Curtis, *Prue and I*

When the two hundred victims in the Denver study were classified in five-year age groups, it was found that the top risk age groups were fifteen to

76

nineteen (51 victims) and twenty to twenty-four (52 victims). Thus over 50 per cent of the victims were between fifteen and twenty-four years of age. Over 80 per cent of the victims were under thirty-five years of age. Twenty-seven victims were under fifteen, and fourteen victims were fifty years or older. The youngest victims were seven and the oldest eighty-five years of age. The median age of the victims was twenty-one, whereas the median age of the offenders was twenty-five. In other studies victims much younger than seven years of age have been reported.

MARITAL STATUS

The majority of victims of rape are single women. In the Denver study only 25 per cent of the victims were married women. The fact that over one third of the two hundred victims were nineteen years of age or younger contributes to the relatively high incidence of unmarried victims but is not a sufficient explanation. Older unmarried women may be exposed to greater risk of rape when they live alone or with other women. As most rapes occur at night, the presence of a husband may well discourage the would-be rapist. Furthermore unmarried women presumably seek male company more often than married women. Such liaisons, especially with strangers, are not without risk.

SOCIAL CLASS

According to Svalastoga most rape victims have a lower working class social background. He found this to be true even when the woman's social class was based upon the occupation of her parents rather than upon her own occupation. Seventy-nine per cent of his 141 victims were from the lower classes and 21 per cent from the upper or middle classes. In contrast less than 5 per cent of the offenders were from the upper or middle social classes.

CRIMINAL RECORDS

The Philadelphia data showed that 19 per cent of the rape victims had an arrest record, the highest proportion of these arrests being for sexual misconduct. Fifty-six per cent of those victims who had an arrest record had been charged with some sort of sexual offense.

VICTIM-OFFENDER RELATIONSHIPS

In Denver 60 per cent of the victims were raped by strangers, in comparison with 54 per cent in Denmark (Svalastoga) and 52 per cent in

Philadelphia (Amir). Seventeen per cent of the Denver victims were raped by casual acquaintances, and almost half of these men picked up their victims in a tavern or restaurant on the day of the rape. Twelve per cent were raped by friends. Thus 90 per cent of the victims were raped by strangers, casual acquaintances or friends.

The remaining 10 per cent of victims were raped by stepfather or mother's boyfriend (4%), employer (2%), neighbor, brother-in-law (each 1%), and ex-husband, future father-in-law, employee, tenant (each 0.5%). Three of the four employers raped babysitters.

VICTIM-PRECIPITATED RAPE

> *"In a sense the victim shapes and moulds the criminal."*
> — Hans von Hentig, *The Criminal and His Victim*

A thirty-year-old married woman was sitting in her apartment late at night watching television. Someone knocked at the door and she answered. Three men were there, and one of them said, "Hello, baby, I'm going to put the make on you." He forced her into the bedroom and raped her. Then the second man raped her. The third man also raped her and struck her on the face, cutting open her chin when she refused to kiss him. The victim had been drinking that evening and all she had on when she opened the door was a blue sweater.

A London judge told a nineteen-year-old girl she should not take her pants off in a laundromat and wash them. "It provokes comment, bothers the police and all sorts of difficulties arise. Next time you go to a laundromat, for goodness sake, don't repeat this performance." A policeman said the girl walked into the laundromat at 10 P.M., took off her clothes and put them in a washing machine. "What? Was she sitting there naked in front of it?" the judge asked. "Well," the policeman replied, "She had on a very small red shirt which came down to her waist." The judge gave the girl a conditional discharge for conduct likely to provoke a disturbance of the peace.

Some women invite rape. By their seductive behavior in dress, bodily movements or suggestive remarks, they convey to men the impression that they are eager or at least willing to indulge in an illicit sexual relationship. Young ladies tempt fate when they have in their possession or wear lapel buttons with inscriptions such as "Help stamp out rape, say yes," "Member Nonvirgins Club" and "Incest, the game the whole family can play." Failure to indicate disapproval of suggestive sexual comments encourages sexual advances which may take the form of forcible rape.

An eighteen-year-old girl was standing in the parking lot of a hamburger drive-in when some men in a car called to her to come over to the car. When she reached the car, she thought she recognized one of the men so she sat in the front seat and started talking to them. Suddenly the driver started the car and drove off. They explained that they were looking for a friend. As they were driving around one of the men asked, "Do you want to fuck?" She laughed and said no.

After stopping briefly at another drive-in, the man sitting alongside her put a gun to her head and said, "Are you scared?" She replied, "I don't like having a gun to my head and I am scared shitless, but I don't feel like crying and begging you because I don't feel like hassling you. You won't get any enjoyment out of being sadistic to me." The man turned to the men in the back of the car and said, "Well, what about it, do you want to or not?" They agreed to go ahead and rape her.

Some women are rape-victim prone, as others are accident prone. While they do not flaunt their sexuality, they nevertheless show a lack of judgment or lack of caution which brings them in peril of rape. They fail to heed warning signs of danger.

A married woman returned a vacuum cleaner which she had borrowed from a neighbor in an apartment house. He asked her to sit down and talk for a minute and then started talking about nudist colonies and said the best way to start is to take clothes off at home. He asked her to play strip poker, but she refused and left the apartment. He followed her to her apartment, put his hand under her blouse, telling her what lovely breasts she had, asked to see her naked and said that he needed her body. She pushed him away saying that "she was not that way." He continued to make suggestive remarks and she asked him to leave. After he left, she shut the apartment door but did not lock it. Shortly afterwards he walked into the apartment again but did not attempt to molest her. She reported the incident to the police.

"The distinction between criminal and victim which in former days appeared as clear cut as that of black and white, actually often becomes vague and blurred in individual cases. The longer and the more deeply the actions of the persons involved are scrutinized, the more doubtful will it occasionally be who is to blame for the tragic outcome. This is especially so in certain cases of homicide" (Mannheim).

Wolfgang found that in 150 (26%) of 588 criminal homicides, the victim was the first to show and use a deadly weapon, or to strike a blow in an altercation. Furthermore, in these cases the victim (62%) was more likely than the offender (54%) to have a previous arrest or police record. He used the term victim-precipitated homicide to refer to these cases.

Amir introduced the term "victim-precipitated rape" to refer to those rape cases in which the victims actually — or so it was interpreted by the offender — agreed to sexual relations but retracted before the actual act or did not resist strongly enough when the suggestion was made by the offenders. The term applies also to cases in which the victim enters vulnerable situations charged with sexuality, especially when she uses what could be interpreted as indecent language and gestures or makes what could be taken as an invitation to sexual relations.

Amir found that 122 (19%) of the 646 forcible rapes in Philadelphia were victim precipitated. The data revealed several significant factors associated with these rapes. Among these factors are alcohol in the rape situation, particularly in the victim, or both in offender and victim; victims with a bad reputation and victims who meet their offenders at a bar, picnic or party.

CLASSES OF VICTIMS

The Young

Children lack the physical strength to defend themselves against assault and do not always appreciate the danger of accepting a ride or gifts from strangers. They are particularly vulnerable to sexual advances by their father, stepfather or other men responsible for their care. Child victims of rape will be considered in the next chapter.

The Elderly

Elderly women, especially those who live alone, are also handicapped in protecting themselves from physical assault. Despite their age some elderly women make vigorous resistance. A seventy-year-old woman was attacked by a thirty-year-old man as she was walking down an alley and forced against a picket fence. She grabbed him and said she would smash his glasses all over his face if he didn't leave her alone. He ran to his car and drove away.

The Lonesome

Loneliness creates a longing for friendship with others. As von Hentig notes, anything is better than the solitude of a lonesome life, and under these circumstances the critical faculties are weakened. The heartbroken girl who has been jilted by her boyfriend and the woman recently divorced or widowed sometimes show extremely poor judgment in their readiness to strike up an acquaintance with a complete stranger.

A single girl reported that she was raped in the back seat of a car by a man she had met in a bar. After leaving the bar with him, she agreed to his suggestion that they sit in a parked car. Once in the car he told her, "I want some, how about giving it to me." She replied, "No, I want to go." He threw her down on the seat, put his elbow on her throat and pulled off her skirt and pants. She told him, "I have a knife in my purse, if you don't let me go I'll stab you." He replied, "You don't have a knife but I do and if you won't be still, I'll use it."

After raping her he went with her to a friend's house but left when she picked up the telephone to call the police. The man on being questioned by the police denied using force. "She gave in willingly. I had to force her just a little bit at first, like anyone making out." The girl later told detectives that she had a hunch what was going to occur when they went to two cars before finding one that was unlocked.

Another girl who was picked up in a tavern reported: He started kissing me, he unbuttoned my sweater, his hands wandered, he undid my bra and forced me to lay down. I started fighting him, I started to scream. When he wanted me to lay down, that did it. I had a feeling at the time I was making a big mistake but I was hoping he would date me. I don't know, I was just stupid.

The Intoxicated

Women under the influence of alcohol or drugs are ready victims for rape. While in an intoxicated state they may use poor judgment in accepting rides home from strangers, rides which are interrupted at a lonely spot for forcible rape. The intoxicated woman is vulnerable to attack, as she is less able to defend herself. One woman who took a taxi home from a party to her apartment was later raped in her apartment by the taxi driver who threatened to kill her.

> I [a middle-aged woman] was walking from the store carrying a sack of groceries when this young fellow came up to me and asked if he could help me carry them. I was a little tight because I had stopped at the tavern. We came up to my apartment and he came in and set the groceries down. I said be my guest. When he finished his coke he came at me like a cat. He grabbed me and started kissing me and I told him to stop because I wasn't that kind. Then he threw me on the floor right in front of the door. He pulled my dress up and panties off. I fought him and tried to scream, but he put his hand over my mouth and raped me.

The Promiscuous

Twenty per cent of the rape victims in Philadelphia were reported by Amir to have a "bad" reputation in the local community. A significantly higher proportion of Negro victims had such a reputation. The assumption was made and later confirmed by Amir that a bad reputation was a factor in victim-precipitated forcible rape. Although Amir does not define the term "bad reputation," presumably he was referring to women with a reputation for sexual promiscuity.

Some men seek out such women with the expectation of easy sexual gratification. These men overlook the fact that promiscuous women may yet exercise some choice in their selection of sexual partners. Furthermore, the reputation for promiscuity may be based upon false claims of sexual conquest made by boastful yet frustrated acquaintances of the victim. Some girls, often attractive in appearance by their choice of revealing dress, readiness to discuss sexual matters and to engage in flirtatious behavior, contribute to the man's expectation of ready sexual compliance. Yet the girl may be virginal and consciously desire to remain in this state. When the man's advances are eventually resisted, he may resort to the use of force.

Hippies

The hippie has been defined [Random House] as a person especially of the late 1960's who rejects established institutions and values and seeks spontaneity, direct personal relations expressing love, and expanded consciousness, most obviously expressed by wearing nonconventional costumes ornamented with flowers, beads and bells and by taking psychedelic drugs. Several hippies were represented in the two hundred victims in the Denver rape study. Two were abducted as they left a well-known hippie cafe; others were raped in their pads or elsewhere while under the influence of drugs as in the following examples.

A sixteen-year-old hippie who had run away from home was brought to a hospital because of vaginal bleeding. At first she said that she just started bleeding and that was all she knew. Later she reported that she had been raped by a youth while under the influence of LSD and Methedrine®. She refused to prosecute her assailant, as she was afraid his friends would retaliate. In her address book the telephone number of the Poison Control Center was listed alongside the notation "In case of too much candy."

*   *   *

A fifteen-year-old white girl who had run away from home wanted to leave the state but decided to stay in Denver at a "crash pad" known as "the Dump." While there she had sexual intercourse with one of the boys. Although she had intercourse willingly, she was later upset about it. A nineteen-year-old Negro boy she met there invited her to his apartment to "clean up" and to try to calm down. She did not suspect trouble and went to a hotel with the youth. There she bathed and dressed again but lay down on the bed because of pain in the vaginal area.

After she laid down, the youth lay down beside her and told her, "You better take them off," while tugging at her clothes. She then became very scared and was unable to move away, but she did remove her slacks and underpants. He said that wasn't enough, so she took off her blouse and bra. She states she kept pushing him away trying to talk him out of it, but he raped her. "That's when I screamed, but it didn't do any good — he just told me to shut up and held his hand over my mouth." Afterwards she ran out the door while the youth was in the bathroom. She said she was given a stick of grass (marihuana) and a glass of whiskey while in the room.

Hitchhikers

Many young girls, especially college students, have been raped after hitching a ride. These girls are either unaware of the dangers of hitchhiking or overly confident of their ability to recognize drivers who might be likely to make sexual advances toward them. Some men intent on rape will drive alongside a girl waiting in the street for a bus, ask for directions to some street on the bus line, then casually, almost as an afterthought, offer the girl a lift. Male hitchhikers sometimes rape female drivers who foolishly respond to their requests for a ride.

Models

Girls who agree to pose in the nude for photographers may find that the man has interests beyond photography. One such girl said that she was raped on the couch in her room. When detectives visited her apartment, they found that the "couch" was a mattress on the floor. The case of Harvey Glatman, who raped and murdered girls who agreed to pose for "cheesecake" photographs, is described in Chapter 9.

The Masochistic

The fascination exerted over some women by sadistic men is of great psychological interest. Many women wrote love letters to the sexual deviate and multiple murderer Peter Kurten while he was in prison awaiting execution. This man, known as the monster of Dusseldorf, murdered or attempted to murder over forty persons. "Brutality belongs to love," he is reported to have said to one girl as he kissed away the blood forced from the mouth of the half-strangled victim. Another girl describes her desire to go with him again despite his homicidal behavior toward her.

> He was very fond of me; only one evening we were walking in the woods round Dusseldorf and I was not of the same mind as he was, he seized me suddenly by the throat and hurt me dreadfully. The pain was so bad and I was so afraid, but then some people came up and he was very quiet and nice again. I told him everything must be over between us, and he was very furious and tried to choke me again so that I had to take back what I had said. Then he took me home and I said I would not see him for another month.
>
> But I could not sleep that night for thinking of him and hoping he would marry me. So I went in the evening to the house where he lived, but the front door was locked and I had to wait. A young girl came along who lived in the house, and when I told her I wanted to get in and see Kurten, she said he had just come home with his wife. I felt as if I'd been struck by lightning. I can't think why he told me such lies. When I think how kindly and sweetly he always spoke — I simply can't understand it. But I said to myself he must be a scoundrel or he could not be so brutal, and I tried to forget all about him. I know he's a scoundrel, but I am certain he is not the Dusseldorf murderer!" (Wagner).

The Sick

Physical illness may not only handicap the woman in her efforts at physical resistance, but also render her less alert and less responsive to situations of danger. A young married woman who lived in a mountain canyon some distance from a neighboring town, sensed danger when a young man came to her home. Because of a debilitating illness she failed to take those precautionary measures which occurred to her at the time. Instead she returned to her bed after the man left. Later the man returned intent on rape and shot her when she tried to escape. She describes her harrowing experience.

I'm always a suspicious person. In my normal state of mind I'm awfully cautious. I was in bed with the flu. I was sicker than I'd ever been with the flu, almost delirious. When he came to the door, it crossed my mind to call the police but I was feeling lousy and I didn't call them. He asked for a Cathy Brown. It was too common a name. I thought he was lying, yet I didn't give it a thought.

I felt his eyes go up and down my nightgown. I thought I won't reach for the door to lock it, he might knock it open. He went back to his car. I heard the door slam and he drove away. I went back to bed. Twenty minutes later I heard someone at the door. I really think it all happened because I was ill. I should have locked the door. If he'd broken the glass in the door to open it, I would have gone out the window or the back door. I knew . . . I froze in bed. He came in my room. I was scared to death, I was whimpering without whimpering.

He did fool me. He said, "Get your purse." I thought it was a robbery. Then he made me take my nightgown off and lie down on the floor. I rose to my feet and said that I heard my neighbor. I told him that she always brought her kids to the house about 3:30. This was not true, I just made it up. I walked quickly to the door, pointed up the hill and said, "That's where she's coming down." When I said, "There she is," I figured it would scare him. He grabbed at me but I ran. I thought when I ran out in the nude he'd take off.

He said, "Stop or I'll shoot." The minute I screamed for help he shot me. I stumbled ten feet and landed in the snow. I saw blood on the snow. He ran beside me. I thought he was going to finish me off. I let my eyes go in a rolling gaze as if I was dead. I thought he'd gone but when I looked up I saw him zipping his pants with one hand, his other hand held the gun pointing at me.

I started to cry and told him, "Look what you've done." I realized that would scare him and I quickly told him. "I'm all right. I'm embarrassed, what will I tell my husband? It's so embarrassing I don't want anyone to catch you. I know you'll get away." I know he believed me. He raised the gun at me, I felt he was contemplating finishing me off. Then he ran.

RESISTANCE

> *"Faint heart never won fair lady."*
> — Cervantes, *Don Quixote*

Ovid has said that a little force is pleasing to a woman and that she is grateful to the ravisher against whom she struggles. Brantome mentions a lady who confessed that she liked to be "half forced" by her husband, and he remarks that a woman who is "a little difficult and resists" gives more pleasure also to her lover than one who yields at once, just as a hard fought battle is a more notable triumph than an easily won victory.

A certain measure of forcefulness is expected by many women in love making or courtship. Likewise the man expects some resistance to his efforts at seduction. It is perhaps not surprising that on occasion misunderstanding results and that the considerable ill-feeling on the part of the woman may lead to a charge of rape.

A twenty-one-year-old man, charged with rape, was six feet tall, weighed 190 pounds and in his work was used to handling objects weighing 140 to 150 pounds with ease. Svalastoga comments, "It is highly probable that a girl's resistance would not penetrate to his consciousness with the same strength as might have been the case had he been weaker, . . . one difficulty in such a situation is that what the stronger partner may perceive as bashful mockery the weaker partner may interpret as a maximum of resistance. He was actually acquitted in court. A contributing factor might be that the girl in question was described as 'loose' by the local authorities."

Amir divided victim behavior into three groups: submission, resistance and fight. In over half of the 646 rapes, the victims displayed only submissive behavior. In 27 per cent of the rapes, victims resisted the offender, and in 18 per cent the victims put up a strong fight against their attackers. Negro and white victims displayed the same proportion of these forms of behavior. The highest proportion of the instances of submissive behavior were cases in which the victim was white and the offender Negro. In most of these cases the victim was older than her attacker.

The younger the age, the more submissive was the victim; the most submissive victims were those aged ten to fourteen years. In the adult age, victims age thirty and over showed significantly more resistance. Victims who were ten or more years younger or older than the offenders were more submissive, while those who were nearly the same age as their assailants (not more than five years older or younger) displayed the highest proportion of fighting behavior. Victims tended to fight more when they were more intimidated in the initial encounter with the offender, or when force was used against them by the offenders. As expected, the presence of alcohol in the victim diminished her capacity to resist, and her behavior was found to be mainly submissive in such cases.

Resistance to rape may take the form of flight, fight, calls or screams for help and efforts to dissuade the assailant from his purpose. The offender may disguise his true intentions by saying that he just wants to rob her or feel her. In this manner he hopes to reduce the likelihood of vigorous defense. The same objective may be obtained by immediate physical assault or threats of violence.

Flight

Flight from the scene may be attempted at the onset of the attack, but many women are so surprised by the assault that they are not immediately able to react effectively. Later when an opportunity presents itself, they may take quick action in spite of risk to life as in the following example.

A young woman and her young baby were forced into her car at knifepoint in the parking lot of a shopping center. She was ordered to drive away, but at the exit from the parking lot she had to stop the car for a stop sign. She jumped out and screamed for help. The man fled on foot and was captured by several men at the scene.

The victim may think of some excuse to leave the scene of the attack and thereby make her escape. She may give the appearance of wishing to cooperate with the offender as in these two cases:

A woman was bathing her baby in the bathroom when a man suddenly entered with his pants unzipped and his penis protruding. He grabbed her by the shoulder, held his knife to her son and threatened to kill the baby if she screamed for help. As he started to remove his jeans, he told her he was going to have sexual intercourse with her. She said, "OK" and told him she would put the baby to bed. On picking up her baby she ran out the front door. The man was last seen running down the alley.

*   *   *

A twenty-eight-year-old woman was offered a ride home from a club by a family friend. The victim's brother was to ride with them, but the friend drove off without waiting for the woman's brother. He stopped in a street and told the woman, "You're going to give me some pussy." When she resisted, he struck her with his fist and pulled off her clothes. He had difficulty inserting his penis in her vagina, and she said, "Come home with me and I'll give you some Vaseline." The man thought for a minute and said, "If you are lying to me, I'll kill you." He drove her to her home and while the man was using the bathroom, she obtained a large butcher knife from the kitchen. When the man came toward her she pulled out the knife. He picked up a broom, but threw it down and ran off.

A common excuse to leave the scene is a request to be allowed to go to the bathroom. This ruse is not always successful, as the man may insist on accompanying the woman or he may tell her to urinate on the floor. "I asked him if I could go to the restroom and he said to do it on the floor. He told me if I didn't he was going to beat me some more. So I did, then he made me wipe it up with my dress." A victim of a man intent on rape said that she heard her neighbor coming and while his attention was distracted she ran out the door.

Fight

Some women fight vigorously to protect themselves from rape and do so from the moment they are attacked. They kick or punch their assailant and not infrequently will direct their attack on his genitals as in the following two cases.

I was getting out of my car when this man grabbed me, tearing my blouse and bruising my arm. He said, "I'm going to have you, I want you." I replied, "Like hell you are" and kicked him in the groin. He doubled over and said, "I'm going to get you for this" and then limped off between two houses.

*   *   *

I was lying down on the couch watching television when I saw a man standing in the living room. I asked him, "What the hell are you doing here?" and went to the bedroom to get my baby. He said, "Do you want to see me jack off?" I said, "Get out of here or I'll call my husband." He said, "You don't have a husband, you live here alone." He put a gun in my side and said, "Why don't you make love to me." He pushed me back on the bed. I jumped up and kicked him in the testicles and pulled his hair, then ran out the back door.

A woman was about to get into her car in a parking lot when a car drove up and the driver got out and placed his hand in his right coat pocket. He told her he had a gun and that she should get in his car. She reached for his hand, felt no gun and told him to get in his car and leave. He said, "We will get into your car." After placing his hands on her shoulders, he attempted to force her into her car. She screamed and he ran to his car and left.

Some women, fearful of rape, carry weapons such as knives, knitting needles and tear gas guns to defend themselves.

I was walking home when a man asked me, "Is that guy following you?" I turned around and saw a man off at a distance. I replied, "No, he is not" and walked on. I pulled a small pocketknife from my purse, as I was scared at this time. In the middle of the next block the man pointed out to me earlier grabbed my throat and held a knife at my side. He said, "Keep your mouth shut." I poked him with my knife and screamed. He jumped back and ran across the street into an alley. I ran to my apartment and called the police. When I went back to the scene with the police, there were two men there who had seen what had happened and had tried without success to catch the man.

Women who have weapons of defense do not always use them but the possession of a weapon may discourage an assailant.

I was walking toward Colfax Avenue when a Negro approached me and patted me saying, "You sure have a nice soft bottom. What do you do nights when you go home?" I said, "Do you see this?" He asked, "What is it?" I said, "It's a tear gas gun." I walked to my car and was sweeping the snow off when he came up to me and said, "I'm not going to hurt you, you're going to come with me." At this time I reached for the ignition key and turned it, causing the car to jump. This threw him off balance; I started screaming and he ran away.

Other women take advantage of any weapon at hand such as a lighted cigarette or hot liquid on the stove as in the following cases.

A man attempted to enter the front door of a doughnut shop in the early hours of the morning. The female employee indicated by gestures that the shop was closed. A few minutes later while working at the grease machine, she saw the man coming toward her from the back room of the shop. He was masturbating as he approached her and he told her as he chased her around the counter, "I need a woman and I need one real bad." She ran back to the grease machine and flipped hot grease on the man with her doughnut sticks. As he reeled back, she ran out the back door and tried to attract the attention of passing motorists. In the meantime the man ran off.

*   *   *

A twenty-year-old woman was walking home when a man drove up alongside the sidewalk and asked her for directions to Colorado Boulevard. He got out of the car and forced her into the front seat at gunpoint. After driving to an alley, he struck her with the gun several times on the side of her face and head. He threatened her and made her remove all her clothing, then made her lie on the front seat and had anal intercourse. Afterwards he put the gun in his pocket and said he was going to rape her. She asked him for a cigarette, hoping for delay and a chance to get away. She lit the cigarette and as the man was removing his pants she burned him on the upper part of his leg and tried to get out the door. He grabbed her and she fought him, hitting him several times in the groin. She managed to get out of the car and ran nude across the alley, jumped a fence and ran up to the rear door of a house. She beat on the door and the occupants let her in and called the police.

*   *   *

I [a twenty-five-year-old married woman] went up to the landlord's apartment to pay my rent and this guy Jim was there. I went back downstairs and went to bed, as I work nights. Jim must have been watching the apartment because he waited until my sister left and before I knew it I woke up and felt someone lying next to me. He was saying and doing obscene things to me. Of course wakening to that is pretty frightening, so I jumped out of bed and told him to get out. I ran out the door and told him I was going to get the police. At that time my baby started crying and he told me to come back or he would hurt my baby. I ran upstairs to a girl friend's apartment and got some bottles and chased him out the door by throwing bottles at him. By this time the girl next door had called the police. She said she knew him by reputation for beating his wife.

Women who have previously been attacked may purchase a revolver to protect themselves from further attack as in the following case.

A twenty-four-year-old divorcee who had been the victim of a burglary and sex attack purchased a gun to defend herself. One month later she was awakened at 2 A.M. by a man armed with a knife. He put his hand over her mouth and asked her if she remembered him. He was the man who had previously attacked her. She reached under her mattress for the gun and fired four shots, hitting him twice. The man struck her and she pretended to be unconscious until he fled with the gun, five dollars and her wedding ring. A short time later the man sought treatment in a hospital for two bullet wounds in the back.

Appeals for Help

Many women scream for help as soon as they are attacked, but few continue to scream after the rapist chokes or strikes them with his fist. The woman who is attacked in her hotel room may hear someone at the door, yet be so fearful of bodily injury that she does not continue to cry for help. A woman attacked in the street may believe that the object sticking into her side is a gun, as indeed it may be, and not call out to passersby in the belief that if she does so she will be shot and killed.

One victim, as she got into her car after work, was seized by a former friend who was a member of a motorcycle gang. She knew his reputation for violence and was afraid to call out to fellow employees in the parking lot. She tried to write the word "help" on the dust on the outside of the car door as she was talking to him, but no one noticed what she was doing. He ordered her to drive off and she told him she would have to stop for gas. While at the gas station she scribbled a note in the women's toilet giving the direction in which they were driving, but the police were unable to find her car in time to prevent the rape.

Persuasion

The victim may attempt to persuade the offender to allow her to go free. Appeals such as "I'm not that kind of a girl." "I'm old enough to be your mother." "I have children." "Would you do this to your mother?" "What would your mother think of it?" and "It will get back to your wife," usually fall on deaf ears. Occasionally prolonged appeals to reason or humanity are successful.

> Two young college girls, both psychology majors, were attacked in their dormitory apartment by a man who recently had been released from a state prison after serving a ten-year sentence for rape, robbery and burglary. The armed intruder settled for a kiss from each after a three-hour interview on their personal lives, their friends, their activities and their college work.
>
> The two girls were able to end the ordeal by announcing they had to go shopping for groceries. The man invited himself along on the trip to the supermarket but when the man saw a parked police car, he told the girls, "Now's your chance" and fled. He was later arrested at his parents' home a few blocks from the girl's apartment. While holding the girls prisoner, he displayed identification cards and told them of his prison record.

The victim who attempts to persuade her assailant to release her may achieve her wish, but there is the danger that such behavior will infuriate the man and provoke him to greater brutality as in the following case. Fortunately the woman realized that a different appeal was indicated.

> He kept saying he was going to kill me. I was crying and pleading with him for our lives and this was just making him more violent. Finally I decided our only hope was for me to go along with him. So I told him he reminded me of my own son. I told him he wasn't so bad and we could go to my apartment. Then he was completely different, apologizing and saying he was sorry.
>
> A taxi driver who was kidnapped at the same time commented, "The woman had plenty of sense and plenty of guts. She started telling him she liked him and it wasn't so bad. I think that this is what got us out alive, because as long as she was crying and screaming, he just got worse and worse, but once she started talking to him, he calmed down, he was entirely different."

To avoid rape women may claim that a husband is expected home any minute or use other stratagems such as the following.

Infectious Disease or Cancer

> He grabbed me by the arm and when I asked him what he wanted, he said to

come into the alley to talk about it. I offered him my purse but he said he didn't want it. He pulled me into the alley, put a knife at my neck and threatened to cut my throat. Then he pushed me on the ground and told me to spread my legs. When I didn't cooperate, he choked me. I told him I had cancer and if he did that he would get it. He told me he could call my bluff, but he wouldn't do it. I tried to get up and he helped me up. He picked up my things and handed them to me. He brushed my coat off, saying if I had cancer I had trouble enough. [This twenty-one-year-old girl did not have cancer.]

Menstruation

I was trying to unlock the front door when a fairly short, slightly built young man in a dark sweater and light brown slacks asked if he could be of assistance, as he saw that I was having trouble with it. I thought nothing was wrong and went on to say, "Watch out for the paint on the door." He tried the key in the door several times and he didn't get it to open. He pulled the key out and said, "Perhaps my knife can help," and he pulled out a large hunting knife. He began cutting at the key and this is when I first became aware of what the implications of his presence might be.

I said, "You look like a professional at this," and at that moment his gloved hand went over my hand and his knife was at my throat and he said, "If you make one sound, I'll kill you. I'm in trouble. I've got to get out of here. If you make one sound, I'll kill you. You have a car and you're going to help me get away and I'll let you go and you'll be able to come back. You'll be all right, I won't hurt you." So I went with him out to the car and I said, "I've got to find out which key it is."

He said, "Come on, hurry it up, hurry it up." As I started to fumble in the lock he said, "I'm going to count one, two, three quite rapidly to ten and if you don't get it open by then. . . ." So I began fumbling with the key and I got the door open. He said, "Get the key and put it in the ignition, I'm going to drive." I put the key in the ignition and scooted over to the seat next to the driver. He said, "Get down on the floor," and shoved me down by the shoulder. He drove off and stopped by a vacant lot.

He said, "Take off your dress," and I said, "Are you going to rape me?" I said to him, "If you are planning to rape me, this would be an inconvenient time to do so." He thought about this for a moment and then he said, "Why would it be an inconvenience?" I said, "Because it's right in the middle of my period, having this flow. Do you know what happens when you have intercourse with someone during this period? They get blistered."

He thought about this a while. Then he handed me my coat and I put it on and he looked at me. He asked me if I had ever taken psychology, then he said, "You are too nice a girl for me to rape. I had no intention of raping you at all. I just did this for my own precaution."

Pregnancy

A young woman who was dragged from the street into some bushes told her assailant that she was pregnant. He informed her that he had raped women who were nine months pregnant and that it had not hurt them. She told him that her doctor had told her husband to stop because it would hurt the baby. He got off her and ordered her to get down on her hands and knees. Then he pushed her head down and attempted anal intercourse. When she attempted to get away, he forced her on her back and raped her.

Another victim was able to persuade her assailant to leave her alone by faking labor pains. The account of her successful resistance is described on page 14.

Fainting

> I feigned a faint. He might possibly have been scared something was wrong with me. After what seemed like an eternity, he finally got up and went in the kitchen. I presume for some ice or water to revive me. At this moment I hopped up and ran to the door and unbolted it (he had put the chain on) and ran down the stairs shouting "Help!" in various apartments but got no response. I finally had to run outside naked and saw a couple and yelled to them. The man started coming to me, but the man who had attacked me came out of the building, saying I was on an LSD trip and to pay no attention to me. Then he left.

Other Forms of Persuasion

> A twenty-year-old girl was attacked in her apartment. The man tore her blouse off and told her he was going to rape her. She said that if he did she would kill herself. He left her apartment without a word to her. A nineteen-year-old girl was walking down a street when a youth accosted her, forced her against a wall and began to kiss her. She said that her mother had just died. He ran off. Another woman told her assailant that her roommate would be willing to have sexual intercourse with him, but he did not accept the offer.

FAILURE TO RESIST

The woman who willingly consents to sexual intercourse may cry rape, but she is not the victim of rape. Some women are so fearful of physical injury or death that they do not resist sexual assault by a stranger. "All I could think of was staying alive, I prayed to God to let me live." Later such women sometimes express surprise and dismay at their failure to resist the offender.

Compliance may be related to great fear of physical injury despite the absence of direct or indirect threats of violence. One such case was a timid, shy, slightly built telephone company employee who was about to leave her car late at night in her apartment house parking lot when a man jumped in the car and instructed her not to scream. She asked him if he was going to rape her and he told her to remove her clothes, which she did without protest.

Failure to resist may also be related to conscious or unconscious desire for sexual intercourse with the rapist. These women sometimes are the most insistent on prosecution and loudest in their denunciation of the defendant on the witness stand. One young married woman whose husband was serving with the U. S. Army in Europe was one of many victims of a rapist. She made an effective witness in his prosecution. Yet the offender claimed that unlike other victims she participated actively in the sexual intercourse. When interviewed by a detective following the rape, she asked him, "What did he say about me?" The detective replied, "Nothing," and her face turned red.

After the rape the victim may fail to seize an opportunity to obtain help or to escape. An offender was driving his victim back to a downtown location where he had abducted her. A police car pulled alongside at an intersection and both drivers waited for the light to turn green. The woman made no effort to attract the attention of the police officers. Another offender purchased gasoline after the rape but the victim made no outcry.

> After he raped me, we drove to a service station. He then bought some gas. This was about 11 P.M. He spoke to both attendants as though he knew them. I didn't scream because he told me, "I wouldn't scream if I were you because you won't get out of this car alive."

The service station attendant recalled the occasion.

> I seen this guy come into the service station. He comes in all the time. I seen him come in this car. I said to myself, "I wonder what that ugly guy is doing with that pretty girl?" He said he needed some gas. I cleaned the windshield. He had his hand on her legs. She looked at me and smiled and pulled down her dress.

THE PERILS OF RAPE

Venereal Disease

Among 1,487 females sexually assaulted in the District of Columbia, 63 (4.2%) became infected with venereal disease. The incidence of venereal disease may have been greater, as many victims did not appear for the follow-up examination. There were fifty-nine cases of gonorrhea, three cases of syphilis and one case of lymphogranuloma as the result of these sexual assaults (Hayman *et al.*).

It is of interest that many victims had preexisting venereal disease. Thirty-nine had gonorrhea, and fifty-six had positive serologic tests for syphilis (which on retesting reduced to six cases of previous unknown or untreated syphilis). Presumably some of the offenders themselves became victims by contracting venereal disease from the women they assaulted.

Pregnancy

Nine of the 1487 victims (0.6%) became pregnant following the sexual assault. In the Denver study 3 per cent of the two hundred victims became pregnant following the rape. Most rape victims who become pregnant as the result of rape request a therapeutic abortion. One rape victim in Colorado, whose husband was sterile as the result of a vasectomy, expressed a desire to keep the baby if she became pregnant. Prevention of pregnancy is reviewed under the section on Medical Treatment.

Physical Injury

Sixty-eight of the 1487 victims (4.6%) were classified as having had severe physical assault, eighteen of whom were admitted to the hospital. Six of these were children two to six years old, admitted because of vaginal or vaginoperineal tears. The twelve adults included nine with fractures and two with stab wounds. Among the fifty victims treated in the emergency room, there were eleven children with vaginal or vaginoperineal lacerations. During the thirty-three-month study period there were four murders in which rape was suspected.

REPORTING THE RAPE

Many victims notify the police at the earliest available opportunity. Others do so only after they have spoken to their husbands, boyfriends, physician, clergyman or employer. Delay in reporting the rape may result from indecision; the victim who dreads the shame of newspaper publicity or appearance in the courtroom may debate with herself before taking action. Fear of retaliation by the assailant, prior friendship with the offender or a blood relationship, awareness of complicity in the offense and a wish to conceal the rape from a jealous husband are other factors.

Delay in notification of the police is more frequent in victim-precipitated rapes and rapes which are later recorded as unfounded by the police. Sutherland and Scherl found that those women who feel there has been no invitation, seduction or willing compliance on their part generally make an immediate telephone call to the police or go to the nearest emergency medical facility. This was true of eight of the thirteen young women studied. The remaining five women who did not immediately notify the police experienced an inner sense of guilty involvement, confirmed by data emerging in subsequent interviews.

Occasionally the police are not informed until the offender either telephones the victim or calls on her as in the following case.

> A middle-aged white woman was invited by a Negro fellow employee to a party in his home. After some drinking, she decided to leave and called a cab. Another Negro offered to drive her home, and the cab driver was dismissed when he arrived. The Negro took her to his car and asked her to stop at his home for another drink. After a short time he made advances to her which she warded off politely. He continued to make advances to her which were rebuffed, whereupon he asked other guests who were present to leave the room and they went into the kitchen.

The man then told her she was going to get the beating of her life. He struck her with his fists, knocking her to the floor and got on top of her and started banging her head on the floor. After striking her in the right eye, which later became swollen and bruised, he dragged her into the bedroom. The victim thought that at this time a finger on her left hand was broken. There was another struggle after he locked the door. After choking her he removed her clothes. Before raping her he asked if she had ever been to bed with a Negro, then told her, "Well, this is one you'll have."

After the rape he told her that she was now his woman and that he wanted her to stay with him. She persuaded him to let her go home so she could obtain treatment for her broken finger and swollen eye. Before calling a cab for her, he threatened to kill her if she told the police. She was treated by her private physician but waited thirty-six hours before calling the police. Her explanation for the delay was that she decided not to do anything about the rape. When the man called her at her home several days later, she decided to prosecute him.

The rape may not be reported until two or three months later when the victim becomes aware that she is pregnant. Police investigation sometimes shows that the sexual intercourse was voluntary and the purpose of claiming rape is to obtain an abortion. In some states abortion is permitted by law upon certification by the district attorney that the woman was the victim of rape.

Many victims of rape do not notify the police. One man raped five women, but only one of them contacted the police. In another case the man who was arrested for the rape of a woman in an apartment house confided to me that he had also raped a woman in an adjacent apartment the same evening. This rape was not reported to the police. Some victims rely on their boyfriends or husbands to revenge the rape. "I wouldn't report it to the police. I told my boyfriend and let him beat him up." Boyfriends do not always react with great understanding when informed of a rape. "I told my boyfriend. He hit me on the head when I told him what happened. He didn't believe me; he said he was going to cut me up if I wasn't telling the truth."

REFUSAL TO PROSECUTE

The victim who reports to the police that she has been raped may later request that no action be taken in court against her assailant. This occurs more frequently among those victims who have reported the rape only after they have been urged to do so by their husbands, relatives, friends, employers or physicians. In some of these cases the accusation of rape has been false (see Chapter 11), in others the victim for some reason has been ambivalent about prosecution from the outset.

A woman who is not greatly upset by the rape may feel that prosecution is not worth the inconvenience of appearance in court. "He tore my dress. If he buys me a new dress, I'll drop the charges." "I'll drop the case if he pays me five dollars for my pants." Fear of publicity often discourages victims from appearing in court. Thus one victim refused to prosecute because she was afraid that her boyfriend or her girl friend would find out what happened to her. Another victim feared that a public trial might reveal information which could be used against her by her recently divorced husband in his efforts to gain custody of their children.

Reluctance to testify in court is another factor. "This letter is to state that I wish to end all proceedings concerning the case of the *People v. R.S.L.* My personal feelings are that the experience of a court trial would be unbearable to me. I find the procedure of quoting every action and word in a courtroom impossible. It seems this would be as trying as the actual experience when this crime was committed."

Some victims, especially those who have known or dated the offender prior to the rape, consider that the arrest or interrogation of the assailant will be sufficient to discourage him from repeating the offense. "He knows now I mean business when I say no, he won't try this again. I would just as soon forget the whole thing." "I want you [the police] to tell him not to do it again."

Pressure from others may deter the victim from prosecution. The offender or his relatives may threaten the victim with violence or use more tactful methods of persuasion. The offender's attorney or family asks the victim if she will drop charges on condition that psychiatric treatment is obtained. One woman gave as her reason the fact that the owner of the tavern she patronized had told her that she could not drink there anymore if she pressed charges.

The victim's family may discourage her from further action when the offender is a relative or close family friend. One girl refused to prosecute, as she said the man was a close friend. Later it was learned that he was her boyfriend's brother. The parents of one girl said they did not wish to pursue the case as "they knew what type of girl she was and they were unable to cope with her." Although the girl was promiscuous, she had on this occasion been raped.

Rarely victims will withdraw charges because they do not wish the offenders to go to prison. One woman said that she had discussed the matter with her husband and did not wish to proceed further, as the man who had assaulted her "was awful drunk and he is married and has two kids and we kind of feel sorry for him." Another woman wondered if her assailant could be charged with a misdemeanor, as she did not want him or anyone else sent to a penitentiary on a felony charge.

Charges of rape may be withdrawn when a pregnancy test is returned negative or if the assailant agrees to marry the victim. Many victims refuse to prosecute because they feel that they contributed in some measure to the rape as in the following example.

She went to a party with her date. After the party he took her home and they sat on a couch for a short time. Then she got up and asked him to leave, at this time he struck her in the mouth with his fist. She started crying and he choked her. He told her he would kill her if she didn't go to bed with him. They struggled and then he pulled her into her bedroom and raped her. He said he was sorry and left. The following day her employer noticed the injury to her face and asked her about it. On his advice she notified the police. Later she refused to prosecute saying, "Maybe it was probably half my fault for even going out with him in the first place."

Some victims blame themselves unjustly for contributing to their victimizations. Others may be aware that by drunken or seductive behavior or by injudicious selection of boyfriends that they are partly responsible for their rape, yet give other reasons for refusal to prosecute. "It doesn't look good, I was up in his apartment in the first place." It would be a mistake to assume that refusal to prosecute indicates that the victim has contributed to her misfortune.

REACTIONS TO RAPE

The diversity of reactions to rape is related to the presence of violence or threats of violence, the age of the victim, her cultural background, personality and prior sexual experiences. Reactions range from lack of concern or deceptive apparent lack of concern, through mild irritation, anger, dismay or depression to major emotional disturbances including severe depression which rarely may lead to suicide or attempts at suicide.

At one extreme is the victim who regards the sexual assault lightly. One such victim, who was very drunk at the time of the rape and had difficulty in recalling all the circumstances, was asked by detectives whether there was any unnatural sexual assault. She replied, "In sex nothing is unnatural." When questioned about fellatio she said that it did not occur, then a moment later added, "By golly, yes, I remember spitting it out." Another woman when asked what happened between the two attacks of rape by her assailant, replied, "We went out for hamburgers." Other victims fall asleep after the rape.

Some victims are more upset over the theft of a purse or other property than they are over the rape. One woman, whose gold ring was stolen, said she would withdraw the charge of rape if the man would return the ring. Another woman raised little objection to the rape, but when the man refused to return her transistor radio to her, she quickly became very outspoken. "When he told me this, I got awfully mad."

One victim became impatient when the man who had threatened to rape her spent much time in fondling her breasts, "I finally told him hurry up and get it over with. . . . He tried to get in me, I helped him by kind of guiding it in but not by touching it. . . . He went for a while and couldn't come. I told him he couldn't seem to get through and laughed at him and he finally got up." Yet another woman was more upset over a black eye than the rape and insisted that the man be charged with assault and not rape. In one case of genuine rape the victim met her assailant a week later and had voluntary sexual relations with him. Another victim later married her assailant, whom she had not met prior to the rape.

A young single girl who was attacked and threatened in her apartment in the early hours of the morning, reported to police that the man was reluctant to answer her questions.

Female(F):   "What's the matter really with making love, I mean this way, it's true natural selection, as in nature, before man corrupted it with his moralizing and prudishness."

Male(M):   "I really like your philosophy."

F: "Don't you want to talk about it?" (He was reluctant to answer my eager questioning.)

M: "I don't talk much, I just say what I have to."

F: "Are you shy?"

M: "No, I just don't talk a lot."

F: "You know it's not the actual fucking, but it's afterwards when you realize you've really established communication between human beings that's so satisfying."

M: "Please don't use that word."

F: "What word, 'human beings'?"

M: "No 'fucking,' I hate that word. I only use it when I'm very mad."

F: "Well, I've always called things by their names, but I'm sorry if it offends you. . . . Do you do this often?"

M: "Oh, I rob people, but this is the first and last time for this (meaning rape). I could get into a lot of trouble by being here, doing this."

F: "Oh, really, why? It's normal to want sex."

M: "Yes, but to break in, that's really against the law and if you called the cops, I could really be in trouble."

F: I assured him in all sincerity (as much as I could muster), "Oh, I won't call the cops, don't worry." I think he did believe me a little . . . I gave him a dissertation on wooing women without having to break into their apartments. (Tell them they're beautiful, he has nothing to offer but his worship of them, etc.) He gave no response to this, but, then most people don't like to hear others preach, especially a woman (on the subject of women) to a man. . . . He was more afraid than I was, or maybe just excited, because with him leaning against me I could feel his heart beating very fast.

An indifferent attitude may hide very great feelings which do not appear until weeks or months later. One victim who was more upset than she realized adopted a fatalistic attitude.

A middle-aged woman was raped by a man who broke into her house and threatened her with a knife. She did not scream, as she was afraid that another member of her family might come to her rescue at the risk of serious injury or death at the hands of her assailant. In a very matter-of-fact way she described the threats and rape. When her apparent unconcern was pointed out to her, she replied, "I'm a fatalist. My theory is what's going to happen is going to happen.

> What comes will come. He didn't hurt me. I might as well be passive, why resist?
> If he kills me, he'll kill me."

The influence of cultural factors is illustrated by the reaction of Chinese women in Hong Kong to rape. While the Chinese living in that city have all been under the direct influence of modern Western culture to a greater or lesser extent, they still have a considerably more conservative attitude and are generally very shy about matters pertaining to sex. The shame suffered by the victims appears to be much more intense than in Western culture. Chinese legends abound with instances of suicides committed by victims after they were raped. Not only were these suicidal acts tolerated, the victims were in fact acclaimed and extolled. It is quite possible that these legends help to intensify the shame and sense of worthlessness in those who are contented to live after they were raped (Wong).

PATTERNS OF RESPONSE TO RAPE

Sutherland and Scherl studied the reactions to rape of thirteen young-adult victims of rape. These white girls, ranging in age from eighteen to twenty-four, had moved into a low income (not necessarily black) community to "do something real" in contemporary society. Follow-up of each of the victims revealed a similar sequence of reactions, falling in three distinct phases, extending over a period of weeks or months. The following account is from their report in the *American Journal of Orthopsychiatry (403*:503, 1970).

Phase One: Acute Reaction

In the moments, hours, and days immediately following the rape, the victim's acute reaction may take a variety of forms such as shock, disbelief and dismay. She often appears at the police station or the hospital in an agitated, incoherent and highly volatile state. Frequently she is unable to talk about what has happened to her or to describe the man who has assaulted her. Sometimes the victim will initially appear stable only to break down at the first unexpected reminder of the incident.

> One day after she had been raped, Louisa was taken by two police detectives to establish the exact location on a country road of her assault. As they were returning to town, a call on the police radio reported the automobile described by Louisa as that of the abductors had been located. They immediately drove to where the auto had been found, unaware of the presence there of two of the assailants. As Louisa got out of the police car to make positive identification of the auto, she saw the men. She began sobbing loudly and uncontrollably and had to be assisted in returning to the police car.

In this early phase of response to rape, shock and dismay are often succeeded by gross anxiety. This frequently occurs at the time the victim must first deal with the consequences of the assault. Notification of parents is one of the early issues to arise during Phase One. A very common statement during the initial interview with the women studied was, "My parents must not know." Immediately following this came one of several other statements of explanation such as "They told me this would happen" or "Now they will make me come home" or "It will kill them." Implicit in these responses seems to be the girl's fear that her own poor judgment precipitated the crisis. However, she is often unable to consider this in any depth until a later time. Seven of the young women studied chose parental illness as the reason why they felt unable to notify their families. In most instances, a marked decrease in the patient's anxiety and other symptoms occurred after she had been able to discuss the incident with her family.

In addition to the concerns the victims raised about telling their parents, the women also focused on a number of other issues during this period of acute anxiety: Should she press legal charges? Will she be able to identify the alleged rapist and how will she feel about seeing him? Will all of her friends and neighbors find out what has happened? What will be the nature of the publicity about the incident? Will she become pregnant? Should she tell her boyfriend or fiance what has happened? What will her clergyman think of her?

The example which follows illustrates a typical Phase One reaction.

Noreen, a twenty-two-year-old woman of middle-class background, was living and working in the ghetto area of a large city. During the night a Negro man broke into her house and raped her at gunpoint while her roommate stood helplessly by. Noreen immediately notified the police and was taken to a local hospital for medical attention.

The following day she told her employer what had happened. She expressed no feelings about the rape even when questioned. At her employer's suggestion, she came to the mental health clinic three days later. She was initially calm and controlled, much as she apparently had been since the assault. However, as she described what had happened she began to cry, saying she wanted to tell her parents but it would "kill" her mother, who had cancer. After a lengthy discussion of possible alternatives, Noreen decided to notify her married sister, who lived approximately forty miles away. By previous arrangement, the girls were to go home for a holiday celebration in about ten days and Noreen thought she could then talk with her parents.

During the time before she went home, Noreen's awareness of her own anxiety increased. She had refused to consider alternate living arrangements during this time, but one night she and her roommate called the police at 3 A.M., saying they were unable to sleep and were afraid the assault might be repeated. The following day both girls moved to a friend's apartment in another part of town.

At Noreen's request she and her sister were seen a few days later to discuss the possible reactions the family might have when they were told about the rape, and the ways in which the girls could deal with these responses. Noreen then revealed her recent fear and anger and her previous loss of appetite and sleeplessness.

The Phase One reaction normally resolves within a period of a few days to a few weeks. There is the expected decline of nonspecific anxiety as the victim turns increasingly away from fantasy and, with support, toward handling the realistic consequences and problems created by the sexual assault. . . .

Phase Two: Outward Adjustment

This phase, often mistakenly thought to represent a successful resolution of the reaction to the rape, includes denial of the impact of the assault and is characterized by pseudoadjustment and return to usual activity. . . . The woman announces all is well and says she needs no further help. It is our impression that this period of pseudoadjustment does not represent a final resolution of the traumatic event and the feelings it has aroused. Instead, it seems to contain a heavy measure of denial or suppression. The personal impact of what has happened is ignored in the interest of protecting self and others.

During this phase the victim must deal with her feelings about the assailant. Anger or resentment are often subdued in the interest of a return to ordinary daily life. The victim may rationalize these feelings by attributing the act to blind chance ("It could have happened to anyone"), to "sickness" on the part of the assailant or to an extension of the social struggle of black against white or of poor against rich. In similar fashion and for the same reasons the victim's doubts about her role in the assault are also set aside.

The following example illustrates the reaction of the victim during Phase Two:

> Denise, a twenty-year-old woman, was working as an "indigenous" neighborhood aide for the local poverty program in the city where she had moved following her high school graduation. One afternoon as she was walking through a deserted park she met a young man who had attended several meetings at the neighborhood center. He introduced her to a friend who was with him, and the three chatted briefly before the first man left. As Denise began to walk away, the remaining man demanded she have intercourse and threatened to kill her if she refused. Denise submitted.
>
> As soon as she was released, Denise reported the incident to her neighborhood center director who notified the police and arranged for medical care. That evening she talked at length with the director and then called her parents who were concerned but supportive. Denise refused professional mental health assistance.
>
> Denise insisted after a two-day "vacation" that she wanted to continue her work at the neighborhood center and refused an offer to be transferred to a similar job in another part of the city. She commented that changing jobs would be an admission of failure and would "let the guy know he really got to me." The neighborhood center director was concerned that perhaps Denise was being "too

brave." At his suggestion, he and Denise discussed this question with the clinic social worker who served as a consultant for the neighborhood center. An evaluation at the clinic was recommended. Denise agreed, provided evaluation, and not treatment, was the intended purpose.

Denise was outwardly calm, composed and reasonable during her clinic interview. She felt a transfer to another part of the city was unnecessary because she would be more careful in the future and thus an assault of this type would not occur again. She decided against pressing legal charges because she felt to do so might limit her ability to work effectively with the people in the neighborhood. Denise said she was not a virgin at the time of the rape, so she was not upset by the incident itself. She denied any sleeping or eating difficulties and said she was annoyed that no one seemed to think she "had the strength to take something like this."

The worker accepted Denise's statements but anticipated with her the likely development of further questions and worries. Shortly after this she failed to keep a follow-up appointment, left her job at the neighborhood center and returned to her parents' home in another state.

The victim has little if any interest in gaining insight through treatment during Phase Two. The woman often strongly asserts she must get back to school or work as if nothing more traumatic than an ankle sprain had occurred. For Denise, an admission of her fear and concern would have seemed to be a sign of her own weakness. Whatever the explanations and rationalizations offered by the victim, they have inherent within them components of the fears from which they spring. Thus for Denise an admission of her fear and concern would have seemed to be a sign of her own weakness.

Phase Three: Integration and Resolution

Phase Three begins when the victim develops an inner sense of depression and of the need to talk. It is during this period that the resolution of the feelings aroused by the rape usually occurs. Concerns which have been dealt with superficially or denied successfully reappear for more comprehensive review. The depression of Phase Three is psychologically normal and occurs for most young women who have been raped. While careful evaluation is always indicated, the depressive feelings should not be interpreted immediately as a sign of illness.

There are two major themes which emerge for resolution in this phase. First, the victim must integrate a new view of herself. She must accept the event and come to a realistic appraisal of her degree of complicity in it. Statements such as "I should have known better than to talk to him or to open the door," "I should have had the lock on the window fixed" and "I should never have been out alone" emerge at this time. Second, the victim must resolve her feelings about the assailant and her relationship to him. Her earlier attitude of "understanding the man's problems" gives way to anger toward him for having "used her" and anger toward herself for in some way having permitted or tolerated this "use."

Phase Three may begin with a specific incident or discovery or with a more general deterioration and breakdown of the successful defenses of Phase Two. Diagnosis of pregnancy, the need to go to a police line-up for identification of the assailant, a marriage proposal, a glimpse of someone who resembles the rapist — these or many other situations may introduce Phase Three. Frequently, however, it is not possible to identify a specific precipitant. Instead, the victim finds herself thinking increasingly about what has happened to her and functioning progressively less well.

The following example illustrates the case of a young woman who handled Phases One and Two by herself and sought professional help only when she encountered the difficulties of Phase Three.

> Alice, age twenty-three, was employed as an adult education teacher at an inner-city school. One night her principal's twenty-year-old son called to say his mother had ready the books she was donating to the night school and wanted Alice to pick them up and have coffee. Alice had met the son once, and accepted his offer to pick her up and drive her to the home. Soon after getting into the car, Alice realized they were not going in the right direction. When she questioned the young man, he stopped the car and raped her. Afterward Alice jumped out of the car and ran home, telling no one what had happened. She went to work the next day and learned the principal's son was moving out of town at the end of the week to take a new job.
>
> Except for occasional nightmares and crying spells, Alice later reported she had rapidly been able to get herself under control. Eight weeks later, after missing two menstrual periods, she discovered she was pregnant.
>
> Alice called the mental health clinic three days later asking to talk with someone about a therapeutic abortion. Following an initial interview with a psychiatrist, she was seen on a daily basis for one week by the social worker and had two additional appointments with the psychiatrist. During this time she realized she had chosen to handle the incident according to her usual pattern of protecting others at great expense to herself. For example, Alice said she could not tell her parents what had happened because they would tell her fiance and "they would all be hurt." Alice was adamant that she could not bear the child both because it was interracial and because of her abiding faith in the sanctity of conception only within circumstances of love and marriage. She was referred to an obstetrician and two weeks later a therapeutic abortion was performed.
>
> While there was no suicidal intent, the week of clinic interviews was marked by feelings of depression with symptoms of frequent crying and loss of appetite. As she considered her recent experience she revealed how overwhelming it had been to her and how scared she was to think about it for fear she would "fall apart." The depression resolved as Alice began to talk about what had happened and to make some decisions about her future. She felt she hadn't handled things too well in the past, but said perhaps this was "the beginning of the new Alice."
>
> Alice returned to the clinic following the abortion to say she was going home. She planned to discuss the situation with her family when she arrived and asked if her parents could call the clinic to talk further. Alice also asked for a referral to a mental health agency in her hometown for further discussion of problems less

immediately connected with the rape. For Alice, the resolution of her depressive reaction involved recognition of a lifelong pattern of punitive self-sacrifice. In addition, the process of recognizing, considering and then terminating the pregnancy consolidated ego capacities and a sense of esteem and self-reliance badly fractured by the traumatic assault.

THE MEDICOLEGAL EXAMINATION

"Voluntary loss of virginity may result in injuries consistent with rape."
– Aleck Bourne

"Medical evidence in sex assaults is chiefly concerned with corroboration – the observations are consistent with the statements that have been made – or not."
– Keith Simpson, *A Doctor's Guide to Court*

Written permission for the medical examination, photographs of injuries and release of information to the police, district attorney or other persons should be obtained from the victim. Parental consent is required in the case of child victims and the consent of the legal guardian should be obtained for a patient who has been committed to a mental hospital. The problem of the mother who brings her daughter to a physician demanding to know whether she is still a virgin and the medical examination of children are considered in the next chapter.

The medical evaluation should be made as soon as possible following the woman's arrival in the hospital. A woman who had been raped was taken to a general hospital for examination and treatment. At the emergency room she had to wait one hour and forty minutes for examination, which was accomplished in ten minutes. The examining physician did not offer a douche or other cleansing materials, and his services were confined to the medicolegal examination. In subsequent statements to the press, the patient complained that the medical search for evidence coldly ignores the patient and that the entire medical procedure is inhumane.

Unfortunately the medical profession cannot complain that this was an isolated incident. Many victims are kept waiting in emergency rooms for much longer periods and receive no better medical care. One victim who was taken to a hospital at 11 P.M. was seen briefly by a physician. At 6:30 A.M. a nursing supervisor discovered the girl still in pain in the emergency room. Thorough examination at this time revealed a laceration of the cervix and hematoma of the uterus.

Haymen comments that "the examinations are usually done by untrained house officers. Victims sometimes wait for hours while other patients are seen and then are examined without privacy, adequate time or understanding and compassion. Little attention is paid to emotional trauma, which is often aggravated by the examination. These patients should be seen by a staff physician or a resident in pediatrics or gynecology, and away from the emergency room."

History Taking

It might seem unnecessary to stress that the history should be obtained in privacy, but too often interviews are conducted in the emergency room within earshot of others. A sympathetic, unhurried attitude is essential. The patient should be allowed to describe the alleged rape in her own words without interruption. After she has finished, direct questions may be required to clarify her account and to explore topics which have not been mentioned such as the use of alcohol or drugs, prior sexual intercourse including the date of the most recent act of intercourse prior to the rape, the date of the last menstrual period, pelvic infections or operations, the use of birth control pills or devices and prior experiences of sexual assault. It is important to know whether she had taken a douche prior to the examination.

Appearance and Behavior

> *"Girls who protest they have fought their way*
> *out of muddy ditches through brambly undergrowth*
> *do not always look as if they have done so."*
> — Keith Simpson, *A Doctor's Guide to Court*

A note should be made of the patient's appearance, behavior and emotional state. Inquiry should be made whether the victim has changed her clothes and washed herself since the assault. Torn, stained or deranged clothing should be described. Police officers will want this clothing for special tests and use in evidence.

Physical Examination

The presence of a nurse during the physical examination protects the physician from false accusations of rape. The history given by the patient will provide a guide to the location of bruises, scratches or other injuries; however, the whole body should be examined.

> The commonest injuries found are bruising and scratches on the face and neck; bruising on wrists, arms and shoulders, where the victim has been gripped or struck; bruising or abrasion on the back where she has been thrown down or forcibly pressed against a hard surface; abrasions on the knees and over other

bony prominences if she has been dragged; bruising and scratches on the thighs and bruising about the shins and ankles sustained while the assailant has attempted to force the legs apart (Sydney Smith). As bruises may not appear until the day after the rape, reexamination may be necessary.

Genital Examination

Search should be made for matting of the pubic hair due to the presence of dried semen and a specimen should be removed for microscopic examination. Foreign hairs or material should also be preserved. In virgins the appearance of the hymen varies considerably and, in the absence of a recent tear which shows evidence of hemorrhage, it is sometimes difficult to determine if it has been injured. Natural notches and fimbriations have been mistaken for rupture. Intercourse sometimes occurs without rupture of the hymen. In nonvirgins there may be no abnormal findings. Elderly women with atrophied tissues are more likely to show evidence of injury than young married women. Serious tears of the vaginal wall may be caused either by rough coitus or by the insertion of fingers, a gun barrel or other object. Lacerations of the perineum and injuries to the bladder or rectum occur infrequently.

Laboratory Tests

Tests for the presence of sperm in the vagina are unlikely to be of value if more than twenty-four hours have elapsed since the rape, unless the victim was murdered. Sperm may be found in rape-murder victims for as long as ten weeks to four months after death (Sharpe). In the living, motile sperm are found in the vagina from one to eight hours after sexual intercourse and nonmotile sperm from one to fourteen hours. In exceptional cases nonmotile sperm have been found eighteen to twenty-four hours after coitus (Sharpe).

Detection of motile sperm is sometimes important in the proof of rape. A woman has sexual intercourse with her husband at 11 P.M. and after he leaves for work at 8 A.M. the following morning, she is raped by a stranger who forces his way into her apartment. The defense attorney will claim that the sperm found in her vagina after the rape were those of her husband. The presence of motile sperm, however, could not be the product of coitus at 11 P.M. the previous night.

There is another technique which can be used to distinguish the husband's sperm from those of an assailant. A young girl and her boyfriend were sitting in the back seat of his car in a lover's lane late at night when they were attacked by three youths and the girl was raped. The youths' attorney claimed that the young couple were having intercourse in the car and that the motile sperm found in her vagina were the product of this sexual intercourse. It was found, however, that the sperm in her vagina did not match the blood group of her boyfriend.

The majority of men are referred to as secretors because their semen (as well as other body fluids) contains the agglutinin of their particular blood group. If the semen contains A or B substance, it must be the product of a man with an A or B blood group. If there is no A or B substance, the sperm could be either from a man with blood group 0 or from a nonsecretor. The technique, therefore, does not always contribute to the medicolegal investigation of rape.

If the rapist has had a vasectomy, his semen will not contain sperm unless the operation was not successful. The presence of seminal fluid in the vagina can be shown by the acid-phosphatase test. Positive reactions can be obtained in vaginal secretions twenty-four hours or longer after sexual intercourse (Rupp). Seminal fluid contains a much higher percentage of acid phosphatase than blood, hence a quantitative determination will distinguish between a positive reaction due to blood in the vagina of a menstruating woman and an elevation due to seminal fluid.

Great care has to be taken in the handling and custody of material for laboratory examination if the results are to be admitted into evidence in court. At Denver General Hospital special kits are prepared which contain a sterile vacuum container and a glass slide which has been initialed by the pathologist to show that it was examined and found free from contamination prior to being placed in the kit. The examining physician etches on the slide the name of the patient, her hospital number, the date of the examination and his own initials. The kit containing the specimens is placed in a special box which is locked. The only key to the lock is in the possession of the pathologist who conducts the special tests. He also initials the slide.

Similar care should be taken in the identification and preservation of clothing, fingernail scrapings, hairs and other material which is kept for special laboratory tests. Clothing stained with semen has a stiff feeling and fluoresces under ultraviolet light. As other stains also fluoresce, this procedure is of value only in showing areas of clothing which should be examined microscopically. Sperm may be detected in clothing many months after the sexual offense; however, under certain conditions they may not be detectable within a short time of the occurrence of the stain. The usual tests are made for venereal disease and pregnancy and should be repeated some weeks after the rape.

Medical Examination of the Suspected Rapist

If the suspect consents to a medical examination, note should be made of bruises, scratches, bite marks and the presence of blood, seminal fluid or other stains. Injuries to the penis may occur in forcible rape. Tests should be made for venereal disease. Foreign hairs or materials should be collected and preserved. The police will take clothing and foreign materials for special examinations.

The Medical Report

"Be assured of this, most excellent Crito,
that to use words in an improper sense is
not only a bad thing in itself but it generates
a bad habit in the soul."
— Plato

Physicians should make a thorough, impartial examination of victims and should leave determination of rape to the court. As police officers in small police departments may be inexperienced in the investigation of rape, it is sometimes necessary to provide full explanation of the significance of the medical findings to aid in the prevention of the twin dangers of criminal investigation of rape: imprisonment of the innocent suspect or failure to prosecute a sexual offender. Explanation of the findings will also be necessary when the physician appears on the witness stand.

Although the physical examination is fraught with difficulties, physicians more often come to grief in the interpretation of their findings. The appearance of a distraught woman in the emergency room with a horrendous tale of sexual assault sometimes arouses great feelings of sympathy for her and anger at her alleged assailant. Such feelings should not be allowed to cloud clinical judgment. The injuries may have been self-inflicted or sustained in a fight with other girls and the history of the sexual assault may be false. Eighteen to twenty-five per cent of rapes reported to the police are determined by police investigation to be unfounded.

It cannot be overemphasized that presence of sperm in the vagina, by itself, is proof of sexual intercourse and not proof of rape; absence of sperm does not exclude rape. Rupture of the hymen may have been caused by a finger, gun barrel or other object. In rape, penetration of the vagina need not be complete, the hymen need not have been ruptured as the slightest penetration is sufficient; sexual emission need not occur. Interpretation of the medical findings should include consideration of the possibility that the genital injuries were either self-inflicted or resulted from voluntary inter-course. Occasionally intercourse with a virgin results in hemorrhage sufficient to require transfusion. Thoinot points out the need for caution in reporting that rape has occurred.

"Suppose, for example, that a virgin yields of her own free will to a lover; she is deflowered. Some hours later she quarrels with her lover, or some other person; she gets a beating and thus has traces of assaults on her body.

For revenge she accuses her lover, or the person who beat her, of having raped her. You are commissioned as an expert; you find recent defloration, traces of assaults on the body, and you conclude from these facts that there has been rape. But later the inquiry demonstrates the trickery, and there you are with your error. You would not have been so badly involved if you had been content to state simply what you had established; on the one hand, defloration; on the other, marks of violence on such and such parts of the body of the girl" (Thoinot).

MEDICAL TREATMENT

The victim should be treated for both physical and psychological injuries. The opportunity to talk at length about her experience to a sympathetic physician is helpful and may do much to prevent an untoward psychological reaction. Time is not always available for this purpose and referral to the Visiting Nurse Service provides the victim with an opportunity to review the experience and obtain the advice and support which she needs (see below).

Since the offender may have venereal disease, consideration should be given to the administration of penicillin to the victim. (Sixty-three women [4.2%] of the victims of sex assault in District of Columbia became infected with venereal disease.) An antiseptic douche should be given to all victims. As women who are not menstruating and who are not using birth control pills or devices may become pregnant as the result of the rape, they should be advised regarding prevention of pregnancy. (Three per cent of the Denver rape victims and 0.6 per cent of the District of Columbia victims became pregnant following rape.)

The risks of endocrine therapy to prevent pregnancy should be explained before obtaining written consent. (Stilbestrol®, 25 mg by mouth daily for five days, followed by Progestron®, 100 mg IM, has been used in one hospital to prevent pregnancy in rape victims. The victims are required to report the rape to the police prior to the medical examination.)

Masters and Johnson have alerted physicians to the possibility of the broad-ligament-laceration syndrome as a cause of disabling pain on intercourse following rape. These authors describe three cases in which individual women were involved in gang rapes with repeated rapes, simultaneous rectal and vaginal rape, and tearing of the soft tissues of the pelvis by introduction of foreign objects into the vagina. For some years after the rape episodes, psychological trauma was assumed to be the cause of the pain on intercourse. Surgical treatment resulted in relief of symptoms.

THE VISITING NURSE SERVICE

In Denver almost all the rape victims are taken by the police to Denver

General Hospital for medical examination and treatment. A few victims either prefer to see their private physician or refuse medical care. At the hospital arrangements are usually made for a home visit by a nurse from the Visiting Nurse Service. This visit is made the day following the rape, as patients seem to appreciate help more readily when it is offered promptly. Several days later, when the emotional crisis has subsided and the need for help is less apparent, the woman may prefer to turn a blind eye to the rape and its consequences.

A few women refuse to see the visiting nurse; some, particularly those in the middle and upper socioeconomic classes, simply tell the nurse that they do not wish to see her; others, usually in low-income Negro or Spanish-American neighborhoods, do not answer the door. The majority of victims welcome the nurse and will often interrupt her explanation for the visit with a torrent of words about the rape and their fears that the man will return or will attack a member of her family in fulfillment of earlier threats to discourage a report to the police.

At first the nurse will make appropriate brief comments in response to the detailed description of the rape and reflect feelings which are voiced or concealed. Later she provides advice on questions regarding venereal disease, pregnancy, police protection, return to work and the need for another visit to Denver General Hospital. Parents of a child victim seek advice on a wide range of topics from school attendance to discipline in the home. When a mother has been raped in her home, she may want to know what she should say to her children who may well have overheard the assault. If psychiatric help is requested, the nurse provides the telephone number and address of the nearest mental health clinic. She will also provide a card with her name and telephone number and, if indicated, arrange for a return visit. The interview usually lasts about an hour.

Home visits are often very revealing. The home reflects the personalities of its occupants, and interruptions to the interview by children and neighbors provide additional insights for the observant nurse. These insights can be utilized in helping the woman cope with the stresses of the rape. On one home visit the author was surprised to see the young school girl who had been brutally assaulted a few days earlier, wearing a white knit pullover with the words "Sock it to me, Sock it to me, Sock it to me" on it in bold letters. It was an attractive pullover, but it did seem rather inappropriate.

COMPENSATION TO VICTIMS OF RAPE

In some countries, including New Zealand, England and Switzerland, under special circumstances victims of criminals may be compensated by the government when the offender is unable to pay damages. In England, for example, the Criminal Injuries Compensation Board awarded $5,656 to an elderly woman who was unlikely to be able to work again following an attack and sexual assault by a stranger. The Board reduces the amount of compensation or rejects the claim in cases of victim-precipitated crimes.

"In cases of rape and sexual assaults, the board considers applications for compensation with respect to pain, suffering, and shock, and also with respect to loss of earnings due to pregnancy resulting from rape. But compensation is not payable for the maintenance of any child born as a result of a sexual offense. Also, offenses committed against a member of the offender's family who is living with him are excluded from compensation" (Schafer).

Chapter 5

CHILD VICTIMS

"Alas! regardless of their doom,
The little victims play;
No sense have they of ills to come,
Nor care beyond to-day."
– Gray, *On a Distant Prospect*
of Eton College

CHILD rape is not a rare crime. One in eight of the two hundred victims in the Denver study were children under fifteen years of age. It is a melancholy fact that the child victim of rape may suffer greater psychological trauma from the ill-advised response of parents, police, court officials and emergency room staff than from the sexual assault itself. It is important to review the care of these children and to explore not only the psychological reactions to rape but also the child's contribution, if any, to her victimization.

Unfortunately the many studies of child victims of adult sex offenders almost invariably group together for research victims of widely differing forms of sexual assault, ranging from rape or attempted rape to fondling of the child and indecent exposure by an exhibitionist. Because of the small number of rape victims in most of these studies, it is difficult to assess the role of the child in provoking rape and to evaluate the aftereffects of this crime.

ROLE OF THE VICTIM

"Man has a horror of imprecise limits and
the clear distinction made between attacker
and victim enables the court to attribute
blame solely to the adult."
– Lindy Burton, *Vulnerable Children*

"Oh, what a tangled web do parents weave
When they think that their children are naive."
– Ogden Nash, *What Makes the Sky Blue?*

Apart from murder no crime against children arouses greater public horror and revulsion than forcible rape or attempted rape. Yet some children behave in a seductive manner toward adults and encourage sexual advances.

Others, in a search for affection, money or other desired object, may place themselves in danger of sexual assault. Lafon *et al.*, in their review of 126 child victims of sex offenders, found some degree of provocation by the victims in 58 per cent of the cases and concluded that the myth of childhood innocence, perpetuated by generations of adults was at variance with reality.

The myth of childhood innocence clouds assessment of sexual offenses against children.

"In many countries, especially in the East, sexual activity among children, particularly of girls, is recognized as normal. The law of the Koran authorized the marriage of girls of nine and of boys at twelve years. In India, infantile marriage has been customary for many centuries; according to the 1921 census, there were 2,000,000 wives and 100,000 widows under ten years. Although it has been claimed that such marriages are rarely consummated before puberty, the contrary has been reported by the Joshi Committee of 1929. This Hindu custom seemed to be popular and did not shock any one until a few years ago when it was investigated from the Western viewpoint. Even our Western laws have fixed the age of consent as low as twelve years. Until 1929 England retained the marriage age at twelve years for girls and fourteen for boys; and in France the age of consent was raised from eleven to thirteen years only in 1863. Similar laws still exist in the United States.

"In addition to the evidence from the early age of marriage in former days, biographical writers and others give numerous instances of the sexual precocity of very young girls and their willingness to indulge in sexual acts, often even before puberty. Typical examples can be found in the Memoirs of Casanova; and in the Confessions of La Marquise de Brinvilliers, the statement is made that she lost her virginity at the age of seven. Guyon notes that the use of child courtesans was at one time quite frequent in China, Russia and Naples, and that travellers have remarked upon the seductive manners of children in many countries where the mores are more lenient regarding sex. Malinowski states that in Melanesia the girls begin sexual intercourse at about the age of six to eight, and ten to twelve in the case of boys. Furthermore, the severity of primitive and modern laws regarding incest (Frazer, Malinowski, Roheim), which refers primarily to relations between parent and child, suggest that such tendencies must exist among humans" (Bender and Blau).

Bender and Blau made a psychiatric study of sixteen unselected successive admissions of prepuberty children to a children's psychiatric ward following sexual relationships with adults. Eleven of the children were females and five were males. "This study seems to indicate that these children undoubtedly do not deserve completely the cloak of innocence with which they have been endowed by moralists, social reformers and legislators. The history of the relationship in our cases usually suggested at least some cooperation of the child in the activity, and in some cases the child assumed an active role in initiating the relationship.

"It is true that the child often rationalized with excuses of fear of physical harm or the enticement of gifts, but these were often secondary reasons. Even in the cases in which physical force may have been applied by the adult, this did not wholly account for the frequent repetition of the practice. In most cases the relationship was not broken until it was discovered by their guardians, and in many the first reprimand did not prevent the development of other similar contacts. Furthermore, the emotional placidity of most of the children would seem to indicate that they derived some fundamental satisfaction from the relationship.

"These children rarely acted as injured parties and often did not show any evidence of guilt, anxiety or shame. Any emotional disturbance they presented could be attributed to external restraint rather than internal guilt. Finally, a most striking feature was that these children were distinguished as unusually charming and attractive in their outward personalities. Thus, it is not remarkable that frequently we considered the possibility that the child might have been the actual seducer rather than the one innocently seduced."

On the basis of their study of seventy-three girl victims of adult sex offenders, Weiss *et al.* concluded that the victims could be divided into two groups: those who took part in initiating and maintaining the relationship (participant victims) and those who did not do so (accidental victims). Forty-four girls were thought to be participant victims and twenty-one were thought to be accidental victims. In eight cases no decision about involvement could be reached.

The typical participant victim, as was noted by Bender and Blau, is often very attractive and appealing. She establishes a superficial relationship with the psychiatrist almost immediately and she may be submissive or sexually seductive. Her fantasies may show masochistic elements, unresolved conflicts over looking and being looked at, and preoccupation with family conspiracies in which father and daughter or mother and daughter share a secret.

Frequently the participant victim's mother is masochistic in her attitude toward her daughter, critical of herself as well as of her daughter and shows conflict not only about strictness and leniency, but also about her attitude toward the child's developing sexuality. At times she feels proud of her daughter's attractive appearance and winning ways, but at other times she labels her a "flirt" or a "prima donna" and fears that the child's attractiveness will lead her into sexual difficulties in adolescence.

"The mother's vacillation in her attitude to her daughter may be understood in terms of her guilt over jealousy of her daughter. This jealousy leads her to deprive and belittle her daughter, whose freedom and attractiveness she feels are at her expense. Her guilt over her jealousy causes her to indulge and flatter her daughter and to humiliate and criticize herself.

"In some cases conflict regarding the child's upbringing appears more prominently as a disagreement between the parents than as an intrapsychic conflict in the mother. For example, a father enjoins modesty and makes certain that he is always fully clothed in the child's presence, while the mother deplores his prudishness and encourages the child to take a more "natural" attitude toward nudity.

"Conflicts within one parent or between the parents as to proper attitudes toward the child's expression of her sexual impulses are confusing to the child and sexually stimulating to her, in that they focus her attention on sex. Her parents' confusion makes it difficult for her to have a stable set of attitudes toward her own sexual impulses, and makes it difficult, therefore, to develop a stable conscience (superego).

"In this discussion of the typical family of a participant victim, the prominence of parental disagreement about the child's sexual upbringing has been stressed. An example will indicate how such parental disagreement may favor the child's tendency to act out sexually with an adult.

"The parents of a six-year-old girl disagreed about what to teach her concerning modesty. Her father encouraged her to go nude in his presence and he went nude in hers. Her mother attempted to counteract the father's influence on the child by teaching her to be modest. In a sense the child's sexual behavior, in which she looked at a man's genitals and allowed him to look at hers, was sanctioned by her father's attitude and forbidden by her mother's, so that this behavior represented on one level the child's alliance with her father in the parental disagreement. The child was able to feel somewhat relieved of responsibility for her sexual activity because this activity seemed to be sanctioned by her father. Nevertheless, she must have known that her father's permissiveness was not meant to lead her to actual sexual activity, so that her behavior was a kind of spiteful obedience to him. Also, she may have been aware that her behavior would prove her mother right in the parental disagreement and thus, in a sense, please her mother. She realized that her father would blame himself rather than her for the sexual activity, and that her mother, too, would blame him. Thus, in her sexual behavior, the child expressed defiance toward each parent and ingratiated herself with each.

"In a number of cases, parental conflicts about the child's expression of her sexuality were not the most striking determinants of the child's sexual acting out. More evident in these cases was the sexually stimulating behavior of the parents toward the child. These parents were actually in conflict about their attitudes in that they did not consciously intend to lead their child to overt sexual behavior. In fact when the child of such parents became a sex victim the parents felt very disturbed and guilty.

"The parents stimulated their children sexually in various ways. In some cases the mother warned her daughter from an early age to avoid men because of the sexual consequences, and in so doing made the child aware of the possibility of sexual relationships with adult men; the mother's warnings were at the same time prohibiting and stimulating to her child. Several mothers directly encouraged their daughters to be "sexy," as, for example, the mother who repeatedly had her six-year-old do a striptease act for company. In some cases, the child's father was very seductive with her and stimulated her physically by kissing, fondling and wrestling. A number of participant victims were stimulated sexually by having the opportunity to watch their parents having sexual intercourse.

"Although these children were able to indulge in sexual activities with adults, they were not free of remorse and guilt about their sexual behavior. Quite the opposite was the case. All the participant victims had guilt about their sexual activities, guilt which, if not expressed directly, was manifest in phobias, nightmares, anxieties, etc. The children's guilt is understandable in terms of their parents' attitudes: The parents both stimulated and prohibited the children's sexual impulses."

"Though sexual conflicts were extremely common among the participant victims, more basic conflicts underlay the sexual ones. Almost all of them felt deprived by their mothers and resentful toward them. Their mothers' masochistic attitudes engendered in the girls intense feelings of guilt and obligation; many felt that they should devote themselves to making their mothers happy, and that they should have no lives apart from their mothers. These girls, feeling trapped by their sense of obligation to their mothers, rebelled against it. Through sexual relationships with adult men, they expressed their defiance of their mothers and gained a feeling of independence. At the same time, they satisfied their longings for approval and attention."

One of their cases is presented here:

Dorothy B., a ten-year-old girl, had a sexual relationship of four years' duration with her stepfather. The relationship began when Dorothy, then aged five, returned to her mother's home after living for two years with her grandmother and her aunt in another city.

The stepfather at first had Dorothy handle his genitals, and when she was about seven, he began having vaginal intercourse with her. He was rough and abusive, threatening to beat her if she told her mother of his actions. Dorothy, nevertheless, attempted several times to tell her mother what was going on, but her mother was reluctant to believe her because she felt Dorothy was merely making a bid for attention. When Mrs. B. finally realized that Dorothy's accusations were justified, she confronted her husband with them. He confessed remorsefully and was sent to prison. Upon his release six months later, he resumed his sexual practices with Dorothy, then aged nine. Dorothy did not tell her mother of this because she did not want to be responsible again for separating her mother and stepfather. Mrs. B. felt uncertain whether she was right in letting her husband return; she decided to leave to Dorothy the final decision as to whether he might stay.

Dorothy was the second of four children; she had two brothers, aged eleven and eight, and a half brother aged nine months. Her birth and early development were uneventful. According to her mother she was a cheerful, friendly child. When she was two-and-a-half, her mother already considered her "a little flirt." She would wander from home and be found by her mother making friends with strange men in a public park. From two-and-a-half to five, Dorothy stayed with her maternal grandmother and her aunt in another city, while her brothers remained at home. This separation was occasioned by her mother's illness and by difficulties between her mother and father, which ended in the latter's desertion of the family. At three Dorothy was given a choice between returning home and remaining with her grandmother and aunt, and she chose the latter alternative. Evidently Dorothy was responding to her mother's rejection by rejecting her mother in return. By her indifference she denied that her mother's rejection hurt her.

At five, following the death of her aunt, Dorothy moved back with her mother and her mother's second husband, the offender. Her mother found her a changed child; she was now ungracious and demanding. "If you gave her shoes, she wanted socks." At times she was affectionate toward her mother and desirous of love, but more often she was sullen and spiteful. It appeared to Mrs. B. that when she and her husband behaved affectionately to each other, Dorothy felt jealous and left out.

According to Mrs. B., Dorothy at the age of five accused an adult male cousin of molesting her sexually, and at the age of seven accused a school janitor of doing so. The janitor defended himself by pointing out that Dorothy had asked him to let her play with his genitals.

With the male psychiatrist, Dorothy was friendly and flirtatious. She talked freely and was mainly preoccupied with the feelings of fear and disgust which her stepfather inspired. Following sexual contacts with him she avoided her friends, fearing that they might smell semen on her. At these times she avoided her stepfather also and could not look him in the eye. She recalled that following her stepfather's return from prison she had nightmares which frequently concerned snakes or other loathsome animals. She dreamed that if she touched these animals she would kill them or be killed herself. She reported the following detailed dream:

"I was going to a social with Lillian (a girl friend). Presents were being given away and I got first choice. I picked the best one. The old man who gave them out didn't want me to have the best one. On the way home I passed a haunted house. Policemen and lots of other people were inside. The man who had passed out the presents was lying dead on the floor; he had no eyes. I looked away from him and left right away. Then he came back to life and came out the door. He touched his finger to the holes where his eyes had been and started to touch me on the shoulder with the gooey stuff. If he had I would have died. Then he fell down, laughed and died in peace."

Dorothy volunteered that the old man in the dream reminded her of her stepfather.

Dorothy remarked that she feared growing up and getting married because neither of her mother's husbands had been any good. Her mother had suffered a great deal and this was to be expected, she said, because good people always suffer.

On one visit Dorothy appeared tense and unhappy. She said that both of her parents seemed sick of her; her stepfather had accused her of being the cause of all his trouble, and her mother had said there was too much hatred in the family and if things did not improve one of the children would have to be sent away. Dorothy assumed that she would be the child to go.

Mrs. B. was, in fact, very critical of Dorothy, who she felt was cold, distant and demanding, and whom she considered her most difficult child. She maintained that Dorothy was vain and too concerned with getting the attention of others, especially of men. She resented Dorothy as the cause of the trouble between herself and her husband.

Mrs. B., however, reproached herself for these attitudes. She felt responsible for Dorothy's difficulties, believing that her resentment of Dorothy and her "martyr" attitude affected the child adversely. She recalled her resentment of her own mother's coldness and martyr-like attitude, and did not want to treat Dorothy as she had been treated. Further, she reproached herself for her inability to discuss sex with Dorothy; she felt that frank sexual discussions might somehow have helped Dorothy avoid the sexual relationship with her stepfather.

When first confronted with them, Mrs. B. had dismissed Dorothy's accusations against her stepfather as a bid for attention in keeping with her flirtatious disposition. After becoming convinced that Dorothy had actually had a sexual relationship with Mr. B., the mother was angry at her and jealous of her. She also felt guilty toward Dorothy, saying, "It was my happiness or Dorothy's, and in letting him remain I was being selfish and not considering my daughter." Further, she blamed herself for refusing to have sexual intercourse with her husband; this refusal she believed tempted him to molest Dorothy.

A detailed discussion of the offender is not relevant. It is sufficient to state that he was a very masochistic man, always ready to feel mistreated. Although he felt intensely guilty toward both Mrs. B. and Dorothy after his sexual activities with the child were discovered, he also felt that they were to blame for these activities: Mrs. B. for refusing him intercourse, and Dorothy for her seductiveness. "She put ideas in my head by climbing on my lap and rubbing against me."

One may ask why specific factors in Dorothy's development have to be considered in order to account for her sexual activities. Would not any child intimidated, as Dorothy was, by her stepfather, submit to him? Despite the relevance of this viewpoint, Dorothy's seductiveness with the janitor shows that she did have a tendency to participate sexually with an adult man, regardless of the factor of intimidation.

It is not necessary again to point out in detail how the child's feeling of rejection by her mother, her hostility to her mother, and her jealousy of her mother were permitted expression in her sexual activities. As in the other cases the mother's jealousy of the child and her conflicting attitudes toward the child were factors that hampered the development of a stable conscience in the child.

Dorothy's situation resembled that of three or four other girls in the research group who had sexual relationships with their stepfathers. In these cases, as in Dorothy's, the mother was unable to intervene and put a stop to the child's activities. Mrs. B. could not "hear" Dorothy's confession of sexual involvement with Mr. B., for she knew that facing the fact would mean that she would have to give up her husband and would also have to feel more guilty toward Dorothy.

Clearly demonstrated in Dorothy's case is the intense anxiety and guilt aroused in her by the sexual experience. Dorothy's dream reveals her disgust and shame over it. Her comments to the psychiatrist show how guilty she felt toward her mother and how intensely she feared that her mother would reject her. She could not tell her mother of the second series of sexual episodes because she did not want to separate her mother and her stepfather again. She feared, too, that if her mother were faced with the choice of rejecting either her or her husband, her mother would reject her.

In some cases, Weiss *et al.* stress specific factors which focus the participant-victim's attention on sex and which permit her to act out sexually. In other cases, sexual acting out is but one aspect of a profound emotional disturbance which is manifest in all areas of the child's life. Children of this type are sexually promiscuous, they steal, play truant from school, run away from home and are subject to extreme fluctuations of mood. Neurotic symptoms are prominent and they react to stress with impulsive, often self-damaging behavior.

In summary, these authors suggest that conflict in one of the parents or between the parents over how to deal with expressions of the child's sexual impulses, make it difficult for the child to develop a consistent and stable conscience that can prohibit the acting out of these impulses. Intense sexual stimulation of the child by the parents also predisposes the child to sexual acting out. It is emphasized that these factors are not in themselves sufficient to account for these activities, as other children with similar backgrounds do not become sex victims.

Understanding of the acting out must also involve consideration of the child's own personality. The suggestion is also made that factors such as maternal deprivation, rejection and inconsistency do not specifically favor sexual acting out but may contribute to generally poor impulse control.

Landis also attempted to study the degree of participation and characteristics of participant assault victims in a university population. He found that the girls who had been involved as children in sexual assaults, as compared with students who had no adult-child sexual contacts, were more likely to have distant relationships with their mothers before the age of fifteen. The "possibly participant" victims came from the unhappiest homes and slightly less of them than students with no adult-child sexual contacts had obtained sexual information from their mothers.

Lafon *et al.* have also emphasized the poor home background and inadequate personality development of children who have provoked sexual attack. Bourdiol and Pettenati noted that child victims frequently had a promiscuous mother or sister. Colin and Bourjade reported that participant victims were profoundly disturbed emotionally and had difficulties arising from the oedipus situation.

Rasmussen (cited by Burton), in her study of fifty-four child victims below the age of fourteen, emphasized an element of passivity or acceptance of the sexual attack. In thirteen cases the girl had remained completely passive during the act, in a further twenty-two cases the offense had been committed more than once and in thirteen of these cases a steady relationship had developed between the man and the girl. In four cases the child had offered herself or provoked sexual intercourse.

Rasmussen accounted for the large number of passive or nonresistant children in his group of victims as follows:

1. Many were lured by money, sweets or small gifts.
2. Many of the attackers were acquaintances and had gained the child's confidence.
3. In many instances the man approached the child carefully, taking care not to arouse fear.
4. Most of the children knew of sexual relationships before the attack, and some desired experience out of curiosity.

Burton in her review of the literature found that the myth of childhood innocence seems in the main to have been rejected and that some degree of participation in the victim group is accepted by all observers. In her own study, Burton found that as a group the child victims showed a significantly greater need for affection both in fantasy and behavior than a comparable control group of children.

It is not clear from this study whether the child's need for affection explains her involvement in a sexual assault. These children may well have sought in a sexual relationship with an adult the warmth that was lacking in their relationship with their own parents but there may be alternative explanations which Burton did not explore.

RAPE AND PERSONALITY DEVELOPMENT

The long-term consequences of rape on the personality development of the child are difficult to assess. Personality problems may precede the rape and may even contribute to the rape. Abnormal personality development after the rape may be related to factors unrelated to the sexual assault. Moses (cited by Burton) traced the development several years later of sixty children, all of whom had been sexually assaulted by adults. In fifty of these children the assault consisted of sexual intercourse.

At the time of the study eight children were thought to be neurotic, five were tending to masturbate, eight had become "preoccupied with sexual things" and sixteen were propelled into heterosexual activities. Moses concluded that the deviant behaviors of well over half of these children were the result of their sexual assault. Burton points out that only twenty-two of the children were supposedly "normal" prior to the assault and that many of the children came from an unsatisfactory background. She notes that there was no control group to determine whether children similar in age and general experience would show similar developmental difficulties.

Burton also draws attention to Rasmussen's results which are in complete disagreement with those of Moses. Fifty-four children who had testified in court against a sexual attacker were interviewed twenty to thirty years later to ascertain the degree of psychic damage sustained. Follow-up was done through the woman's doctor, who rated her mental health and social adjustment in adult life. All but eight subjects were well adjusted. Three of the eight had become psychotic, three had become prostitutes, one was considered "hysterical" and one was very "nervous."

Rasmussen concluded that there was no evidence to link the later personality disintegration of these eight subjects with the attack. Instead the evidence suggested an independent constitutional predisposition to breakdown. In only a few cases had the child been surprised and brutally overcome, and even in these cases no evidence existed to suggest that the child had suffered psychic or physical damage as a result.

Bender and Blau found that "the most remarkable feature presented by children who had experienced sexual relations with adults was that they showed less evidence of fear, anxiety, guilt or psychic trauma than might be expected. On the contrary, they more frequently exhibited either a frank, objective attitude, or they were bold, flaunting and even brazen about the situation. This was particularly noteworthy considering the circumstances of the observation which in all the children except two followed or was coincident with legal procedures.

"At first the children often showed no guilt, but this tended to develop as they were separated from their sex object and means of gratification and as they were exposed to the opinion of parents and court officials. It occurred especially with the more intelligent children and seemed in part a reflection of adult censure and not to carry any real conviction to the child. In some instances this seemed to result in an intellectual and emotional bewilderment resulting from their effort to reconcile their personal experience with the attitude of authority. But in other children it appeared to be a normal reparative process in bringing them to reject and repress their sexual desires, with a return to the usual childhood interest."

"The emotional reaction of these children was in marked contrast to that manifested to the same situation by their adult guardians, which was one of horrified anxiety and apprehensiveness regarding the future of the child. The probation reports from the court frequently remarked about their brazen poise, which was interpreted as an especially inexcusable and deplorable attitude and one indicating their fundamental incorrigibility." The past behavior of these children usually included behavior difficulties in addition to the more recently discovered sex delinquency. Hyperactivity, general restlessness and a rebellious, disobedient and disrespectful attitude toward the parents were commonly noted.

Ten female child victims in this study were followed up fifteen years later by Bender and Grugett. Eight of these women had made satisfactory adjustments, some better than others. One had become chronically psychotic and another, with previous psychotic episodes, was dependent on public support. None of the ten needed social correction or attention because of sex activities in adult life. The authors conclude that overt sex activity in childhood with adult partners was in one way a deflection of the normally developing sexual impulses and that such a deflection was responsive to social and clinical treatment.

Burton notes that "the literature on the subject of the sexually assaulted child has originated in many different areas of study and has approached the problem with different degrees of scientific exactness, very few studies being satisfactory from this point of view. Generally the conclusions reached must be considered extremely tentative. No distinctions are possible in many of the studies between personality characteristics before the assault, which may have precipitated it, and those seen after the assault, and possibly resulting from it. Generally no information is given about the time lapse between assault and the personality assessment, or about the effect this might have on the observed personality variables. Most often no controls free of sexual assault are used, and without them no reliable assessment can be made of the abnormality of the sexual behaviours and preoccupations perceived."

In her retrospective controlled study in which child victims were examined on an average three years after the assault, Burton substantiated the following general viewpoint of other research workers.

"Most children so involved make an adequate personality adjustment: only a few of the more disturbed children for whom the sexual acting out was undoubtedly symptomatic of a general disintegration of personality, make a poor adjustment."

MEDICAL EXAMINATION OF THE VICTIM

"In some states it is a misdemeanor for a physician to fail to report a case of suspected sexual molestation or rape or to examine the presumed victim before she has been examined by a coroner's or state attorney's physician. Laws of this sort have been passed because so often the evidence needed to establish guilt in such circumstances is lost or rendered worthless by a well-intentioned but unthinking examiner. Also, an understandable desire to protect the child and her family from being publicly involved may make the family physician hesitate to notify the police. It would seem wise for any physician who may be called for such cases to acquaint himself with the regulations which the state attorney or the coroner in his locality has established for emergencies of this type. Otherwise, despite his best intentions, he may destroy the very evidence upon which the conviction of a guilty person or the exoneration of an innocent one would depend" (Huffman).

The child victim of rape or alleged rape is often taken by her parents or the police to the emergency room of a general hospital for medical examination. Too often this examination is restricted to a medical determination of evidence of sexual intercourse and physical injury. As emergency rooms are very busy and as physicians are reluctant to become involved in legal proceedings, the unfortunate child victim sometimes is kept waiting an unduly long time before she is seen by the physician.

Two child psychiatrists, Lipton and Roth, who acted as consultants on all child victims of alleged rape admitted to a university pediatric emergency room, make critical comments on the handling of these children.

"Problems arising in the handling of these cases range from the feelings of the staff to the physical structure of the department. Since many people are involved in any case presenting in the emergency room, for example secretary, orderly, nurse, physician, the patient and her parents may be exposed to many variations of attitude before being seen by their definitive physician. Often an undercurrent of horror or excitement develops as it becomes known that a "child rape case" is in the ward; this may affect handling of the patient. Frequently we have seen patients needlessly exposed with scant consideration for feelings. One of our patients sat through several interviews in a backless hospital gown with a blood-stained sanitary napkin in a dish at her side.

"We found that upset feelings among the staff might lead them to be impatient with the time spent sorting out the problem, so that untoward interruptions occurred. Occasionally the interviewer was met with hostility for wasting the time and space of a busy emergency ward. At other times the anxiety expressed itself in the form of coarse humor which could sometimes be overheard by the patient."

The medical evaluation should extend beyond the legal requirements, as the child and her parents may be in need of psychiatric guidance. A routine quick medical evaluation may further traumatize the child.

History Taking

Lipton and Roth note that obtaining a history from the patient is not a routine matter. The child needs to feel that the physician "respects her and is interested in her feelings and general adaptation rather than being interested only in the concrete details of the rape, or in quickly examining her. Techniques which communicate this respect and interest include assuring the patient of confidentiality, giving her time to get over her initial anxiety about talking with a physician, interviewing her in private surroundings and having a nonjudgmental attitude . . . .

"History taking should be in comfortable, private surroundings and should be as unrushed as possible. Although initially the parents and patient may be interviewed together, the patient should be given the opportunity for a separate interview. The aims of history taking should be (a) to ascertain the facts of the present episode as well as the past history leading up to it; this would include a brief overview of the general functioning and development of the child, including the problem areas, (b) to assess the degree of emotional impact of the situation on the patient with attention to her particular concerns, (c) to permit the patient to acknowledge her main concerns, which may help direct the physician in his management and (d) to allow the parents to develop more perspective in the current situation."

The need for a private interview with the child is illustrated by a thirteen-year-old who revealed that she did not want an examination because of embarrassment and for fear that this would reveal evidence of previous sexual activity to her mother. The mother subsequently revealed that she had become pregnant at thirteen and feared the same occurrence in her daughter. She accepted a referral to a psychiatric agency. Another thirteen-year-old confided to the physician that she wanted protection from her father. Although he had tried twice to molest her and was known to have molested another daughter, the mother found it difficult to see the necessity for protecting the girl. The patient was very relieved when her complaint was handled seriously and steps were taken to afford her protection.

One girl who cried rape in fact had voluntary intercourse with her date who then took her home. One-half hour later she discovered vaginal bleeding and then charged that she had been raped. Another girl who asked to be interviewed alone expressed concern regarding a kidney infection which had persisted for six months despite repeated treatment. She revealed that she had had intercourse six months before and, having seen a sexual hygiene film the previous day, was concerned that she had gonorrhea and perhaps syphilis. She also asked many questions about sex and was worried about her sexual control.

A visual examination of her genitals revealed no trauma, but an aspirate revealed the presence of gonorrhea. Appropriate medical treatment was instituted; both patient and mother accepted referral to a social agency.

The Physical Examination

The physical examination can appear to the child as yet another sexual assault. Rothchild points out that in general the younger the adolescent, the more acutely sensitive she is to any genital investigation. Her modesty is affronted by it, and in the sense that the conditions of the examination require her to submit passively to a genital penetration, she may — consciously or not — imagine the experience as a seduction or even as a sexual attack.

> A fifteen-year-old, confiding to a friend her first experience with vaginal examination, reported solemnly, "I lost my virginity today." Beneath the apparent jest lay the girl's equation of the examination with intercourse.

Rothchild urges caution when parents bring a child to the emergency room for a pelvic examination. "Although pelvic examinations may be quite feasible mechanically, it is the psychological significance which checks the routine examining hand.

"One examination to be most cautiously approached is that requested by the overly interested parent, anxious to check on the virginal condition of the girl's genitals. Anatomically the establishment of virginity is often problematic, and in any case the examination is scarcely a guarantee against future intercourse. The physician who accedes to such a parental request becomes partner to the parent's excitement, thereby reinforcing the effects of the parental concern on the girl. A somewhat similar situation can arise in a hospital emergency room when an anxious family rushes in the child who has allegedly been raped.

"A hasty vaginal investigation, undertaken under highly emotionally charged circumstances, can feel to the girl like a repetition of the real or imagined experience, thus cementing in her mind the psychological effects. Though harder and more time-consuming than a pelvic examination in both situations, a verbal examination with both parents and child, individually, may be more diagnostic. A single talk with the too intimately interested parent seldom diminishes the excitement for long; when such parents subsequently feel the urge to cross-examine the girl after a date, for instance, I have suggested they call me instead. When rape is in question, preventive medicine can sometimes be practiced by postponement or omission of the vaginal examination, though each case must be individually judged."

Many physicians require not only parental consent but also the informed consent of the daughter before making a pelvic examination. They believe that the daughter is the patient, that their primary responsibility is to this patient, that her wishes must be respected and that her confidential statements as well as the findings on physical examination should not be revealed to the parents without her consent.

The Pelvic Examination

Evaluation of genital injuries in children is often fraught with difficulties which have been well described by Schauffler:

"Trauma to the hymen and other vulvar structures may involve medicolegal considerations which can be embarrassing to the physician who is not well informed about such matters. It should be understood that frequently even small children will present, for no apparent reason, a flat, widely patent, almost nonvirginal hymen. This condition may occasionally be contingent on confirmed masturbation or other such practice. It is our experience, however, that developmental factors frequently account for confusing appearances in this respect. We advise the utmost conservatism in drawing serious deductions from anything but frankly visible traumatic conditions such as a bruised or bleeding vulva or a freshly and characteristically traumatized hymen.

"Minor injuries caused by attempted penetration are nearly always the direct result of circumferential pressure resulting in linear splits of the hymen and mucosa similar to those seen after childbirth. The more massive injuries will involve deeper structures and can scarcely be attributed to such confusing factors as self-manipulation or voluntary attempts at sex performance. Injury to bladder or urethra, rupture of the bladder and second to third degree tears of the perineum are, of course, most often due to penetration by the male organ, but may be by traumatic foreign body, which is not rape . . . .

"The rather daunting developments reported among adolescents have made it necessary to use far more care in convicting of actual rather than statutory rape in teen-age girls. The use of tampons and frequent voluntary indulgence in sex practice by even very young girls, must be considered as a possibility when the charge of rape is made and the hymen and vagina are not virginal. I am often puzzled at the apparent ease with which some physicians, particularly police doctors, seem to be able to make a pat diagnosis of rape. I find it quite difficult, in the absence of typical marks of injury, to feel sure of such a diagnosis, and more so as time goes on and the sex age of teen-agers moves down. The finding of sperm in a nonvirginal vagina which is not injured, is doubtless a determining factor, but, even so, permissiveness or even solicitation cannot be ruled out, and the charge must most often, in justice, become statutory rather than actual rape or criminal assault."

Laboratory Tests

These tests have been described in Chapter 4. The physician should remember to retain stained or torn clothing for examination by the police.

Venereal Disease

As the offender may have venereal disease, consideration should be given to the use of penicillin as well as the routine antiseptic douche. Among 1,448 victims of sexual assault in Washington, D. C. reported by Hayman *et al.,* sixty-three contracted venereal disease. One of them, a four-year-old girl, became infected with primary syphilis. Tests for venereal disease should be repeated later.

Pregnancy

Large doses of estrogen should be given to the postmenarchal adolescent to prevent pregnancy. It should be noted that pregnancy has been reported in very young girls. Dewhurst has reviewed the literature on precocious motherhood. In 1939 Escomel described the case of the youngest mother in the world. A short time before her fifth birthday she was found to be six months' pregnant. She was later delivered by Caesarean section of a baby weighing almost six pounds. The mother had her first period at eight months. Prior to this report the youngest mother had been a child six and a half years old, who, it was believed, was seduced by her sixty-eight-year-old grandfather (Chaschinsky and Jerschow). The pregnancy continued normally and labor commenced but prolapse of the umbilical cord caused death of the baby, who weighed six pounds nine ounces.

The account includes a heart-rending description of the child in labor who, immediately after contraction, with tears in her eyes, ran about the room after a butterfly which had found its way there. The girl herself had no idea whatever that she was pregnant or, later, that she had been delivered. Dewhurst comments that the delivery of a baby of this size *per vaginam* in such a young girl is an astonishing event, even allowing for the more rapid growth and development of precocious puberty. He quotes other cases of pregnancy in seven- and nine-year-old girls. One seven-year-old girl gave birth to twin boys, both dead.

THE POLICE

The police may add to the patient's stress by repeated interrogations between medical interviews and examinations. Experienced detectives on the sex detail are unlikely to behave in this manner. Furthermore they have a sound understanding of the requirements and limitations of a medical examination in the prosecution of rape. Those police officers in small departments who are not familiar with this crime may have little understanding of the medicolegal aspects of rape.

Lipton and Roth note that it sometimes becomes the task of the physician to inform the police of the limitations of genital examinations as evidence; for example the absence of sperm does not rule out rape and should not lead to dismissal of the charge. Cases were observed by these authors in which police pressure led a physician to compromise his judgment and even to provide them with medical information without due and written permission from the parents.

THE PARENTS

In most of the cases reported by Lipton and Roth the problems presented by the parents were an integral part of the situation. "The reactions seen in all parents were varying degrees of anger, guilt and helplessness, sometimes compounded by excitement. Although most of these feelings were the result of parental concern, they also led to parental behavior detrimental to the child. Most parents felt helpless and needed definitive guidance in the current episode. Some recognized difficulties preceding the current event and wished for more general assistance. As might be expected, guilt was present in most of the parents and in some cases undoubtedly contributed to excessive anger."

In those cases where the child by her behavior contributes to her victimization, parents are often quite unable to recognize the child's participation in the offense. By implying that the child is quite guiltless, parental hostility to the child is allayed and the child's anxiety decreased. On the other hand, some parents either blame the child or disbelieve her accusations as in the following case reported by Schauffler.

A girl, fourteen, was placed in a foster home by her divorced mother, who could not care for her. The foster-parents were devoted to her and frequently took her to the country to spend weekends with the foster-mother's parents, Mr. and Mrs. B. Mr. B. initiated the child into various acts of sex perversion. The child never told her foster-parents or her own mother of these practices but did describe them to some friends at school. The complaints of the parents of these children led to a police investigation, and the child related her story to the police. The matter was taken to the district attorney in the county where Mr. B. lived, and then a confusing and unhappy time began for the child.

Like all children who are witnesses in criminal cases against adults, she was required to tell her experiences many times; first to the police, the district attorney, to the grand jury and then again in public at the preliminary hearing and the final trial under cross-examination. And this was not all. In the state where this crime was committed, the law permits the defense attorney to question the child in the presence of the defendant, so she was subjected to that ordeal.

Her mother entered the case. The mother was loyal to the foster-parents and Mr. B. and frequently implored the girl to tell the truth to her. She told the truth. Her mother disbelieved her and gave her long lectures on girls who lied and sent innocent men to jail. The foster-parents followed the same line of emotional appeal to the child until she was removed from their custody by the juvenile court.

By the time this case came to trial, the girl was emotionally upset and was almost physically ill, but she told her story well and Mr. B. was convicted. The social workers in charge breathed a sigh of relief and felt they could at last begin to help her to settle down and lead a more normal life. They were too optimistic. The mother continued to plead with her. Mr. B. appealed his conviction to the Supreme Court and hired private investigators to accost the child on the way to school, to interrogate and threaten her. At last, emotionally and physically ill, she was taken to the hospital. By some misrepresentation, Mrs. B. visited her there and exhorted her to write a statement that would exonerate Mr. B.

This case is perhaps unusual in the amount of pressure that was placed on a child trying to tell the truth and in the number of times she had to repeat the details of an unhappy and unnatural experience. The social worker supervising the case counted at least thirteen times that she was interrogated on this subject. But any child under like circumstances is required to tell his or her experiences many times during a prosecution and is subjected to much of the same emotional appeal and pressure (Schauffler).

THE CHILD IN COURT

Appearance on the witness stand is an experience which few adults relish. The strain on a child may be easily imagined. Emotional conflicts and anxiety previously mastered are reactivated at the trial which may occur months or even a year after the offense. A particularly stressful experience occurs when the accused insists on defending himself and conducts the cross-examination of his victim. Cross-examination by an attorney may be no less stressful when the attorney adopts a bullying manner or unfairly attempts to discredit the character of the victim.

The child should not be required to wait in the courtroom corridor but even if she waits in a room, on her way to and from this room she may overhear ribald comments or other statements which cause further distress. When the assailant is a relative or former friend toward whom the child has positive as well as negative feelings, her emotional conflict may be further magnified as in the following case described by Schauffler.

An intelligent, sensitive girl of thirteen was brought to the juvenile court by her mother, who wished her placed in a boarding home. She said that placement was imperative for the child's welfare but failed or refused to give any convincing reason. The child, however, told the caseworker that her stepfather had seduced her and had been having sex relations with her for months.

She was placed in a boarding home and later taken before the grand jury who indicted the stepfather on a charge of statutory rape. After this indictment, the child, who had previously been an exemplary little girl in her boarding home, began to display behavior manifestations common to children who are emotionally upset. She developed enuresis, talked in her sleep, was periodically moody and tearful. At other times she was tempestuous and rebellious. A sympathetic foster-home mother with the help of a child guidance clinic managed to help her through this difficult period of her life.

Although she maintained that the story of her relationship with her stepfather was true, she frequently expressed the wish that the "trial" was over or that she need not testify at the "trial." She worried about her stepfather being detained in the county jail.

The day of the trial was one of long torture and hardship. Between fits of weeping and frequent side-glances at her stepfather, she told her story to the jury. The jury convicted her stepfather, but the trial judge was impressed by the child's evident emotional disturbance and unhappiness and requested to talk to her before he pronounced sentence. The caseworker who accompanied her to the judge heard her make this plea: "I have told the truth, Judge – it is the truth. But I don't want my stepfather punished. I don't want him sent to jail. Can't you keep him from going to the penitentiary? He has been good to all of us. Now my mother will have to work."

The judge did send the girl's stepfather to the penitentiary. Her behavior problems increased. She was continuously in rebellion against her foster-mother, her own mother and any other adult who attempted to supervise her. It will be a long time, even with the most sympathetic and expert care, before she will be able to adjust emotionally to a level of normal behavior.

Such emotional conflicts are common to children who are called on to testify against adults for whom they have affection. They are frequently too young to comprehend the moral implications of the adult offender's behavior. They view their own part in the prosecution as an act that has sent a friend or a loved one to jail.

Such emotional disturbances are often increased if the mother or other members of the family disbelieve the child's accusations or are not in sympathy with the prosecution of the offender. In the case of the child here described, it is significant that her mother opposed the prosecution of the stepfather although she believed the child's statement and even said the stepfather had carried on illicit affairs with other young girls. Because of his excellent earning capacity and his generosity to her, she was unwilling to have him prosecuted. Her indecision and her unsympathetic attitude toward the child undoubtedly increased the child's confusion (Schauffler).

In an effort to protect children against traumatic experiences not only in the courtroom but also during police investigations, the parliament of Israel passed a law called the "Law of Evidence Revision," which came into force in 1955. The major points in this law have been described by Reifen.

1. No child under fourteen years shall be investigated, examined or heard as a witness in the matter of an offence against morality, save with the permission of a youth examiner (an expert trained in the field of mental hygiene); 2. A statement by a child as to an offence against morality committed upon his person, or in his presence, or of which he is suspected, shall not be admitted as evidence, save with the permission of the youth examiner; 3. For the purpose of the law, youth examiners shall be appointed after consultation with an Appointment Committee. This Committee shall consist of a Judge in the Juvenile Court (Chairman), an expert in mental hygiene, an educator and an expert in child care; 4. Evidence as to an offence against morality taken and recorded by a youth examiner, and any minutes or report of an examination as to such an offence prepared by a youth examiner, are admissible as evidence in court; 5. Where evidence as referred to above has been submitted to the court, the youth examiner may be required to re-examine the child and ask him a particular question, but he may refuse to do so if he is of the opinion that further questioning is likely to cause psychic harm to the child; 6. A person shall not be convicted on evidence by a youth examiner

unless it is supported by other evidence.

A radical reform on the lines of the system in Israel raises formidable legal difficulties, especially in interfering with the fundamental right of the offender to defend himself. Many children invent elaborate and circumstantial fantasies about assault, especially in incest cases, and the greatest care is certainly necessary. But is seems questionable whether the well-tried procedure of examination and cross-examination before a jury is as successful in reaching the truth in the child witnesses as with adults. After two or three months' delay, with frequent repetitions, memory becomes stereotyped; and the jury unfamiliar with such extraordinary offenses may find the facts difficult to believe. *(Brit Med J, 2:* 1623, 1961).

PSYCHIATRIC TREATMENT

The child may be in need of psychotherapy and this need may not be apparent at the time of the medical examination following the alleged rape.

An excellent procedure is to arrange for home visits by the Visiting Nurse Service. Ideally the first visit should be on the day following the medical examination. At this visit and on subsequent visits the experienced public health nurse can arrange for psychiatric treatment if the need arises and with the approval of the parents. (The Visiting Nurse Service role has been reviewed in Chapter 4.)

Untoward psychological reaction to the rape may be delayed or may be exacerbated by subsequent events. "In many cases the most traumatic aspects of the assault are the unaccountable change of attitude in some of the parents, the interrogations and physical examinations, and the repetitions and rehearsals, perhaps lasting for weeks or months, which precede appearance in court. Even more important, especially in older children, is the painful and confusing process of learning to look at the offense and the offender through adult eyes. There may also be a sense of guilt about the extent to which participation was willing" *(Brit Med J, 2:* 1623, 1961).

Although the victim is often spoken of as "wonderfully brave," "surprisingly composed" when giving evidence in court, Gibbens and Prince note that there may be a reaction later, as in their following case of statutory rape.

> An attractive but emotionally immature girl of fifteen, from a respectable but restrictive home, began to be interested in boys; she was told firmly that she was far too young to accept any dates. She met a young man of twenty-three secretly. He probably pursued her fairly relentlessly, for she said later that he always wanted to go somewhere where they could kiss and cuddle, while she only wanted to go dancing or to the pictures. Her parents found out and forbade her to see him. As so often, this led to protest and rebellion and had the effect of making

her start to have sexual intercourse with him.

When this was discovered, there was a family crisis; she ran away, was brought before the court as in need of care or protection and sent to a hostel to remove her from this association. The young man was prosecuted, no doubt mainly because of the father's relentless insistence. In the hostel the girl appeared very anxious and unsettled, and after many weeks had to go and give evidence against her lover, much against her will. She was still very much in love with him, and never had the slightest resentment against him.

The warden of the hostel who accompanied her remembered how cool and self-possessed she was during the trial. Her lover was sent to prison for a year. On return to the hostel the girl was much more unsettled. Two older girls exposed her to a great deal of pseudosophisticated talk about lesbian habits, and may have taken her to lesbian clubs. She became completely confused and paranoid about friendships with other girls, imagined herself about to be seduced homosexually, and after a few weeks, in an hysterical scene, rushed from the hostel and tried to throw herself under a bus.

The report to the court recommended that she be sent home and referred for psychiatric treatment. Her breakdown, very unusual in a case of seduction which does not lead to court, was attributed to having to give evidence against her lover. She had not only to submit completely to the discipline of parents against whom she was rebelling, but to make a public confession of rejecting all that was most worthwhile in her experience (however romantic and misguided it may have been). It is not surprising that this led temporarily to a rejection of hetero-sexuality altogether and a state of acute emotional confusion which had quite dangerous results (Gibbens and Prince).

Chapter 6

PSYCHOLOGY OF RAPE

"A man in passion rides a horse that runs away with him."
— C. H. Spurgeon, *Ploughman's Pictures*

THE explanation of rape is usually sought in the obvious conscious motivation of sexual desire, perhaps associated with other motives as envy, revenge, anger and sadism. Often indeed there is clear evidence of such factors, but even when they are present they do not always provide an adequate explanation for the crime. The offender himself may seek to explain his conduct in like manner. Yet the mainsprings of human conduct are so complex as to cast doubt on such simple solutions.

The conscious confessions of criminals and a statement of the circumstances of the crime, be it ever so complete, will never sufficiently explain why the individual in the given circumstances had to commit just that act. External circumstances very often do not motivate the deed at all, and the doer, did he wish to be frank, would mostly have to acknowledge that he really did not himself exactly know what impelled him to do it; most often, however, he is not so frank, not even to himself, but subsequently looks for and finds explanation of his conduct, which was in many ways incomprehensible, and psychically only imperfectly motivated, that is to say, he rationalizes something irrational (Ferenczi).

For example, a young man who was arrested after he had made several homicidal assaults on women was quick to agree with the district attorney that his assaults were for the purpose of sexual gratification. At first sight this explanation appears satisfactory. After rendering his victims unconscious he would proceed to rape them. But surely sexual intercourse can be achieved at less cost. The man was of pleasing appearance and experienced little difficulty in establishing social relations with members of the opposite sex. He lived in a large city where it was relatively easy to make the acquaintance of prostitutes. Furthermore, intercourse with an unconscious woman in a dark alley with the ever-present risk of detection can scarcely be pleasurable.

Not all his victims were rendered unconscious. He would pick up a young girl at a drive-in or on the city streets and drive her to a lover's lane. On arrival without any attempt at seduction he would tell the girl to remove her underclothing. Removing a large hunting knife from the glove compartment he would ostentatiously clean his fingernails while commenting on the dangers of physical resistance. In these circumstances one would not expect to find a loving embrace. On psychiatric examination it was pointed out to the young man that he must harbor considerable feelings of hostility toward the opposite sex.

When he rejected this suggestion, he was reminded that he had fractured the skulls of two women, attacked others with a hatchet and in other ways physically assaulted a number of women. Grudgingly he agreed that perhaps he had acted in a hostile manner toward a number of women. He acknowledged that the fleeting tense moments with his victims were not the most appropriate circumstances for sexual union. He was then asked if any woman had made sexual advances to him. There was indeed one such instance, an attractive young woman who, while on a date, made it clear that she was willing to have sexual relations with him. He added rather primly that this suggestion upset him and he drove her straight back to her home.

After further discussion he began to realize that sexual gratification was not the explanation for his assaults on women. He requested psychiatric treatment for which he was eligible under a sexual psychopath law. It was pointed out that treatment would mean exploration of the source of his hostility to women and that this hostility probably originated in his childhood. As the only significant members of the opposite sex in his early life were his mother and his grandmother, attention would be focused upon them. At this he became extremely angry and, flexing his biceps, shouted out that he would bust the teeth out of any blankety blank psychiatrist who suggested that his mother had anything to do with his problem. His extreme reaction brought to mind Shakespeare's comment "The lady doth protest too much, me thinks." When his anger subsided he became very anxious and volunteered that he had committed a number of assaults which the police did not know about; stating, "I'm cutting my throat by doing this," he gave time, place and circumstance of these earlier crimes.

Although he claimed that his relationship with his mother was a good one and that she disapproved of his wayward behavior, it was significant from his account that she had in the past shielded him from the police and hence from detection and that she gave tacit approval for his delinquent behavior. When she visited him on the ward, she would sit close to him in a conspiratory manner and the pair would stop talking whenever a nurse approached within earshot. On one occasion, however, the two were overheard reviewing with obvious pleasure one of his earlier offenses. His mother in her childhood had been placed in a home for delinquents.

Sexual and aggressive instincts or drives sometimes find expression in forcible rape. Rape is rare in those societies where promiscuity is socially approved and usually occurs when the man, because of physical disfigurement, mental disease or retardation, is unable to find a willing partner.

Under special circumstances, which temporarily weaken self-control, men who have no sexual deviation may resort to rape. Psychological controls over the sexual and aggressive drives may be weakened temporarily by acute mental illness, alcohol, drugs or other factors. The restraining influence of the conscience is reduced when the victim behaves in a sexually provocative manner ("She asked for it"). Social restraints against unlawful behavior may be relaxed in wartime when a conquering army seizes and plunders an enemy city. It is also stated that some men will rape a young virgin in the superstitious belief that this will cure their venereal disease.

Our interest is in those men with serious sexual psychopathology who have the urge to rape women. Not all these men commit rape. Psychological defenses against the urge to rape include *fantasy* ("The bad do what the good dream"), *sublimation* through writing about rape or through the detection of rapists, *overcompensation* with great concern for the protection of women against sexual assault and *obsessional neurosis* in which the forbidden impulses find verbal expression but responsibility for them is disowned (for example, the patient talks about impulses to rape his mother but attributes these impulses to a mental problem rather than to an actual desire for sex with mother). The man may find strength in religious beliefs or escape from temptation in a monastery.

Other men with serious sexual psychopathology will rape once or twice and some will repeat the crime time and time again. It might be thought that these men have abnormally strong sexual drives, and indeed a minority of rapists give a history of an incredible number of acts of sexual intercourse either on a voluntary basis or in the form of forcible rape. Their wives complain of the tedium of intercourse after breakfast, during the lunch hour as well as at night. On the other hand many rapists have difficulty either obtaining or maintaining an erection at the time of the rape as well as in voluntary sexual intercourse.

Johnson and Szurek, in a series of papers, have drawn attention to the unwitting sanction by parents of antisocial behavior in their children. The parents find vicarious gratification of their own poorly integrated forbidden impulses in the acting out of the child, through their conscious or more often unconscious permissiveness or inconsistency toward the child in a particular sphere of behavior. In the child there is rarely a generalized weakness of the superego, but rather a lack of superego in certain circumscribed areas of behavior.

For instance, a child may be entirely dependable about regular school attendance or honesty at work, but engage in petty stealing or serious sexual acting out. The parent's unconscious condoning of the acting out of asocial impulses by the child may serve the twofold purpose of allowing the parent vicarious gratification of forbidden impulses, as well as allowing the expression of hostile destructive impulses felt toward the child. One child in a family of several children might unconsciously be singled out as the scapegoat to act out the parent's poorly integrated forbidden impulses.

Johnson and Robinson note the role of parental equivocation in fostering antisocial behavior in the child. When the child reports such behavior, he meets with "double talk" rather than a clear direct prohibition.

"Antisocial behavior of almost any kind may be fostered by vacillation, ambiguity, equivocation or "double talk" on the part of parents, such as the following examples show: 'Fire-setting is prohibited, but, if you must light a fire, let us burn papers in the sink.' 'You must not steal, but if you do take money, take it from my purse instead of the neighbors'.' 'Do not lie,' but a half-hour later the parent will say, 'Perhaps we should tell teacher you were sick that day we went riding.'

"A spurious admonition to right behavior, prompted by a fragile parental conscience, is rendered futile by the permissive, 'but if you must. . . .' Such ambiguities occurring in individual delinquency have been reported extensively elsewhere.

"These techniques are also employed in the fostering of behavior oriented toward sexual deviations. A request to 'sonny' to wear his bathrobe becomes ineffective when coupled with mother's 'cute' reference to the charms of the boy's nudity. Orders to 'stay out of the bathroom until Dad has finished' are more appropriate in a family than open doors.

"A transvestite boy of fourteen years of age, at the age of five, had been found smelling assorted laundry items belonging to his mother. Instead of an unequivocal prohibition, the mother urged only that the boy substitute her clean underclothing.

"Children sense the anxious, vacillating permission and seduction in such parental double talk. Another manifestation of double talk is the parentally expressed concern for imagined future misdeeds by the child — the imagination deriving from the parent's mind but taking root in that of the child. There may be dire warnings of future sexual misconduct quite foreign to the child's conscious inclinations. A consciously guileless adolescent who is subjected to suspicious, suggestive, unfriendly quizzing angrily apprehends the destructive lack of faith on the part of the parent. The child senses that he is expected to misbehave sexually. The parents' fantasy that their small child will probably get into sexual trouble during adolescence provides a compelling guide. Unconsciously, the parents gradually maneuver this child into adolescent sexual acting out."

These authors also note that deviant sexual behavior is fostered by sensual tempting and sexual stimulation of the child. This seduction may be as subtle as a caress or as blatant as actual incest.

"The simplest unwitting seductions occurring in a family often reflect confused parental efforts to be 'modern' and hide nothing from the child. The conventional restraints of common modesty respected outside the home are ignored when the children are concerned. The parents parade about the house in all degrees of nudity, sleep with the child, bathe with the child and respect no bathroom privacy. The child's normal but tentative efforts at privacy are disregarded. The behavior may extend to such more frankly seductive practices as playing with the child's genitals or permitting an intimate physical examination of the parent. Initial reluctance by the puzzled child gives way to compliance in the climate of permissiveness, and the parent and child stimulate each other.

"In such families, no consistent attitude toward conversation about sex is displayed. A vague sense of guilt may rigidly proscribe all mention of sex, or 'freedom from prudery' may foster excessive discussion of sex, providing unconscious gratifications to parent and child, with supercharged, unhealthy but exciting tension."

The seductive mother arouses overwhelming anxiety in her son with great anger which may be expressed directly toward her but more often is displaced on to other women. When this seductive behavior is combined with parental encouragement of assaultive behavior, the setting is provided for personality development in the child which may result in sadistic, homicidal sexual attacks on women in adolescence or adult life.

The sadistic component in rape stands out among those rapists who do not merely threaten their victims to obtain compliance but resort to physical violence even in the absence of resistance. Indeed the violence may occur after the rape. The epitome of sadism is seen in those men who both rape and murder, particularly those who repeat these crimes over and over again. The so-called Boston strangler, De Salvo, claimed to have assaulted eight hundred to a thousand women and to have murdered twelve of them. A further victim died of a heart attack.

Easson and Steinhilber reported that among seven children and adolescents who showed murderous aggression, lack of privacy, physical overcloseness and, at times, the grossest seduction were repeatedly found. For example, the mother of one thirteen-year-old boy had for five or six years been in the habit of getting into bed with the boy and, face to face with him, massaging his back.

The mother of another thirteen-year-old boy gave him details of her first intercourse. Repeatedly this boy had pleaded for firm discipline and definite limit setting. Despite his murderous outbursts and his requests for control he was allowed to retain his collection of knives and guns. Repeatedly the parents indicated to this boy that they expected from him aggressive and dangerous behavior.

> As he stood behind me stroking my neck, he asked, "Mother, can I have intercourse with you?" I was scared he was going to choke me, so I answered, "Yes, but it would be horrible."
> Thus the mother of a thirteen-year-old boy described her experiences in the hotel room which she shared with this patient during his evaluation at the Mayo

Clinic. Since the age of five years, this boy had had classic temporal lobe epileptiform seizures about once every three months. He was grossly obese, weighing 205 pounds, with a height of five feet nine inches. The results of neurologic examination were unremarkable. X-ray examination and laboratory tests all gave normal results. The electroencephalogram showed frequent sharp-wave bitemporal discharges maximally in the left temporal region; these were increased by hyperventilation and in a recording during sleep.

The patient was the youngest of four children with a sister aged thirty-three and brothers aged thirty-one and twenty. He was conceived within three months of the marriage of his sister. His parents said they had wanted, in this pregnancy, "a roly-poly girl." The boy had had repeated temper tantrums from early childhood. He was enuretic until age seven and he still bit his fingernails and toenails at the time of this psychiatric evaluation. By the time he started school at age six he was obese and was mocked by the other children because of his obesity and femininity. His mother refused to let him fight back against his tormentors. All his life she had controlled his bowels with laxatives and she still bathed him. From the time of starting in school, the patient had become increasingly aggressive and demanding. His father would beat him brutally, at times until he bled, because of his use of swear words with a sexual connotation.

From age twelve he had asked his mother repeated questions about her sexual activities. On many occasions he asked if he could have intercourse with her. Her standard answer was, "Yes, but it would be horrible." This statement was agreed on by the patient and by both parents in their histories. The boy obtained from his mother details of her first intercourse and details as to how she felt during intercourse when his sister was conceived.

During the year prior to his visit to the clinic, his aggression had been much more marked and there had been at least ten episodes during which he stabbed or attempted to stab members of his family. He had knifed his twenty-year-old brother after a breakfast table argument. He stabbed his father in the back once after his father had brutally beaten him. He stuck a knife into his mother when she refused to drive him to town. Other episodes were similar. All these stab wounds were superficial. When the mother went to the hospital six months before the boy was seen at the clinic, his father told him that he would not sleep with him because he felt that his son might kill him in his sleep. Several times when the boy had threatened his father with a knife, the father deliberately turned his back on the boy "to give him a better target if he wanted one."

To the patient, incest was a real possibility. The father agreed, too, that the boy could have intercourse with the mother because "he is physically able." He also said that he had thought that perhaps the boy might rape his mother, but he did not mention it to her because "it might scare her." He was aware that on this trip the boy and his mother were sharing the same hotel room.

The patient's father described his own father as sadistic and brutal and related how brutal beatings had had little effect on himself. He said that he had stopped beating the patient, his son, "because I felt I might kill him." The patient's mother told how her own father was arrested for child neglect and how her mother had told her dying sister that she had been prenuptially conceived.

The patient had an IQ of 112. The Rorschach test showed marked impulsivity, with distortion of reality and poor insight; there were no indications of a schizophrenic process in the projective test results.

The boys in this study were set the pattern of physical violence either by parental example or parental approval. Most of these boys had collections of knives and guns; these collections they were allowed to retain and, in some cases, to augment, even after several episodes of extremely violent and menacing behavior. In each case the child was repeatedly given to realize that his parents expected him to be physically violent and antisocially aggressive, even to the point of murder.

Even if one finds a striking incidence of parental brutality and parental seduction in the life histories of homicide offenders and rapists, some caution should be exercised in the interpretation of this finding. One cannot assume that such factors inevitably lead to homicidal behavior or rape. The author studied three matched groups — convicted homicide offenders, hospital patients who had made homicidal threats and hospital patients who had no history of homicidal behavior. Individual members of each group were matched according to age, sex, race and parental social class.

Parental brutality was recorded when whippings or other punishment caused bruises, welts or blood loss or when the child was struck with a closed fist. Parental seduction was recorded when the parent of the opposite sex slept in the same room or bed with a child to the age of five or beyond; exposed breasts or genitals; had sexual relations with marital partner or lovers in the presence of the child; discussed sex in a pathological manner or sexually assaulted the child. Statistical analysis showed no significant differences among the three groups in the incidence of parental brutality and parental seduction.

Anger toward a brutal father may also be directed toward the mother who did not protect her child from physical assault. Even when there is no physical brutality or maternal seduction, there may yet be very great anger toward mother because of her domineering possessive control over the child. This anger may be displaced on to other women. Some mothers exert almost unbelievable dominance over their children and this dominance continues into adult life. Some children are able to maintain their independence despite the maternal efforts to manipulate them. Others submit passively and never rebel within the home.

As children and adults they report their every action to mother, follow her suggestions for choice of career and remain no more than puppets responsive to mother's every whim and gesture. If they do step out of line, mother becomes ill, talks of her heart attacks and quickly stifles any independent strivings by arousing feelings of guilt. These children usually are not consciously aware of their resentment and speak only in loving terms of mother. Slips of the tongue and ill-considered remarks or acts under the influence of alcohol reveal hidden feelings.

If during an alcoholic bout the son destroys mother's prized possessions, mother and son are united in seeking an explanation in mental illness and neither will consider the possibility that anger at mother is a factor. In their rapes these men often brutally ill treat their victims and show great control over the women by tying them with ropes and forcing them to take part in humiliating perverse sexual acts.

Bromberg points out that psychological understanding of rape is enhanced by analysis of the meaning of the victim in terms of the offender's ego. "Study shows that the victim is a source of unconscious gratification for the aggressive sex offender quite apart from her value as a sexual object. By placing the sexual object in an inferior, degrading role through rape or sadistic and perverse acts, the offender satisfies his need for a position of sexual dominance. This sense of dominance, implied in rape or any form of sexual crime, has the corollary effect of belittling the sexual object. To the sexual pervert, belittlement of the sexual partner is a source of unconscious gratification because it satisfies hostile impulses directed toward women."

Careful psychiatric examination of the rapist who has committed repeated sexual offenses may provide an apparently convincing explanation of the psychological factors leading to this behavior. It is less easy to explain why others with similar backgrounds do not resort to rape. Care should be taken not to seize upon certain factors then to use Procrustes' bed to fit each rapist into one of several stock formulations of the psychodynamics of rape.

It has been suggested that latent or overt homosexuality contributes to rape. According to this theory the man has to prove to himself that he is not a homosexual by repeated acts of intercourse with willing or unwilling members of the opposite sex. Halleck notes that quite frequently in our society latent homosexual fears are associated with paranoid attitudes toward the world and particularly toward females, who threaten the deviate's masculine image. The rapist tends to see all women as seductive, depriving and dangerous. He frequently vacillates between perceiving them as frightening giantesses or as lesser beings. In his attacks upon women, he both conquers his fears and confirms their inferiority.

Many rapists do give a history of homosexual behavior or thoughts and temptations. Alternatively their aversion to any physical contact, however slight, with other men; excessive anger at homosexuals or their great delight in encouraging homosexuals to make advances then beating them savagely, suggest an overreaction based upon their conscious or unconscious fear of this tendency within themselves.

One rapist, unsure of his masculinity, joined the Marine Corps, to prove "I was a man." He worried that his penis was small (not true) and in his rapes he feared that he would not be able to satisfy his victims. Twice a year he arranged for a sperm count and despite reassuring reports he ruminated over his failure to impregnate his girl friend over a period of two years. She became pregnant shortly after her marriage to another man. When another girl friend refused to marry him because she wanted to go to college, he felt that the real reason for her refusal was because "she thought my intercourse was no good. She wanted something better."

He described his mother as "a sexy babe with a big bosom," his wife as "she's just like my mother, like two peas in a pod, always telling me what's best for me, her waist is real small like my mother's," and his victims as "sexy looking, filled out real nice." He said that his mother dyed her hair blond when he started dating blond girls. She objected to his choice of girl friends, saying they were just tramps, and she showed great interest in his activities outside the home and was always wondering if he was on a date. He had fantasies of cutting off the breasts of his victims, and he mentioned that he would enjoy having a room in which breasts were mounted like trophies on the wall. "I don't know how you could mount a vagina. How could you cut a vagina off?"

The forcible rape of a woman previously unknown to the rapist may involve an attempt to establish a loving relationship with a woman. At first sight, this concept appears to be absurd. Coercion is not conducive to a loving response, although one of my forcible rape victims later married her assailant. We should remember that the perceptions and logic of the rapist may be seriously affected by distortions in his personality. His inability to initiate or to maintain personal relationships may lead him to actions which would appear most inappropriate to others not similarly handicapped.

Sexual intercourse is a symbol of a loving relationship of a deep personal attachment. The man who lacks such an affectionate attachment may endeavor to achieve it through enforced sexual relations. But the symbol is not the reality, and the offender continues his rape in an endless, inevitably fruitless search to fill the void within himself.

Bowlby speculated that young girls of affectionless character, who show a remarkable lack of affection or warmth of feeling for anyone, might become prostitutes in later life. This speculation was founded on the fact that many prostitutes have the same combination of a desire for libidinal satisfaction and an inability to make affectionate personal relationships which characterizes the affectionless thief. The latter so often steals the symbols of affection, for example toys and candy. But the stealing proves ineffective because the symbol of love has been mistaken for the real thing.

Two clinical studies may contribute to our understanding of the psychology of rape.

CLINICAL STUDY ONE

A young man was questioned by a police officer after he had been seen walking around a well-to-do apartment house neighborhood in the early hours of the morning. The area was under close police surveillance, as a number of rapes had been committed in the same manner, within an area of just a few blocks. The man appeared to be ill at ease and he was therefore taken to police headquarters for further questioning. After about forty-five minutes interrogation, he confessed to nine or ten rapes or attempted rapes, as well as numerous acts of window-peeping.

There was a sense of relief after this confession. He had been feeling tense and uncomfortable for some months and had attempted to keep himself busy by holding two part-time jobs in addition to his work as a construction laborer. At night when not working he would prowl the apartment house area which was close to his own home. Prowling, which would continue for three to five hours at a time, consisted of a search for young women. He would peep at them through windows. Many of the girls either did not draw their blinds or they left venetian blinds partially closed so that he could see between the slots.

He became familiar with the small area he prowled around and he came to know when people would be away from their apartments. Usually one window would be left unlocked and he never had difficulty pulling open the unlocked crank-type window, then dislodging the screen. Once inside an apartment, he would steal items which caught his fancy. At first he broke into apartments in the absence of the owners. Later he broke into apartments to rape girls he had previously observed while window-peeping.

In these rapes he followed a stereotyped procedure. Through his window-peeping he would establish that the woman appeared attractive to him, that she had gone to bed and fallen asleep and that a way of entry was available. Sometimes he knew from his window-peeping that the victim had not locked her apartment door after returning home late at night. He would take his .32 caliber nickel-plated revolver in his hand and approach the bed. Sometimes he would leave the gun in his pocket.

Almost ten years after his arrest, this man described to the author his sexual offenses and life history.

The Offender Looks at Himself

I'd see a light, I'd go peak in a window. I had devious ways of doing it. I developed sneaky underhand ways of doing things. No one would question a car being parked there. I'd act like I was supposed to be there. I'd just sit and watch for someone coming home. I'd watch people's patterns. I was quite brazen sometimes. People are careless. People aren't conscious of what they are doing. People don't dwell on protecting themselves from deviates, from sick, twisted minds. They leave blinds open, carry on quite openly. I'd masturbate as I watched them undress.

I'd find a woman and observe her till I felt I saw a pattern and an opportunity to be able to rape her successfully. If I didn't follow this procedure, I'd usually fail completely and not get in actual contact with the woman, or I'd find I'd picked a woman I didn't desire. I'd want her in bed and asleep. I'd try to wake her with caution, want to control her to keep her from becoming too scared. I thought she would submit, even hoped she'd want me, love me, give herself willingly. I had a fantasy women secretly like to be kissed on their vagina. I thought this would please them. I was actually desperately wanting to please the woman, win her over. I'd concentrate on this.

I would try to make sure the victim was covered with blankets so I could control her movements when she woke up. I would lay my weight on her and pin her arms to her body to hold her still and set the pillow over her head ready to push down on her mouth if she tried to scream or anything. I'd start talking to her right away as soon as she woke up. "Be still, be still, don't move, do just exactly what you're told and you won't get hurt. I've got a gun." These phrases I might repeat several times and interchange, depending on how much resistance I felt from the woman.

Then I'd squeeze her tighter, depending on the resistance I got, hold her. The next thing I'd usually do right away would be blindfold her. I'd look for a scarf or pillowcase. The object was to blindfold her so she couldn't see me. I'd warn her not to look at me while I was doing this, I didn't want her to see me. That was very important to me. Sometimes I'd say, "Don't look at me if you don't want to get hurt, just do as I say." Then I'd ask, "Where's your money, I want your money." I'd be gruff and demanding about this, insistent, I'd demand to know where the money is, tell them not to lie or hold out on me.

I'd get whatever money they had at that time. I'd be telling them that's all I want is your money, just be still and be quiet. When I got the money, I'd go back and sit down on the bed by the victim, take ahold of her, start talking to her. "Don't be scared, don't be afraid, just relax, don't make any noise." Sometimes I'd press the gun against them on the leg or on the arm or someplace to let them feel the gun and know that I had it. I'd tell them I had a gun "just do what I say and you'll be all right."

If the victim had not put up any strong resistance, I wouldn't let them feel the gun in this way, I'd just leave it in my pocket. I'd start caressing them first through the bedclothes, their outer limbs, the feel of their hair. Try to kiss them. Tell them to be still and take it easy. If I didn't get too much resistance, like strike at me, try to tear off the blindfold, look at me or try to get out from under the bedclothes, I'd go on caressing them.

Then I'd take the bedclothes down and start caressing them, warning them to hold still, and if they weren't putting up too much resistance, I'd start talking to them about how soft and warm they were, that everything would be all right. I'd continue to caress them. I'd start caressing their breasts, their stomach and start taking off any night clothes they would have on. I'd tell them I wanted to look at them, warning them again to be still, to be quiet. I'd start caressing their vagina and stroking their pubic hair, telling them to open their legs, telling them to be still, trying to kiss them on the lips.

Usually I'd have to start forcing their legs open using my hand, sometimes I'd have to put a knee between their legs keeping my weight and body close to them, controlling them physically. I might hold my position at this time for a while, caressing them, holding my weight on them, talking, telling them I wanted them. I was aware of my victims talking to me. They would plead, sometimes they would make caustic remarks to me, curse me. I was sensitive to what they would say in a way, but it wouldn't back me off from my intentions.

I'd answer them. One girl, I was caressing her breasts and she made a remark it must be a disappointment her breasts were so small. I told her they were beautiful and went on caressing her. I had to make sure they were under control physically because I was going to perform cunnilingus on them and I needed them to lay still. Once I was certain they would be still I'd get their legs open. I'd try to keep the action smooth to keep the woman under control.

I'd be kissing her, sucking on her breasts as I opened her legs, telling her you're beautiful, you're warm, you're soft, kissing her stomach. I'd put a leg in each arm with my face over her vagina, warning her a last time to lay still and keep her blindfold on, holding a leg firmly in each arm. I'd begin to brush her pubic hair and inner thighs with my face and lips, gradually I would kiss her vagina directly. I'd do this for maybe five to ten minutes. I'd tell her to respond, to let herself go. I thought that this appealed to the women, that they would like it.

How long I would do this would depend on her response, how cooperative she was. If a woman resisted this cunnilingus I might stop in a minute and I'd open up my pants, never take them off. I did take them off one time, that was an exception. I'd have an erection or semi-erection when I couldn't obtain a full erection, this would bother me some. I'd warn the woman to be still, to be quiet, telling her she was good, tell her to open up. I'd insert my penis in her vagina.

I would tell her to respond, to let go and to have a climax with me. I'd be trying to talk seductively to her whenever I could, whenever I had control. I would climax pretty shortly and I tried to hold the woman after climax, soothing my own feelings, relaxing, telling her to be still, to be quiet, to stay in bed while I was getting off of her and straightening my trousers. By this time usually the woman would be quite still. Sometimes I'd thank her. If they'd been passive, I'd tell them they were good. Tell them to be still and be quiet, that I was leaving.

Sometimes I would leave out the window the way I entered; on a couple of occasions I left through the apartment door. How fast I would leave would depend on how still I sensed the victim would remain. I usually knew beforehand how far I had to go to my car and how to leave the immediate neighborhood and get home.

When I'd go back to the car, that was when the turmoil of feelings would start, I'd feel a big thrill, deep self-gratification. I'd be scared I'd get caught and I'd have to hurry to get home, longing, wishing I could have stayed with the woman. Frustration and anger that it had to end. About the time of getting home, depression would start to set in. Some guilt feelings about the victim, but very little, what she was doing and how she was feeling now. Some disgust with myself. A feeling of "Here I am back where I was, another damn day." I'd really get depressed looking at the day ahead.

Some girls I didn't rape. There were two girls in an apartment. The first girl that I woke was the most beautiful girl in these rapes, also the youngest, like a beauty queen; she offered no resistance. I started to caress her, she shook and showed she was quite frightened. I removed her panties and I kissed her and was going to rape her and she asked me to please, please stop, she was a virgin and was going to be married next week, to please let her go. She was crying then and she repeated how important it was for her to be a virgin. She choked me up, she really got to me and I felt terrible. I told her I would quit and started reassuring her that I would quit, then I left.

She was the only one who talked me out of it, others scared me out of it. There was another occasion, two girls in an apartment in the same bed. I woke them both up, concentrated on one of them and demanded to know where their money was. They only had a few dollars and it made me pretty angry. When I returned to the bed to rape this one girl, she was very rigid and tense as I started to caress her. Her roommate called her by name, raised up in bed and told me what did I think I was doing in there. She stood up on the bed and started hitting me with her fists. The girl I had been attempting to rape started kicking at me with her legs and tried to hit me with her fists.

As soon as this started happening, I wanted to get away, but I was pretty much out of control and started pushing at them and hitting at them, telling them okay I would go. By this time they were yelling to get out, get out and I went back out the window, dove out the window head first. If they'd have had a gun around, they would have shot me with it.

(Following his arrest the man spent four years in jail and during most of this time he was in the maximum security section of a state penitentiary. He had previously served time for burglary and was aware that rapists were abused and looked down on by other inmates.)

All the hatred, disgust other cons have with themselves, they take it out on these guys. I expected it but I didn't get it. I scared them with my physical strength, size and reputation from being in the penitentiary before. I conned other cons, manipulated my way into a tier porter's job and I got extra food, extra books, did favors for other guys, this bought them off. No matter what feelings they had, they kept them to themselves. The combination of these two approaches kept me exempt from the ridicule and abuse sex offenders experience from other convicts.

Before anybody could confront me, I'd confront them. That was one of my tactics, pick a weak spot and let them know I had it on them. I'd leave them alone and be helpful to them if they didn't threaten me. I played a stereotyped hard arsed role. I built up walls to keep people away from me, I'm really scared of fighting, some people don't believe me when I say that, but I don't like it. That's why I built up that combination of tactics.

I was scared of one guy, he was the ringleader in the cell house, he called himself the boss con. Several other guys in the cell house antagonized him towards me and I heard he was going to kill me. It really scared me, it was either him or me. I got a knife and went to him. He backed off and said that there was no hard feelings. I also said there was no hard feelings, but I didn't trust him. I was still scared and angry, but I would not admit this to myself. I pretended that everything was all right and so did he.

About a month later I was mopping the tier at the time I was supposed to do this and he was playing cards. He refused to move when I asked him. After asking him to move once, I deliberately provoked him by splashing mop water on him. He jumped up and attacked me. He knocked me about three cells down the tier. Then he crushed me against the bars and started to strangle me. He would have killed me if he could. I turned loose all my anger and I beat the hell out of him.

I feel now, looking back on it, I was waiting for an opportunity to get my feelings out, my fear and my angry feelings. I had to hide my own fear and anger from myself. I'm sure I set the fight up deliberately as I look back. I baited him to attack me when I was in the right, then I let everything out. After that the others were afraid of me.

I hit the end of my rope in cell house three; lay there and rot or change. I saw myself as being in there the rest of my life. I began to look at myself and what I was going to do. The doctors told me I was sick, but I wouldn't talk to them – a combination of things, my lawyer told me not to tell the doctors anything, that they'd use it to prosecute me in court, that gave me a good excuse but the real reason was I was scared to open up. I didn't know what would come out, I thought I was a monster, a sex maniac.

I started writing short stories – the schoolteacher took an interest in my writing, he kept telling me about the good feelings in my stories and I got to thinking I had some good feelings for myself and people and my life wasn't all bad. I tested this out for a year and a half. It started bothering me. I got to feeling the psychologist, Mr. Stock, cared about me. He came once a month, but I still wouldn't open up. But I got to thinking he really cares, maybe he can help me. I started trusting him with my good feelings. He'd accept them but every once in a while he'd try to get me to talk about my angry feelings. I'd freeze, I'd clam up, I wouldn't admit them to myself.

Lieutenant McDaniel, the officer in charge of cell house three, he helped too. He was a strong stable figure of authority. I became conscious he liked me. He did his job, you couldn't play on his feelings, he couldn't be manipulated. Regardless of my behavior he was consistent. He could take my foolishness, nonsense, gripes, pettiness, put up with me. He was firm. I couldn't get away from him. If you were wrong, no matter how much he liked you, he'd put his foot down, make you take your medicine. I had thirty-one months with him. I've never forgotten him.

I wouldn't admit angry feelings, but I felt bad about what I'd done. I asked to go to the hospital but I thought I saw an angle to get me out of the tight spot I was in. They saw through this, but after about nine months I was transferred to the hospital. I began to see that I did have angry feelings to my mother and to my dad. She was a gentle, kind, devoted, religious mother, but she frightened me with her religious concepts. She talked about turning the other cheek and not judging people, but she screamed at my father and called the police on him.

She prayed for her sister, my Aunt Betty, but she called the police to arrest her for drinking. She wasn't drunk or anything. I liked this Aunt Betty. She took us swimming and played with us. My mother never played with us. She was in church two or three times a week, as well as Saturday and all day Sunday. It built up a lot of anger in me. I wished her dead, I didn't want her as my mother. I had a great big frog, I wanted to show him to Mum but she wouldn't come out. She wouldn't even come to the window. This happened all the time. She'd be reading her Bible or talking with her women about who was going to be saved. We took it to the neighbor boy's house, his mom and dad came out and looked at it. I preferred to be around their home.

I secretly admired my father, but I talked about what an s.o.b. he was. When I was four or five years old he'd put boxing gloves on me and get down on his knees and make me fight him. The way he'd do it he'd keep punching me and make me hit him. He'd hit me harder and I'd have to get up and fight him. If he was drinking and I was playing with Joyce, a neighbor kid, he'd say, "Come with me, you're no pansy, you're a man." He'd knock me on the ear with his fist, boy, that hurt. If I cried, he'd hit me again, say men don't cry.

He'd lecture me, "What the hell's the matter with you? I don't treat you like a son, I treat you like a brother, I treat you like a man." He'd tell me when he was a kid he could whip anyone in the neighborhood. He'd drive around, find two or three kids, then he'd say you go whip them and whip them good. I'd try to squirm out of it. He'd double his fist up and hit me in the ear or in the ribs and knock the air out of me. "Go out and whip them kids, if you don't, I'll beat the shit out of you. You're no pansy, do I have to be ashamed of you?" I'd go, crying, pick a fight, I was scared stiff and I didn't want to fight.

I'd fight in sheer desperation. When I got back to the car, he'd pat me on the back and hug me and make me feel good. I'd feel relieved. He'd make me drink when I was six or seven. He'd buy a bottle of whiskey and make me drive. I was big for my age but I don't know how I did it. He'd cry and tell me my mother was trying to cut his throat and he'd stop and park and tell me about his father. His mother died, his father committed suicide and he had to be a man when he was seven. His five sisters were all cutthroat bitches and he had to go on his own and be a man. He'd tell me to have a drink with him. I was scared I'd go to hell if I drank with him. He hit me, he didn't have to hit me many times and I'd drink with him.

He didn't care how he beat me, he'd just start swinging on me like I was another man. If I went down, he'd boot me. He broke my nose, busted my mouth open, blackened my eyes, put lumps on my head, kicked me in the ribs and broke them, stood on my hand and broke it. The contrast was so extreme between my father and mother. He'd roll drunks for their money and brag about it to me, about how good a fighter he was.

He bragged about his infidelity, you didn't dare trust women because they'd cut your throat, you couldn't be a pal to them. Point out what he thought was good-looking women to me, tell me that short-waisted, long-legged women were the best piece of ass. They were all hypocritical, you could screw any of them, the only one faithful was my mother.

He burned the house down for insurance and told me not to tell my mother because she'd have him sent to prison. I was hurt about the things I lost in the fire. My mother would cry and pray to God and ask why this happened. She asked God what had she done. It put me in a bind. They didn't have friends, they dumped a lot of feelings on me.

I didn't associate a lot with my sister, I was proud of her, but I didn't like to play with her. She was five years younger than I was. I did watch out and see that she didn't get hurt by the other kids. At times I'd tease her and play with her. My mother threatened to get a divorce because his drinking had increased and they were fighting constantly. Things were really miserable around home. By this time I had taken my father's side. One day he came up to school and had me called out of class and told me he was leaving the old lady, meaning my mother. "What are you going to do, stay here and be saved and be a pansy or go with your old man and see the world?"

I had a lot of mixed feelings, but I chose to go with him. I got a big thrill out of how permissive he was with me, letting me go to shows which was a sin with my mother. I wasn't attending school, we were living out in the woods with one of his friends. It was a lot of fun and this went on for two to three months before I started missing my mother and started to have a lot of guilty feelings about what I was doing. I was drinking with my father and he was dumping his feelings on me — "a lousy world, don't trust nobody, you've got to be tough."

Finally I asked to go home; my dad told me I was cutting his throat, but he allowed me to go home. I was happy to get home and I started back to school. It seems I was resentful being told what to do and my uncle said I was a smart aleck. I told him I was going to be a bum when I grew up. For a while I was glad to be home, but I never got close to my mother again. One day at school I was told to hurry home because my mother was ill. When I got there an ambulance was driving away. There was a bunch of women there and they had been praying when she keeled over with a cerebral hemorrhage.

My aunt took care of my sister and I. My mother lived for seventeen days. I did want to see her. I had a lot of guilt feelings because my aunt would say, "Where is your father? He should be here, you're just like your father, driving your mother to the grave." I snapped back at her and voiced faults about my mother and her religion, but I had a lot of feelings and I felt very guilty. Not being allowed to see her confused me; I knew she was alive, but my aunt said she didn't want to see us children. I never believed that. I'd never let myself believe that.

When she was buried, there was a sense of relief and a sense of feeling very alone. I started telling myself I didn't care. I didn't care if she was dead. School didn't mean anything to me anymore. I wouldn't let my aunt comfort me. I felt she didn't care about me and I thought my dad's attitude about life was right. We were living in a small trailer and I saw her undressing. I started imagining having sex with her, I had just turned thirteen. I started stealing her money and her underclothes. She said I was a bum, I lived up to it. She continued to blame me for my mother's death. I'd tell her I don't care, but inside I felt I was responsible.

About this time I began going in the neighbors' home when they weren't there and watch their television. I started window-peeping. After four or five months, my dad came home and said he was going to take care of us kids. My dad made me stay at home and look after him while he was drinking. He'd have wild hallucinations or nightmares and would beat me. I had sexual feelings about the wife in the house next door. I was babysitting, they came home drunk one night. I stayed there and went in the bedroom, kissed her, fondled her and caressed her all over her body. The second time I did it she woke up.

They raised hell with me, and my father went along with it. In privacy he made light of it and said what a good screw the neighbor's wife would be. Later in an angry drunken state he beat me for it and told me what a degenerate bastard I was. They got a lady babysitter. I went in the house when she was asleep, but she woke up and I lied, said I thought there was a fire. The neighbors raised hell again. I stuck with my lie. Shortly after, I quit school as I didn't have any friends at school and I couldn't study.

I really started window peeping and prowling. I'd just turned fifteen. A cousin introduced me to a twenty-year-old girl. I took her home and she lived with me for three months. My dad treated it as a joke. "Are you going to let me have some when you get done?" I didn't get any satisfaction out of it, and while she was still living with me I started window peeping again. My father beat her in a drunken rage for no reason, so I took her home to her parents. Shortly after, I left home with some money my dad had rolled from a drunk.

He came and got me when I was arrested for mail theft. The neighbors complained about my window peeping, my dad would make light of it but at other times he'd beat me for it, say I wasn't a man. Life was a drudgery and the minute I was seventeen I joined the Army. For a time I enjoyed it. I was doing some window-peeping, but I started stealing cars. I got a thrill out of it, felt I was getting even with people. I'd steal the car, drive it at a high speed for a short distance, steal things, sometimes throw them in the owner's trash can. I stole seventy cars in four or five months and broke into four or five homes. I'd prowl through their belongings, eat out of their icebox, watch their television, take jewelry, snapshots, souvenir letter openers and clothing. I was sent to a reformatory for car theft, it didn't affect me. I thought it was another of these things you have to go through.

When I'd break into a home, I would fantasize it was my home, fantasize about the people who owned the home similarly to how I fantasized while window peeping. I think I was trying to share their lives and feel safe too. I felt safe peeping at them, I didn't feel safe being with people and doing things with people. Many times I've spent an hour watching television with a family, watch them eat dinner, read newspapers, kids running in and out, watch women do their housework, watch people entertain and have parties.

I'd fantasize about what work the man did, where they'd come from, what they liked to do, did they fight, were they happy, why were they happy? Why other people seemed happy bugged the hell out of me. I didn't really believe it. The sexual thing come in there, watching women disrobe, get ready for bed, bathe, I used to be anxious to see what they did when they were alone.

When I'd break into a home, I would take things; I realize now I was taking things of sentimental value, mementoes and other items which could not easily be replaced. I would take the object, feeling very strongly at the time that I would have what the owner had, always to experience bitter disappointment later and find the sentimental object was empty to me and I would throw it away. Sometimes I'd knock things over, lamps and, at the time, I thought it was accidental. Sometimes I'd destroy things. Looking back on it, I think I was striking back at people, they had things I didn't have.

I was arrested for prowling and they charged me with vagrancy. In a routine lineup, I was picked out by a woman as the man who had raped her. The lineup had a specific suspect but she looked me right in the eye and said

I did it. She said there was no question about it in her mind, no doubt about it. This was after the lineup face to face. They told me afterwards she continued to say it was me even though I was at work at the time and she had been told this. I was nearly sent up for rape before I started.

I got a sixteen-year-old girl pregnant, so I married her and had the marriage annulled, no guilty feelings or remorse. I did more prowling, more peeking and more burglaries and started taking money from commercial buildings. I stepped out of one building right into the police and got a two- to ten-year sentence. I felt it was a dog-eat-dog society and I had no real remorse. I was becoming very manipulative of people. While I was in the penitentiary I was eager to get out and resume my window peeping. I daydreamed about raping and I had fantasies of raping young sophisticated, good-looking, independent, working girls. I had fantasies the girls would like it, would accept me, but they had to be caught off guard and taken.

They had to be feminine. My mother's sister, the one who cared for us when my mother died, she was a soft and feminine woman, at first appearance quite sophisticated. As I see it now she had quite a lot of the bitch in her. She enticed me, I don't think she was aware of it, disrobing in close proximity to me. These women I picked, they were feminine but there was a strong strain of bitchiness in them. I didn't realize it. I feel I missed the boat with my mom and this aunt. I got left out by women, that's when I got downright hateful. The only difference between the women I selected and my aunt was the age.

In the act of rape I would try to pretend to myself I was a fine man. An impossible task, as I had just enough contact with reality to feel wrong and this caused tremendous tension of feeling during the act. This caused much of the guilt afterwards which also had to be escaped. I never accepted anyone in faith, I saw people as cold, selfish and uncaring. I never opened up, give a real feeling of myself to anyone, other than anger. I had no rewarding image of myself or anyone else. I could not see or take pride in anything I accomplished or anything others shared of themselves with me. So everyday living, socializing, whatever I did, alone or with others, was empty and unrewarding.

I had a complete fantasy life that involved my being stronger than all men, irresistible to all women, a doer of great things. I had no sensitive contact with either men or women, men were something to beat at all cost, women were something to screw if at all possible. People, men and women, were strictly things to outsmart, things you must take what you want from and consider myself better than.

I obtained the same basic emotional pleasure from rapes, robbery and voyeurism that healthy people derive from various acceptable contacts with others and sharing of feelings or competing with one another. A rape was like a daring businessman pulling off a successful business coup. This was some of the feeling before and during the act. High excitement, boldness, masculine images at stake, putting it over on someone. At times during criminal acts, such as rape and all the rest, I even felt I belonged with other people. However, shortly after, I would feel cut off again, in the dark — unaccepted, unwanted.

In one instance where the woman was very responsive, I spent the whole night with her and had the fantasy that she was my wife, a devoted lover and mother. I almost couldn't pull myself out of the fantasy to leave, although I knew she would have company early the next morning. She had to encourage me to leave. I also had fantasies in which I justified what I was doing to people and I supported my anger by rationalizing that people were all like myself and I was doing what others were afraid to do.

I had fantasies about the woman I was raping, how she felt physically, where she had been in life, some resentment that she'd done things in life without me. I had a longing to do things in general with people. Sometimes I'd verbalize these fantasies if the woman was quite submissive, otherwise I'd just take the trip within myself.

CLINICAL STUDY TWO

One afternoon a man with a stocking mask on his face and a gun in his hand entered the home of a young married woman with the intention of raping her. Although only thirty-one years of age he had served a two- to five-year sentence for a burglary, a five- to eight-year sentence of indecent liberties and he had committed almost two hundred criminal offenses. These crimes included approximately fifteen rapes or attempted rapes, the armed holdup of a jewelry store, fifty to sixty burglaries, twenty to thirty thefts of five-year sentence for a burglary, a five- to eight-year sentence for indecent exposure and the destruction by fire of a warehouse and a garage.

The woman was forced to undress, but she succeeded in distracting his attention for a moment, and she fled from her house in the nude. When she screamed for help, he shot her (see page 84 for her account of the attack). Following his arrest some days later, the man described his childhood background and criminal career to the author.

The Offender Looks at Himself

My mother didn't think I could do anything wrong. She overprotected me, wouldn't let me play ball, play football, wouldn't even let me ride a bicycle. She even wanted me to stay inside. She taught me embroidery, stuff like that, cooking, trying to make a real sissy out of me. Maybe that's one of the reasons I'm scared to death of a fight now. She dressed me in baby dresses for quite a while. She got dolls for me. She told me I played with them for quite a while.

This overprotectiveness, my mother would do things to humiliate me, spit on her handkerchief, clean my face in a bus, in church, in front of other people. I'd feel downright humiliated. To this day I don't know how to tie a necktie, she always done this. I used to sleep in her room. My stepfather slept in another room. When I was about eleven or twelve, I saw her naked a few times. It didn't embarrass her. She was always trying to hold me when I was younger. Thirteen or fourteen on I wouldn't like to kiss her. When I went to the Navy, I felt embarrassed just hugging her. I knew she wanted to kiss me goodbye. I wanted her to do it on the cheek, she did it on the lips. . . . Sex was definitely not talked about in the home.

My father died when I was about five and I don't remember too much about him. Sometimes I blame myself for his death. I know I didn't kill him. Sometimes I think because of me he had to die. I should have died. He was head of the family, everyone loved him; I didn't belong to the family (see below). I came close to dying of double pneumonia. They prayed to God I wouldn't die, I didn't die, after that my father died.

My mother remarried when I was seven but he died within about a year. Seems like she married again less than a year later. He used to whip me. He'd threaten to kill me, he'd threaten to kill somebody as a matter of speech. He threatened to kill my brother-in-law when I was fifteen and I took the gun from him. I think the argument was over me. I never got to know him until I was in the penitentiary. I always had a fear of him, but he wrote me a letter when I was in the pen that he loved me, then I expressed love for him.

Around eleven or twelve if I was masturbating, I'd use a picture from a catalogue, but I'd get visions of my mother naked and I'd feel funny, very unpleasant, guilty. I'd try to get rid of that vision of her and finish masturbating. As long as I had that vision of her I couldn't masturbate and that's still the same way today. When I was fourteen or fifteen, I had these fantasies my mother would be sitting in a chair with nothing on but a garter belt and stockings and would have her legs spread. When I had these fantasies, it was sickening.

At thirteen my "mother" told me I was adopted. I mixed up a bunch of poison. I don't know what all there was, there was some weed killer. I tried it out, it killed the flowers, next day they were dead. I drank the rest. Nothing happened, I got sick.

After I found out I was adopted, I felt I didn't belong to the family. I felt I was in the way. Lots of times I've thought about it. When I was told I was adopted, the best way I can describe it, it was as if your wife would say, "I don't love you." I felt rejected I guess. I felt I wasn't worthy of their love, like a stray dog somebody would pick up. I ran away from home but I didn't get very far.

If I knew who my mother was, I'd feel like somebody then. I don't feel

I'm anything, just a piece of garbage. I couldn't take no kidding, like somebody call me a bastard, I'd be mad enough to fight, that's funny because I'm a coward. It never did turn into a fight, I bluffed them down. I thought my real mother was a prostitute who hadn't taken precautions. All my birth certificate says is "Baby boy Smith." I used to have daydreams of breaking into the hospital where I was born and find out who my mother was. I'd find out where she lived, knock on the door. When she answered it, I'd tell her who I was, stick the revolver right in her gut and just shoot her dead. Hell, she threw me away. My girl friend had a child and she kept him.

My problem with women must have started around thirteen or fourteen. The first thing I ever done was to a woman walking down the street. I felt underneath her dress between her legs. Then I ran off. I done that quite a few times, then I started exposing myself. There are certain kinds of women I can't expose myself to, it's not so much their physical looks but what I think their personality is. It's hard to explain, just a feeling I get. If I think she's really fussy about things, kind of bitchy; I've had opportunities to expose myself to women like that, but there's no desire to do it.

Others have been protected all their lives, churchgoers, they know nothing about sex. I can expose myself to that kind. They've got to be shocked into knowing there's such a thing as sex. Then there's the matter of calling the police. The kind that are shocked by it are too ashamed to call the police and they're not going to. Some women, you think they wouldn't mind it, even enjoy it. The kind that like to see you, they're certainly not going to call the police. Those bitchy ones don't go along with it.

When I talked to a doctor about that, it turned out I did it when I was angry at my mother. My mother would write me a letter, "be sure and eat, do this, do that." That would build up an anger in me. I've been chased about twenty times for that and for peeping tom. You can always spot an apartment with girls in it. They put a teddy bear, a snoopy dog, funny bottles or wigs on head racks in the window. Window-peeping and indecent exposure — if I would think about my mother, it would put an absolute stop to it.

My first marriage (age twenty-two), I didn't feel close to her until the night before the marriage when she told me she had once been raped. During this time I would be driving along the road, see a woman or child and expose myself. I also did considerable window peeping. On one occasion someone got a description of my truck or the license number and I was picked up. There were no charges and I told my wife, she was sympathetic. She seemed like a dull person and I divorced her after about a year.

My first attempted rape, I was about twenty-four, the girl was pretty nice. I doubled up my fist and hit her in the face as hard as I could. She just stood there screaming, it scared me off I guess. Then there was a twelve-year-old girl, I couldn't get in her. The next time I used a gun. I was being a peeping tom but I noticed her park her car. I couldn't get in her and I made her use her hand until I reached a climax. I stopped a girl but she acted like she was going to start going again, before she could I cocked the gun so she could hear it. I asked her for her money, she didn't have any. I told her to take her panties off. I told her to turn around and I raped her from behind. She said she didn't want to do it like an animal. I got done and left.

I didn't think too much of my second wife. I'd known her for over a year, one night she told me she was pregnant by another man. It hit me like a ton of bricks, then I fell in love with her. Before we'd had sex, but I didn't feel nothing toward her. She had the baby, put it up for adoption. I had mixed feelings about that, I wanted to keep it.

She divorced me while I was in the penitentiary. It really hurt me. I was really in love with her, the way she did it, came down on a Sunday, said, "I love you." She said she'd be down again next Sunday. Tuesday I got a set of divorce papers. She had it all planned. It takes longer than two days to get divorce papers and get them sent down to the penitentiary. It really hurt me, I had fantasies of killing her.

She was a beautician and after I left the pen I rang up a whole bunch of beauty shops to find her. I wonder if that doesn't mean something, the places I held up were beauty shops. I was serious about wanting to kill her. It was the only time I had sadistic fantasies, tying her down over an ant pile, just like the Indians, keeping her alive a long time, cut her eyelids off so she couldn't close her eyes, keeping her alive and torturing her.

I'd been in the pen for burglary, most of the burglaries I've pulled, my main objective is to get underclothes. I used to dress up in the clothes and masturbate. I've even exposed myself like that. I've even attempted rape dressed up like that too. One burglary, I went in, took my clothes off, put her clothes on. I took a broom handle, put it in my rectum and masturbated. I wanted to feel what a woman would feel from me, but I don't think that was a homosexual thing. There were times especially in the pen, plenty of time to daydream, I actually had the wish I was a woman and a lesbian making love to another woman. Picture arcades would fascinate me, spend around twenty dollars in no time flat. I would masturbate as I watched women kiss women.

When I was in the pen the second time, most of the guys thought I was in for burglary, that's what I told everybody. It was for indecent liberties, I took her panties down and touched her. I think she was five. I've done pretty fantastic things, but basically my moral standards are higher than most people's. I don't like to see women running around in shorts. Things like that, I don't especially care to see them smoking in public. As far as law and order goes, I'm for law and order. I'm right wing. I realize these student demonstrators have a right to express their opinion, but there shouldn't be all this looting and rioting.

I thought my father was watching me from heaven. It's unusual, but deep down inside of me I still believe it. I think God has punished me – indecent exposure, masturbating in church, because after doing something like that I'd always have real bad luck. When this urge – indecent exposure, burglary, rape – hits me I have an urge to have a bowel motion. Often in a burglary I stop and have a bowel motion. I had a bowel motion once with my clothes on, I couldn't hold it. It happened just as I stepped out of the house. A lot of places I go in with gloves on, but a lot of places I take them off. I leave fingerprints, I make a game of it. . . . If I came out and told you how wrong it is, I'd break down.

There were other rapes and attempted rapes. I was married when some of them happened. There were two attempts in a row, I didn't have no gun. I jumped out of the bushes, stuck the pliers in her back and told her it was a gun . . . a fourteen-year-old girl waiting for a bus, I put my hand over her mouth, stuck a door handle in her back and said, "This is a gun". . . . A fifteen-year-old girl in a laundromat. I started masturbating in front of her. She started to leave and I caught her. I had a little knife and I threatened her with it. She said the knife wasn't big enough to hurt her. I said it was if it was in the right place. She took her panties off . . .

After I came out of the penitentiary the second time, the first place was a wig shop. I went in the back door with a gun and stocking over my face. There was about eight women in the place. I took their money. I just went in and robbed them, then I told them I wanted them all in the back room. I told them all to undress. I was going to rape one of them and the other women said she was pregnant so I left her alone. I took the second one standing up. There was a third one looked better so I took her further back, made her lay down on the floor. When I was in the pen I used to dream about almost exactly what I'd done. . . .

A girl sitting in her car at a park. She got out of the car and started climbing down some rocks, so I followed her. It was daytime, she had a bunch of friends further down. I stopped her, pointed the gun at her. Finally I had to threaten to kill her before she'd go ahead and do it. She told me she had poison ivy. I never did get it. . . . I'd been visiting my mom. On the way back I saw this young girl walking down the street. I walked up behind her, grabbed her by the hair, put the gun at the back of her head. I told her, "Keep quiet or I'll blow your brains out. . . ."

I held up a beauty shop in Cheyenne, Wyoming. I wanted to rape a woman but I got scared. I went in and told them it was a holdup. I took their money and had all of them lay down on the floor. But there was too many of them, at least twenty. I didn't know it was such a big place. I got scared. . . . I burglarized three beauty shops, one of them twice. In one shop, it was just turning dark, the door was locked but I could see the key in the door. So I picked up a rock, broke the window and opened the lock. There were two women, I made them go to the back. I molested one, felt up under her dress, and left. I think I took a wig.

The Day of the Shooting

I was in my car driving north of Denver. I guess I was looking for a place to burglarize. I was driving around not going any place in particular, then I thought I ought to go to Boulder. I remember seeing a girl in a car up by the university, I was just riding by when I seen her. She was real attractive. I remember thinking, I would, well like to rape her. She was really good looking, almost knock you out to look at her. I was going to park by her car, by the time I got there (I had to turn around) she was already gone.

So I just drove around town, I'd never been there before. I was kind of looking it over. I stopped in a store and bought a pair of women's stockings. I did commit a burglary near the edge of town. I took some stuff. One of the things was a pistol and a little television set, it wasn't very many things. While I was committing the burglary, I had a bowel movement. I had my clothes on and I just couldn't hold it. It happened just as I stepped out of the house, I couldn't hold it. So I went driving down some road that led out of town. I cleaned myself up with a towel that I had.

As I was driving back toward town I seen these houses kind of up on a hill. I decided I'd burglarize them. I parked my car in front of them. I went up to the first one to make sure nobody was there and a woman answered the door. I asked her if so and so lives there. She answered no. So then I went to the next house; nobody answered so I went in, the door was unlocked. I didn't find nothing to take. I went back down to my car and I got one of the stockings that I bought and a pistol.

I went back up to the first house where the woman had answered the door. When she answered the door, she said she was sick, that she'd been in bed. Her front door was unlocked so I went in real quiet. I was going to go to the bedroom, point the gun at her. I asked her if she had any money, to make her think it was a holdup. It's kind of a psychological deal if you get a person off guard. If you're trying to sell something to somebody, get them to say yes to something else, then it's easier to get them to say yes to what you're selling. Kind of an old Dale Carnegie kind of thing.

She gave me the money she had. There was only a dollar and some change. I told her to take her nightgown off. She did. I told her to get down on her knees. She said she heard somebody coming. She said she was going to look out the door and then when she got to the door, she opened it and started running. It was about twenty feet to a bunch of stairs that went down to the road. Right at the top of the stairs I caught her. I had my gun in my right hand and I grabbed her with my left hand. I didn't want to hurt her, so I told her to get back in the house and I'll leave.

She broke away from me and started running down the stairs. I begged her to stop. I went running down the stairs after her, somehow the gun went off. When the gun went off, she fell and it was right at the bottom of the stairs. It seemed like it was an accident, like I didn't shoot her. I went running past where she was up to my car. She was screaming something at me. I don't know what it was. I got right to my car and I realized that I still had this stocking on and the gun in my hand and there were cars going by and everything.

I said I didn't have no memory of the gun going off, but I'm sure I must have, my reasoning tells me. It seems like I feel bad, at the same time I feel she shouldn't have run like that. She brought it on herself. I know it's serious, but I don't feel like it's serious. This girl I shot, she had a real good resemblance of the image I had in my mind of what I thought my mother looked like. Looking at her face from the side she looked like Mrs. – – –, that I think is my real mother. When I went to the door the first time, the way she was kind of leaning out was the kind of action I've seen Mrs. – – – do lots of times. When she leans out the door, she has her hands between her legs leaning over.

So I got back in the car and started it. I stayed on the road, it took me all the way through town. I stopped some place for gas. About a block from there I seen a little girl five or six years old. I wanted to touch her and expose myself to her. But I was too late, when I got back she was gone. I couldn't find her. So I got back in the car and started driving some more. I came to another town, there was a beauty parlor on the street. I seen two women through the front window as I drove by.

So I went down to the corner, turned in the alley and parked. Before I got out of the car I got the gun and a stocking, knocked on the back door. I tried the door but it was locked. A woman asked who was there, I told her I had a package. So she said to bring it around the front. So I walked around and went in the front door and there were the two women that I seen in the front window. I told them to get in the back room. Just then another woman came out from the back. I got all three in the back.

I made all three take their clothes off. I didn't want them to know what I was going to do. I asked them if they had any money, so they gave me some money. I asked them if this was all of it, they said yes. I still didn't want them to know what I had in mind. So I made a pretense of looking for some other things. I found about two hundred dollars. Then I took the third one and raped her. I made all three get in the bathroom, the one I raped I tied her hands behind her.

I wound up in Denver again. I found out the police were looking for me. I hid out at this girl friend's house. She offered to alibi me, say I had been with her at the time of the shooting. I went to a motel and the police got me.

COMMENT

The perceptive reader will draw his own conclusions regarding the origins of rape in these two men. The reader would like to have the observations of members of the offenders' families. Their recollections of the offenders' early childhood experiences, although also subject to distortions and blind spots, are essential to an informed evaluation of the origins of the urge to rape. The first offender has drawn his own conclusions, which may have been influenced by the views of his therapist. The second offender mentions only the conclusion of the therapist, who treated him for indecent exposure, and has not explored in depth his problem of rape.

THE RAPIST'S VISITING CARD

The second offender mentioned that often in a burglary* he would stop and have a bowel motion. At one burglary he had an involuntary bowel motion in his pants. Other rape offenders known to the author have defecated on the ground outside the rooms of their victims. Feces which the criminal leaves at the scene of his crime have been called the criminal's *carte de visite odorante.*

Explanations of this peculiar visiting card have been reviewed by Theodore Reik, who discounts the theory that feces are a visible sign of the criminal's lighthearted impudence and intention to mock authority. Some criminals believe that they will delay their pursuit if they leave their feces behind, and to lengthen their respite they cover their feces with various objects. Popular names for feces in foreign countries (watchman, sentry, night watchman) are cited in support of this superstition. The custom is also attributed to the criminal's superstitious belief that something must be left behind if he is to escape, the underlying conviction being that every crime must be expiated, and by making this sacrifice he propitiates the gods.

Reik maintains that if the custom goes back to superstition, there must be a deeper psychological explanation and suggests that it is an expression of the unconscious impulse to confess. The feces, which are part of the person, represent the culprit himself and are left behind for the purpose of self-betrayal. Indeed, on rare occasions, identification of intestinal parasites in the feces may lead to conviction of the criminal. Reik cites the case of a dangerous criminal, recently released from prison, who defecated at the

---

*Guttmacher contends that burglary, the offense of breaking and entering — the very words suggest the possible symbolism — is far more likely to be a forerunner of rape than homosexuality, voyeurism, exhibitionism or any other type of sexual offense. One third of his rapists had been previously involved in burglaries. Heirens, the seventeen-year-old University of Chicago student who committed more than five hundred burglaries and three murders, used to have an erection at the sight of the window through which he was to enter and had an emission as he went through.

scene of his crime and cleaned himself with his prison discharge papers. Self-betrayal may take the form of leaving not feces but clothing or some other article which can be traced to the offender.

RETURN TO THE SCENE OF THE CRIME

The criminal's return to the scene of his crime has also been attributed to his unconscious need to confess. Although rapists seldom return to the homes of their victims to repeat the rape, a few do so and may return again and again until their almost inevitable arrest. The mass murderer Kurten, who raped some of his victims, has recorded his pleasure in returning to the scene of one of his murders.

"Next evening I went back to the spot and thought over where I could bury the body. I thought how nice it would be if I had something of the kind to go and sit by when I took a walk. I dug a deep hole in a woody corner of the field. I took the body and laid it just as one would lay an ordinary corpse in a grave. . . . I had a feeling of solemn tenderness all the time. I stroked her hair and shoveled in the first spadeful of earth very evenly and carefully. . . . I went to the grave many times afterwards and kept on improving it. Later on I must have been to the spot at least thirty times, and every time when I thought of what was lying there I had a feeling of satisfaction" (Wagner).

Chapter 7

GROUP RAPE.

"Birds of a feather will gather together."
— Robert Burton, *Anatomy of Melancholy*

GROUP rape is an especially terrifying and humiliating experience for a woman. The girl who is seized as she is walking home on a dark street and forced into a car by several men is usually too frightened to resist, and if she does, her efforts are more likely to result in injury than escape from her fate. In fear of her life she will probably be .made to participate in perverse sexual acts which add to her humiliation.

Group rape is much more frequent than is generally recognized. Sixteen per cent of the victims in Denmark (Svalastoga), 18.5 per cent in Denver, 43 per cent in Philadelphia (Amir), 50 per cent in Toronto (Mohr) and about 66 per cent in Finland (Antilla *et al.*) were raped by groups of two or more men. A recent drastic increase in the number of rapes in Finland from 144 in 1950 to 371 in 1966 has been attributed to an increase in the number of juvenile offenders associated with an increase in the proportion of juveniles in the population. Some studies have shown that younger offenders are more likely to be involved in group rapes than are older offenders.

Ten per cent of the victims in Denmark, 8.5 per cent in Denver, 16 per cent in Philadelphia and 28.5 per cent in Toronto were raped by groups of two offenders (sometimes referred to as pair offenders). Six per cent of the victims in Denmark, 10 per cent in Denver, 21.4 per cent in Toronto and 26.5 per cent in Philadelphia were raped by groups of three or more offenders.

In both Philadelphia and Toronto 71 per cent of the rape offenders were involved in group rapes, compared with 38 per cent in Denver. Group rapes involving two offenders accounted for 12.6 per cent of the rape offenders in Denver, 16 per cent in Philadelphia and 21 per cent in Toronto. Group rapes involving three or more offenders accounted for 25.7 per cent of the offenders in Denver, 50 per cent in Toronto and 55 per cent in Philadelphia.

A common pattern of group rape in Denver consists of a group of three or four youths, usually Spanish-Americans, who pick up one or two Spanish-American girls outside their homes, on the street or at an amusement park. They persuade the girls to go in their car for a ride or to visit a hamburger stand. After stopping to pick up other companions and beer or wine, they will drive into the mountains or to a suitable lonely location. The girls will be encouraged or forced to drink alcohol, smoke marihauna or take drugs and then forcibly raped.

The girls will be returned to their homes and they tell their parents that they were abducted and raped. They claim that they were forced into the car at gun or knife point. Skillful interviewing or a lie detector test at the police department leads to an admission that they entered the car voluntarily. Occasionally one of the girls has had prior sexual experiences with one member of the group.

Another pattern of group rape is for the youths to call at a girl's home. One member of the group claims to know a brother or cousin of the girl's brother. Once inside the home, they take advantage of the absence of the parents and other family members to rape the girl. Sometimes the girl goes to the home of a girl friend. There she finds a group of boys who tell her that her girl friend is out but is expected back shortly. She is encouraged to come in and wait for her friend. One or more of the boys who are high on marihuana or alcohol start making suggestive remarks. The girl becomes uncomfortable and starts to leave but is taken to a bedroom and raped.

Young girls who go to a drinking party in a home after school soon find, as they probably anticipated, that petting is a feature of the party. One girl will be taken around the house by one of the boys. A petting session in a bedroom ends up in group rape while the party continues in the living room.

The young woman at a drinking party who consumes too much alcohol and remains long after all the other girls have left may find that the men take advantage of the situation. Often the girl reports the group rape to the police but later refuses to prosecute, doubtless because she is aware of the damage to her reputation which might result from cross-examination on the extent of her drinking and on her behavior prior to the group rape.

Another pattern of group rape involves women who have been drinking in a tavern. The victim may be seized by several men as she leaves the tavern and driven away in their car. Sometimes two or three women who are together will be offered a ride home. One woman, two if there are three women, will be driven to their homes, but the last woman in the car will be driven to a suitable location and raped by all the men as in the following example:

> I went out with my girl friend Barbara; first we went to a tavern, then we went to a party. The party was too crowded, so we went to this club about half an hour before closing time. A soldier introduced himself to me; he said his name was Bob. The other guy with him said they came from Fort Carson and were staying for the weekend. Bob kept asking me if I wanted to party some more after we left here. I said I was supposed to be home and usually didn't stay this long.
>
> I fast danced with him and when we were getting ready to leave he asked Barbara if we had a ride home. She said no, so he asked me could he take us home. Barbara said yes, so we started out to the car. A guy was drunk asleep in the back seat, another was standing by the door. They pushed the drunk one up, then Bob got in the back and I got in sitting next to him. Then the driver got in,

Barbara sat in the middle in the front. Then Bob said, "Get straight men, there are women present," so the drunk one sat up straight.

The driver said to Barbara, "Where do you live?" She told him, so they took her there. She got out and the driver walked her to the door. He got back in and said, "Where do you live?" I told him and he said, "You'll have to direct me." So I directed him, then Bob put his arm around me. I sat up, he pulled me back and said, "I want you." "Don't take her home, man." Then the one in the front seat said, "Man, let me drive." Instead of turning where I said, he went the other way. I started screaming, then Bob held one hand on my neck and the other on my head and started kissing me. The more I screamed the more he squeezed my neck.

The man sitting next to Bob said, "Knock her out, man." But he didn't, he kept saying, "I'm going to get you." Then they drove up to this motel. They got out of the car and Bob told them to wait in the motel. He threw me down and had a hand over my mouth and the other hand taking my pants, then my panties off. Then he put his nasty penis into my vagina. Then the other two came out and said "Let's bring her in." Bob carried me in and said, "You'd better be quiet." I started crying louder but it didn't seem to do no good. They put me on the bed.

So the next one was the drunk, he said, "Make it." I told them to let me go home that I was getting bad pains in the abdomen. The drunk one said, "Make it, it's my turn. Take your clothes off." I said no, so he took them off and laid on me. He said, "Kiss me." I didn't and he hit me on the side of my head. He put his nasty penis in my vagina. The other two walked in on him and he told them to wait in the bathroom until he was finished, so they did. I never stopped crying. I said, "Why me? Why don't you get someone who is willing, like a prostitute?"

Then Bob said, "We don't want no prostitute. We want you. We go out for what we want, and I want you." Then the last one said, "It's my turn, go get some hamburgers." So the other two left and he said, "What do you want from me?" I said, "Take me home, please." He said, "They took the car, make another suggestion." I said, "Let me run." He said, "Go." I started up and he pushed me back on the bed. He said, "I'm not going to touch you." I said, "I don't have any money." He said, "You wouldn't have enough." Then he came closer and started kissing me. I started screaming and never stopped until the others came back. They carried me back to the car and drove me home.

Occasionally a girl will be seized as she is walking home alone in the evening and forced into a car. She is warned not to cry out under threat of physical violence and is driven to a deserted spot where she is raped by the three or four men in the car. In the case described on page 20 a woman and her boyfriend were both forced into a car and the man was knifed and otherwise intimidated so that he could not come to her aid.

A not infrequent pattern is for a man who has had prior sexual relations with a girl to set her up for rape by some of his friends. The man invites the girl to a party. On arrival she finds that no other girls are present and if she expresses concern, she will be told that others are expected to arrive shortly. After some drinking she is forcibly raped by all present except her boyfriend. His companions go through the motions of threatening him with a gun to prevent his intervention on behalf of the girl, who usually has no idea of his role in the group rape. She is threatened with bodily injury or death if she reports the rape to the police.

If despite these threats she does inform the police, she will often omit mentioning that her boyfriend was present. She will make up a story of abduction in the street by complete strangers and will say she was taken to the house where the rape occurred. Extensive police investigation may bring to light the true story and then the girl or her parents will decide to withdraw the charges of rape. One girl later admitted to the police that her boyfriend played an active role. "I lied, my boyfriend was in on it. It was no kidnapping. He was the first one [to have sexual intercourse]."

Girls with a reputation for promiscuity are likely victims of group rape. A group of school boys or youths who have recently graduated from school seize the girl at a dance or as she leaves her job as a carhop at a hamburger stand and later rape her. A twenty-year-old girl who was known to have had sexual relations with many men was abducted by a group of school boys and raped. She was extremely upset by the incident and informed the police. The boys were arrested and she was charged with contributing to the delinquency of minors.

In group rape situations, especially when the girl has joined the men of her own free will, the decision to rape the girl may not be made until some time after the girl joined the group. When the girl is told what is about to take place, it is not unusual for one or more men to leave the group because they do not wish to be involved. They seldom take any steps to help the girl. The man who does not wish to participate may be afraid to leave.

The reluctant rapist, fearful of the scorn of his companions, or of physical violence at the hands of the group leader, may whisper to the girl that he is not going to assault her. "I don't want to do this, but Nick will stab me if I don't." Frequently a member of the group has difficulty in obtaining an erection, especially if others are watching. Usually he is unceremoniously pushed aside after a brief time by impatient companions, including others who have already raped the girl and wish to repeat their performance.

A group of Negroes who raped a white girl took photographs of some of the rapes and warned the girl that if she told anyone about the rapes they would give the pictures to the Black Panthers for publication in their newspaper. They also said they would send pictures to her mother and blow up her house.

In group rapes there may be some degree of privacy. Only one man at a time remains in the room or car with the girl. Initially all may be present to help subdue the girl should she attempt to resist. Resistance, however, is unusual as the girl is intimidated by the number of men arrayed against her and also by the threats of physical violence. Alcohol and drugs play a significant role in group rapes. Almost invariably the men have been drinking. Nine of the twenty group-rape victims in Denver had been drinking prior to the rape.

Upon hearing the knock at my door, I [a thirty-year-old divorced woman] woke up, got out of bed and went to the door. I looked through the glass and at first I didn't see anyone. I started back to bed and heard a knock again and I looked out and saw a guy I know named Butch. I let him in and I'd started to the bathroom when I heard him saying, "Come in." I turned and saw another kid. Then three others came in one by one. They looked very young to me and I asked Butch why he brought them here. He knew I didn't like to be around a whole bunch of guys.

Butch asked for smokes and someone held out some brown cigarettes and asked me if I wanted one. I asked what they were and they laughed. I had been looking at their faces to determine for myself what was going on and I noticed their eyes seemed glassy to me. "Is that grass?" I asked; again dumb laughs. By this time two in leather jackets were sitting by me on the sectional. The guy sitting to my left said something to the effect of "Get her, Butch." His face was expressionless and I looked down wondering if they were going to smoke grass when I felt a hot flash over my right eye.

He hit me again in some place and I remember saying, "Butch, what are they doing to me?" Because the two in leather jackets were trying to hold me down by my legs while I was attempting to get up from the couch. My nose began bleeding from the repeated blows Butch gave me and I said, "Stop hitting me, why are you making me bleed? What do you guys want?" No one answered, Butch kept punching me and I said "Do you want sex?"

Then they talked. "Yeah, right." I begged them to quit hitting me and I would give in. Then two guys said, "Leave her alone, Butch," and it seemed like three guys were going to go on me at once. I said, "Not in front of everyone, please. Not all at once." Butch grabbed my arm and said, "Alright, where?" I pointed to my bedroom. He took me in the room and turned on the light and I pleaded for the light to go off. He turned it off and told me to take off my pants. I didn't respond fast enough I guess so he started hitting me in the face again until I told him I couldn't if he kept hitting me, so he stopped.

He then told me to get on the bed and lay on my back. By then he was naked too. He raped me, then he told me to eat him and again I didn't move fast enough and he hit me again. Then he tried for my rectum. I held my buttocks tight so he hit me. I tried to stay quiet as I could and he hit me again. Then he asked if I was cherry there and I said yes. He seemed to understand and he said "Just relax." Soon he had me roll on my back and he finished in my vagina. He got dressed and told me to stay there.

I got up and the two in leather jackets came in. I turned to leave and Butch hit me in the head again and told me to get back on the bed. I asked if I could go to the bathroom. Seeing the front door open, I bolted and ran out. Butch said, "Grab her," by then I was outside and I don't know who chased me but I made it to my neighbors. They streamed out running to their car. Butch sauntered out and made like he wasn't in a hurry and the car left and sped off.

Some group rapes are planned beforehand, although the victim may not be selected at the planning stage. Thus the group may cruise the streets in their car in search of a suitable woman for rape. Other group rapes are committed on impulse following the suggestion of a member of the group. This is likely to occur when the men are in the company of a woman who is without female companions. A man who picks up a girl in a street or at a tavern may drive her to the homes of some of his friends in order to have others to aid in the rape.

The leader of the group is usually the man who suggests commission of the offense and he is usually the first to attack and the first to rape the victim. Often he is the most brutal assailant but not invariably. Indeed he may restrain some of his associates from hurting the woman.

Group rapes usually consist of from three to five offenders. Altogether there were sixty-five men involved in the twenty group rapes in the Denver study. Gang rapes may involve twenty or more offenders.

GANG RAPES

"Pleasures afford more delight when shared with others;
to enjoy them in solitude is a dreary thing."
— Dio Chrysostom, *Third Discourse in Kingship*

"Gang-bangs" or "lineups" are a feature of the social life of youthful street gangs in the larger cities. Over forty years ago Thrasher described a gang rape in Chicago.

> A Jewish girl, eighteen years of age, on her way home from work flirted with two young men and finally accepted a ride. Instead of driving her home, they stopped in front of a poolroom where soft drinks were served and coaxed her to come inside.
> This was the hangout of a gang of about seventeen Italian boys ranging in age from seventeen to twenty-one. The door was locked and the girl was attacked by six or seven of the group. The proprietor of the poolroom in the meantime called up the remainder of the gang, seventeen in all, and the girl was attacked by this number within an hour. The girl was three months in a hospital before she recovered. The men were sent to the Joliet penitentiary.

Yablonsky, in his study *The Violent Gang,* notes that for the violent-gang boy a close, warm relationship with a female entailing mutual responsibility and empathy is rare. He describes three extreme patterns of sexual behavior:

1. *"Gang-bangs".* A promiscuous female is "lined up" and often as many as fifteen or twenty boys will indulge themselves with her in some form of sexual act. The "victim" is generally a mentally defective or severely disturbed girl, sometimes violated by forcible rape. The assault may occur on one occasion, or may be repeated over several days.

2. *"Idolatrous" love.* The gang youth romantically "falls in love" and fantasizes a perfect female ideal. The allusion by another gang member that "his girl" is prone to promiscuous relations produces an explosive response. The "boyfriend" attempts to maintain an illusion of virginity and perfection about his girl friend that is usually in conflict with the facts. Here again he relates, not in significant human interaction, but on what approaches an unfeeling fantasy level.

3. *Overt disdain.* In this pattern there is an overt disdain for girls, combined with homosexual overtones. Exploitation of girls is used for "rep" making and ego gratification. The girl becomes a target for hostility and physical brutality which, when reported back to the gang, confers prestige on the violator. "Why waste your time with broads?" "You can't trust them," "I belted her a few times" are common expressions that reflect the gang's general opinion.

PUBERTY RITES AND GANG RAPES

Many primitive societies have puberty rites which prepare the adolescent youth for the responsibilities of manhood. These rites usually require the youth to undergo some painful experience to prove his courage. Circumcision is frequently a painful feature of these rites, but among the Kikuyu tribes of Kenya a more pleasurable demand is made of the youths who are required to perform the act of ceremonial rape. The youths wander the countryside in bands, usually well away from their homes. The object of each band is to find a woman who must be of married status and a stranger to them, on whom to commit rape.

The ideal woman, according to Lambert, would be of the Kamba tribe, which was persistently at enmity with the Kikuyu, but failing a Kamba or other foreign woman a Kikuyu from a distant area would serve. As suitable women were not readily available, the first one caught would be raped by each of them and by any other bands who might be attracted by her screams. The initiate who failed to prove his manhood could never have lawful intercourse with a Kikuyu woman.

Fortunately for the unfortunate victims, in practice the ceremonial rape was ritually reduced for most of the band, to a masturbatory ejaculation on the woman's body or in her presence. Immediately after performing the act, each youth threw away the wooden earlobe plug and bundle of sticks which indicate the status of neophyte. Lambert notes that a plea of *kuihaka muunyu* (ceremonial rape) would not have been considered by a native court a sufficient answer to a charge of rape, if the woman's guardian was inconsiderate enough to make that charge.

Bloch and Niederhoffer suggest that "informal rituals of contemporary adolescent gangs are very similar to puberty rites in primitive society and represent spontaneous attempts to find psychologically supportive devices to assist the maturing male to weather the crisis of adolescence. When adolescent youths, as in our own society, find it difficult to enter the adult status, for reasons of delay, social or technical obstacles, or because of the lack of an orderly facilitating process, they will attempt to embrace the symbolic equivalents of the adult behavior denied them. . . .

"Thus, the adolescent drinking, sexual escapades, wild automobile rides, immature assertiveness, violent reactions to parental restraints, protests against authority, and the other forms of intransigence which, to the youth at any rate, appear to be the prerogatives of the mature adult. . . . Thus, we may conceive of much of gang practice and the spontaneous, informal rituals of gang behavior as arising because our culture has been unable, or has refused, to meet the adolescent's needs during a critical juncture in his life."

MOTORCYCLE GANGS

Members of motorcycle gangs such as Hell's Angels and the Devil's Disciples are usually much older than members of the youthful street gangs of the larger cities. Victims of their "gang-bangs" are seldom chance victims seized as they are walking along a street. Usually they are girls who have sought out the company of the gang, and many of them have indicated readiness to participate in sexual intercourse. Some of them do not always appreciate the fact that desire for intercourse with one member of the gang is accepted as willingness for intercourse with other gang members. Thus they become ready victims for rape, but they may find it difficult on account of their character and reputation, to seek redress in court.

The following case illustrates the humiliation which motorcycle gangs inflict on their victims, in this case a nineteen-year-old girl.

There were other boys there and about five girls. Merv said to me, "You gotta turn out for us or we'll punch you." I asked him what he meant and he said, "You're going to have to hole with all of us tonight." I've heard that phrase before, it means intercourse. I told him I didn't go for that and to let me out. Then one of them grabbed me and pulled me in the bedroom. Merv said, "Hey, get her to drink this and it'll be easier." Then one of them said, "There's going to be a turnout, go get everyone."

I drank the beer. They told me I had taken LSD and I could call it acid. I kept trying to get away but one was standing at the door. There was no way I could get out. The one at the door said, "Let me punch her. I haven't punched any broad for a long time." Merv told him no, to be cool. They started pulling off my clothes and I fought them, but they told me if I didn't do as they wanted, they would punch me to death. They pushed me on the bed. One of them kept hitting me on the legs.

Merv finally managed to take all my clothes off. He said he wanted me to be his old lady and he started singing, "Look it, isn't she one of the sights." Merv pulled me up toward the pillow on the bed. He got on top of me and rolled over me. He laid beside me, one leg over me so I couldn't move. One of them brought some cake back into the bedroom. They took pieces of the cake and put it inside my vagina and started to lick the cake out of my vagina. About six of them did this.

At the beginning of this one or two of them held my legs spread apart while each individual one shoved his piece of cake into my vagina. After that was all through, Merve said he wanted to give me a "header." He unbuckled his pants, then he took out his penis and he forced me to kiss it and put it inside my mouth. I kept telling him to leave me alone, but he wouldn't. He kept making me to use my mouth until he climaxed, but he didn't climax in my mouth.

Red was second. He made me use my mouth until he climaxed. They would climax over themselves because I pulled away. I'm not sure the number that made me do it. While I would do it to one, the rest were sitting around drinking beer and wine and watching. They would pour beer and wine over me and would lick it up. After that each one pulled his jeans down and had intercourse with me.

I just remember seeing different faces on top of me. I would know each one that had intercourse with me if I saw them again. As soon as one would climax, another would get on me. After they had all had intercourse with me, they all left the room. I put my clothes on and started to leave. Merv said he'd take me home. They were all members of motorcycle gangs. He told me again he wanted me to be his old lady.

Perverse sexual acts are a feature of motorcycle gang "rapes." The pilot's wing insignia on the jackets of gang members come in red for having engaged in cunnilingus with a menstruating woman, black for cunnilingus with a Negro woman, and brown for sodomy. An excellent account of the sexual behavior of the Hell's Angels is reported by Hunter S. Thompson in Chapter 8.

PAIR RAPES

> *"Company, villainous company, hath been*
> *the spoil of me."*
> — Shakespeare, *Henry IV*

As in group rapes, one offender often stands out as the leader and he is usually the first to attack and the first to rape the victim. He may know the victim and he may arrange a meeting with his companion in order to have assistance in the rape. Alternatively the companion may be the one to plan the rape and he may overcome the scruples of the girl's boyfriend. There may be no planning and the rape may occur on impulse under favorable circumstances.

A twenty-one-year-old girl complained to police that she was kidnapped while attending a party and later raped by a man and his companion.

It was so stuffy and hot in the house that I went outside to sit for a while.

George came out and sat beside me and told me that he liked me. I said, "Thank you." He asked if I would go out with him and I told him, "Sorry, I've already got a man." He said that it didn't matter we could still go together and I told him I was going to another party. He didn't reply to that statement but changed the subject and asked if I'd ever felt so low as to die. I told him that I didn't think about such things and he said that he did, and that when he was ready to die he'd like to take someone with him.

I told him that some day he'd probably find someone and he said, "I already have." When he said that I got scared and started to leave. As I started to leave, he placed both of his hands around my neck so tight that I thought I was going to die right there. He dragged me to his car which was two or three cars away from the house. We got in the car through the driver's side. Then he said to keep quiet or he would kill me.

I moved toward the door on the other side of the car. I opened the door and he grabbed hold of me. He said not to do that again or he'd kill me. Then he hit me in the face with his fist and I was crying. We drove one car length and then this other fellow, Mike, appeared and got in the back seat. George told Mike to get the knife out to kill me if I screamed anymore. Mike passed something to George, I didn't see what it was.

Then Mike started ripping off my clothes from the back seat. Then he got in the front seat and finished ripping off my clothes until he had removed all my clothes. Then George stopped the car, they had kept me down on the seat so I don't know where we stopped. Mike started to insert his finger in my vagina. They took turns doing this to me. I kept screaming, I didn't know what to do. George sucked my vagina with his mouth. The other guy wanted to try it, so George quit.

Then Mike tried, but couldn't get between my legs. While Mike was trying to do this, George made me hold his penis. At that time I opened the door of the car and screamed for help. They pulled me back in the car. Then they decided to change positions. George tried to rape me. Mike told me to suck his penis, and told me that if I bit him that would be the end, and that if I didn't suck his penis, they would kill me like the other girl. Mike started hitting me, so I had to do it.

I think the one that was having sexual intercourse reached a climax because he asked me if I could feel his juice. Then they decided to stop because it was getting light and the cars were driving around. Mike wanted to let me go and George wanted to kill me. I jumped out of the car and ran off carrying my clothes.

RACE AND GROUP RAPE

When the relative proportions of racial and ethnic groups in Denver were considered, it was found that there was less than half the expected number of white group offenders, two and one-half times the expected number of Negro group offenders and over six times the expected number of Spanish-American group offenders. The Negro group-offender rate was six times and the *Spanish-American group-offender rate over fifteen times the white group offender rate.* Thirty-three of the eighty-six Spanish-American rape offenders were involved in group rapes.

There was half the expected number of white victims of group rape, almost twice the expected number of Negro victims and over five and one-half times the expected number of Spanish-American victims of group rape. In Denver Spanish-American women are over ten times more likely to be the victims of rape by a group of men than are white women. Negro girls are over three times more likely to be raped by a group of men than are white women. Thus in Denver Spanish-Americans are more likely to appear as offenders or victims in group rape than are whites or Negroes.

RACE AND PAIR RAPE

When the relative proportions of racial and ethnic groups in Denver were considered, it was found that there was less than half the expected number of white pair offenders, over three times the expected number of Negro pair offenders and five and one-half times the expected number of Spanish-American offenders. The Negro pair-offender rate was seven and one-half times, and *the Spanish-American pair-offender rate twelve and one-half times the white pair offender rate.* Fourteen of the eighty-six Spanish-American rape offenders were involved in pair rapes.

There were almost three times as many Spanish-American victims of pair rape as would be expected, considering their proportion in the population. Spanish-American girls are over three times more likely to be victims of pair rapes than white girls. Curiously there were no Negro victims of pair-rape offenders.

AGES OF OFFENDERS

Analysis of offenders was made by five-year age classifications. It was found that solitary offenders and groups of three or more offenders have their highest incidence between ages twenty and twenty-four and their second highest incidence between ages twenty-five and twenty-nine. Groups of two (pair) offenders have their highest incidence between twenty-five and twenty-nine and their second highest incidence between ages twenty and twenty-four. In the age classification fifteen to nineteen years, the percentage of offenders was highest in groups of three or more offenders (23%) and lowest in solitary offenders (12.5%). Groups of two offenders were second highest (18.8%). This finding may be explained by the greater need of younger offenders for assistance in carrying out this crime (see Table V).

AGES OF VICTIMS

Analysis of victims was made by five-year age classifications. Victims of solitary and pair offenders have their highest incidence between twenty and twenty-four and their second highest between fifteen and nineteen. Victims

TABLE V

AGES OF RAPE OFFENDERS
(in per cent)

AGE	OFFENDERS		
	Solitary	*Group of Two*	*Group of Three or More*
	(N. 136*)	*(N. 32)*	*(N. 65)*
Under 15	–	–	1.5
15-19	12.5	18.8	23.0
20-24	34.6	31.3	33.8
25-29	21.3	34.4	24.6
30-34	8.8	9.4	9.2
35-39	12.5	–	3.0
40-44	4.4	–	3.0
45-49	2.9	3.1	–
50-54	1.5	–	1.5
55-59	.7	3.1	–
60 +	.7	–	–

*Ages were not available on twenty solitary offenders.

of three or more offenders have their highest incidence between fifteen and nineteen and their second highest between twenty and twenty-four. In pair rapes half the victims were the same age or younger than the offenders and half the victims were older than the offenders. In rapes by three or more offenders almost three out of four of the victims were younger than the offenders (see Table VI).

Rape

TABLE VI

AGES OF VICTIMS
(in per cent)

AGE	VICTIMS OF		
	Solitary Offenders (N. 163)	*Group of Two Offenders (N. 17)*	*Group of Three or More Offenders (N. 20)*
Under 15	13.5	5.9	20
15-19	24.5	17.6	40
20-24	25.8	29.4	25
25-29	9.8	17.6	
30-34	8.0		5
35-39	4.9	5.9	
40-44	4.3	11.8	5
45-49	1.2	11.8	
50-54	3.1		
55-59	2.4		
60 +	2.4		5

Chapter 8

HOMICIDE AND RAPE

"Murder most foul, as in the best it is;
But this most foul, strange and unnatural."
— Shakespeare, *Hamlet*

Rapists seldom murder their victims. It is difficult to obtain statistics on rape-murders as the offenders are usually charged with murder and the associated rape is not listed in court or penitentiary statistics. Force used to subdue the woman may result in death, although this outcome may not have been intended by the assailant. Pressure on the neck of the victim, insufficient to cause strangulation, may cause death from reflex causes. The offender, either deliberately or in panic, may kill in order to avoid detection as in the following case.

A twenty-five-year-old man who was not on speaking terms with his wife spent Saturday afternoon drinking with a buddy. He had been feeling depressed that day because of a quarrel with his wife. During the evening he returned home to obtain his rifle, but exchanged no words with his wife. After visiting several bars he drove to a lake where he swam for about an hour. After this he shot one or two rabbits that were caught in the lights of his car. He drove around aimlessly and finally drove alongside a dam. On a sudden impulse he shot at the headlights, tires and windows of a car which was parked there. "I guess I was angry, I can't remember now what it was. It wasn't exactly anger, I kind of felt tense." He did not think there was anyone in the car and he was surprised to find two young couples huddled inside.

At gunpoint he robbed the men of their wallets; and as he feared they might attack him while he was turning his car around, he decided to take one of the girls as a hostage. The girl he chose, a slim attractive blonde, on his instruction drove his car farther into the mountains. After about forty-five minutes they were forced to stop because of a flat tire. He then raped her. While he was changing the tire, the girl ran down the road which was illuminated by the headlights.

"I hollered at her to stop. She didn't, I panicked, got scared or something, I fired twice. With a rifle I'm an expert, I aimed right at her head — her blonde hair showed out better than anything else — that's what I shot at. I wanted to stop her, I didn't want her to run away. I went out, she was kind of kicking, one of her legs was moving, I shot her again. I felt her pulse. If I felt it once, I felt it a dozen times. I must have killed her instantly. I knew I

173

had to hide her then. As far as thinking about the law, I wasn't thinking about the law; I never thought about the consequences till it was all over. I've imagined that this is all a bad dream. I knew I done this, but I can't make myself believe I did it."

After burying the body some eight hundred feet up a steep slope in the mountains, he remained there for three or four hours wondering what he should do. He then drove to Wyoming, where he decided to return to his home in Colorado and "get it over." He realized, correctly, that his car would be traced, and he was arrested the following day. Within thirty minutes he confessed the crime and later he led the officers to the burial spot, since he thought his victim deserved a decent burial.

On psychiatric examination he cooperated readily. He appeared depressed over his situation and expressed considerable remorse for his crime.

A rather taciturn man, he described himself as a person who preferred to get on with the job rather than talk about it. "I never speak my opinion on anything. I just go along with the crowd. I'm not one to judge other people. What other people do is their business. It's hard to get me mad; I seldom argue." Review of his personal history revealed that he was smaller than other children of his age and this always made him "feel out of place." He complained that the older school children used to pick on him. At ten years of age he became very friendly with a blonde girl; they always liked to do things together. It was agreed some years later that they would marry when they were old enough. At the age of seventeen he returned home after a week's absence to learn that his girl friend had married another man. At first he could not believe the news and when he realized it was true he became very angry. "I could have strangled her at the time, I really got mad at her. After she jilted me, I didn't have anything to do with blonde girls."

A year later he married a girl who was about the complete opposite of his former girl friend in appearance and character. The marriage was not a success. There were three children of the marriage. Since his wife did not want any more children, he underwent a sterilization operation. Although he denied any regrets about this operation, the psychological effects of this operation may have been of some importance.

Although he blamed himself for the failure of the marriage, he complained that his wife was moody and sexually cold. There had been no sexual relations for the three months preceeding the tragedy. They seldom argued, but for periods of up to a week at a time they would hardly exchange a word. Following one argument he fired seven or eight shots at his mother-in-law's picture which was hanging on the wall of the living room. Following another argument he drove to the dam where he later abducted the girl and swallowed the contents of a bottle of his wife's sleeping tablets. He was discovered unconscious and rushed to a hospital.

Psychological test results were reported as follows: "Basic feelings of inadequacy were present. While he has strong wishes to be successful and assertive, he feels very incapable of attaining these. He has marked feelings of deprivation, together with much underlying anger at being deprived. He tends to react to situations in a passive-dependent manner. Interpersonal relationships are perceived by him as being very conflicted, particularly relationships between men and women. While he does not appear to be able to relate well to others, he has difficulty in expressing his anger overtly. His general conflict seemed to be one in which he was too angry to get along with others, yet too dependent to stand alone."

It is significant that his victim closely resembled his former girl friend. He claimed that the resemblance did not occur to him until after his arrest. It is likely that his crime has unconscious determinants in his anger at his rejecting wife and his deep resentment toward his former childhood sweetheart. It is of interest that twice following arguments with his wife he drove to the same dam: the first time his hostile impulses were turned on himself in the form of a determined attempt at suicide; the second time his anger found expression in shooting up an apparently unoccupied car and later in rape and murder.

He was found guilty of murder in the first degree and sentenced to life imprisonment.

The psychological origins of rape combined with homicidal aggression were reviewed in Chapter six. Hyatt Williams, who has treated a number of rape-murderers, emphasizes the phenomena of splitting, shown by a predominance of destructive cruelty in an individual who at another time may show love, devotion and compassion, and projective identification in which aspects of the offender are seen in the victim. (See Williams' case history below of a man with a long history of sexual crime, including rape and finally murder.) Alternately there may be an explosive element within the personality which erupts with homicidal violence; the victim who is raped and murdered may represent a hated mother or sister. All the rapists seen by this writer showed feelings of inferiority and unconscious feminine tendencies.

CASE OF B*

This man, whom we shall call B, was twenty-six years of age when he was convicted for the murder of a late middle-aged woman whom he strangled while giving her a lift in a truck he was driving. B had a long history of delinquency which included rape, attempted rape and an episode of violence against men and property while in the Forces overseas. Then he had been rejected by a girl and in the rage which followed he got drunk, was affronted

*Reprinted from Rape-Murder by Arthur Hyatt Williams, M.D. In *Sexual Behavior and the Law* by Ralph Slovenko, with the permission of Doctor Williams and Charles C Thomas, Publisher.

by someone and then ran amok and perpetrated indiscriminate violence, hitting a man over the head with a bottle and smashing up the bar. This seemed to represent an attack upon the young brother of his childhood and then upon the bar representing the breasts in the early feeding situation. The difference between these crimes of violence was in its more apparent object only, the underlying factors being very much the same as in the crimes directed against women.

B was a short, strong, muscular man. His mother and father were living. He was the eldest of a family of six, there being a young brother, three sisters and then two brothers. He showed strong loyalty and devotion to his family and to anyone who became his friend, and ruthless destructive enmity to anyone who had attacked or affronted him in any way. This polarized relationship consisting of idealized good persons and denigrated and even daemonified bad persons prevaded all his human relationships. Early in therapy he showed himself to be a strong lover of truth and he would go over and over a piece of information until it was felt to be true both in external and internal reality. Nevertheless, he was a violent man who could become a murderer when affronted by a slight or insult from anyone, be he prison official or fellow prisoner. B had a considerable tendency to nurse grievances, sometimes for long periods, but also he cherished, nurtured and was able to act upon feelings of gratitude. He could be generous and devoted as well as savagely destructive. Before discussion and attempted elucidation of the contradictory aspects of his character a summary of his life situation will be given.

B was a slightly premature baby; he developed a rather poor breast-feeding situation followed by bottle feeding when he became a hungry and voracious feeder. At the age of eight years he was evacuated with his brother eighteen months his junior and after several disturbing changes of foster home he was billeted upon a farm. The austere and forbidding foster mother singled out B for dislike, deprivation and rebuke while giving the younger boy such affection and good things as could be squeezed out of her grudging personality. B gave way to open jealousy of his brother only once. It was when the latter was allowed to ride a large farm horse, an indulgence ruthlessly denied to B. At school he showed the first signs of femininity playing games with the girls and avoiding the fights and rough and tumbles of the boys. He remembers wishing he had been born a girl. Masculinity was equated with aggressiveness, naughtiness and trouble. On one occasion after a particularly severe scolding from his foster-mother and while still fugitive from her piercing and accusing eyes, he decided to run away, and was pursued by villagers who hounded him down like a animal. When he was exhausted, he dived into a bed of nettles despite being lightly clad, and was stung from head to foot. That was the end of the chase and he was taken back. Soon the swelling caused by the nettle stings became so alarming that his mother had to be summoned to visit him.

When B eventually returned from wartime evacuation to his home, he appeared to adjust comparatively well, but his mother noticed that he had developed a quiet and remorseless side to his character. At puberty he made advances towards first one then to another of his three sisters, who rebuffed his attempts but decided not to tell their parents of his activities because, apart from his sexual advances, he was such a kind and likeable brother. He made advances to other girls, attempted to rape an adolescent girl and finally at seventeen he was convicted for the rape of a young adult woman. The crime in fact was not rape, as the woman helped him to have intercourse and then asked him to stay with her. He suspected a plan to trap him and escaped from her. She was offended and reported the assault as rape. He did not dispute her evidence, as his intention had been to rape her.

Early in treatment it was realized that B was at his most hostile and dangerous when he felt deprived. Deprivation was felt when he was left and then later became important in the transference relationship as it flared up and became almost uncontrollable whenever the therapist was ill or on leave. Rejection, devaluation, absence and sometimes criticism, if felt to be motivated by hostility, were regarded as affronts. Grievances were nursed and revengeful toll exacted. At this point a particular *modus operandi* was typical. If offended by a loved person, the act of vengeance would be enacted upon a scapegoat, otherwise it would be inflicted directly upon the persecutor. It became apparent that he had a tender and compassionate side to his personality as well as a murderously aggressive and destructive one. This problem had afflicted him for most of his life. A childhood incident will illustrate this point. He had returned from being evacuated and along a river bank he found a wounded dove. He tried to repair its broken wing and leg but without success. He could not tolerate the sad-eyed reproach of the dove's unblinking eyes, felt the bird to be irreparable and so killed it. The guilty feelings which developed were very painful and he felt haunted by the reproachful eyes of the dying bird. The link here was with the good mother in both external and internal aspects, but mainly the latter whom he had lost during the period of war-time separation owing to evacuation. Inside him her kind eyes had been replaced by the piercing, accusing, persecutory eyes of the bad foster mother.

One way in which he attempted unconsciously to cope with his savage destructive part was by becoming intensely feminine and by denying the masculine part of himself to which he ascribed all the intense destructive and aggressive activities. During late adolescence he experienced a homosexual phase in which he felt himself to be a girl both psychologically and sexually. He adopted a girl's name, which he realized later was that of his mother. It was as if he had become totally possessed by the internalized woman so that the masculine components of his personality were obliterated. During this phase he had felt attracted as a woman to men, had been passive in homosexual relationships, had dressed as a young woman down to the most meticulous detail of dress and makeup and had enjoyed the whole procedure as a strange and largely unreal experience. He felt sad and forlorn that he should be unable to have real breasts. When a boy complained of their small size, he whispered the hope that they might grow in time, but he was wounded and reproached by the remark. Eventually the feminine phase broke down when he had relationships with a cruel man during which he seemed to incorporate and therefore be possessed by a cruel penis.

During therapy he developed another intensely feminine phase during which he could be seen to alter facial expression. He had little or no control over the change from masculine to feminine and vice versa but knew when it was taking place. His face would soften and his mouth alter. His voice would become higher and the air of brooding and truculent defiance would wane. A certain wistful sadness would then prevail. His phantasies and dreams became feminine. Again these feminine phases were brought to an end either by aggressive behavior witnessed or suffered. This kind of experience appeared to get inside him. Also, the surge of biological masculinity manifesting itself by erections and nocturnal emissions sometimes made the feminine illusion no longer convincing to him. One of the results of therapy has been the setting of the feminine component against the stronger masculine one, mitigating and softening the brutality of the latter, a process which had not appeared possible previously. He was dominated by powerful feelings of envy of both men and women, standing for father and mother, brothers and sisters and for both masculine and feminine aspects of the therapist. Envy of women was more powerful and fundamental involving as it did his attitude towards the breasts, the genitals, the biological receptivity and the capacity to conceive and bring to viability new human beings inside them. He attempted to deal with these powerful feelings of envy of the woman as well as to mitigate his dangerously aggressive masculine drives by a very full working out of his feminine identification in phantasy and action. Phantasies and feelings of pregnancy occurred and were described in great detail. The working out of a phantasy to the last detail characterized B's masculine as well as his feminine side.

In the masculine phase, aggressive destructiveness mainly but not exclusively directed against females would be mitigated if a woman or girl yielded willingly to his demands and gave generously in response to his needs. Refusal, resulting in deprivation, whether in the external world or worked out in the internal world of phantasy, evoked all the furious destructive and murderous proclivities of B. Each crime he had committed could be related to a refusal or the abandoning of him by an important person. The rape when he was about sixteen was after a girl had rejected him following his emergence from the long spell of feminine identification previously mentioned. An attempted rape in the Services overseas had been when a young woman to whom he had been engaged rejected him after hearing about his criminal record. Also, at this time, his mother had just given birth to another son. The murder took place closely upon the heels of another rejection by a girl. It has already been mentioned that the absences of the therapist were occasions when explosive outbursts occurred. The infantile prototype of the situation which set into motion the powerful unconscious compulsion to reenact the revenge with every repetition of the original rejection and deprivation has not yet been delineated, but the birth of the brother eighteen months his junior and subsequent neglect of B seem to be the most obvious events. Moreover, this brother, handsome, charming and loved by everyone including B himself, by his very qualities contrives to be an object of both jealousy and envy. B's real mother for a long time tended to be idealized, but eventually when he saw the glint of sunlight upon her hair he realized with horror that his mother's hair was like that of the woman he killed. Early in his life there must have been a splitting of the image of mother into a good idealized one and a bad daemonified one. It is clear that during the period of wartime evacuation the real mother was felt to be a good mother but she was away. The actual hostility of the foster mother probably was accentuated by B's sulky truculence. It became easy for B to project the image of bad mother into her and hate her relatively violently. There were murderous feelings which were by no means unconscious and this murderous hatred was not mitigated and detoxicated by the loving feelings he had towards his real mother. Here then in the foster mother he found the first scapegoat and indeed this relationship figured decisively when the scapegoat woman in the image of the bad foster mother was singled out for her murderous fate.

This woman had a peculiar hair winding tic. He had given her a lift once before. The bad foster mother with the piercing eyes had also a hair winding tic. It was thought that this tic was a powerful factor in his choice of this particular woman as his victim by facilitating the projection into her of the image of bad foster mother. She also had piercing eyes and a plaintive voice. It is significant also that his brother had a similar hair winding habit. He gave the woman a lift, intending to rape her and then kill her, but during the struggle his desire to rape her waned and he strangled her. She said to him that she was too old for sexuality and this may well have put him off by unconsciously fitting her into the image of mother too vividly. Some considerable time after the therapist had been told most of the story of the murder, B remembered an important fact. He found that his victim was clutching a sixpenny piece in her hand. He felt that this coin had been intended for him. He was seized by sickening panic and overwhelming remorse as he realized that the daemonified image which he had projected upon and into this aging woman did not really fit his victim but by then she was dead. He nearly gave himself up to the police at this juncture but was able to rationalize his feelings of remorse at least to some extent by the thought that perhaps she had intended the coin as bus fare.

The destructive and aggressive impulses were not always enacted upon a victim but sometimes upon himself. The most dramatic occasion was when he drove a truck into an obstruction with the intention of killing himself. He was intercepted and ordered to stop and so was injured but not killed. During therapy he developed a severe attack of angio-neurotic oedema at a time when the interpretations were so "getting under his skin" that he felt murderous towards the therapist, but also wanted to preserve him. The oedema repeated the incident in which, feeling hunted and haunted, he fled from the farm during wartime evacuation and when at bay, flung himself into a bed of nettles. He showed that the image of the therapist had come to represent not the somewhat idealized real mother of his childhood but the diabolic foster mother with the penetrating eyes. When he was visited by the therapist the linkages between the two aspects of mother and of the therapist were able to be shown and the alarming swelling began to subside.

The predatory relationship which in his masculine phases B displayed consisted mainly of a drive to get for himself objects or rather part objects. This desire for part objects can be demonstrated by recounting one of his daydreams. He owned a woman farm which consisted of a house with an upper floor, a ground floor and a basement. On the upper floor he kept lovely girls to provide for his sexual needs. On the ground floor he kept large breasted girls whose babies had been taken away from them during lactation so that they could provide him with all the milk he could possibly need. The basement was where rebellious and homosexual girls were kept. They were treated cruelly and if recalcitrant subjected to torture, starvation and death. This phantasy shows how different attitudes have to be expressed toward different objects. The girls in the basement were bad because they were rebellious and wanted each other and not him. The girls on the upper floor were for the gratification of the recently acquired more genital masculine needs. Those on the ground floor were for the satisfaction of his oral needs to suck and get milk as nourishment. It is significant that all the girls were in one house. This shows a tendency towards integration but there is still much splitting and compartmentalization in his personality. It is significant that he is still grounded at an oral level; the genital level being above and to be aspired to. Below and base were his feelings towards the devalued denigrated women who were bad because they opposed or refused him.

B was aware that he had profound personality difficulties. He found it painful to contain and attempt to control the violent part of himself and unlike other cases did not have long periods of relief from the explosive pressure of the split-off part of his personality which in fact always threatened to break loose. His attacks upon women whether token actions or major crimes of rape, attempted or actual murder, did relieve the pressure of impulses for a short time only. Even so, remorse and persecutory feelings prevailed during the periods after the crimes had been committed. There were feelings of triumph and omnipotence too, but these were transitory. Whenever guilt became unbearable B became paranoid, angry and destructive. When depressive anxiety derived from concern for objects either external or internally represented, or both, mounted, and became unbearable, a switch to persecutory anxiety took place. Increasing pain occurred when external or particularly internal objects were felt to be irreparable. When persecutory anxiety began to predominate again, further attacks were made upon the internal object causing the pain to mount still further and at this point a violent projection was liable to take place into an external object, usually a scapegoat. The preexistant internal phantasy constellation was then worked out, sometimes in great detail upon the external object as in the case of the actual murder.

After some years of therapy B shows signs of personality integration and the profound disturbance of the internal situation has been mitigated to a marked extent. It is felt that if such an improvement has been possible by means of psychoanalytically orientated psychotherapy in this very disturbed man, the prognosis should be a good deal better with milder cases and improved technique. On the other hand it must be emphasized that B's love of and capacity to face the truth in himself did make him a promising and encouraging case for study and for therapy.

ALBERT DESALVO

> "Albert was truly a remarkable man . . . .
> He was completely lovable to every individual
> while working for me. Never was there any
> deviation from the highest proper sense of
> things."
> — DeSalvo's employer

On June 14, 1962, a fifty-five-year-old woman was found strangled to death in her Boston apartment. On June 30, two women, one sixty-five-years old and the other sixty-eight, were strangled to death in the Boston area. There was no evidence of rape, but all three women had been sexually molested and a bottle had been forced into the vagina of one victim. On August 19, a seventy-five-year-old woman was strangled, and on the following day a sixty-seven-year-old woman was also strangled. By this date the older ladies in Boston had good reason to fear the Boston strangler. In December two girls in their twenties were strangled and sexually assaulted.

The slayings continued in 1963 and 1964. One girl was only nineteen. The victims were strangled in their apartments which showed no signs of forcible entry. They were discovered with a nylon stocking or other article of clothing tied around the neck, nude or partially undressed with evidence of rape or sexual molestation. There were variations on this theme. One victim had a broomstick in her vagina. Two victims were stabbed, and one had twenty-two wounds in her throat and left breast ("She made me feel unclean the way she talked to me.") She had also been strangled. The body of one victim was covered with bedclothes ("She treated me like a man.") Some victims had been gagged and tied.

On October 27, 1964, a young woman was attacked in her apartment, gagged, tied to her bed and molested sexually. Her assailant, who was armed with a knife, left after extracting a promise from her that she would not tell anyone. She informed her husband and the police, who arranged for an artist's sketch of the man based on her description. The sketch resembled thirty-two-year-old Albert DeSalvo, who was known to the Cambridge police as the "measuring man."

Three years earlier, following his arrest as a housebreaker, he admitted that he had been measuring women on the pretext of determining whether they had suitable figures for employment as models. He was given a psychiatric examination in a state hospital and a diagnosis was made of sociopathic personality. In May 1961 he was sentenced to two years imprisonment for assault and battery (which was the charge used in connection with his measuring activities) and for attempted burglary. In his youth he had been a window peeper. In 1955 he had been arrested for molesting a nine-year-old girl but was released when the girl's mother refused to press charges. Two months later he was arrested for peeping and charged with disorderly conduct; however, the charge was dropped.

DeSalvo was questioned about the strangulation murders but he denied involvement and was committed to the Bridgewater State Hospital for pretrial psychiatric examination. While in the hospital he confessed to his attorney that he had committed thirteen homicides in the Boston area and in nearby Lawrence. The first homicide occurred two months after his release from prison in 1962. Subsequently he made a detailed confession to John Bottomly, assistant Attorney General of Massachusetts, who had been appointed to coordinate the search for the Boston strangler. He also confessed that he had raped many of his homicide victims and claimed that he had sexually assaulted between eight hundred and one thousand women.

DeSalvo was sentenced to life imprisonment for assault with a dangerous weapon, assault with intent to commit rape and other charges related to his October 27, 1964, attack on the young woman whom he did not kill. It is unlikely that he will ever be charged with the thirteen homicides, as his confession was obtained under conditions which precluded use of the confession in evidence against him.

Gerold Frank in *The Boston Strangler* has provided a fascinating, encyclopedic account of DeSalvo, his crimes and the extensive prolonged police search for the strangler. This search was complicated by false accusations (some Boston women suspected their husbands) as well as by false confessions made by men who had memorized newspaper accounts of the crimes.

Frank notes that despite the climate of fear in Boston during this period, women continued to permit strangers to enter their apartments. DeSalvo would press the buzzers of an apartment house. The woman who opened the door first became his victim. He would say that he had been sent to do some work in her apartment. If she hesitated or refused to let him in, he would say, "If you don't want the work done, forget it" or tell her to call the apartment house manager. These comments served to reassure the suspicious victim. One fifty-eight-year-old woman, apologizing for her caution, mentioned the danger posed by the Boston strangler. She was the eleventh victim.

DeSalvo, who was diagnosed at Bridgewater State Hospital as having a sociopathic personality disorder marked by sexual deviation with prominent schizoid features and depressive trends, had a rather unusual home background. His father, who used to go around with prostitutes in front of his children, had been arrested five times for assault and battery on his wife. One time he broke her fingers. He had also been arrested for nonsupport, larceny as well as breaking and entering and had served time in jail. The children were frequently beaten by their father, according to Albert, who mentioned that his sisters "always had blacked eyes." Albert was involved in sex play with girls at ten years of age and he was seduced by a married woman at the age of fifteen.

While serving in the Army, he married a German girl. (He was a military policeman and the Army's middle-weight boxing champion of Europe.) He claimed that his wife frequently refused to have sexual relations with him; she in her turn mentioned that he wanted to have sexual intercourse from four to six times a day. He complained that she "would put me down in front of others, make me feel like nothing in front of friends and give me an inferiority complex" (Frank). DeSalvo, like many other multiple murderers, did not smoke or drink.

HARVEY GLATMAN

In August 1957 the parents of a young model reported that she was missing from her home in Los Angeles. She was last seen in the company of a man who wished to take photographs of her. Eight months later a young divorcee disappeared after going out with a man she met through a lonely hearts club. In July 1958 another model, a former striptease dancer, disappeared from her apartment in Los Angeles. Three months later thirty-year-old Harvey Glatman was arrested on a country road by a highway patrolman who caught him struggling with a girl for possession of a revolver.

The girl informed police that she was a model and that she had agreed to pose for some "cheesecake" photos for twenty dollars. Instead of driving her to a studio, Glatman drove away from Los Angeles, and he then attempted to tie her up. She resisted his efforts and in the struggle for the gun a shot was fired which caused a superficial wound on her leg.

In Glatman's apartment were found pictures of the missing divorcee and missing models. The pictures showed the girls, fully clothed, gagged and bound with rope. Other pictures showed the girls nude or partially clothed. There was a picture of each victim with a sash cord around her throat. Curiously one series of pictures included Glatman's driver's license. He explained that this was to identify himself. He confessed that he lured his victims to their death by posing as a photographer. His first victim agreed to being tied up when he said he was taking pictures for a crime magazine. The pictures were to portray a terrified girl at the mercy of a rapist. The pictures he took were very realistic. The girls were disrobed, photographed, sexually assaulted, then strangled.

On being charged with the murder of two of his victims, Glatman pleaded guilty and blocked all efforts of his attorney to enter a plea of not guilty by reason of insanity. When he was sentenced to die for each of the two murders, the defendant jokingly asked, "How can they carry out two death penalties?"

He was first arrested in Denver at the age of seventeen after he had tied up and robbed two Denver women. While awaiting trial, he kidnapped a young girl from a street in Boulder, Colorado, and drove her to a canyon near the town where he tied her up and sat beside her all night. He left her in the morning, but at nightfall he returned and released her unharmed. The girl did not press charges, but he was sentenced to one to five years for his first crime. In 1946 he was arrested in New York for stealing purses from women as they were walking home late at night from bus stops. A five- to ten-year sentence was imposed and he was released in 1951.

Some modelling agencies and free lance models in their newspaper advertisements welcome amateur as well as professional photographers; others go even further and offer to lend or rent cameras to those "photographers" who do not have their own equipment. Following the Glatman killings the Los Angeles City Council drafted an ordinance requiring models and photographers, specializing in nudes, to register with the police and show evidence of good moral character.

Chapter 9

INCEST

"Every prohibition must conceal a desire."
— Freud

INCEST is sexual intercourse between relatives within the prohibited degrees of relationship defined by the law. Most statutes in the United States include within the sweep of incest all relationships nearer than first cousins, some include first cousins (Mueller). Incest was not a criminal offense in England until 1908, except for a short period from 1650 to 1660. Prior to 1908 incest was punishable by the ecclesiastical courts. In England it is unlawful for a man to have sexual intercourse with a woman he knows to be his granddaughter, daughter, sister, half sister or mother. Presumably intercourse with a grandmother is not unlawful. Similar restrictions are imposed on women.

Most societies prohibit incest, but there have been exceptions. According to Herodotus, Cambyses, King of Persia from 529 to 522 B.C., wishing to marry one of his sisters, summoned the royal judges and asked them if there was any law permitting a brother to marry his sister. The royal judges gave the safe answer that they could find no law permitting such a marriage, but they had discovered another law which permitted the King of Persia to do whatever he pleased. He then married first his eldest sister and later a younger one as well. Heraclius permitted uncle-niece marriages when he married his own niece. The people, however, disapproved of the marriage and attributed the defects of his children to divine wrath (Weinberg).

Many of the Ptolemies, who ruled Egypt from 320 to 30 B.C., married their sisters or half sisters. Cleopatra, the child of brother-sister marriages through several generations and the mistress of Julius Caesar and Mark Antony, married her younger brother, Ptolemy the third. Brother-sister marriages also occurred among the Incas of Peru, and in Hawaii. Anthropologists have long maintained that these exceptions to the universal taboo upon brother-sister and parent-child marriages were sanctioned only for the royalty and never for commoners.

"The marriage of brothers and sisters, they argue functioned to preserve the purity of the royal blood line, to keep privilege and rank within the group and to set the divine rulers apart from their mundane subjects who were required to observe the taboos. Ordinarily the authors do not recognize any cases of parent-child marriage, though a few do cite the case of father-daughter marriage among the Azande kings and the case of the orgiastic father-daughter incest among the Thonga" (Middleton).

Middleton, however, points out that these anthropologists remain almost totally unaware of the evidence painstakingly uncovered by Egyptologists regarding father-daughter marriage among the kings and brother-sister marriage among the commoners. During the period of Roman rule, there is very strong evidence that brother-sister marriages occurred among commoners with some frequency. Middleton also notes that there is evidence that societies which have sanctioned union between brothers and sisters or between parents and children have not been nearly as rare as has been generally supposed in recent years.

INCIDENCE

Despite the strong legal and cultural prohibitions against incest, this offense occurs much more often than is generally recognized. In 1937 New Zealand had the highest rate of detected cases, about nine cases per million population, compared with five and less than four cases respectively in Canada and Scotland. In 1930 there were 1.1 cases per million in the United States. These figures do not reflect the actual incidence of incest.

Child victims are often afraid or ashamed to report the crime to the police, and their mothers may conceal the offense when it comes to their attention. Medlicott, on the basis of his experience, believes that father-daughter incest is at least five times as frequent as court statistics would suggest. Adult victims of seduction by their children or siblings are unlikely to reveal their participation in a sexual activity which arouses almost universal repugnance.

Father-daughter incest is much more frequent than mother-son incest. Weinberg, in his study of 203 cases of incest brought to the attention of authorities in Illinois, found that there were 159 cases of father-daughter incest in contrast to two cases of mother-son incest. Brother-sister incest accounted for thirty-seven cases, and there were five cases of combined father-daughter and brother-sister incest. Prevalent opinion is that brother-sister relationships are the most frequent type of incestuous contact. However, being relatively transient and having fewer disturbing consequences, sibling relationships are less likely to come to the attention of investigators than other forms of incest (Weiner).

OEDIPUS AND HIS MOTHER

> *"And loudly o'er the bed she wailed where she*
> *In twofold wedlock, hapless, had brought forth*
> *Husband from a husband, children from a child.*
> *We could not know the moment of her death*
> *Which followed soon."*
> *— Sophocles, King Oedipus*

According to Greek legend, Laius, king of Thebes, was warned by the

Delphic oracle that his son would one day kill him. Later when his son was born, he pierced the infant's feet with a nail and left him to die on a mountainside. But a shepherd found the boy and named him Oedipus, because his feet were deformed. As a young man Oedipus learned his terrible destiny from the oracle at Delphi. He was told, "Away from the shrine, wretch, you will kill your father and marry your mother."

Oedipus believed that he could escape this fate by leaving Corinth, the home of the couple whom he assumed to be his true parents. But in his travels he quarreled with a stranger and killed him. The stranger was his father, Laius. Unaware that the first part of the prediction had been fulfilled, Oedipus continued on his way. When he killed the Sphinx, a monster with a woman's head, lion's body and eagle's wings, which had been terrorizing the countryside, he was rewarded with the kingdom of Thebes. He married Jocasta, the widow of Laius, unaware that she was his mother. On discovering his crime, he blinded himself as punishment and Jocasta hanged herself.

The term "Oedipus complex" has been used to describe attachment of the child for the parent of the opposite sex, together with aggressive feelings toward the parent of the same sex. These forbidden feelings may be banned from consciousness; exceptionally the death wishes for the parent of the same sex find expression in murder. The victim may be either the hated parent or some parental figure whose behavior reactivates earlier feelings of overwhelming hostility.

The forbidden sexual feelings are more likely to find expression in the choice of a wife who resembles mother than in incest.

PHAEDRA AND HER STEPSON

> *"How could I commit that crime whose very mention*
> *Makes me feel polluted?"*
> — Euripides, *Hippolytus*

When Hippolytus, the illegitimate son of Theseus, King of Athens, raised a temple to Artemis, the goddess of virtue; Aphrodite, the goddess of love, was offended because he did not bestow the honor upon herself. She plotted the death of Hippolytus and sought an odious revenge by causing Phaedra, the stepmother of Hippolytus, to be overcome by incestuous desires for her stepson. Although Phaedra did not tell anyone of her love for her stepson, she used to spy upon him as he exercised daily in the gymnasium.

Phaedra, recognizing the hopelessness of her incestuous love, decided that the only honorable escape from her passion was death from starvation. On her sick bed she tells her nurse that she intends to take her own life rather than to dishonor her husband. The nurse senses that she is in love with Hippolytus and encourages her to reveal her love in a note to her stepson.

When Hippolytus treats her with contempt she turns against him.

> *"She will triumph at my death — my murderess.*
> *She will smile, the goddess Aphrodite. As for me,*
> *I am full of a love that has turned to poison;*
> *But at least my death will hurt him, yes,*
> *It will teach him not to look down at me. For that height*
> *On which he stands, his reason, is as dangerous*
> *As my disease. I will teach him moderation,*
> *And make him share the agony of my own sickness."*
> — Euripides, *Hippolytus,* translated by Kenneth Cavander

Phaedra hangs herself but leaves behind a note accusing her stepson of dishonorable proposals and monstrous crimes. Theseus, on reading the note, banishes his son from Athens. Later, recalling the three wishes granted to him by his father, Poseidon, he requests the death of his son. Hippolytus is killed while fleeing from Athens. The horses of his chariot, frightened by a monster, stampede in terror. The chariot is overturned and Hippolytus is dragged to his death by the horses. This Greek legend forms the subject of tragedies by Sophocles, Euripides and Racine.

Messer notes that the Phaedra complex should engage our attention in view of the increase in the number of families broken by divorce, desertion and death. Over half a million divorces or annulments are granted each year in the United States. The result of the high divorce rate is an increase in the number of remarriages. The stepparent and stepchild are not blood relatives and the incest taboo is thus diluted.

LOT AND HIS DAUGHTERS

In Genesis 19 we are told that the elder daughter of Lot said to the younger, "Our father is old and there is not a man in the country to come to us in the usual way. Come now, let us make our father drink wine and then lie with him and in this way keep the family alive through our father" *(New English Bible).* The story of Lot and his daughters was chosen by Medlicott as the prototype of parent-child incest because it is more directly related to actual clinical incest than the Oedipus story. Medlicott reviews this early case of incest.

> The father, Lot, was a nephew of Abraham. Both were wanderers in search of green pastures and entered Canaan together. Their shepherds quarrelled and it became necessary to part. Abraham offered the choice of pastures to Lot who chose the richer pastures but met with disaster. His ungodly neighbors marauded his flocks and his sojourn in Sodom was unhappy. When Lot was warned to leave Sodom prior to its destruction by the Lord, his married daughters and his sons-in-law refused to leave, the family broke up, and he was finally led out by an angel with only his wife and his two unmarried daughters. His wife, Idith, was turned into a pillar of salt because she disobeyed the Lord and looked back at the destruction of Sodom. Lot and his daughters sought refuge in a cave and it was

here that the incestuous behavior took place.

In reviewing this story we must accept the incest as actual rather than alleged. The setting was that of a catastrophic situation with the daughters believing the world of man destroyed as in the story of Noah and the flood. In addition there was, of course, the lack of privacy of the cave similar to the primitive housing situation in some cases of clinical incest. As will be discussed below, the family structure was seriously disrupted.

The role of Lot as the incestuous father is that of a man who has lost his status as the all-powerful patriarchal father who holds his family together. Like so many incestuous fathers, Lot had a serious problem with alcohol, as shown by allowing himself to get drunk two nights running. Indeed, alcohol and incest appear to be closely allied. Rashi (1929-32), an eleventh century French Rabbi, commenting on the Lot story, states: "Anyone who allows himself to be overcome with wine consumes his own flesh." By "consuming his own flesh," no doubt, Rashi meant committing incest.

The daughters in this instance were clearly the active initiators of the incestuous behavior. The Bilder Lexikon (1961) does describe Lot's daughters as still virgins and longing for masculine embrace. They distinguish the story not only as the oldest example of conscious incest, but also of incest as the result of feminine aggression. In clinical incest it is not uncommon for daughters to provoke their fathers. The significance of there being two daughters, not one, is doubtful unless it is that forbidden wishes are more easily acted out in the presence of an accomplice. More than one daughter being involved, however, does bring the story again into line with clinical incest where the incestuous father commonly moves from older to younger daughters.

The role of Lot's wife, Idith, is not out of keeping with clinical incest stories. It appears that she was at cross purposes with her husband and sided very largely with the people of Sodom. It is reported that when asked by Lot to give a little salt to strangers she replied, "Do you mean to introduce this bad custom also into our city?" On the basis of this story Rashi (1929-32), commenting on Idith's being turned into a pillar of salt, said: "By salt had she sinned and by salt was she punished." Jones (1912) writes of the remarkably close association between the ideas of salt and fecundity but points out that salt, both in absence and excess, prevents fruitfulness and sexuality. He comments that it is thus appropriate that Lot's wife, as a punishment for regretting the (homosexual) sins of Sodom, was turned into a pillar (phallus) of salt. In many myths and rituals looking is tabooed. Her "looking back" could also be interpreted as the looking away from what is going on between father and daughters, which is common in clinical incest.

We have no information as to the general effect of their incestuous behavior on Lot's daughters except that they both become pregnant. Their incestuously conceived sons fathered two tribes who were persistently thorns in Israel's flesh.

SOCIOLOGICAL FACTORS

A number of reports have contributed to the belief that incest occurs mainly in remote rural areas among backward people, or is induced mainly by poverty and gross overcrowding, or involves primarily families with low moral standards. Weiner, in his excellent, thorough survey of publications on incest, sharply questions these sociological generalizations which are based upon criminal and prison records. Lower-class offenders are more likely to be arrested, convicted and sentenced to prison than middle- or upper-class offenders. A high incidence of crowded living quarters is to be expected among lower-class offenders, whether or not they had committed incest, simply as a function of their low social position and marginal economic status.

Weiner believes that it is an error to infer that incest is relatively rare in the middle and upper classes merely because known incest offenders are mainly of the working class. In an earlier study by Weiner which was limited to incestuous fathers applying voluntarily for assistance to a psychiatric clinic, all the men seen were of the middle class. In his knowledge, there currently exists no sound basis for affixing the relative frequency of incest behavior in the various socioeconomic strata.

COMPLAINTS OF INCEST

Cases of father-daughter incest are usually reported to the police by the wife of the offender. She is often aware of the incest behavior long before she notifies the police, and when she does take action her motivation is more likely to be anger at her husband over some unrelated matter than concern for the welfare of her daughter. Pregnancy or abortion, which cannot easily be concealed, may bring the offense to light as in six of the twenty cases reported by Tormes. The child, under threats of punishment by her father, may conceal his offense by blaming her condition on rape or sexual intercourse with a boyfriend.

The children may confide in a schoolteacher, neighbor or relative. An older daughter who wishes to protect a younger sister or who resents being replaced as the sexual partner by the sister may reveal her incestuous relations with her father. In Tormes' study eight of the twenty cases were reported by the mothers, five by public agencies including schools, two by relatives, two by older sisters and the remaining three by the child victim herself, a neighbor and a private doctor.

Occasionally incest behavior may be detected in progress by the police as in the following case.

> A brother, aged twenty-six, went with his sister, aged twenty, to the local public house for the evening a few days before Christmas. On the way home they decided to go and collect holly on the nearby common. There they were caught in the act of intercourse by a policeman. They admitted to the police that they had had intercourse on a large number of occasions (Radzinowicz).

After a complaint has been made to the police, it is not uncommon for the wife and daughter to refuse to testify in court. If the complaint is made to a public agency, the family may quickly leave the state to forestall the possibility of criminal proceedings. The wife will often say that she reported the offense because she wants treatment for her husband and does not want him to go to prison.

FATHER-DAUGHTER INCEST

Father-daughter incest usually begins about the time the eldest daughter reaches puberty, when the father is between thirty-five and forty-five years of age. It may, however, start when the girl is only three or four years of age or be delayed until she is an adult as in the following case.

> A twenty-year-old girl was visited in her apartment by her father, who had been drinking. After making some suggestive remarks, he grabbed her, forced her down on her bed and raped her. She lay as "still as a corpse" but did not make a determined effort to escape. Nor did she call for the help of her landlady, who was in the adjacent apartment, as she wanted "to avoid the embarrassment of revealing that her father was attempting to rape her."
>
> Some months earlier she had left her parents' home, as he had twice tried to assault her. She had been her father's favorite until she reached the age of puberty, when he turned agiainst her and later he accused her of being a whore. This was before she became promiscuous. Presumably his friendliness turned to dislike as a protection against his own sexual temptations which he projected onto her by calling her a whore.

Most of the fathers are living at home with their wives and children when the incest occurs. Incest may start when the wife is pregnant, sick or in the hospital. In homes broken by separation or divorce, or death of the mother, the father may seek sexual gratification within the home. Incest is seldom confined to a few acts of sexual intercourse but continues over months or years. As one daughter grows up and leaves home, her place is taken by a younger daughter. One man had sexual relations with each of his five daughters when they reached the age of twelve or thirteen. Another man began intercourse with three of his four daughters when they attained puberty. It is difficult to believe that the mothers in these cases were unaware of the incest. A father who said that his wife was "an old haybag" and would have nothing more to do with her had four children by his mentally retarded daughter (Weinberg).

THE FATHERS

Weinberg describes three types of fathers involved in father-daughter incest: (a) the father whose social and sexual activities are confined within his own home. He does not seek or pursue women outside the family. (b) The pedophilic father who seeks sexual gratification from young girls in preference to adult women. He may or may not concentrate his sexual attentions upon his daughters but usually seduces a daughter because she is most accessible. Presumably he loses interest in his daughter when she reaches adolescence. (c) The indiscriminately promiscuous psychopath who seeks sexual gratification whenever he can find it. Young girls and adult women, within and without the home, attract his attention.

A minority of the fathers are described as being affectionate, responsible breadwinners who are very helpful in the home. ("He polished all the furniture, waxed the floors, took out the garbage and did all the shopping.") Presumably these offenders prompted the following comment of a prison official. "Experienced guards who see a 'fish' (a newcomer) come through the gate carrying a Bible know he is an incest offender . . . Such individuals carefully obey rules and conform strictly to prison regulations . . . They are rarely disciplinary problems."

The majority of the fathers in Tormes' study combined incest, chronic brutality and alcoholism. Thirteen of the twenty mothers described brutal behavior, and Tormes gives the following examples:

> "Breaking a radio over the mother's head; burning the children with hot irons; chasing the mother out of the house with a gun (on three occasions); locking the mother or children in closets while he sexually abused the child victim; keeping the family out of the house until very late hours of the night; throwing knives, bottles, or other heavy objects at the mother or children; forcing sexual intercourse with the daughter in the mother's presence; forcing sexual intercourse with the mother in the children's presence; attempting to strangle the mother with a handkerchief; forcing the daughter to submit to a crude abortion that resulted in prolonged debilitating illness . . .
>
> All of the children in these families claimed to have submitted to the fathers' sexual demands either because of personal threats to them or fear of future violence. In the words of a twelve year old victim: "He is twice as big as I am . . . I can't fight with him. I've seen him beat the hell out of my mother, who's as big as he is! Why won't he beat the hell out of me?"
>
> In spite of the father's record of brutality in the home, there were only two cases of previous arrests for violence outside the home among the twenty father-offenders.

Other writers also report that many of these fathers have no prior criminal record, although Weinberg noted that 50 per cent of the father participants in his survey had previous criminal records, usually for personal offenses such as disorderly conduct rather than for property offenses.

Psychosis is rare. Krafft-Ebing gives the following example of paranoia in a father who impregnated his daughter and attributed his incest to divine command. "It was revealed to me that I should beget the Eternal Son with my daughter. Then a man of flesh and blood would arise by my faith, who would be 1,800 years old. He would be a bridge between the Old and the New Testament." There is a high incidence of character disorder and emotional immaturity among incestuous fathers. They rationalize their behavior, and feelings of guilt are not readily apparent.

"Many even argue that they would have been remiss as fathers had they not engaged their daughters sexually. One father explained to his wife, concerning his sexual activity with their daughter, that the girl needed to be taught the facts of life and he was exercising the parental privilege; another explained that incest began in his conscientious parental effort to give his daughter a sexual education so that she would 'not grow up to be frigid like my wife'; a third justified the sexual relationship as his attempt to make his daughter, a hostile and withdrawn girl, feel less angry toward him. A man, described by Reinhardt, whose two daughters' promiscuity was known to him, said about his incest with them, 'I wouldn't have if they were virgins, but what's the difference if it's me or some other guy?' The capacity to evolve and defend such flagrant rationalizations may be of central importance in influencing a nonpsychotic man with otherwise good impulse control to act upon his incestuous urges" (Weiner).

The following statements by men serving sentences in a penitentiary for incest reveal a wide range of response to their behavior.

> I am not guilty of this offense. I have never had sexual relations with my daughter or bothered her in any way. I was blamed by my daughter because I refused to let her go out with boys due to the fact that some of the things I had heard when I did let her go out and the fact that she ran up a high telephone bill calling her friends.
>
> * * *
>
> I was alleged to have had sexual intercourse with all three of my older daughters but never had. Some years ago I was tried on a similar charge and found not guilty. I have never had any sexual abnormalities. I firmly believe that Nancy became angry with me because I wanted her to attend school, and behave properly, and that is why she put me here. My wife told the authorities that I did not do such a thing. The district attorney confused my daughter while she was on the stand and he put me here. He claimed that I had had sexual relations with some of my daughters since their ages of six years but this is not true. I am absolutely not guilty of these offenses. (Records showed that there was an eyewitness to the man's abnormal sexual behavior.)
>
> * * *
>
> I don't remember doing anything like this. I might be guilty, I don't know. I was supposed to have had intercourse with my fourteen-year-old daughter and they say she is pregnant. I really don't know what I did, I guess I had intercourse with my daughter. I wasn't in my right mind. I'm sorry for what I did. I probably had intercourse with her three times or something like that. She never fought me off and always acted like she enjoyed it. She would come to me and ask me to do it, most of it was her own idea. She even told me once that if she caught me with another girl she was going to stick a knife in my back. (The daughter reported that her father had forced her to have sexual relations and had threatened to kill her if she told anyone.)
>
> * * *
>
> I had been drinking on this particular day that I took my daughter into the bedroom and had intercourse with her. She had sat on my lap earlier and I took her into the bedroom and removed her panties. She did verbally resist me. I have engaged in intercourse with her on occasions for five or six years. Sometimes once a week and sometimes twice. On other occasions, once a month. I had a

vasectomy about nine years ago hoping it would curb my desires. I have had these urges, I thought they were normal, and have been able to suppress them. I tried to seek help but couldn't bring myself to tell my wife or anyone.

*   *   *

During that evening I had drank heavily and after drinking so much, I sometimes black out and do not recall what has taken place thereafter for several hours. I went to bed with my wife during the evening and evidently sometime during the night I arose and went into the bedroom where my fourteen-year-old daughter was sleeping and allegedly had intercourse with her. I do not recall doing this and the next thing I remember is the police getting me out of bed. This is the only time this happened and I had no good reason for this other than I had been drinking heavily and was not having adequate sexual relations with my wife because she was sick. I had no excuse for my behavior. I allegedly reached a climax with my daughter. She is very well developed for her age.

THE WIVES

Often there is clear evidence that the wives turn a blind eye to the incestuous behavior because they are fearful of their husband's violence, wish to be relieved of sexual relations or do not wish to lose their husbands to a penitentiary. The following excerpts from some of the twenty incest cases reported by Tormes graphically depict the reactions of the wives to their knowledge of the sexual molestations.

Case No. 1. The daughter, when she was eight years old, told the mother that she was being molested by the father. The mother slapped her face and called her a bad girl. The case was reported by the mother, seven years later, when the victim attempted to commit suicide. (Father returned to the home one month after the initial complaint was filed).

Case No. 2. The mother was informed by a younger sister that the father locked them (the children) in a room while he stayed out with the oldest daughter. A younger brother mentioned that once he had looked in through a window and had seen them together in bed. The case was reported after six years of regular sexual activity, by the mother's brother. The girl was pregnant.

Case No. 3. The mother, while watching television, fell asleep. When she awoke, she went to look for her husband. Peeking through the keyhole of her own room, she saw her husband on top of the daughter. The mother then returned to the television and went back to sleep. Shortly after this, she went to the hospital to have a baby and she left all the children in the care of the father. One day, she was visited by a social investigator (the family was receiving public assistance, as the father had not worked in ten years), who filed a neglect petition because of the atrocious conditions in the home. On investigation of the neglect case, the mother mentioned the incest, six months after the keyhole incident. (This father also returned to the home after conviction.)

Case No. 4. All four daughters complained to the mother that the father was manipulating (or attempted to manipulate) their breasts and vaginas. The mother told them that they misunderstood their father, he was merely trying to show affection. The case was reported by a relative when the oldest girl became pregnant by the father.

Case No. 5. The mother, after being informed by the child of the father's molestations, sent the child away to a school for the mentally retarded. The child, however, would come back to the home for weekend visits. The mother went out leaving all the children in the care of the father. The child reported her own case at Willowbrook. (One other younger child was found to have been molested in this family.)

Case No. 6. The mother noticed that nearly every day the father spent two hours locked in the bathroom with the daughter. The other children in the family complained that they were always late to school because of this. The case was reported by the victim herself after a family quarrel.

Case No. 7. The mother awoke in the night and discovered that the father was not next to her in bed. For reasons which she was unable to explain, she went straight to the younger children's bedroom where she saw the father in bed with the victim. The mother then returned to her own room and went back to sleep. The case was reported by an older sister after a family quarrel which took place four months after this incident.

Case No. 8. The mother had seen, on several occasions, the father in bed with the daughter with his private parts exposed. She admitted being suspicious. The case was reported by the mother herself two and one-half years later when the girl became pregnant by the father.

Other writers cited by Weiner have also described the contribution of the wife to her husband's incestuous behavior. One husband, with the approval of his wife, slept with their daughter during the wife's pregnancy. One wife, who slept in a bedroom separate from her husband because she was unable to tolerate his snoring, sent her oldest daughter in to sleep with him "so he wouldn't be lonely." In another case the wife not only willingly accepted her husband's rationalizations for the incest but encouraged and observed the incestuous activity.

Psychological tests (Thematic Apperception Test) administered to daughters involved in father-daughter incest showed that the girls uniformly saw the mother figure as cruel, unjust and depriving. In contrast father figures were sometimes described as nurturant, sometimes as weak and ineffectual, sometimes as frightening (Kaufman *et al.*).

The wives studied by Kaufman and his associates were infantile and extremely dependent. They sought from their children the affection they had not received from their own mothers. These wives singled out one daughter who was encouraged to resume responsibility beyond her years, a responsibility which included sexual relationships with her father. There is reversal of the dependency role. Instead of the mother taking care of the child, the child is expected to take care of the emotional needs of her parents. These wives, when confronted with evidence of incest, would blame the daughters rather than the husbands.

THE DAUGHTERS

The daughters are usually between six and fifteen years of age, although some are younger and others either continue into adult life or participate in incest for the first time as an adult. The majority are coerced or seduced by their fathers; a few seduce their fathers. Although some children are too terrified of their fathers to report the incest, the surprising failure of so many to seek help suggests that the experience is not without its satisfactions. When the daughter finally complained to others, it may be because her father has prevented her from dating boys, punished her severely or transferred his sexual attentions to a younger daughter.

An adult patient of Karpman has described her willing participation in her own seduction at the age of fifteen.

> There was no further sex talk or play until bedtime that evening. We both undressed for bed at the same time. After I had on my nightgown, but before I had taken down the covers on my bed, Dad came for me and led me into his bedroom. It seemed quite natural that he should do this. I think I rather expected it. I may even have hesitated to get into my own bed in anticipation of some kind of advance from him.
>
> I let Dad take the initiative, and complied willingly with everything he suggested. He told me where in his bed to lie — next to the wall. I scrambled into place quickly, following his instructions. It was a hot summer night and, as he usually did on the hottest nights, he had placed the pillows at the foot of the bed where there was more breeze from the windows. At first, we merely repeated the play we had enjoyed so much during the afternoon trip homeward. Dad then again assumed the "teacher" role. This was to overcome the guilt of further intimacies in which we were about to indulge.
>
> I use the plural "we" advisedly. Both of us were anticipating greater pleasures. He wanted to show me the position the man assumes in sex relations. He had me spread my legs far apart until he was able to touch the opening to the vagina with his penis. I did as I was told, assuming the role of an obedient child. Although I had participated actively in mutual masturbation play in the car with pleasure which must have been apparent, I now concealed my enjoyment . . . He fell asleep first. I lay for a long time thinking about what had happened and enjoying my thoughts . . . By assuming my role of passive acquiescence to assuage my own guilt and deflect accountability from myself, I increased Dad's guilt and probably brought on his acute anxiety.

Although there have been a number of reports on the long-term effects on the incestuous daughter of sexual relationships with her father, satisfactory studies on a large number of cases are lacking. Promiscuity, aversion to heterosexual relationships, homosexuality, antisocial behavior and absence of untoward effects have all been reported. In those cases in which little or no anxiety could be observed, Barry and Johnson found evidence that the incest was condoned and fostered by the nonparticipating parent as well as the incestuous parent. Allen, presumably referring to adult incest, suggests that there can be no psychic trauma if there is no knowledge of any blood relationship, and points out that Oedipus himself was happy until his dreadful secret was revealed to him.

Weiner suggests that the conflicting reports on the consequences of incest arise from differences in the age of onset in the populations studied. In his opinion, the likelihood of detrimental effect might depend on whether the girl is adolescent or preadolescent at the onset of the incest. Noting that published reports do not contain sufficient data to test this hypothesis, he draws attention to the impression of Sloane and Karpinski that the potential for psychological damage to the daughter is greater when incest begins in adolescence than it is with preadolescent onset. Adolescents have greater awareness that this behavior is socially reprehensible and their inhibiting forces are stronger.

Promiscuity is frequently mentioned as an outcome of father-daughter incest. A report of the Chicago Vice Commission showed that fifty-one of the 103 promiscuous women examined reported having had their first sexual experiences with their own fathers. Halleck estimates that about 15 per cent of the total population of a training school for delinquent girls were seduced by their own fathers or stepfathers. As many girls are reluctant to report incestual acts, the actual number of cases could be much higher. He states that those girls exposed to incestual experience show serious behavioral problems throughout adolescence, hysterical personality traits and promiscuity. Aversion to sexual relationships with men and frank homosexuality can be understood as a flight from a heterosexual relationship which might reawaken psychological conflicts over the earlier incestuous encounter.

MOTHER-SON INCEST

Cases of mother-son incest seldom come to the attention of the police and very few cases have been reported in the literature. Commenting on the seeming rarity of mother-son incest, Barry states that it seems inadequate to assume that this is merely because there are no indifferent, fostering or permissive fathers. To ascribe the infrequency to the assumption that mothers are less attractive to sexually capable sons than fathers are to daughters would seem to Barry to be only masculine chauvinism. He finds a possible answer in the close biological dependency between mother and son.

Weinberg has emphasized the role of the dominant mother who has ambivalent feelings toward her son — intimate yet hostile. Some mothers by their promiscuous sexual behavior in the presence of their sons have aroused their incestuous impulses. Although absence of father from the home has been suggested as a contributing factor, Weiner cites Tramer's report of a case in which the father, far from being absent, was the instigator of the incest.

This man forced his two teen-age sons to have intercourse with their mother while he watched. This man had become impotent after an initially good sexual adjustment in his marriage and watching his sons having intercourse with his wife stimulated him to the extent where he was able himself to copulate. The father was schizophrenic and the mother, although not psychotic, was partly responsible for the incestuous relationship. Weiner wonders whether the sons could have been "forced" into the incestuous acts had they not to some extent been willing. Hence, he suggests that this case is reminiscent of the family collusion observed in father-daughter incest.

Barry and Johnson have described a family in which the father periodically deserted the family and was often in jail. They lived in an isolated Kentucky mountain community. The family physician told the boy that since he was the eldest, he should take his father's place in every way and help his sick mother become well. The young man was not mentally deficient and recounted the details of his sexual relationship with his mother with no apparent feeling that it was of any particular significance. Irene Josselyn, the psychiatrist who examined the twenty-three-year-old son, found no evidence of psychopathology.

Profound psychopathology is usually noted in one of the participants in mother-son incest. In three of four cases known to the writer, the sons later became schizophrenic, but it was not possible to assess the role of the incestuous relationship in the origins of this disorder. One mother, when approached sexually by her son, refused sexual relations saying, "What would the neighbors think if I became pregnant?" Two cases involving sons who became schizophrenic have been described by Wahl.

The first case was a twenty-seven-year-old schizophrenic soldier who responded to treatment but relapsed after home visits. On three occasions prior to a home visit he lacerated himself on a window. His mother's attitude was grossly overprotective, alternating with severe rejection each time she would form a new marital or extramarital relationship. She would become furious when the doctors would not permit her son to return home, writing her congressman and the American Legion, accusing the hospital of attempting to interfere with "mother love."

The mother was extremely physically affectionate on hospital visits, called her son "Lover" and was observed lying on the ground wrapped with him in a blanket. Another time she was observed opening his fly and playing with his penis. After each visit the patient would be extremely disturbed. Later he described with great emotion many occasions in which mother would initiate sexual intercourse with him. She threatened him with the fears of homosexuality unless she gave him this "special training."

The second case was a twenty-seven-year-old chronic schizophrenic Korean War veteran. In his youth he frequently observed his mother having sexual relations with a variety of men. He also had frequent opportunity to observe her nude and insensible after alcoholic debauches. Although he had never been close to his mother and was repulsed by her behavior, he began to feel sexual attraction toward her. He became psychotic in Korea after seeing the bodies of several hostages who had been shot and mutilated by the enemy. One man had been castrated. He recovered quickly but relapsed after an act of incest with his mother. One evening he returned home and found his mother naked and in an alcoholic stupor. According to the patient and another informant he had intercourse with her.

BROTHER-SISTER INCEST

Weinberg found that the average sister participant in thirty-seven cases of brother-sister incest was about nineteen years old, or four years older than the average daughter participant in incest. The age range was from twelve to thirty-six. The brothers averaged about twenty-four years of age, the youngest was twelve and the oldest forty-four. Sister participants were more promiscuous than daughter participants and were more likely to become pregnant. The usual brother-sister relationship is replaced by a courting relationship which sometimes leads to marriage under an assumed name. A famous case of sibling incest is that of the poet Lord Byron and Augusta Leigh his half sister. The Bible relates that Abraham married Sarah, his half sister.

In thirteen cases of brother-sister incest reported by Doshay, the parents were found to have contributed to the incest through lack of supervision and guidance of their children. Sloane and Karpinski described a seventeen-year-old girl who complained to her mother that she had been attacked by her brother. Her mother merely laughed and said, "You, a great big girl, and couldn't fight him off." The girl then admitted that she had been having intercourse with her brother ever since she was fourteen. The mother did not seem at all disturbed by this announcement of incest.

An unusual case was that of a twenty-four-year-old man who had for a long time desired sexual relations with a younger sister but feared his parents' reaction. One night when his parents were away from home, he went to his sister's room on an impulse, woke her up and told her he wanted her. She thought he was joking and started laughing. He then stabbed her repeatedly with a knife, causing deep lacerations of her neck, chest and hand. One laceration to her neck was seven inches long. He did not carry out his plan to attempt incest, leaving the room after another sister responded to the victim's screams.

He had previously been arrested for burglary and arson. There was a history of setting fires to buildings as well as to articles of female underclothing. He was a window peeper and had written "poison pen" letters to girls in which he made threats "to cut them up." He had recurring dreams and fantasies of raping girls and then cutting them into little pieces.

FAMILY INCEST

In rare cases the whole family indulges in incestuous behavior. A thirty-four-year-old man was arrested after his wife reported to the police that he had been having sexual relations with his fifteen-year-old daughter during the previous five years. She said she had not reported the incest earlier because she was afraid of her husband. Interviews with the children revealed that the father would have intercourse with his daughter in the presence of other members of the family. It was verified that his wife used to have sexual relations with her two adolescent sons, who also had sexual relations with their sister.

Another man who was charged with incest reported, "I am guilty of having intercourse with my daughter. This was caused by my wife's unwillingness to enter into sexual relations with me. My daughter, the victim, is actually more developed than her mother and probably her willingness to perform the act with me led to my involvement. My daughter admitted that she had committed this act with both of her brothers, in addition to other boys in the neighborhood. This happened on several occasions. This daughter is presently pregnant." This man's two sons reported that the father had committed acts of anal sodomy on them.

Raphling has described an extraordinary case of family incest spanning three generations. A thirty-nine-year-old man was referred for psychiatric treatment by his physician because of incestuous relations with his daughters. At the age of eleven he observed sexual relations between his father and his oldest sister. Later he also had sexual relations with this sister. When he was fourteen, his mother seduced him and urged him to manipulate her genitals. At eighteen he followed in his father's footsteps and began to have sexual relations with his two younger sisters.

Following his marriage he had both vaginal and rectal intercourse with his wife. When his first daughter reached puberty at the age of twelve, he initiated her into sexual relations while his wife was in the hospital delivering their youngest child. Subsequently he had intercourse with her two to three times a week for five years. The daughter states that she allowed this relationship to continue because her father expected her to participate, because she felt sorry for him after she refused him and because she feared she would lose any affection he might have for her if she did not submit.

When he approached his second eldest daughter, he was vehemently refused by her; consequently, he has rarely been able to complete the sexual act with her. His third daughter, age eight, protested so strenuously that he made no further sexual advances to her. When his only son reached puberty, the patient urged him to have sexual relations with his own mother. The son did eventually make vague sexual advances to his mother which greatly angered her. In addition, the patient implicitly gave his son permission to have sexual relations with his sisters. The eldest complied with her brother's demands. The next eldest daughter denied having submitted to her brother, despite his claims to the contrary.

The patient revealed the intimacies of his life with a smile that reflected a mixture of pride and shame. He believes that he is an ideal father and husband and that he is doing his daughters a favor by initiating them into sexual relations. Paradoxically, he is a prudish man who dictates high moral standards to his family at the same time he commits incest. He exerts a rigid social control over the life of his daughters. Approximately three years prior to his sexual involvement with his daughters, he turned to "God and the church" seeking moral principles by which to guide his life. He realizes that his sexual behavior is bizarre, but attributes it to the example he learned from his parents.

Chapter 10

FALSE ACCUSATIONS OF RAPE

IT is easy to claim rape falsely, but exposure of the imposture may be very difficult. The frequency of unfounded claims of rape provides a serious problem for law enforcement agencies. In 1968, as a national average, 18 per cent of all forcible rapes were determined by police investigation to be unfounded. In Denver 25 per cent of forcible rapes reported to the police over a period of one year were unfounded. These are conservative figures, as the police do not record a rape as unfounded so long as there is doubt. In the Denver study a further 20 per cent of the complaints of forcible rape were open to considerable question.

The conscious motivations for false accusations are reviewed below. It would be erroneous to assume that in all cases these motivations explain the falsehood. The psychological basis for the false claims of rape may be much more complex than the woman realizes. The presence of such factors as revenge, blackmail, protection of reputation and jealousy do not always provide an adequate explanation. Unconscious factors may also contribute beyond the girl's awareness. Repressed erotic wishes or fantasies may be converted into beliefs and the girl may be convinced of the reality of her claim of rape despite convincing evidence to the contrary.

JEALOUSY

A twenty-three-year-old woman reported that a man came up to her as she was leaving work and told her, "I've got a gun, now get in the car." He took her to a room in a hotel and began beating her about the face and head. When she refused his demands for money, he stuffed his handkerchief in her mouth and raped her. The suspect told police that he had known her for two years. On the day of the alleged rape she called him on the telephone and asked him to pick her up at work. While he was driving her home, she suggested that they go to a hotel but he refused, as he did not have the money to pay for a room.

She said that she would pay for the room and they went to a hotel. He did not lock the door, as the desk clerk did not give him a key. She undressed, they had intercourse and then he drove her home. The next day she called him and told him she had heard that he was trying to pick up another girl and she said that she would shoot him if he did. Physical examination of the woman did not reveal any bruises. The hotel clerk remembered that no one was with the man when he checked in the hotel and a witness noted that she was waiting outside in the car. The man appeared to be telling the truth on a polygraph examination.

A married woman brought her six-year-old daughter to the police station and claimed that she had caught her husband attempting to rape the child. The father was asked to come to the police station and he said that he had never touched his child. While the detectives were talking to him, his wife called on the telephone and said that she had seen her husband with another woman. She was jealous and had made up the story of attempted rape.

LOVERS' QUARREL

A sixteen-year-old girl called the police to report that a man had forced her into his car and had taken her to a house where he raped her and forced her to remain with him for eleven hours. The following day she came to the detective bureau and said that she had not been raped. The assault consisted of a light slap and she described the incident as "nothing other than a lovers' quarrel." She had been dating the man but had stopped seeing him. He persuaded her to enter his car after he saw her returning home late at night in the company of two other men, and they spent the night in his apartment.

A WOMAN SCORNED

> *"Heav'n has no rage like love to hatred turn'd,*
> *Nor hell a fury like a woman scorn'd."*
> — William Congreve, *The Mourning Bride*

A woman who wanted a ride home from her girl friend's apartment called on a former boyfriend who lived nearby. She complained to the police that instead of driving her home, he drove by the stockyards and told her she would have to walk home if she did not agree to have sexual intercourse with him. When she started to get out, he pulled her back in the car and raped her. The man, on questioning by the police, denied raping her and said that she had lived with him for two months. Recently he had thrown her out because of her excessive drinking. The woman refused to come to the police department to provide further information.

The woman who agrees to sexual intercourse after prolonged courting and promise of marriage may become somewhat peevish when her boyfriend stops calling on her. She may respond by threatening to report to the police that he raped her unless he agrees to marry her. She may, in fact, go to the police with a fabricated story of forcible rape if the man fails to marry her.

PREGNANCY

Pregnancy in an unmarried girl, in a woman who is divorced or separated from her husband or in a married woman whose husband has been sterilized or was overseas, confined in a penitentiary or otherwise away from home at the time of conception is an awkward situation for which some acceptable explanation is desirable. False claims of rape often do much to maintain family harmony.

A twenty-one-year-old single girl reported to police that as she was walking to her apartment house a car passed her slowly then stopped near the corner. When she reached the corner, three of the four Spanish-Americans in the car jumped out and forced her into the car. They pushed her down on the floor and then drove around in circles for fifteen minutes. Then they stopped at a motel and the driver went into the office. He returned in a few minutes and drove the car to one of the units. She was taken inside where the men took off her clothes.

Three men held her down and all four took turns "fondling and putting their fingers in my privates." Only one man had sexual relations with her. Afterwards she was driven back to the vicinity of her apartment. She did not tell anyone about the rape, as she felt so ashamed. When she realized that she was pregnant, she decided to report the rape to the police. The detectives were puzzled why only one of four men had intercourse with her and why they bothered to register at a motel when they were near the outskirts of the city. On further questioning, the woman decided, "It is not my desire to prosecute, because the report I made is false. I know the man that is responsible for my pregnancy, but I won't reveal his name."

LEGAL ABORTION

In those states which permit medical termination of pregnancy resulting from rape, women may falsely claim rape to obtain a therapeutic abortion. In Colorado, for example, pregnancy resulting from forcible rape, incest or statutory rape may be terminated providing less than sixteen weeks of gestation have passed. A certificate is required from the District Attorney stating that there is probable cause to believe that the alleged violation did occur.

A woman, whose husband had been serving in the U. S. Air Force in Viet Nam complained to an Air Force physician that she had been raped. She commented that she hoped her husband would be given compassionate leave to return home. Her efforts to gain the threefold advantages of a legal abortion, the return of her husband from Viet Nam and an acceptable explanation for her pregnancy failed when it was determined that her complaint of rape was not true.

A young woman reported that she visited the apartment of a friend and when she rebuffed his advances, he pushed her down on the couch and raped her. She had known the man for less than a month and had only been out with him once before. Curiously she could not recall his surname and apart from his general appearance she was unable to give information which might aid in his identification; however, she thought he was employed by the public service company.

Her reason for reporting the rape was to obtain a legal abortion. She did not volunteer any explanation for the five-week delay in reporting the rape to the police. After declining to submit to a polygraph (lie detector examination), she asked the detective if he knew how she could get an abortion, then she acknowledged that she consented to sexual intercourse although "originally I was opposed to sexual intercourse with him."

WELFARE PAYMENTS

Some welfare departments penalize female recipients of welfare who have illegitimate pregnancies. One woman reported to police that while walking home from a supermarket, she was followed by a man. She assumed that they were both walking in the same direction and she did not become alarmed until he followed her into her apartment house. As she entered her apartment, she was pushed inside by the man. He shut the door, turned on the light in the living room and asked her to make some coffee. While she was doing this, he grabbed her by her right arm and pushed her into her bedroom where he removed her pants and raped her. When the detectives asked her to take a lie detector test, she revealed that the pregnancy was the result of sexual relations with her boyfriend and she was fearful of losing her welfare payments.

CHILD CUSTODY

Promiscuous wives, involved in divorce suits, sometimes make false claims of rape to protect their reputation, especially when they anticipate a courtroom battle over custody of their children. A woman separated from her husband claimed that a Negro called at her home one evening while the children were asleep. He claimed to be an encyclopedia salesman, but once inside her home he forced her down on the couch and raped her repeatedly over a period of several hours. Later she admitted that she had made up the story after she learned that her husband had hired a private detective to watch her home. She did not want the fact this Negro had visited her to be revealed at the child-custody hearing.

VENEREAL DISEASE

The married woman who contracts venereal disease from her lover may try to avoid detection of her infidelity by telling her husband that she had been raped. In order to convince him, she feels obliged to make a false report of rape to the police.

PROTECTION OF REPUTATION

Women detected in the act of sexual intercourse and married women found in the company of a man other than their husband may attempt to protect their reputation by false claims of abduction and rape. A state highway patrolman stopped a car for speeding in the early hours of the morning. A woman in the car screamed that she had been raped. She said that she had just left a tavern and was getting into her car when a man grabbed her and forced her into his car. He drove her into the country and raped her. However a policeman who worked at the tavern recalled seeing her leave the tavern in the company of the man. When confronted with this information, she admitted that she panicked when the car was stopped by the patrolman, as she was fearful that her husband would learn of her escapade.

Another woman, who operated a collection agency, claimed that after driving away from a client's home she was attacked by a Negro who had been hiding in the back seat of her car. He jumped in the front seat and said, "Bitch, I'm going to have you, I've been watching you for four months." He told her to drive the car to a lonely spot where he twisted her arms behind her back and forced her to submit to him.

The man described was later arrested but claimed that he had spent the afternoon drinking with her in a tavern. When confronted with this information, the woman admitted that she had been drinking with the man and that she had made up the story of rape. She said that if she had not made the complaint of rape, "her collection agency might have suffered along with her reputation."

THE OUTRAGED HUSBAND

Married women, fearful of physical assault or other punishment by their husbands, may attempt to explain their arrival home late at night or in the early hours of the morning with false accounts of rape and abduction. They are often reluctant to report the rape to the police and may do so only upon the insistence of their husbands. Some of these women quickly reveal the truth when questioned by detectives in the absence of the husband.

One such woman reported to the police that she was in the restroom of a tavern when a Negro walked in, grabbed her and forced her into his car. He then drove her to an apartment house, took off her clothes and raped her. He then left the room and another Negro appeared and raped her. When he left, yet another Negro came in and raped her. Then the Negro who had abducted her raped her a second time. After she dressed, he drove her home. The following day she quickly told the detectives that she had been drinking in a tavern with her husband, who left after an argument. Another man in the tavern bought her several drinks, then they went to his apartment where they had sexual intercourse.

She became upset when three Negroes came to the apartment and took their turns having sexual relations with her. She told her husband that she had been raped, because she feared a beating. He called the police. "I actually had a little too much to drink and I want to drop the case. I wasn't forced to have sexual relations."

Sometimes long-suffering husbands, suspicious of the claim of rape, are the first to suggest to detectives the possibility of fabrication. A forty-six-year-old woman claimed that two men forced their way into her car as she was waiting for signal lights to turn to green. They made her drive to a parking lot, where they were joined by four other men. All six men raped her and she then drove home and went to bed. In the morning she told her husband and then notified the police. Her husband confided his suspicions to the police, who asked her to take a lie detector test. She then said that her car had slid in the ice and she had been unable to drive back on the road. A passing motorist and his companion helped to push her car back on the road. The two men then had sexual intercourse with her consent.

THE OUTRAGED WIFE

A woman at a drinking party could not find her husband and went to look for him. She checked their car and discovered her husband having intercourse in the back seat with another guest. The guest screamed that she had been raped, and the man was arrested. He proclaimed his innocence, but the woman told a convincing story of being dragged to the car and being threatened with death if she resisted. Later the woman admitted in the privacy of the detective's office that it was not rape, but that she became frightened when the man's wife started screaming and tried to attack her. "When his wife appeared I had to say something."

LOSS OF A BOYFRIEND OR HUSBAND

Young ladies who have lost the affection of a boyfriend may attempt to regain it by a dramatic appeal for sympathy. Thus a girl calls her boyfriend in a distraught state claiming that she has been sexually assaulted and appealing to him for help in this crisis. Married women threatened with divorce may also act in this manner.

A thirty-six-year-old woman, separated from her husband, telephoned him and asked him if he could come to her home and help her. On arrival he found his wife lying in her underclothes on the floor moaning and crying out, "No, don't do it, don't do it, leave me alone." Her clothing was torn and some of the furniture in the living room had been overturned. Later she told detectives that three Negroes had broken into her home and raped her. Inconsistencies in her accounts of the incident raised considerable doubt about the genuineness of her complaint.

THE UNWELCOME LOVER

Some women have difficulty in breaking off love affairs. Often they have ambivalent feelings toward the man and react ambivalently, one day announcing that all is over and the next day permitting the man to stay for dinner. When the discarded lover resorts to violence to obtain the sexual relations previously readily available, the woman may appeal to the police for help in her dilemma. She makes a report of rape but neglects to mention her seductive-rejecting relationship and prior acts of intercourse.

One such woman complained that the man had been raping her for years and she was sick and tired of it. Another woman complained that when she refused to open the door of her apartment, the man forced the door open, damaging the lock. She said later that she would withdraw the charge of rape but she wanted the police to stop her former boyfriend from calling on her.

ASSAULT DURING VOLUNTARY SEXUAL RELATIONS

Some women who complain to the police of rape do so because they have been handled roughly or physically assaulted during voluntary sexual intercourse. These women do not reveal that they agreed to the sexual act at the time they make the complaint. A twenty-two-year-old woman reported that three men abducted her as she was leaving a downtown tavern. She was driven to an unknown location and raped by two of the men. The third man was unable to have an erection and in his anger he struck her on the abdomen with his fists. One of the men burned her on the buttocks with a lighted cigarette.

A few days after making the report she said that she did not want to prosecute. At this time she revealed that she willingly went to the car with one of the men and had sexual relationships with him. After they had finished, two of the man's friends came to the car and also had sexual intercourse with her. "This wasn't a forcible rape. I made the report because one of the men got rough with me."

A young woman who reported that she had been raped by a boyfriend in his apartment was found on physical examination to have prominent scratches and bruises in several places on her back and arms. Subsequent investigation revealed that she had agreed to have sexual relations but that her boyfriend physically assaulted her repeatedly despite her complaints of pain and efforts to escape from him. The man admitted the physical assault and in explanation simply said, "While making love, I got carried away and scratched her a little bit and bruised her." The girl later said that she intended to make an assault report until the doctor told her she had been raped. "I didn't know that was what you called it." In another similar case the girl had bite marks around both nipples.

CONCEALMENT OF ASSAULT BY THE HUSBAND

A young married woman with a black eye and numerous bruises on her face and body complained to police that an intruder had broken into her home while her husband was at work and raped her. Despite her vigorous resistance she had been overcome by the man, who also stole the money in her purse. Her husband, who accompanied her to the police station, did not seem to be concerned, and later it was learned that there had been an argument between the husband and wife over her spending habits. The argument was terminated by her husband beating her. Neither of them wished her parents to know about the physical assault and they concocted the story of rape.

SELF-INJURY

Women who make false accusations of rape may not only rip their clothing and overturn furniture but also inflict injuries on themselves to give the appearance of a struggle. A sixteen-year-old-girl told police that two men drove alongside her in a car as she was walking to the library. They yelled out to her, asking where she was going, but she ignored them. The car stopped and a thin man got out, holding a long knife in one hand. He grabbed her with his other hand and forced her in the car, after warning her not to call out. Once inside the car she was told to close her eyes, and the car drove off at a high rate of speed.

There was no conversation during the drive which lasted five to ten minutes. She was taken to a small brick house, location unknown, which the thin man opened with a skeleton key. She was made to sit on a chair, the only furniture in the living room. One man went to the back of the house and the thin man put his knife to her side and told her to sit still. He started to remove her clothing, meanwhile asking her if she had ever had sexual relations, if she had a boyfriend and similar questions. While talking to her, he cut the skin over her chest. When he lifted her skirt, she jumped up and ran out the door. He grabbed her, tearing the buttons off her sweater, but she managed to break free and ran to a public telephone to call her parents.

An experienced detective had some reservations about her story, but she appeared to be in genuine distress during the interview shortly after the alleged attempted rape. Medical examination showed superficial knife wounds over her upper chest and abdomen. Some days later she admitted that the account of the assault was a hoax. She had visited the house in the company of two young men whom she declined to name. She said she lied because she was fearful of what her parents would do if they found that she had been out with these men.

RESENTMENT

The man who is very attentive and considerate while seducing a girl may pay dearly for his inconsiderate behavior after the sexual intercourse. An eighteen-year-old girl reported to the police that a man had stopped her as she was walking to work and forced her into his car at knifepoint. He drove off and started feeling her body as he was driving. After parking the car in a vacant lot he told her, "If you don't take your clothes off, I'll put this knife through your throat." She began taking off her underclothes while he unzipped her dress. After fondling her breasts, he raped her. The day after making the report, the girl admitted to detectives that she entered the car voluntarily and had sexual relations of her own free will. She added, "I got mad at him when he made me get out of his car and catch a bus. This was my reason for calling the police."

BLACKMAIL

Although the author has not encountered blackmail as a motive for rape, Bronson in 1918 reported that it was a frequent motive. He cited the two following cases: A woman, after trying to get money from a wealthy man by accusing him of an assault on her child, gave the child up to her own lover, who, she knew, was infected with gonorrhea, so that the accusation in future could have material basis of fact.

A woman accused several individuals of having raped her child, aged nine and a half years. The expert showed that this had no foundation. The genital organs of the child were healthy, but there was noticed on the superior portion of the vulva a red circle, of recent origin, as large as a silver half dollar. The woman herself had bruised her child to form a ground for her accusation, the motive being blackmail.

In England, when there had been a number of sexual assaults on women in railway trains and the daily papers had taken the matter up with considerable excitement, demanding the exemplary punishment of the offenders and the introduction of special measures for the safety of female travelers, an English judge laconically remarked that in his opinion men traveling on the railways were in greater danger from women's attempts at blackmail than were women from men's attempts at rape.

DESIRE FOR ATTENTION

A twelve-year-old girl was brought to the police department by her parents with the story that she had been raped the previous day. She was walking home from school with two friends when a dog ran out from a yard toward them. The other girls ran away and when they were out of sight, a man ran out from behind some bushes, dragged her into the bushes, pulled down her pants and raped her. She screamed for help, but no one appeared. After the rape the man told her, "Don't tell anyone about this or I'll kill you." She ran home but was too scared to tell her parents until the following day.

Medical examination showed no evidence of sexual intercourse. On subsequent interview with a detective and review of her story, she admitted that the report was not true. "I made this up because my mother doesn't pay attention to me, neither does my dad. They're closer to my brother. He's five years old."

A woman felt neglected by her husband who held two jobs. She gave an elaborate but fictitious account of rape in her home in the early hours of the morning. Her ruse succeeded, as her husband gave up his night work.

DESIRE FOR PUBLICITY

Szurek has described the case of a fourteen-year-old girl who accused her father of having intercourse with her. She eagerly looked forward to the front page publicity she would receive as a result of her father's trial. The girl's mother testified in his defense and he was acquitted. When the girl was five years old, she frequently "snuggled up and burrowed into adults" in a way that her father thought was more than "childish affectionateness." When the girl was eight, male neighbors complained to the mother that her daughter was too provocative with them in their homes, and asked the mother not to permit her to visit.

When the mother confronted her with these complaints, the girl accused the neighbors of sexually approaching her. However, she also hugged and kissed several of her mother's boyfriends so effusively that some of them never returned. When she was eleven years of age, she was so sexually provocative with a married Japanese male houseservant that he left. She sneaked out of windows at night to meet boys or invited them into the house when her parents were away, using her allowance to buy them liquor.

She later boasted of having had her first coitus at twelve with a man twice her age. When taken to a therapist who gave a poor prognosis, she told him that her mother and grandmother performed cunnilingus upon her. She told other girls she was pregnant and needed an abortion. She said the father of the "child" could have been any one of thirty or forty men, either black or white, although upon examination she was found not to be pregnant. Later she boasted that she had "taken on six or more teen-agers in a gang-bang on a dare." While confined in a juvenile court detention home, she accused her father of having one of his female friends perform cunnilingus upon her, then of having a male friend have intercourse with her, and finally of the father himself having intercourse with her.

FALSE ACCUSATIONS BY PARENTS AND DAUGHTER

Bronson notes that young girls may be the complainants in false accusations of assault or rape at the instigation of hysterical parents. A girl comes home from school or play crying, having been roughly handled by some young man of the neighborhood, although with no evil intent. Forthwith the mother, in anger, conceives the notion that the young man had impure designs; she may influence the child to tell a story corroborative of her own suspicions.

Under repeated cross-questionings and repetitions of the framework of a story, the child's account of what actually took place fits more accurately with the mother's accusation, and thus a case develops requiring the attention of physician and court. In a case of this kind, known to Bronson, there was a feud of long standing between the parents of the supposed assailant and the girl's parents. The accusation was all that was required for a bitter and vicious outbreak of hostilities between the two camps.

Sutherland describes the case of a young girl who claimed that she had been raped by an old man. On medical examination it was found that she had a slight trickle of blood from the vulva down on her thigh. The blood was found to come from a small linear wound inside the vagina. She volubly described what had happened. The doctor, becoming suspicious that the story she told was false, asked her to repeat her tale, which she at once proceeded to do in exactly the same words. Suddenly he interrupted her and then asked her to continue. This she did by beginning at the beginning again. When he asked her who had scratched her inside her vagina, she at once replied, "My mother, with her fingernail." The man was exonerated.

Other illustrations of false accusations by parents and their daughters are described above in the section on blackmail.

THE UNWELCOME STEPFATHER

Young girls who are very attached to their fathers and distressed over the divorce of their parents on occasion falsely accuse an unwelcome stepfather of rape. Presumably there is an underlying expectation that the accusation will lead to a reunion of the mother and father. In other cases the intention may be simply to separate mother from a drunken, cruel and overbearing stepfather.

A fourteen-year-old girl, on returning home from school, asked her stepfather for some money. He replied, "You will have to give me some" and took her to his bedroom and told her to lay on the bed. He removed her underclothing and had sexual relations. Afterwards he told her not to say anything to her mother. The stepfather who appeared surprised by the accusation was very cooperative with the police and requested a polygraph test. Later the girl admitted that she had been having sexual relations with a boyfriend and that she made up the story, as she had not menstruated for some months. Medical examination showed that she was pregnant.

FALSE REPORT OF INCEST

Thoinot has reported the case of an innocent man falsely accused of rape by his own daughter. Mr. B and his wife took into their household a friend who had just lost his wife, a Mr. H, aged sixty years, and his daughter Lucie, aged eleven. Some time later Mr. B and his wife lodged a complaint with the court in which they accused Mr. H of having raped his own daughter.

At the hearing, Lucie unhesitatingly accused her father of having had sexual relations with her since she was nine years old. She also said that he practiced cunnilingus and the child did not merely accuse him orally, she wrote to a little girl friend and told her all the horrors of which she had been the victim; she wrote to the police commissioner, telling him that sooner than return to her abominable father she would prefer to kill herself.

The physical examination showed that she was a virgin and the case was dismissed. It was not until several months later that the child, on the eve of her first communion, confessed that B and his wife had fabricated the entire charge, and that she had been their accomplice on the promise that they would give her money that she might become an actress. The motive that had actuated B and his wife to accuse H falsely was the wish to appropriate to themselves a considerable sum of money that they owed H. B and his wife were prosecuted and convicted.

Resentment toward a drunken, cruel father may lead a daughter to make false claims of rape against her own father.

TO AVOID PARENTAL PUNISHMENT

A young girl who behaves in a guilty manner after a date with her boyfriend confesses that she has had sexual relations when questioned by a suspicious parent. However, to avoid blame she may cry rape. Discovery of blood-stained underclothing by the mother may also lead to false claims of rape. This is rather awkward for the boyfriend, especially if the girl is under the legal age of consent, because even if the girl later admits that she gave her consent, her boyfriend can still be charged with statutory rape.

The girl who is required to be home by 11 P.M. but does not return until the early hours of the morning may seek to avoid punishment by claiming that she was kidnapped while walking home from her girl friend's house and raped. She gives an elaborate description of her abduction by three men who stopped their car alongside her and offered her a ride. When she refused, two men jumped out, forced her into the car, drove her out in the country and raped her repeatedly.

Gebhard recalls that Dr. Kinsey often said the difference between a "good time" and a "rape" may hinge on whether the girl's parents were awake when she finally arrived home.

THE FIRST MENSTRUAL PERIOD

A mother brought her twelve-year-old daughter to the police department and reported that her daughter had been raped by a visitor to the house where she was employed as a babysitter. The girl said that the man asked her to show him where the light switch was in the bathroom. When she showed him, he asked her if she had menstruated yet and when she replied no, he pulled her pants down and raped her. Afterwards she noticed blood dripping from her vagina.

The man who was arrested denied the rape but said that he had asked an older woman in the home to tell him where the bathroom was and she had shown him and turned the light on. This woman confirmed his story and added that this was the only time the man left her company while he was in the home. He was only gone a very short time. On questioning by the detective, the girl admitted that she had not told the truth. She said she was late returning home and her parents had gone to look for her. After finding her, they took her home and examined her underclothing. On finding blood on her panties, her parents became very angry and her father threatened to spank her. Because of her fear of a spanking she made up the story. Apparently her parents did not realize that this was her first menstruation.

CURFEW VIOLATION

A fourteen-year-old girl claimed that she was dragged from a bus stop late at night to a house by two young men. One man told her, "I want you to help me celebrate my twenty-fifth birthday." She said no, but one of the men struck her about the head and neck. She started kicking the man but the other man held her hands and both of them forced her into a bedroom and raped her. She dressed, then picked up a bottle, hit one man over the head and ran out of the house. When questioned later she admitted that she had been in the company of the men during the evening and when a police car pulled up alongside her, as she was walking home alone, she quickly made up the story, as she was afraid she would be arrested for curfew violation.

CHILDREN AND THEIR SCHOOLTEACHERS

Schoolteachers are not infrequently the victims of accusations by hysterical girls who have a secret attachment for them. Bronson gives the following example. A schoolteacher was charged with having committed a rape on a child of thirteen years of age. The child was unusually precocious for her age and swore very distinctly to a rape having been committed. She made no complaint, however, for a week or ten days. On examination there was no mark of violence about her, either recent or remote. The girl's story was inconsistent and not supported by evidence.

On cross-examination she said the prisoner committed the rape while they were standing up. The girl was short, and the schoolteacher, who was sixty years of age was tall. She was quite sure that she was never placed on the ground. She resisted all she could but could not help herself. Her statement of the mode in which the act was perpetrated involved so many inconsistencies and improbabilities that the jury acquitted the prisoner.

A CHILD'S FANTASY

Thoinot describes the case of a little child who was adopted by Mr. and Mrs. X, highly honorable people. One day Mr. X read about the story of a scandal that was making a good deal of noise in a certain city in France. The little girl was present but was playing with her doll and, besides, appeared to pay no attention to what was said in her presence. The husband and wife commented on the story, supposing that the child was incapable of understanding the conversation which was held in veiled terms.

Several days afterward Mr. X surprised the little girl in the act of holding her doll and kissing it passionately on the upper part of its legs which she held wide apart. Mrs. X asked the child who could have taught her to do such a thing. In no way disconcerted she replied that she was doing to her doll what had already been done to herself. She declared further that when she was with her nurse, the nurse's little boy had lain with her and that they had acted like husband and wife. After the little boy, his father had come, and then the grandfather, and they had taken the same liberties as the little boy.

There was a great uproar in the house. The little girl was submitted to an examination by an able physician, who declared that no assault had been committed on her. The girl admitted that there was no truth in her story and that she had simply wished to do like the ladies whom they told about in the newspapers.

FALSE ACCUSATIONS BY PROSTITUTES

A surprising number of false accusations of rape are made by prostitutes. As police usually check to see whether complainants of rape have prior criminal convictions, these women are likely to find their complaints regarded with some skepticism, especially when they have a record of multiple convictions for prostitution, drunkenness and vagrancy. Factors commonly underlying these false accusations are failure of the client to pay the fee, roughness or brutality during or following sexual intercourse, the use of force to secure participation in perverse sexual acts, blackmail and attempts to discredit police officers.

Failure to Pay

A forty-year-old woman who looked much older claimed that a man grabbed her as she was entering her apartment house, forced her into her apartment, then forced her to remove all her clothes and to participate in fellatio and sexual intercourse. The alleged rapist, a twenty-eight-year-old man, told police that she propositioned him, naming a fee of ten dollars. He did not have this much money and after some haggling a fee of six dollars was agreed upon. After fellatio and sexual relations he refused to pay her and she became enraged, throwing a glass at the door and raising so much noise that the landlord appeared. A check on her criminal record showed that she had seven arrests for prostitution, sixteen arrests for drunkenness and one arrest each for indecent exposure and resistance.

Another woman, with numerous arrests for prostitution and drunkenness, claimed that she had been raped by four men who forced her to accompany them to a hotel room then raped her ten times. When confronted with the information provided by the hotel manager that she entered the hotel willingly, she admitted that she had claimed rape because the man did not pay her. As she had made previous false accusations of rape, the detectives patiently explained to her that when her clients did not pay her, this was just prostitution without being paid and not rape.

Assault

A twenty-five-year-old woman with several convictions for prostitution and unlawful occupancy of a hotel room claimed that a man forced her to accompany her to a hotel room where he raped and assaulted her. She had a black eye as a result of the assault. The man admitted having sexual intercourse with her and striking her. The blow was struck during an argument over the fee. She refused to press charges of simple assault. In a similar case the man claimed that he struck the prostitute when he discovered that she had stolen his wallet.

Perverse Sexual Acts

Some prostitutes draw the line on request for certain sexually perverse acts. When force is used to obtain their cooperation, they may later attempt to gain revenge by making false accusations of rape. A woman who claimed that she had been raped and assaulted later acknowledged that she had agreed to have sexual intercourse with the man for fifteen dollars. "He told me to get my clothes off. He told me to lay down, so I did. So then he had this wax dill and tried putting it in me. I said no and I pushed this thing out and threw it against the wall and I got the telephone and hit him with it on the forehead and cut his head. He told me, 'You son of a bitch, why did you hit me? You took it [the dill] the first time [referring to a previous occasion].' I said, 'How should I know, I was drunk.'

"I got my coat and purse and started walking toward the bathroom and he grabbed me and hit me on the face and head and then he made me lay down and started to let me have it with the wax dill. Then he put his penis through the rectum, so I told him that it hurt real bad and he said, 'Shut up, I don't care if it hurts.' So he told me to get dressed and I told him to forget about the fifteen dollars.' "

A twenty-year-old girl reported to police that while she was standing in the parking lot alongside a nightclub, two men about twenty-five to thirty years of age asked her to come with them. When she refused to spread her legs, both men hit her several times. "I was tired of being hit so I gave in." Both men raped her and took her back to the car. After a short drive one man left the car and the other man prevented her from getting out. However, she later jumped out of the car at an intersection.

She began to run from the car but slipped and fell. The man caught her and later raped her again. "After this he made me 69 him. I got sick and threw up when he put it in my mouth." He told her to commit several unnatural acts and when she refused he struck her again. She was driven downtown and allowed to leave the car. When examined at a hospital, she was found to have scratches and abrasions on her face.

The following day, when interviewed by detectives, she eventually gave a much different account of her experience. She was not forced to accompany the men to the house but was offered two hundred dollars if she would allow the men to "go all the way" while an unknown man would be peeking at her. She was told that an elderly white man "got his kicks" from watching Negroes having sexual relations with white girls. This man was going to pay eight hundred dollars and her share would be two hundred dollars.

One man was unable to have an erection and the other man hurt her when he attempted intercourse. When she complained of the pain, she was told not to think about it, but she began to cry and the man struck her in the face. "I guess this guy was watching through a peephole. I heard him say, 'You guys aren't fucking her right, the deal's off." Afterwards the man who struck her asked her, "What's wrong with you, you messed up a good thing" and she replied, "I just couldn't go through with it."

This man later forced her to have sexual relations with him and forced her to commit various unnatural acts. He struck her several times because of her refusal to cooperate. Afterwards he drove her downtown and she took a cab to a hospital where she called the police and made the complaint of rape.

Attempts To Discredit Police Officers

A police officer who has to arrest a woman may find himself the victim of a false accusation of rape. The owner of a tavern who was in danger of losing his license for serving alcohol to minors felt that he was being victimized by the officer who inspected his tavern frequently for liquor code violations. In an attempt to have the officer removed from the force, he arranged for a prostitute to make false accusations of rape against him.

DELUSIONAL STATES

A forty-six-year-old woman reported to the police that her husband had been having sexual relations with their youngest daughter. The husband denied the accusation and medical examination of the young girl showed that there was no basis for the charge. Psychiatric examination of the mother showed the presence of numerous delusions. She was convinced that her husband was plotting to kill her or drive her insane by giving her aspirins which contained poison. She also believed that their home was being used as the headquarters of a gang. On one occasion eight members of the gang, armed with loaded pistols, surrounded her house and demanded to see her daughter.

After several months' treatment in a psychiatric hospital, she was discharged against medical advice on the request of her husband. However, she continued to believe that her husband was committing incest. She also thought that he had hired the doctors to weaken her mind. Other paranoid delusions included the belief that the gang were storing money in her house, confusing her daughter, and calling her filthy names over the telephone. She purchased a pistol and several days later she shot and killed her husband while he was sleeping.

"We quarreled two times that afternoon and night about some property he was keeping secret from me. I had bad impulses. I wanted to take revenge because he harmed my health, used me as a guinea pig for experiments. He was doing that to my daughter, having intercourse. I was so sure I was going to die. I didn't think I was going to live at all. I was so sure I was going to drop dead I turned in my keys to the deposit box I had.

"I didn't want him around my children. He had betrayed me. He would enjoy watching my funeral. I didn't want to let him enjoy that, I just can't figure it out myself. Something overpowered me. I just couldn't control myself. I try to think if I really did shoot him. I must have. I guess I did. I went in and told my daughter I had shot him."

False complaints of rape are not infrequently made by middle-aged women suffering from paranoid psychoses. One woman made several calls to the police department with complaints ranging from obscene telephone calls, theft and threats to attempted rape. On one occasion she was convinced that a man had broken into her home because a perfume bottle had been moved a few inches on her bathroom shelf. Many of these women accuse their doctors of rape or attempted rape. Medlicott mentions a fifty-six-year-old married woman who for five years had believed that two doctors were using "rays" and telepathic influences to seduce her. This author has also reported the two following cases.

A minister's wife, a quiet, repressed, very likable woman, was receiving carbon dioxide coma treatment. On waking, the doctor was impressed by the odd way she looked at him and by the questions she asked. Because of shortage of staff he did not have anyone in the room at the time but merely left the door into the corridor open. Feeling uneasy he had the receptionist present on the next occasion and she was interrogated by the patient as to where she was standing during the treatment. On the next occasion he brought a more senior member of the staff in and again the patient wakened in a suspicious state. Fortunately he had a good relationship with the patient, otherwise she would probably not have come back. Although earlier questioning had not elicited the cause of her suspicion, she now broke down and said she had been quite certain on each occasion the doctor had interfered with her sexually. She respected him but the reality was overpowering and it was only after the second witness had been present that her good sense told her she must have been imagining it. With this she was able to ventilate some disturbing sexual phantasies and conflicts she had previously suppressed. A doctor's reputation could well have been harmed, not by malicious intent, but merely by his becoming the vehicle for the suppressed sexual impulses of a highly respectable woman.

A university graduate of forty-two years had a short illness of an obvious hysterical origin at twenty-one years, but had married successfully and been a capable housewife and mother. She was very attached to her family doctor, who had a large obstetric practice and had delivered her children. A few months before she was seen, she maintained she visited his rooms one evening and was shocked when he kissed her and wanted intercourse. Two weeks later she went back again at night, when she said he pricked her arms with a pin to test for hysteria. This extended after she took her dress off, to more general pricking and he demonstrated that the right side of her body was not as sensitive to pin pricking as the left. He then said he had the right answer for hysteria and started to massage her. This, she said, nearly produced a stupor, but before she lost consciousness she was able to stop him and save her honor. Superficially, the story was plausible, but she was an inveterate reader of medical books and her phantasy tied in with other odd ideas. She shortly became frankly psychotic. On recovery from the psychosis she still maintained the truth of this story. Knowledge of the patient left no doubt, however, that this false accusation arose upon the basis of an erotic phantasy which had become real to her.

Alcoholic delirium (delirium tremens) may also lead to false accusations of rape. A forty-nine-year-old woman reported to police that three men broke into her home and demanded her money. They threatened to come back for money later, then took all her clothes off her and raped her. They also forced a broom handle into her vagina and also the sharp end of a large meat fork. There was no evidence of rape or injury to her vagina. She was in a delirious state due to alcoholism.

HYSTERIA

The dissociative reactions of hysteria may be associated with unfounded accusation of rapes. Bronson states that "an hysterical woman under such circumstances may even show minute extravasations of blood as in a bruise, upon her limbs and body as evidence of struggle. Nor are such stigmata always self-inflicted. They may appear automatically." This author quotes the case of a married woman who accused a physician of raping her during a vaginal examination.

The woman testified as follows: "The doctor came to the house at about half past eleven. Upon his arrival he said, 'Getting along any better?' I answered, 'I am about the same; I am weak and the flow still continues, but I have no pain.' He said he will have to examine me and he put his hand inside me and asked me whether I felt any pain. I answered no; then he touched me, I do not know just where, and suddenly I felt myself weak and falling into his arms; he put me on my bed and when I felt his organ inside of me and very deep I came to myself; I cried out, "My God!" and I pushed him away with my knees so that he had to draw back. When I saw that it was the doctor who did it I fainted again; just as I was losing consciousness I felt that he was trying to start all over again."

Witnesses testified regarding an incident in which a physician, a druggist and a priest were called hurriedly to her house. She seemed in a deep faint, her eyes were closed, her body apparently lifeless. The druggist who reached the scene first felt for the pulse and found it strong and bounding. The priest asked why he was sent for and it was the woman who answered him; although she seemed dead a few minutes before, she now engaged in conversation. The woman had not fainted. Although a medical expert testified for the defense that she was simulating illness, the diagnosis would appear to be hysteria. The physician accused of rape was acquitted.

THE HYSTERICAL PERSONALITY

Women who have an hysterical personality (which should not be confused with the illness hysteria) are inclined to be very demanding, dependent, immature, vain and self-centered. They are very suggestible and are subject to vivid emotional outbursts, but their moods change as quickly as April showers. Within moments lighthearted laughter and composure can replace apparent great distress with copious tears. Their exhibitionistic, dramatic behavior is accompanied by a remarkable capacity for self-deception and sometimes by considerable disregard for the truth.

Persons unfamiliar with this character disorder may be greatly impressed by their apparent candor and sincerity when they make accusations against others. Thus false claims of rape may arouse immediate sympathy and concern for the girl and anger against the alleged assailant. Feeling runs high and the unfortunate man may be quickly arrested and imprisoned.

These women, who are often very attractive, in their words, gestures and choice of clothing create an aura of sexuality. Yet their sexually provocative behavior, although designed to arouse the male companion, is suddenly terminated when the man becomes too eager in his advances or when he wants to go beyond the threshold to her apartment after an evening together. Teasing of the man and not desire for sexual intercourse is the motivation behind the seductive behavior. If in the course of petting the man succeeds in removing the girl's panties, the girl may suddenly panic and cry rape.

An attractive slim twenty-five-year-old fashion model was introduced, at a wedding reception, to a young man who showered attention on her. He neglected to mention that he was a married man visiting the city for several days to attend a business convention. On their third date in three days he took her to an expensive restaurant and then to a nightclub. He boasted about his financial success as a stockbroker, claimed that he was a cousin of the actor Paul Newman and talked of flying her in his private plane to Las Vegas to see the shows. She could bring another girl and boyfriend so the guys and the girls could stay in different rooms and "not have to worry."

Lavishing praise on her appearance and personality, he expressed surprise that she was not already married. Indeed he talked about marriage and what good-looking children they would have. During the evening he drank a considerable amount of alcohol and although he did not appear to be drunk, she doubted whether he was sober enough to drive.

Despite her misgivings, he was able to drive her to her apartment where she invited him in for coffee. After a short time she told him she had to work the next day and leaned over to kiss him goodnight and thank him for the evening. He put his arms around her and forced her back on the couch. She resisted him and started screaming. He told her that if she did not cooperate he would have to hurt her and she became even more alarmed. She picked up an ornament with a sharp point and tried to "rip his eyes out."

Other residents of the apartment house who had heard her screams banged on the door and the man released her and let them in. The man who was accused of rape later told police they had been petting and after she had allowed him to remove her panty hose she suddenly told him to leave her alone or she would start screaming. Without waiting to see his response, she started screaming at the top of her voice.

He denied having made any threats of physical harm, and he denied having raped her. There was no medical evidence to support a charge of rape and the man passed a polygraph test which he requested. The girl later withdrew the charges of rape "as he had a lot to drink and I don't think he meant to hurt me."

REPEATED FALSE CLAIMS OF RAPE

Women who return again and again to police departments with false claims of rape have usually had prior psychiatric treatment or diagnostic evaluation. This information is not always volunteered to the investigating officers. The middle-aged repeaters usually have a chronic paranoid delusional state. Despite their bizarre ideas they may make a satisfactory adjustment in the community; occasionally some of them take the law into their own hands, with tragic outcome, when they feel that the police or courts are not providing adequate protection for them from their imagined assailants.

Adolescent girls and younger women who make repeated false reports of rape are usually hysterical personalities. The hysterical character disorder may be accompanied by or overshadowed by features of a sociopathic or antisocial character. Many of these girls are of average or bright intelligence but a few are mentally retarded promiscuous girls, some of whom have difficulty in appreciating that the police department cannot be used to punish clients who have failed to pay for sexual favors.

An eighteen-year-old girl of average intelligence within a few years made eight false reports of rape to police departments. Once she reported that a physician tried to force her to go to bed with a Negro. Another time she gave an elaborate account of rape by two Negroes. Her recollection included a multitude of details on the appearance, behavior and conversation of the men, the circumstances of her abduction, the car which was used and the house to which she was taken, yet she could not recall how many times the men had intercourse with her. She refused to take a polygraph test. Over the years she accused over sixty men of having raped her.

A twenty-three-year-old girl of average intelligence at various times accused her father, her stepfather, as well as a number of casual acquaintances and strangers of rape. She was known to be promiscuous and she had boasted of her employment as a prostitute. Her imagination rivaled that of Baron Munchausen. She told the most improbable tales, yet her life had not been without incident and not all her dramatic experiences could be dismissed as figments of her imagination. Although she frequently contradicted herself, it was not always easy to separate fact from fiction and there was reason to believe that she had on occasion been the victim of rape. From adolescence her life was punctuated by admissions to hospitals for drinking, drug abuse and attempted suicide. Unfortunately treatment failed to halt her self-destructive behavior.

> *"There is no lie so reckless as to be without some proof."*
> — Pliny the Elder, *History*.

Girls who make repeated claims of rape may not make more than one report to any single police department. If the girl tells an apparently convincing story, the unfortunate victim of her false accusation may be arrested and taken to jail as in the following case described by Schauffler.

A worker from a protective agency was called to a suburban school to listen to the story of a little girl who had confided to her teacher that the father had attempted to molest her sexually. The child was eleven years old and the adopted child of an elderly couple. She readily told the same story to the worker, and she was brought to the office for further questioning.

Inquiry revealed that her father was a man of excellent reputation who held a responsible position in his community. Because it was difficult to suspect this man of such a crime and also because of the implausible story that the child related, the workers of the agency decided to make further investigation before the matter was taken to the district attorney's office.

The investigation in her home and former neighborhood disclosed that the child had made this accusation before. She had accused a crippled foster brother, a high school boy and the janitor in the school she had previously attended. She had become so unpopular in the community that her parents had moved, hoping that a new school and neighborhood would help her. Evidently the child had used this device as an escape from unpleasant situations. She had accused the school janitor at a time when she was having difficulty in school. Her father had recently punished her.

This case was not prosecuted, but the parents felt inadequate to cope with the child and placed her in a boarding school. Three years later the father retired and bought a home in a distant part of the state and the parents took the child with them.

It is interesting that after three months in the new community she made the same accusation against the town handyman who was repairing the school building. An enraged populace caused this man to be placed in jail and the case was taken before the grand jury, at which time the child's propensity to tell this story was disclosed by the records of the juvenile court in her former community.

Sometimes the claims of rape by these girls are easily detected. One fourteen-year-old girl accused her stepfather of raping her, but investigation showed that at the time of the alleged rape he was attending a union meeting. A nineteen-year-old girl accused her employer, but there were obvious inconsistencies in her account of the rape. Later she accused a police officer of rape when he arrested her for shoplifting. When the man accused by the girl is known to have been in her company and has previous convictions for rape, there is a greater possibility of injustice, as he may decide not to testify in his defense in order to avoid the cross-examination which would reveal his prior convictions. A national file on women who make false accusations of rape would appear to be desirable to protect the innocent.

The methods used by police to detect false complaints of rape are reviewed in Chapter 14.

THE LAW ON RAPE

"Laws were made that the stronger might not in
all things have his way."
— Ovid, *Fasti*

R<small>APE</small> may be defined as unlawful sexual intercourse between a male and a female, not the wife of the perpetrator, under circumstances which render the female legally incapable of consenting to the act; or where the female's resistance to the act is overcome by force or violence, or threats of bodily harm; or where her consent is induced by trick, fraud or the administration of intoxicating or stupefying substances (see Michael and Wechsler).

Some statutes still use the old term "carnal knowledge" to refer to sexual intercourse. Penetration of the vagina need not be complete, the slightest penetration is sufficient, and in virgins the hymen need not be ruptured. Ploscowe suggests that the law should require more than "the slightest penetration of the women's person" to make the act of attempting to have intercourse, rape.

"Courts and legislators sometimes forget that attempted rape and assault are also crimes, though they are punishable less severely than rape. Sexual intercourse, which is the essence of rape, is not present where there has been only the slightest of sexual contacts. The rule as to slight penetration also complicates the problem of proof. In one case in which a man was convicted of rape largely on the uncorroborated testimony of a woman, a doctor examined her two hours after the alleged assault took place and could find no evidence of sexual intercourse. Nevertheless, the conviction for rape was sustained, since the slight sexual touching required for rape under the law did not necessarily leave any physical evidence" (Ploscowe).

Sexual emission need not occur; however, an occasional suggestion may be found that emission must be established. Perkins comments: "If the theory back of this idea was pressed far enough, it might reach the point of recognizing the effective use of a contraceptive as a complete defense to a prosecution for either rape or carnal knowledge of a child. It is safe to assume that no court would go this far. In fact, the premise itself is false. The sound rule, which prevails very generally, if not uniformly today, is that emission is neither necessary nor sufficient to establish guilt in these cases. The essential element is penetration."

A wife who refuses to have sexual intercourse with her husband cannot appeal to the law that she has been raped because her husband overcomes her resistance with force. If, however, her husband helps another man to rape her, he can be convicted of rape as in the following case. A husband growing weary of his wife of ten months, for the purpose of obtaining grounds for divorce, paid a lodger in his home twenty-five dollars to commit adultery with his wife. The husband and his brother hid in an adjoining room and made no effort to aid the woman when they heard her screams and witnessed her unsuccessful struggles to avoid rape by the lodger.

The wife testified that the lodger caught her by the throat, threw her down and raped her. She tried her best to struggle against the man and screamed for help. When her husband came in she said to him, "Oh, dear, kill him," but her husband pushed her away from him and soon thereafter went away with the other two men, apparently on friendly terms. Three days later he filed for divorce on the ground of adultery and took no steps to prosecute the man who had raped his wife. The husband was later convicted and sentenced to prison for seven years.

A husband who attempted to force another man to rape his wife was convicted of an assault with intent to commit rape. The circumstances of the assault are described with some indignation by the Supreme Court of North Carolina *(State v. Dowell,* 106 N.C. 722, 11 S.E. 525, 1890).

> The facts are abhorrently simple. The white husband of a white wife, under menace of death to both parties in case of refusal, and supporting his threat by a loaded gun held over the parties, constrains a colored man to undertake, and his wife to submit to, an attempted sexual connection. The details of this shocking transaction are so disgusting that we will not stain the pages of our reports with their particular recital.
>
> Suffice it to say that, under the coercion of the defendant, Lowery, the colored man, did actually make the attempt. Indeed, he did everything necessary to constitute the crime of rape except actual penetration. Fortunately the fright and excitement rendered him incapable of consummating the outrage, which, as we understand the case, he would otherwise have perpetrated; and, alike fortunately, at perhaps the critical moment, the gun discharging itself in the hands of the unnatural husband, the enforced assailant was enabled to effect his escape.

In *R. v. Miller* the judge held that when a wife had left her husband and filed a petition for divorce against him but no decree and not even an interim order had been made by the court, the wife's implied consent to intercourse had not been revoked and the husband who had intercourse with her against her will could not be guilty of rape. But he held that the husband was not entitled to use force or violence in the exercise of his right to marital intercourse and that if he did so he would make himself liable for whatever other offense the facts of the particular case might warrant. The jury convicted the husband of assault.

CONSENT

If a female consciously consents to the act of intercourse, however tardily or reluctantly, and however persistently she may resist for a time, the act is not rape, provided she is of such an age and condition as to be capable of giving a valid consent . . . the important distinction lies between consent and submission; the latter does not preclude a prosecution for rape (Clark and Marshall). Submission to force or as the result of being put in fear and terror is not consent.

Juries considering the issue of consent would do well to keep in mind the admonition of Sir Matthew Hale, lord chief justice of England from 1670 to 1676. "It is true rape is a most detestable crime, and therefore ought severely and impartially to be punished with death; but it must be remembered that it is an accusation easily to be made and hard to be proved, and harder to be defended by the party accused, though never so innocent."

FORCE AND THREATS OF FORCE

Physical force or threats of bodily injury show that the sexual act was rape. An old rule required that the woman must have resisted "to the uttermost." But to make the crime hinge on the uttermost exertion the woman was physically capable of making would be a reproach to the law as well as to common sense. As the court stated in People v. Connor:

> It is quite impossible to lay down any general rule which shall define the exact line of conduct which should be pursued by an assaulted female under all circumstances, as the power and strength of the aggressor, and the physical and mental ability of the female to interpose resistance to the unlawful assault, and the situation of the parties, must vary in each case. What would be the proper measure of resistance in one case would be inapplicable in another situation accompanied by different circumstances. One person would be paralyzed by fear and rendered voiceless and helpless by circumstances which would only inspire another with higher courage and greater strength of will to resist an assault.

The instructions to the jury in *State v. Dill* provide a comprehensive review of the problem of resistance to rape.

> As showing consent, or want of consent, the nature and extent of the resistance offered by the woman is a most important consideration. Generally if the woman assaulted is physically and mentally able to resist, is not terrified by threats, nor in a place and position that resistance would have been useless, it must be shown that she did, in fact, resist the assault made upon her person. In the absence of fear and terror induced by force or threats of force, or of other circumstances which would make resistance unnecessary, as where the futility of resistance is reasonably apparent, an entire want of mental assent or consent on the part of the prosecutrix must be shown.
>
> Resistance, however, is relative; and the amount of resistance required to negative consent depends on the circumstances of the particular case; and there is

frequently presented the question whether the woman ultimately consented to the intercourse, or refrained from resistance, or ceased to resist, because it was useless or dangerous. Generally, the resistance offered by the woman must be reasonably proportionate to her strength and opportunities. In the absence of excusing circumstances it must be shown that the woman did resent the attack made upon her in good faith and without pretense, with an active determination to prevent the violation of her person, and was not merely passive and perfunctory in her resistance.

It is not necessary that the woman use in opposition to the assault all of the physical force of which, in the estimation of the jury, she was capable. It is sufficient if her acts and conduct show a want of consent made manifest by actual, unfeigned resistance resolutely maintained until penetration has been accomplished.

Again, as bearing on the question of consent whether the person assaulted called for help or made other outcry, especially where help may reasonably be expected. Marks of violence upon the person of the woman, the condition of her clothing, and whether she made prompt complaint of the alleged outrage to those to whom she would naturally complain are facts to be considered.

You will, therefore, consider carefully the age and mental condition of the prosecutrix and her size and strength as compared to that of the accused, the testimony relating to the nature and extent of the resistance made by her, the place where the alleged assault took place, the proximity of persons or passersby, calls for help or other outcry, the condition of her clothing, marks of violence on her person, if any, and that she made prompt complaint to her husband and to the police.

The issue of consent is seldom a problem when a woman is attacked in the street by an armed stranger. When, however, the woman has been dating the alleged assailant and has invited him to her apartment, it is sometimes difficult to evaluate the claim of rape. This vexatious problem has been well reviewed in an unsigned article in the *Yale Law Journal (62*:56, 1952) which is quoted below.

When her behavior looks like resistance although her attitude is one of consent, injustice may be done the man by the woman's subsequent accusation. Many women, for example, require as a part of preliminary "love play" aggressive overtures by the man. Often their erotic pleasure may be enhanced by, or even depend upon, an accompanying physical struggle. The "love bite" is a common, if mild, sign of the aggressive component in the sex act. And the tangible signs of struggle may survive to support a subsequent accusation by the woman.

In some cases, the woman's conscious response to the sexual demands of a man may not accurately be labeled either "consent" or "nonconsent" in the sense of a definite positive or negative reaction. Consent, like any other conscious attitude, results from a particular organization of needs in an individual at any given moment, but — especially where sexual stimuli are involved — a person may have no clear attitude. The complex set of personality needs, many of them rooted in the unconscious and often competing with each other, may produce an ambivalent and unclear mixture of desire and fear even in the "normal" person. For instance, a woman's need for sexual satisfaction may lead to the unconscious desire for forceful penetration, the coercion serving neatly to avoid the guilt feelings which might arise after willing participation. But the desire thus generated for the "attack" is likely to clash with the civilized "superego" which vehemently rejects such unrestrained sexuality. At the moment of genital entry, neither force may have gained dominance and no positive or negative attitude formulated.

Where such an attitude of ambivalence exists, the woman may, nonetheless, exhibit behavior which would lead the fact finder to conclude that she opposed the act. To illustrate: a woman whose sexual desire and superego are in conflict may alternate rapidly between "approach" and "rejection" responses to the man, first scratching and pushing him, at the next moment soliciting his caress. In other women, the anxiety resulting from this conflict of needs may cause her to flee from the situation of discomfort, either physically by running away, or symbolically by retreating to such infantile behavior as crying. The scratches, flight and crying constitute admissible and compelling evidence of nonconsent. But the conclusion of rape in this situation may be inconsistent with the meaning of the consent standard and unjust to the man. There is no explicit provision in the law for the woman's attitude of ambivalence. But the universal rule that the state has the burden of proving the woman's nonconsent indicates that if she lacks a definite negative attitude, the law will consider the woman to have consented. And fairness to the male suggests a conclusion of not guilty, despite signs of aggression, if his act was not contrary to the woman's formulated wishes.

The woman's unreliable behavior presents less serious dangers for the man if she later accurately recalls her attitude at the time of the sexual adventure. But since the memory process commonly alters the content of a perception, the woman's recall will often be tailored to fit personality needs which become dominant after the act. The stronger these needs and the more ambivalent the original attitude, the greater is the subsequent distortion. Most women probably have a strong need to adopt the socially acceptable motive and thus some may honestly believe that they were forced to submit over their mental opposition. Particularly since most reports and complaints are made to parents, police or prosecutors, the woman is likely to recall her attitude as one of opposition. Reporting to such "authority figures" encourages the dominance of superego needs in the woman. The distorted recall bypasses the explicit legal pronouncement that a *post facto* attitude toward the act has no legal significance.

OTHER THREATS

Many threats other than direct bodily harm, such as loss of a job or suitor, may coerce a girl into submission, and though she may consider herself opposed to the act, the law does not treat these situations as rape. Unlike American jurisdictions, some other countries — U.S.S.R., Switzerland and Yugoslavia — regard sexual intercourse induced by economic coercion as a form of rape.

The Soviet Code punishes "coercion of a woman by any person on whom she is dependent materially or by reason of her employment." The Swiss Code provides that "whoever influences a woman to copulate with him by abuse of her emergency or her dependency caused through an official or an employment relation or through other similar situation, shall be confined in the prison." In Yugoslavia "whoever through misuse of his position procures a female person subordinated or dependent upon him to have carnal knowledge shall be punished by detention for no more than three years. The penalty for forcible rape is imprisonment for not more than eight years" (Donelly, R.G.: *Yale Law J, 61*:510, 1952).

INTOXICATION

> *"Candy is dandy*
> *But liquor is quicker."*
> *— Ogden Nash,*
> *Reflection on Ice Breaking*

Intercourse with a woman who is so intoxicated from alcohol or drugs as to be incapable of consenting is rape. An English judge expressed the opinion that "it would be monstrous to say that these poor females are to be subjected to such violence, without the parties inflicting it being liable to be indicted. If so, every drunken woman returning from market, and happening to fall down on the road side, may be ravished at the will of the passersby" (*Regina v. Fletcher,* 8 Cox c.c. 131, 1859). But, as Ploscowe notes, there is unquestionably a difference in iniquity between a man who has sexual intercourse with a drinking partner and the rapist who brutally violates a complete stranger.

Ploscowe points out that a man who is drunk cannot defend himself by saying, "If I had been sober and in full command of my faculties, I would not have committed this brutal rape." Similarly a woman who drinks herself into a stage of intoxication should not be permitted to claim, "If I had been sober and in full command of my faculties, I would not have consented to the sexual intercourse." By getting drunk she took a chance that she would be tampered with sexually. When a woman drinks with a man to the point of intoxication, she practically invites him to take advantage of her person. She should not be permitted to yell when she is sober, "I was raped!"

While intoxication is no excuse under the law for a particular criminal act; nevertheless, where the crime requires a particular state of mind with respect to the act committed, intoxication might constitute a defense. For instance, in the case of forcible rape, not only must the perpetrator intend to have sexual intercourse with the victim, but he must also intend to overcome her resistance by force and violence in achieving the intercourse. It is conceivable that a person might be intoxicated and yet capable of achieving intercourse, but at the same time his intoxication might preclude him from consciously forming the intent to overcome the resistance of the victim by force and violence. In such a case the question of specific intent would be for the jury to resolve.

MENTAL ILLNESS

Unlawful sexual intercourse with a female who is so mentally ill or mentally retarded as to be incapable of giving legal consent is rape. In general, the disability must affect the ability to know the nature and consequences of the act so that she is not capable of rational consent (75 CJS 480). Perr describes the case of a twenty-year-old mentally retarded epileptic girl who did not know her address, the date or the year of her birth. She had no knowledge of sexual activities and their consequences. She thought that babies came from the hospital but had no idea how they got there. Her IQ was forty-five.

Men intent on sexual intercourse do not always make careful inquiry into the mental state of the woman of their choice. Nor indeed are they always able to make such an evaluation. If the man himself is mentally retarded or of borderline intelligence, he can hardly be expected to determine the woman's capacity for legal consent. All women are presumed to be sane and since a presumption of sanity exists, even one charged with rape is entitled to be protected by the assumption unless he had reason to know otherwise *(State v. Helderle,* 186 S.W. 699 LRA, 1916F, 735).

Lee Wilson was fixing a flat tire on his car when a forty-four-year-old woman called to him from her home, invited him in and assisted his entry through a window. A brother-in-law of the woman entered the home and found her having sexual intercourse with Wilson. He was convicted of rape and sentenced to ten years in a penitentiary. At the trial relatives of the woman testified that she could not carry on an intelligent conversation and had never learned to read or write. One witness described her as "man crazy" and said she would hang out the window and call to men.

Wilson in his appeal against his conviction and sentence contended that he did not have reasonable grounds for believing that she was incapable of consenting to sexual intercourse. The Court of Appeals of Kentucky agreed with him and stated in its opinion: "Sexual intercourse with an idiot or insane woman is not rape unless the man knows she is insane or an idiot and takes advantage of that fact to accomplish his purpose" (*Wilson v. Commonwealth,* 160 S.W. 2d, 649, 1942).

FRAUD

The use of fraud to obtain sexual intercourse may lead to prosecution for rape. The man who impersonates a woman's husband by getting into her bed late at night is guilty of rape when the woman submits because she falsely supposes that he is her husband. In the absence of statute, sexual intercourse with a woman procured by deceiving her with a "sham wedding" has been held to be not rape on the theory that she knows she is having sexual intercourse with this very person and is deceived only as to a collateral matter.

Another type of fraud involves pretended medical treatment either by a physician or a bogus physician. Illustrative cases of pretended medical treatment cited in legal texts are usually from Victorian times and show remarkable gullibility on the part of the victim, her parents, or all three. Take, for example, the following cases. In the first case a John Flattery was convicted of the rape of nineteen-year-old Lavinia Thompson at the Winter Assizes in Leeds, England, in 1876 *(Regina v. Flattery,* 13 Cox C.C. 388, 1877).

> On and for some time previous to the 4th of November last she was in ill health and subject to fits. On the 4th of November, 1876 (being market day at Halifax), with a view to obtain medical and surgical advice and relief, she went with her mother to Halifax to consult the prisoner, who kept an open stall in the market, at which he professed for money consideration to give medical and surgical advice.
>
> They went together to the prisoner's stall, and there saw him; and in the presence and hearing of the prosecutrix her mother told the prisoner her condition as aforesaid, and that she was subject to fits, and consulted him as to a remedy.
>
> The prisoner expressed a desire to examine the prosecutrix with a view to giving the advice sought, and requested the prosecutrix, and her mother, to follow him to the Peacock Inn, which was close by, for that purpose, and they did so.
>
> At the Peacock Inn the prisoner put several questions to her mother touching the condition of the prosecutrix, and made some examination of her person. Having done this, the prisoner not believing that the advice he was about to give would be of any service to the prosecutrix, nor intending, nor with any view to perform a medical or surgical operation, but solely with a view to gratify his lust and have that carnal sexual knowledge of her person which he afterwards had, as after stated, fraudulently, and knowing that he was speaking falsely, told the mother in the presence and hearing of the prosecutrix that "It was Nature's string

wanted breaking," and asked if he might break it.

The mother replied that she did not know what he meant (as in fact she swore she did not), but that she did not mind, if it would do her daughter any good. At that moment the prosecutrix, in the prisoner's presence, had a fit, and fainted away. When she came to herself again the prisoner, in the prosecutrix's presence and hearing, fraudulently and falsely repeated that "Nature's string wanted breaking," and added, if that didn't do her good nothing would, and he again then asked if he might break it. Again the mother said she did not mind if it would do her daughter, the prosecutrix, any good.

On this the prisoner said to the mother, "You stay here and I'll try." He then went into a small adjoining room followed by the prosecutrix, solely in order as he represented, and as prosecutrix and her mother believed, that he might perform the operation he had advised, which both prosecutrix and her mother, on prisoner's representations aforesaid, believed would probably effect her cure, and not with any intention on the part of the prosecutrix that the prisoner should have sexual connection.

In that room the prisoner put the prosecutrix on the floor, and then and there had carnal sexual connection with her, the prosecutrix making but feeble resistance, believing (as she swore) that the prisoner was merely treating her medically, and performing a surgical operation, as he had advised, to cure her of her illness and fits, and submitting to his treatment solely because she so believed, such belief having been wilfully and fraudulently induced by the prisoner as aforesaid.

The following case from Indiana in 1893 is rather unusual *(Eberhart v. State,* 134 Ind. 651, 34 N.E. 637, 1893).

The prosecuting witness, Lottie G. Mohler, was thirteen years of age, past, and for two or three years had been subject to epileptic fits. Her father was a day laborer, while both father and mother were ignorant and credulous to an extreme degree, though apparently well-minded persons. The girl herself had not gone to school since she had been afflicted with epilepsy, and had gone out nowhere, except when accompanied by her father.

Appellant was a pretended traveling doctor, and about fifty years of age. He had traveled over parts of Illinois and Michigan, as well as in this state, professing to cure diseases by charms or spells, but not laying claim to any great medical knowledge. The parents of the prosecuting witness were advised to make trial of his powers to relieve her of her malady, and called him to treat her, during one of his visits to the neighborhood.

His first treatment was to take her to a private room, and tie a string of woolen yarn around her person, charging her to tell no one what he had done. She did not tell this to her mother, and the mother did not want to know what the doctor had done when she learned that he told the girl not to tell. This was in December, 1892. In January, and also in February, he came again, and the treatment was repeated. Before the February visit he wrote the following letter to the mother:

"Perth, Ind., Feb. 1st, 1892. Mrs. Mattie Mohler: This night I received your letter, and would say it would be necessary for me to see her again, and sleep in the same room with her now and then. You will see the change, for I make it a point to operate on these cases the third time after night, and, if possible, when the spell is on. It is possible that I may see you before Saturday night, and have a room to ourselves. Yours, truly, Lewis Eberhart.

"Try and get out of her what makes her cry. I am of a notion that her disease is
a curse. Does she make any religious profession, or not? Look for me, and ask her
if she is very anxious to see me, or not. I will use Latin phrases altogether on
behalf of her. Yours, L.E."

The parents consented to this astounding proposition. The prosecuting witness
slept in a small room downstairs on a couch, while the doctor slept in the same
room on a bed. The rest of the family slept upstairs. On the fifth night that they
so slept in the same room, he waked her up, after she had been some time asleep,
and called her to his bed, saying he had something to tell her that would cure her
of her fits.

As soon as she reached his bed, she testifies, he pulled her in, and committed
the crime charged; she trying, as she says, "to make him quit, but he would not
do it." Her mother and sister-in-law found evidence of the truth of her statement,
although at first she refused to tell because, as she says, the doctor forbade her to
say anything about it.

In 1872 the following case was described by the Supreme Court of
Michigan *(Don Moran v. People,* 25 Mich. 356, 1872).

> The People, to maintain the issue on their part, introduced evidence which
> tended to prove that the father of the complaining witness, shortly before she was
> sixteen years of age, brought her to the house of the defendant, in Detroit, to be
> treated for consumption, the defendant claiming to be skilled in the treatment of
> diseases of that kind; that her father left her at defendant's house; that the
> defendant made an examination of her, and, after such examination, told her that
> the "whites" had collected in her stomach; that she was ulcerated; that her uterus
> was inverted; that to save her life it would be necessary to enlarge her "parts," so
> that the "whites" might pass off, to break the ulcers, and to turn the uterus; that
> he could do this with instruments, but the operation would probably kill her; that
> the only way would be for him to have carnal connection with her; that when she
> objected, he told her that it was what he did to all women who came to be treated
> by him; that he had told her father that it would be necessary, and he understood
> all about it, and had authorized the defendant to have connection with his
> daughter; that she relying upon these representations, and believing them to be
> true, permitted the defendant to have connection with her; that if it had not been
> for such representations she would not have yielded; and that said representations
> were false, and known by the defendant to be so.

A more recent case from Missouri in 1925 cost the accused physician a
sentence of five years in the State Penitentiary for the rape of a
forty-four-year-old widow. *(State v. Atkins,* 292 S.W. 422 Mo. 1926).

> The story told by prosecutrix is that, when she came to appellant's office on
> February 20th, there was no one in the waiting room, and appellant invited her
> into his private office, closed the doors to the waiting room, and the hall, and told
> her to take a chair. Prosecutrix was not satisfied with bifocal lenses for her glasses,
> and asked for others, and appellant said he wanted to go over her first and see if
> he could find the cause of her eye trouble before he changed the lenses. He
> weighed her, took her temperature and examined her lungs.
>
> He then laid the chair-back down. The rest for the feet and legs was not raised.
> Appellant said he wanted to make an examination. It appeared that he had made
> a similar examination on February 6th. He put her heels in the stirrups of the

chair, and thus drew her legs up and apart. Appellant began his examination by pressing on her stomach and sides. He asked if she knew she had a tumor, and if any other doctor had told her that. She answered in the negative. She had been examined by physicians several times before.

Appellant then took her bloomers off of one leg. Prosecutrix, because of embarrassment, closed her eyes, and covered them with her arm, and did not see what appellant was doing. He applied something to her person, which she thought was medicine of some kind. She assumed he was going to make a vaginal examination. He began to press against her sides, and then prosecutrix felt something press against her private parts. Her exact testimony in this respect was as follows:

"Being a married woman, I realized, thought I did, what it was, and the next instant I knew what it was. His privates were entering mine. I jumped out of the chair as quick as I could, pushed him back, as I leaped out of the chair the back of the chair flew up . . .

"Q. And you say at that time his privates entered your privates? A. Yes, sir; he entered me just as I jumped up. I says, 'I am done with you.' He said, 'What is the matter, Mrs. McQuerter.' I says, 'You know what is the matter; you have insulted me.' 'Why, Mrs. McQuerter, you are mistaken,' he says. I says, 'I am not mistaken, you insulted me.' I says, 'You would stand on a stack of Bibles, wouldn't you, and swear you didn't insult me.' He said, 'Yes, I would;' and I said, 'Well, I would stand there and swear you did.'

"Q. Did you see anything? A. Yes, sir; he had on a white jumper; his pants were undone, and the white underclothing was pulled out of his pants.

"Q. You noticed his pants unbuttoned in front? A. Yes, sir' they were showing and his white underclothing was showing. I said, 'Why do you deny it; your underclothing shows what you were doing;' and he stepped into this little room, and when he came out his clothing was buttoned.

"Q. Then what was done? A. I went to the door to this reception room.

THE CHOIRMASTER OF LIVERPOOL

In contrast to the above cases, this one involves a choirmaster and not a physician or bogus physician. He had sexual intercourse with a girl under the pretense that her breathing was not quite right and that he had to perform an operation to produce her voice properly. The Court of Criminal Appeals held that he was properly convicted of rape *(Rex v. Williams,* 27 Cox C.C. 350, 1922).

The appellant, who was the choirmaster of a Presbyterian church, by reason of that fact became acquainted about Christmas, 1921, with Vera Howley, a girl of sixteen years of age, and it was arranged by her parents that she should take lessons in singing and voice production from him. On the occasion of the second singing lesson on January 17 the appellant said that she was not singing as she should and was not getting her notes properly and told her to lie down on a settee.

He then removed a portion of her clothing and placed upon the lower part of her body an instrument — which was in the nature of an aneroid barometer and according to the evidence was not in working order and would not in any event have been affected by the breathing of the girl — and then told her to take a deep breath three times. He looked at the instrument and purported to write something in a book. He then dropped on to her and proceeded to have sexual intercourse with her.

She said, "What are you going to do?" He said, "It is quite all right; do not worry. I am going to make an air passage. This is my method of training. Your breathing is not quite right and I have to make an air passage to make it right. Your parents know all about it, it has all been arranged; before God, Vera, it is quite right. I will not do you any harm." The girl made no resistance, as she believed what he told her and did not know that what he did was wrong – nor did she know that he was having sexual intercourse with her. The appellant had sexual intercourse with the girl a second time on April 28 in similar circumstances.

The appellant also on two occasions committed an indecent assault upon Ada Mary Cannell, a girl of nineteen years of age, to whom he was also giving lessons in singing and voice production. Upon the pretence that her breathing was not right he put his finger up her private parts, saying that he was making an opening for the air to pass up.

The jury convicted the appellant upon each of the counts and he was sentenced to seven years' penal servitude in respect of the charges of rape and to twelve months' imprisonment in respect of the charges of indecent assault.

A PERSONNEL MANAGER IN DENVER

A man struck up a conversation with an eighteen-year-old girl on a Denver street and invited her to join him for coffee in the cafeteria of a nearby department store. He said that he was the personnel manager of the store and told her, "I don't usually go around picking staff up on the street. I have never done it. I could get into a lot of trouble, but you just look like the intelligent type we could use. I think I could really use you as a model. We have a spring sale coming up and we need some models." He said I should be more friendly because I was kind of straight faced. "If you're going to be a model, you'll have to smile."

He told me the store would provide clothes for me and that I would be paid even during the training. After the coffee he drove me back to my apartment. He said, "You would make a great model," then he said, "I guess I will measure you now – Well, take off your boots so I can measure your legs." So I took off my boots and then he said, "Oh, you've got real nice legs." Then he said, "Well, you know, you've got to have a diaphragm," and I said, "I do?" He replied, "Yes, we started making it a rule, the stores started getting too many girls getting pregnant."

"From January to October there were about thirty-three girls and nine of them were models and all of them pregnant. Yes, you have to have one." I said, "O.K., I guess you know what you are doing, at least I don't." So he said, "Well, I'm going to have to measure you, you are going to have to take your underwear off." He stuck his finger in me and he said, "You are tense, relax." Then he said, "Well, I can't do it, I will have to use myself."

I told him I did not approve of that and he said, "If you are going to be a model, you'll have to have a diaphragm." I told him I didn't want one, I would chuck the whole thing. He said, "I will just write down a nine and leave it at that. He just kept making notes on his card. I said, "How do you know what you are writing, have you taken any courses." He said he had gone to college for four or five years, "You know in medicine."

Another girl aged twenty was approached in the street by a man who said he worked for a department store and he offered her a job as a model, providing he was allowed to take measurements of her body. These measurements were made in the girl's apartment and then he told her that the manager would not consider her for a position unless she was measured for and wore a diaphragm due to the fact that many of the models were getting pregnant. The girl consented and he produced an instrument from his bag to measure her vagina.

The man informed her that she was a size nine and too small for a diaphragm and that she would need to be a size sixteen or seventeen. The only way to do this was through intercourse. She also consented to this. The following day he called on her and told her that she would have to be bonded in order to secure this position and that the price of the bond was twenty-five dollars, but if she put up fifty dollars this would give her the status of a professional model and entitle her to a greater weekly salary. He returned later to say that all positions were filled and she would have to wait till the following week to obtain a position. Although he said he would call again and tell her where to report, this was the last she saw of him.

A third girl was approached in the same manner. After examining her vagina, he told her she had an unusual disease which had come to the United States from Viet Nam. He said that she had probably caught the disease from a toilet seat and he offered to treat the disease with pills which would cost the girl eighty dollars. Not one of the three girls had the presence of mind to note the number on the license plate of his car.

The rarity of rape by fraud cases today may be partly explained by the difficulty of presenting a convincing picture of such grossly impeded comprehension to skeptical jurors; the scene depicted may resemble more an artful seduction than forcible intercourse. *(Yale Law Journal, 62:63, 1952)*

PROSTITUTES AND RAPE

> *"Just as it is possible for a very wicked man*
> *to be murdered, so it is possible for a*
> *prostitute to be raped."*
> — Rollin M. Perkins, *Criminal Law*

The analogy quoted above leaves much to be desired as Perkins himself points out in his discussion of prostitution and rape. He adds, "to speak of sexual intercourse with a prostitute without her consent as an outrage to her person and feelings is in the nature of mockery. Her unlawful career has not placed her beyond the protection of the law, it is true; but when her only grievance is that she was taken without being paid, the law of assault and battery would seem more appropriate than to include such an act within the scope of one of the gravest felonies, which is still a capital crime in a number of states."

A victim of alleged rape may be cross-examined regarding her chastity to aid the jury in determining whether or not she gave consent for the act of sexual intercourse. In some jurisdictions a single girl cannot be asked whether she has had prior sexual intercourse.

The following discussion on this problem appears in 75 CJS, Rape #63:

> Evidence of the prosecutrix's unchastity is admissible to show the probability of consent where want of consent is an element of the offense charged, and such unchastity may be proved by showing her bad reputation. To rebut corroborating circumstances such as pregnancy, the accused may prove specific acts of intercourse by the prosecutrix with other men.
>
> In order to show the probability of consent, the general reputation of prosecutrix for immorality and unchastity and her general immoral habits and character may be shown, as by showing that she was a common prostitute, generally promiscuous, or drunk and dissipated. Further, while some authority holds that specific acts of intercourse or lewdness committed by the prosecutrix with other persons may be shown, other authority requires prosecutrix's want of chastity to be shown by evidence of general reputation for unchastity and not by proof of specific acts.

STATUTORY RAPE

> *"The concept of Tennessee law that an act of sexual*
> *intercourse with a girl under twenty-one with her consent*
> *is rape would, if Professor Kinsey's researches are accurate,*
> *require the imprisonment of a substantial part of the*
> *Tennessee male population if the law could be enforced."*
> — Morris Ploscowe, *Sex and the Law*

> *"If the law supposes that," said Mr. Bumble, "the law is an ass."*
> — Dickens, *Oliver Twist*

Even though a girl has consented to sexual intercourse, the man can be convicted of statutory rape if she was below the legal age of consent which ranges from seven years of age in Delaware to twenty-one years in Tennessee. Thus sexual intercourse with a sixteen-year-old girl may be legal in one state and illegal in an adjoining state and the maximum penalty may be life imprisonment. In many states a girl can legally marry long before her consent to sexual intercourse can shield a man from a rape charge. Nor, in many jurisdictions, does the man's mistaken belief that the girl was above the age of consent shield him from prosecution. There is a growing body of law which recognizes as a defense to the crime of statutory rape a reasonable mistake in fact by the defendant with respect to the age of the victim. (See *People v. Hernandez,* 61 Calif. 2d 529, 393 P. 2d 673, 1964).

In some courts when the charge is statutory rape, the defense is not permitted to show that the prosecuting witness has a bad reputation. This may lead to grave injustice.

Even though the girl is a prostitute, the man can still be charged with statutory rape. In 1967 a man in Indianapolis met a fourteen-year-old girl in a cocktail lounge where she and a girl friend had been for two hours. He took her to a hotel which adjoined the lounge and had sexual intercourse with her. At his trial the girl admitted she had engaged in prostitution in Louisville, Kentucky, as well as in Indianapolis. The man was convicted of statutory rape and sentenced to two to twenty-one years in the Indiana State Prison.

The appeal court noted that cross-examination of the girl established that "she was sufficiently experienced in the delicate and sensitive matter of sex, and that she had no lack of either the vocabulary or understanding of these matters which one might expect from her tender years." However, the appeal court upheld the conviction and sentence of the trial court *(Montgomery v. State,* 229 N.E. 2d 466, 1967).

Ploscowe cites the case of a man who had sexual intercourse with a girl, not quite sixteen years of age, who was being prostituted by her husband. The defendant was one of several men who had visited with her and had sexual intercourse with her. Neither the girl's marriage, nor her lack of chastity, nor the fact that sexual intercourse grew out of a prostitutional situation sufficed to save the defendant from a long prison sentence.

Perkins notes that it shocks the moral sense to see a normal and socially minded boy convicted of a felony for having been picked up on the street and led astray by a common prostitute who merely happened to be under the age mentioned in the statute, particularly if she was actually older than he. Almost fifty years ago a judge expressed a similar opinion in language which would not be universally followed today.

> There are not a few sober-minded fathers and mothers who feel that the statute is more drastic than sound public policy requires. The purpose of the lawmakers in its enactment is manifest. Experience has shown that girls under the age of sixteen, as the statute now reads, are not always able to resist temptation. They lack the discretion and firmness that comes with maturer years. Fathers and mothers know that this is true of boys as well. It is too true that many immature boys do not have the moral fiber and discretion of a Joseph. A lecherous woman is a social menace; she is more dangerous than T.N.T.; more deadly than the "pestilence that walketh in darkness or the destruction that wasteth at noonday."
>
> "For the lips of a strange woman drop as an honeycomb, and her mouth is smoother than oil;
> "But her end is bitter as wormwood, sharp as a two-edged sword.

"Her feet go down to death, her steps take hold on hell."

— Proverbs 5:3-5.

We have in this case a condition and not a theory. This wretched girl was young in years but old in sin and shame. A number of callow youths, of otherwise blameless lives so far as this record shows, fell under her seductive influence. They flocked about her, if her story is to be believed, like moths about the flame of a lighted candle and probably with the same result. The girl was a common prostitute as the record shows. The boys were immature and doubtless more sinned against than sinning. They did not defile the girl. She was a mere "cistern for foul toads to knot and gender in." Why should the boys, misled by her, be sacrificed? What sound public policy can be subserved by branding them as felons? . . . But that is a question solely for the lawmakers; courts must construe the statute as they find it *(State v. Snow,* 252 S.W. 630, 1922).

It is encouraging to note that some recent statutes do not permit imprisonment of men who have had sexual intercourse with the consent of older girls of bad reputation who are below the age of consent. The Kentucky Revised Statutes (KRS, 435, 100, 1963) state that if the child is of the age of sixteen years and under eighteen and if it can be shown that she is sexually immoral or has a reputation for sexual immorality, the punishment shall be a fine and not imprisonment.

MARRIAGE AS A DEFENSE TO RAPE

It is not unusual for the parents of a pregnant unmarried daughter to threaten her lover with a charge of statutory rape unless he agrees to marry the girl. This is not always a sound basis for marriage. A man charged with statutory rape does not invariably escape prosecution through marriage. A man was charged with statutory rape but the prosecution was dismissed when he married the girl. Some time after the birth of a child he deserted his wife, as he had been told that he was not the father of the child. He was charged with having committed statutory rape prior to the marriage and later sentenced to five years' imprisonment in the Kansas State Penitentiary. His conviction and sentence were upheld by the Kansas Supreme Court.

ABORTION LAWS AND STATUTORY RAPE

Some states have abortion laws which authorize abortion in cases of statutory, as well as forcible, rape. Some parents of unmarried pregnant daughters do not wish to force a marriage by threatening criminal proceedings against the daughter's boyfriend (or rather former boyfriend, as pregnancy often terminates adolescent love affairs). However, in order to obtain a legal abortion it usually becomes necessary to charge the youth responsible for the pregnancy with statutory rape. Only then will the district attorney authorize the abortion.

In Colorado many district attorneys do not relish their involuntary involvement in these abortion proceedings. Often the girls are reluctant to testify and not infrequently refuse to testify after the abortion has been performed. Some girls claim that they do not know the name of the man responsible for their pregnancy and invent a story of forcible rape by an unknown man of average height wearing a mask. In this manner they save the boyfriend from criminal prosecution and provide additional work for busy police officers and district attorneys.

THE RELUCTANT WITNESS

> *"Give your evidence," said the King, "and don't be nervous, or*
> *I'll have you executed upon the spot."*
> — Lewis Carroll, *Alice's Adventures in Wonderland*

In Missouri in 1921 a fifteen-year-old promiscuous girl refused to testify in court against a man accused of having carnal knowledge of her. The method employed by the trial court in persuading her to testify is not likely to be employed today.

The witness repeatedly refused to answer questions. Finally the court took the matter in hand and admonished her, but she still declined to answer. Thereupon, by direction of the court, the jury retired.

"The Court: Of course, you gentlemen understand the court can punish her for contempt of court by sending the witness to jail, but that wouldn't be any penalty for this witness, because she has been confined in jail and the reform school for months; if I have a right to, I'll instruct the sheriff or her mother to give her a good licking between now and 1 o'clock.

"Mr. Hall: I would suggest that she be sent to jail and not given anything to eat but water and bread.

"The Court: Mrs. Smith, you are her mother; if I put her in your charge, will you give her a good licking between now and 1 o'clock?

"Mrs. Smith: I'll get her to answer questions, if I can.

"The Court: This is the way she did before; I think she just needs a good licking; I think she ought to have the fear of God and the law put into her heart.

"Mr. Bradley (prosecuting attorney): I do too, Judge.

"The Court: If I have the power to do it, I'll order the sheriff to give her a good licking between now and 1 o'clock.

"Mr. Bradley: I would be glad to see it; if she don't talk. I've got my patience exhausted. I think she needs a whipping.

"The Court: Mr. Sheriff, will you lick this witness between now and 1 o'clock? Miss Marler, will you answer these questions, or had you rather be whipped by the sheriff?

"Witness: It don't make any difference to me.

"The Court: Will you answer these questions if the jury is brought back?

"Witness: (No answer).

"The Court: Mr. Sheriff, we have a witness here who won't answer questions, and we are discussing some method of making her answer questions. Sending her to jail, we think, wouldn't do much good, because she has been in jail for several months, and she is fourteen years old, and I want to know if you will — if the court orders it, if you will take her out in the presence of her mother and give her a good licking, with a good, strong switch? You might want to consult counsel before you decide about it though.

"The Sheriff: I'll say, off the reel, I refuse to do that; but I'll take the girl out and talk to her. She promised me she would talk.

"The Court: That wouldn't do a bit of good.

"The Sheriff: I'll tell you what I would prefer to do: I prefer to take her back to jail and put her in the dungeon and keep her there until she decides to talk. I'll do that rather than give her a licking.

"The Court: I know whippings have gone out of fashion, even in our schools. This generation is being raised to think they are too good to be whipped. I don't know what to do, gentlemen; I'll do whatever you say, if it is right.

"Mr. Hall: I would suggest, if you want her whipped, let her mother whip her. She has a right to, and I think she is the only one that has the right.

"Mr. Billings: Her mother could give her consent for her being whipped.

"The Court: She is really in the charge of the juvenile court. I think the court could order her licked, but I don't know whether it would be obeyed or not.

"Mr. Hall: I don't think he has a right to order her licked, but he could have her tied up by the thumbs.

"The Court: No, the warden of the penitentiary got into trouble for tying them up by the thumbs. What do you say, Mrs. Smith? Will you whip this girl between now and 1 o'clock?

"The Sheriff: I'm going to suggest one thing: Nannie knows we have a crazy man down there, and I'll put her in with that crazy man unless she will talk. She must talk or do something. You told me before you were going to tell this whole thing, and I don't want to punish you, but I'm going to have to do something. I'll put her up there and let her wait on that crazy man; he is sick.

"The Court: All right, Miss Marler, what do you say? Will you talk if the jury is brought back?

"Witness: Yes, sir.

"The Court: All right, let the jury come in, Mr. Sheriff." *(State v. Snow* 252, S.W. 630, 1922).

MALES INCAPABLE OF RAPE

In England and in some American courts a boy under fourteen years of age is presumed to be physically incapable of committing rape and no evidence can be introduced to show capacity in fact. Some American courts have assumed that this rule resulted from the belief that boys in England seldom attain puberty before the age of fourteen, but Perkins states that the special rule in regard to rape resulted from the unwillingness of early judges to hang one so young for this type of misconduct.

In some states a boy under fourteen cannot be convicted of rape unless his physical ability to accomplish penetration is proved as an independent fact and beyond a reasonable doubt. The statutes do not state the manner of proof and in the unlikely event of the youth being willing to provide a practical demonstration he would have to break the law to do so. The apocryphal story is told that a man in a paternity suit was judged to be the father of an illegitimate child, at the same time in an adjoining courtroom his wife was granted a divorce on the ground that he was impotent.

WOMEN AS OFFENDERS

A woman who helps a man to commit rape, for example by helping to restrain or subdue the victim, can be convicted of rape. An adult female who entices a youth to have sexual relations can be prosecuted for statutory rape in a few jurisdictions in the United States. In Colorado, for example, a female may be charged with rape if she obtains sexual intercourse with a male under the age of eighteen years by "solicitation, inducement, importuning or connivance." A prostitute may also be charged with rape if the male under eighteen years was "prior and up to the time of the commission of the offense, of good moral character." In Norway the definition of rape also covers a woman forcing a man to sexual intercourse, but as the Norwegian Professor Aedenaes notes, this is improbable in fact.

LIABILITY FOR RAPE

The rape offender may be sued in a civil court in addition to being convicted and sentenced in a criminal court. A fourteen-year-old girl complained that a man for whom she had been babysitting before taking her home drove her to the sixth floor of an indoor downtown Denver parking garage and forcibly raped her. The man, who claimed that the girl encouraged his advances, was convicted of statutory rape and placed on probation. The girl who subsequently underwent an abortion operation, sued the man. The civil court awarded $7,500 to the girl and $2,500 to her mother for medical expenses.

The state was not liable to a mental hospital patient who gave birth to a child as the result of being raped on the hospital grounds, a New York appellate court ruled. The evidence established that the hospital was not negligent in keeping the patient in an open ward.

> The patient also contended that the hospital should have discovered her pregnancy sooner and should have offered her an abortion. The court said that the hospital was under no duty to prevent the birth of the child.
>
> The twenty-two-year-old patient was admitted to the hospital suffering from a psychosis with mental deficiency. She was five months' pregnant, was unmarried, and had given birth to an illegitimate child five years earlier. The record of a previous hospitalization stated that she was promiscuous and that her personality was hostile and aggressive. She was placed in a closed ward on admission.
>
> After her child was delivered, the patient was transferred to an open ward. The hospital grounds consisted of approximately seventy-two acres which were on an island. Patients could not leave the grounds and persons not connected with the hospital were present only with permission. The grounds were patrolled by a force

of from six to ten men during the daylight.

There were a church and stores on the grounds in an area that was open and within a ten minute walk of the building where the patient was housed. She was permitted to go to the church and stores, but only in the company of at least two other patients who were considered capable of looking after her.

After she had been in the open ward for almost a year, her mental condition was reviewed and it was noted that she was nice and cooperative and followed instructions well. Seven months later it was discovered that she was between three and four months' pregnant. There was testimony that the patient had said that when she went to church, she slipped away from the other patients and went with a boy.

The physician who was the director of the hospital testified that its policy with regard to open wards was in accordance with the policy promulgated by the Department of Mental Hygiene. He stated that the purpose of open wards was to help those patients considered psychiatrically suitable in regaining their dignity and readjusting to responsibility and free movement about the community. He said that if the patient had been kept under lock and key in a closed ward, it would have had a harmful effect on her psychiatric condition, and that the risk of any of the patients in the patient's ward coming into contact with a man alone was infinitesimal. He stated the opinion that the treatment and supervision given the patient conformed to accepted standards of practice.

The open-door policy has been widely accepted as favoring rehabilitation of the mentally ill. The decision to place the patient in an open ward was a medical judgment. Since she was considered a proper patient for an open ward, there was no reason to place more restraints on her than was usual in such a ward. The state would not be liable, even if it could be said that the hospital's medical judgment as to the patient's suitability for an open ward was erroneous. *(Williams v. State of New York,* 290 N.Y.S. 2d 263 N.Y., May 21, 1968).

PSYCHIATRIC EXAMINATION OF THE VICTIM

Donnelly notes that the lack of witnesses to alleged sex offenses makes them singularly susceptible to false complaints, which because of judge and jury bias in favor of the complaining witness are frequently sustained. Since what appears on the surface to be a straightforward and convincing story is often the fabrication of a disturbed personality, he suggests that rules of evidence should be liberalized to permit adequate probing of the personality of complaining witnesses. Present rules of evidence, in his opinion, hinder rather than aid a proper inquiry into the veracity of complaints of sexual misconduct.

Many lawyers have suggested the need for psychiatric examination of the victim especially when there have been no witnesses and no evidence of injury to the victim or evidence to indicate a struggle. It was Dean Wigmore's view, concurred in by a committee of the American Bar Association, that in all cases charging sex offenses, the complaining witness should be examined before the trial by competent psychiatrists as to her (or his) credibility.

ADMINISTRATION OF THE LAW

District attorneys exercise much greater power in the administration of the law than is generally recognized. Although the jury decides whether a person is guilty of rape and the judge fixes the sentence, a district attorney decides whether or not the case will ever come before the court and jury. Davis believes that justice is administered more outside the courts than in them and he proposes that the discretionary power of police and prosecutors should be curbed:

"The enormous and much-abused power of prosecutors not to prosecute is almost completely uncontrolled, even though I can find no reason to believe that anyone planned it that way — or that anyone would. Prosecutions are often withheld, sometimes on the basis of political, personal or other ulterior influence, without guiding rules as to what will or will not be prosecuted, without meaningful standards stemming from either legislative bodies or from prosecutors themselves, through decisions secretly made and free from criticism, without supporting findings of fact, unexplained by reasoned opinions, and free from any requirement that the decisions be related to precedents. Furthermore, decisions of a top prosecutor are usually unsupervised by any other administrative authority, and decisions not to prosecute are customarily immune to judicial review. The discretionary power of public officers to confer privileges or to be lenient is always intrinsically a discretionary power not to confer a privilege or not to be lenient and is susceptible to many kinds of abuse, including the worst sort of discrimination, favoritism or caprice, and may be extremely damaging to private interests."

The district attorney bears a heavy responsibility, and it is not always a simple matter to decide upon the filing of criminal charges. Some cases of rape clearly demand prosecution, for example the brutal rape and bodily injury of a woman by a complete stranger who gains entry to her home by forcing open a locked door. But what of the alleged assailant who is invited into the woman's apartment, offered alcohol and encouraged to make sexual advances? Here it becomes the word of the woman who claims rape against the word of the man who claims consent. There may be a narrow line indeed between allowing rape to go unpunished and subjecting an innocent man to the ordeal and expense of a criminal prosecution.

In making his decision the district attorney will consider the circumstances of the alleged rape, as well as the attitudes and reputations of the parties involved. Did the woman make a reasonable effort to resist? Resistance may be both futile and dangerous when a man strikes a woman down with a blow on the jaw and then threatens her with a knife. But what of the woman who tells her boyfriend, "Stop it, quit it, you must be kidding," and permits removal of her underclothing because the boyfriend was "tugging on them."

Did the victim seize any opportunity to call for help or to escape from her attacker? Why did she not seek help when her abductor permitted her to use the toilet at a gasoline station? Was the rape reported promptly to the police or reluctantly after several hours delay on the urging of her husband? Is the victim a reliable informant? Why does she say that she was attacked by a complete stranger after leaving a restaurant late at night and omit to mention that she paid for this man's coffee and that she left the restaurant in his company?

The woman who volunteers to police that she is currently the mistress of a prominent business man and that she has had twenty-five lovers since her divorce may have a difficult time on the witness stand. Likewise the victim who claims that she was raped five times and that both the man and herself reached a climax each time may not find a sympathetic jury. Why does the victim refuse to take a lie detector test when the man accused insists on being given the test? What are the results of the medical examination and laboratory tests?

Have the police made a thorough and impartial investigation of the rape? Is the police officer's judgment clouded by sympathy for the woman or prejudice against the accused? Why did the officer have the man arrested at his place of employment rather than request him to come to police headquarters for an interview when scrutiny of the woman's account of the alleged rape should have raised immediate skepticism; for example, the woman does not report the first "rape" to the police and continues to live in the home of the alleged assailant, and she reports the second "rape" after a delay of some hours. Her clothing is not torn and there are no bruises or other injuries. Alternatively the officer may be prejudiced against the victim.

What are the prospects of successful prosecution? Just administration of the law demands a high level of experience, skill and judgment upon the part of both police officers and district attorneys. Since most public prosecutors are elected officials and may have political ambitions, many are likely to be influenced by the "scandal quality of an accusation." The prominent position given to forcible rape charges by many newspapers may excite a public demand for retribution, which the prosecutor can ill afford to ignore.

Chapter 12

INJUSTICE IN THE COURTS

"Justice consists in doing injury to no men."
– Cicero

T HE greatest danger of conviction of the innocent in rape results from mistaken identification of the assailant by the victim. In a distressing number of cases perjury has sent innocent men to the penitentiary. Erroneous convictions on circumstantial evidence also occur. Failure of the police to make a thorough inquiry may lead to failure to elicit evidence which would exonerate the man wrongfully accused of rape. False confessions by the mentally ill or mentally retarded add to the melancholy number of false convictions.

The overzealous district attorney, in his eagerness to secure a conviction, may overlook evidence which does not support his cause and not make it available to the court and jury. Deliberate suppression of evidence favorable to the accused is not unknown. The lax or incompetent defense attorney may send his innocent client to the penitentiary. Public indignation over a brutal rape, or trial by newspapers, may influence the minds of jurors and lead to injustice in the courtroom.

MISTAKEN IDENTIFICATION

A favorite device of college psychology professors is to arrange for a lecture to be interrupted by a stranger who commits an apparent criminal act before quickly disappearing. When the students are asked to describe the supposed criminal, widely varying accounts are given of his physical appearance and behavior. In his account of sixty-five criminal prosecutions and convictions of completely innocent persons, Borchard found that the major source of these tragic errors was a mistaken identification of the accused by the victim of a crime of violence.

In eight of these cases the wrongfully accused and the really guilty criminal bore not the slightest resemblance to each other; whereas in twelve other cases, the resemblance, while fair, was still not at all close. In only two cases could the resemblance be called striking. Borchard intentionally omitted from his collection cases of alleged rape presumably because of the frequency with which the innocent are convicted. He comments further upon the problem of mistaken identification:

"Juries seem disposed more readily to credit the veracity and reliability of the victims of an outrage than any amount of contrary evidence by or on behalf of the accused, whether by way of alibi, character witnesses, or other testimony. These cases illustrate the fact that the emotional balance of the victim or eyewitness is so disturbed by his extraordinary experience that his powers of perception become distorted and his identification is frequently most untrustworthy. Into the identification enter other motives, not necessarily stimulated originally by the accused personally — the desire to requite a crime, to exact vengeance upon the person believed guilty, to find a scapegoat, to support, consciously or unconsciously, an identification already made by another. Thus doubts are resolved against the accused."

In February 1969 Gordon J. Ragan, imprisoned three years before in Philadelphia on a seven- to twenty-year sentence for the rape of the wife of a University of Pennsylvania professor, was freed after Fred A. Conyers admitted the crime. The resemblance between the two men was so striking that neither the victim nor relatives of Ragan were able to tell the men apart. A chance encounter between some relatives of Ragan and Conyers at a Philadelphia police station in 1967 led to the reopening of the case. Conyers was serving a two- to ten-year sentence for another rape when he confessed.

In April 1969 in Fort Worth, Texas, Danny Drew was stopped by a patrolman for a traffic violation. While he was sitting in the patrol car, he heard an announcement over the police radio describing a person of his appearance; five feet eight, blond and dirty. "I'd just got off the job and I was dirty." Police found a pistol in his car and he was arrested. Then came a lie detector test. "It didn't turn out right for me." A young schoolteacher identified him in the line-up as the man who had raped her.

Some days later the schoolteacher saw the photograph on television and in the newspapers of another man who had been charged with three cases of rape. She decided she might have been wrong in her identification and notified the district attorney. A second line-up was arranged and the girl identified the other man. The district attorney said he would drop the case against Drew, who had paid three thousand dollars for bail bond, lawyer's fees and other expenses.

In Denver in 1936 twenty-two-year-old Margaret Cyckose was about to cross the street on her way home from work when a car pulled over to the curb. There were two young men in the car and the driver asked her the best way to get to Fourteenth Street. She gave the directions but the man did not drive on, instead he invited her to go for a ride. When she hesitated, the men dragged her to the car as she fought and screamed. She was driven into the countryside where she was beaten and raped. The men then brought her back to Denver, where she was found lying on the sidewalk with her nose broken and her face badly bruised.

The following evening the parents of two young girls complained to police that the girls had been taken to a party by four strangers. The girls, who were not molested, recalled the name of the driver, a Mr. Mattice. He was arrested and charged with attempting to corrupt the morals of the girls. Mrs. Cyckose identified him as her assailant. He protested his innocence, saying that he was asleep in a hotel at the time of the rape. The hotel clerk confirmed that he had answered the phone at 6 A.M. However, the crime was committed four hours earlier and he was convicted and sentenced to life imprisonment.

A few months after the trial two police officers began to doubt Mattice's guilt. After his conviction three more rape attempts occurred and in each case the police found an abandoned stolen car. The officers checked Mattice's alibi by driving to the place where the rape occurred. They found that Mattice could not have made the trip, much less committed the crime, and returned to his hotel by 6 A.M. Furthermore, they found that Mrs. Cyckose had told the police officers who brought her to headquarters after the attack that her assailants were clean shaven. Mattice had a moustache.

On checking police photographs of two well-known car thieves, it was found that one of them closely resembled Mattice. This man was arrested and interrogated. Finally he confessed, naming his partner in the rape of Mrs. Cyckose. His account of the crime matched additional information which had not previously been revealed by the victim. Mattice was pardoned and later awarded four thousand dollars compensation for false arrest, conviction and imprisonment. This case involved not only mistaken identification but inadequate investigation by the police and defense attorney of Mattice's alibi. Heightened feelings in the community over the brutal rape doubtless played a role.

PERJURY

> *"You told a lie, an odious, damned lie:*
> *Upon my soul, a lie, a wicked lie."*
> — Shakespeare, *Othello*

In 1968 in Oklahoma John Severs, a forty-five-year-old pastor and oil field worker, was convicted of the rape of his duaghter in 1966 when she was fifteen. He was sentenced to ninety-nine years imprisonment, and the prosecutor said that ten members of the jury panel that heard the case voted to give Severs the electric chair. In 1969, in a hearing ordered by the Court of Criminal Appeals, his daughter, now seventeen, testified that she had lied. She said she was angry with her father because he beat her mother and she lied to get even with him.

The girl told the court, "Although I still have no love for my father, by reason of his acts over the years towards my mother and myself, I realize my wrong is as great or greater than his. I have been informed by a lawyer in the presence of my mother that I could be prosecuted under the law of the State of Oklahoma for perjury. Being fully advised of this, I am still compelled to make this statement to clear my conscience of what I have done." The girl volunteered to take a lie detector test.

Judge Jerome Frank and Barbara Frank in *Not Guilty* describe the following cases of perjury.

In May 1935 twenty-six-year-old Arthur O'Connell was brought to trial in Boston for a sexual attack on a thirteen-year-old girl. Convicted on the testimony of the alleged victim and that of her thirteen-year-old companion, who testified that she had witnessed the crime, O'Connell was sentenced to a term of not less than eight and not more than twelve years. In June of the same year the "victim's" companion confessed that the crime had never occurred. O'Connell had merely stopped to talk to the girls for a moment. They had perjured themselves "just for fun." After a month's imprisonment O'Connell was released.

In Kansas City, Missouri, in the year 1948 sixty-year-old Edward Oscar, brought to trial for an attempted rape of an eleven-year-old girl, was convicted on the alleged victim's testimony and sentenced to twenty years in prison. Five years later, in 1953, the state's witness confessed that she had perjured herself at Oscar's trial; there had been no crime. In March 1953 the court set aside Oscar's conviction and found him not guilty.

FALSE CONFESSIONS

False confessions of murder are not uncommon, especially in those unsolved murders which attract considerable newspaper publicity. The Black Dahlia murder is a case in point. Twenty-two-year-old Elizabeth Short, a fast-living young woman, acquired the soubriquet Black Dahlia because of her penchant for black dresses and black underclothing. On January 15, 1947, her nude body, cut in half at the waist and mutilated with twenty stab wounds, was found in a vacant lot in Los Angeles. More than thirty persons have confessed responsibility for her death, but the crime has yet to be solved. A wish for publicity and notoriety is evident in some of these confessions.

Persons who seek out the police to volunteer false confessions of crime choose relatively respectable crimes such as murder and armed robbery not sexual offenses such as rape and incest. An exception has been described by Popella. This man, who charged himself twelve times with rape and murder or robbery and murder, in the end embarked on manslaughter and murder.

False confessions of rape by a schizophrenic are usually readily recognized as the product of a mind diseased. A young man informed his family that he was being punished by avenging angels for the rape of young girls. Later he talked about battling with the devil in hell and said that he had witnessed heaven for a short period of time. He was brought to the hospital after he ran naked into the street. The middle-aged man in a psychotic depression who berates himself for real or imagined sexual offenses in childhood, talks of suicide, refuses to eat and is unable to sleep at night is also likely to be taken to a hospital rather than to a police station.

Police tend to be somewhat skeptical when approached by a stranger who confesses a major crime. Jack Chester, the young man who shot his fiance in Boston in 1957, had some difficulty in persuading a patrolman directing traffic that he had just committed murder. When, however, police are questioning someone suspected of crime, they are sometimes too quick to believe a confession to the crime. The mentally ill and the mentally retarded may respond to prolonged interrogation by admitting offenses which they have not committed.

In 1965 Ronald Avard, a twenty-two-year-old man of Rugby, England, after questioning at a police station confessed to the attempted rape of a six-year-old girl and the indecent assault of another girl, aged eleven. At his trial a psychiatrist testified that he had a mental age of seven and he was found unfit to plead to charges of attempted rape and indecent assault. He was committed to a special hospital reserved for people of "a dangerous, violent or criminal nature." Avard had no previous convictions, no history of violence, and because he was found unfit to plead was never convicted. The only evidence against him was his own confession.

In 1968 a Rugby insurance agent, whose calls included the homes of Avard's parents, the girl assaulted and a boy who had been with her at the time, became convinced from conversations with the families that something was wrong about the case. He persuaded Avard's father to write to Mr. William Price, the member of parliament for Rugby, who met with the children and their parents. The girl said that she had known Ronald Avard for seven or eight years and he was not the man who attacked her. She said that when interviewed by the police she was not asked about Ronald Avard and did not say that it was him.

The boy with her at the time of the offense said that the man was older and taller than Avard whose name was not mentioned by the police. Evidently Avard was not suspected at this stage of the investigation. The mothers also made statements saying that the children had told inconsistent stories from the start. The statements were sent to the home office. An official reply stated that photographs shown to the girl and the boy did not include Avard's but following Avard's arrest his photograph was shown to the boy who commented that it was similar to the man who had assaulted the girl.

The home office refused to set up an investigation, as the officials were satisfied the law had taken a proper course. Mr. Price eventually made a complaint under the Police Act for an inquiry which was conducted by a Detective Chief Superintendent from another police district. This officer concluded that Avard was not responsible for the assault and he was released from the hospital. The home office also revealed that the police had considered charging another man for the offenses with which Avard was originally charged but "it had been decided on the advice of the Director of Public Prosecutions not to take any action."

Disquieting features of this case are that this mentally retarded man was brought to trial and sent to the hospital when the only evidence was his own confession. He was so mentally retarded that he was not aware of the capital of England, nor the reigning sovereign, nor the fact that he was in prison. Yet he was regarded quite capable of making statements which, as Mr. Price pointed out, would get him locked up for the rest of his life.

Under the Children and Young Person's Act, children in England are protected from having to appear personally in court in cases involving sexual offenses unless the defense counsel insists. In this case, if they had appeared or been shown Avard's picture for positive identification, the case would almost certainly have been dropped. The mother of the girl in a statement claims that she tried to tell "police officers that my daughter made it clear it was not Ronald Avard, but they did not appear to be interested."

GUILTY BEHAVIOR

The innocent man who behaves in a guilty manner following the crime may be arrested and convicted. He may draw attention to himself by talking at length about the crime and by making comments which suggest that he has more knowledge of the circumstances of the crime than are available from newspaper and television reports. Refusal to speak to the police or to take a lie detector test may strengthen the suspicions of the police and prompt the district attorney to file charges. Proof at the trial that his alibi is false may lead to a verdict of guilty even though he may have had nothing to do with the crime.

SUPPRESSION OF EVIDENCE

In Waukegan, Illinois, in 1923 Mamie Snow, a sixty-two-year-old spinster who sold notions door-to-door, told the police that James Montgomery, a twenty-six-year-old Negro, had attacked and raped her. He was immediately arrested. The victim was examined by a physician who found no evidence of rape, but the prosecutor suppressed this evidence when he presented his case to the grand jury. It is perhaps significant that the previous year Montgomery won a civil suit against the prosecutor, who was a member of the Ku Klux Klan.

According to Judge Jerome Frank, who described this case at length, on the eve of the trial Montgomery and his lawyer were threatened with the violent wrath of the Klan if Montgomery set up a serious defense. The threat had its intended effect. The lawyer did not examine prospective jurors and accepted a jury picked by the prosecutor. He did not cross-examine the witnesses and offered no evidence. Montgomery was convicted and sentenced to a life term in the penitentiary.

Montgomery spent twenty-four years in prison. In 1947 a Chicago lawyer visiting a client in the penitentiary was told that Montgomery needed help as a belief prevailed among the prisoners that he was innocent. It took the lawyer two years to complete his investigation. He found that Mamie Snow, who died later in a mental hospital, did not recognize Montgomery on the day after she identified him at police headquarters. He obtained evidence of the Klan-inspired threats to Montgomery and his lawyer. He spoke to the physician who told him of the evidence the prosecutor had suppressed.

In 1949 the lawyer filed a petition for a writ of habeus corpus in the United States District Court of Chicago. The judge, after an intensive study of the evidence, handed down his opinion in which he said that Montgomery's innocence was clear, as was also the prosecutor's guilt. The judge ordered his release on the ground that, because of the gross unfairness of his trial, he had been denied his constitutional rights. The state did not seek to try him again. Through his lawyer he brought suit against the state for $250,000 in the Illinois Court of Claims. But that court turned Montgomery down on the ground that, since the prosecutor was an employee of the county, the state had no responsibility for the methods he pursued.

THE GILES-JOHNSON CASE

"He who decides a case with the other side unheard,
Though he decides justly, is himself unjust."
— Seneca *Medea*

On July 21, 1961, local newspapers reported that a pretty sixteen-year-old girl was raped twice and her escort beaten near Spencerville, Maryland, after three Negroes dragged them from their car. The girl, her date, Stewart Foster, and two other young men had driven to a swimming and fishing spot on the Patuxent River in a secluded wooded area shortly before midnight. Their car ran out of gasoline and the girl and Foster remained in the car while the other young men went for gasoline.

They later testified that they had been seated in the back seat of the car for some fifteen minutes after the two young men left when Johnson, one of the Negroes, approached the stranded car. Two other Negroes, James and John Giles, also came to the car. Foster rolled up the windows and locked the doors. The girl and Foster testified that the three Negroes demanded his money and his girl then smashed the car windows with rocks to open the car doors. Foster unlocked the door on his side and told the girl to get out her side and run while he held off the three.

Foster was knocked unconscious when he left the car. The girl ran into the woods where she was found by John Giles. His brother, James Giles, and Johnson joined them a few minutes later. She testified that when one of the trio attempted to remove her clothes, she disrobed herself below the waist and submitted to all three youths without resistance because of fear.

The Giles brothers, who were tried before Johnson, testified in their own defense. Their version of the events was that the three young men approached the car and asked Foster for a cigarette, that Foster called them insulting names and reached down as if to pick up a gun or other weapon, and that they broke the windows to prevent his getting it. They said they did not know it was a girl who fled into the woods.

John Giles testified that when he caught up with her, she offered to submit to him if he would help her escape from the others, but that he declined. James Giles testified that when he and Johnson joined the couple, the girl told the three that she had had relations with sixteen or seventeen boys that week and two or three more wouldn't make any difference, that she disrobed herself and invited all three of them to have relations with her, and that he and Johnson, but not John Giles, had relations with her.

Both John and James Giles testified that the girl said that if they were caught in the woods she would have to say she had been raped because she was on a year's probation and was in trouble. The girl denied having made the above statements.

The prosecutor ridiculed the claim by the defendants that the girl had not only consented but also encouraged them. He told the jury that this was the most vicious rape case he had ever prosecuted and asked them to return a verdict of guilty and not to tie the judge's hands with respect to the sentence. The jury returned a verdict of guilty and did not add to its verdict the words "without capital punishment."

This verdict permitted the judge in his discretion to impose the death penalty. He was also free to sentence the men to life imprisonment or imprisonment of not less than eighteen months nor more than twenty-one years. The trial judge sentenced the Giles brothers to death in the gas chamber. Subsequently Johnson was also convicted and sentenced to death.

The *Washington Post* in an editorial (May 14, 1963) noting the sentence of death must soon be carried out, described the crime as a vicious one but questioned the death penalty.

> Most troublesome of all is the severity of the sentence. Without minimizing in any way the ugliness and seriousness of rape, the death penalty seems excessive where death was not a consequence of the crime. Early this year in Federal District Court, Judge Alexander Holtzoff sentenced three young men for an almost identical crime; they had raped a seventeen-year-old girl after breaking into

a parked car and dragging her from it. The sentences imposed were from five to fifteen years for one assailant, six to eighteen years for a second and seven to twenty-one years for the third.

The one conspicuous difference between the two crimes was that the victim as well as the three culprits in the District of Columbia were colored, while in Maryland the victim was white, while those who attacked her were Negroes.

Did this difference affect the jury verdicts in the Giles-Johnson cases? Did it influence the severity of the sentences in these cases? Unless these questions can be answered in the negative beyond a reasonable doubt, Maryland cannot in good conscience take the lives of the Giles brothers and of Joseph Johnson.

The Giles-Johnson Defense Committee was organized by prominent citizens, many of whom did not question the verdict but felt under the circumstances of the case the sentences were harsh and excessive. After all appeals were exhausted, and the execution date of the Giles brothers was only three weeks away, new evidence was discovered which corroborated the story told by the defendants, and raised the gravest questions concerning the manner in which their conviction was obtained.

In August 1963 the Defense Committee asked the Governor of Maryland to grant the men immediate release from prison and conduct a searching inquiry to see if a full pardon should not be granted. Five jurors also wrote to the Governor to say they now had reasonable doubt as to the guilt of the condemned men. One juror wrote, "We had no idea of the character and police record and previous sexual history of the girl or the police record and character of her escort." Another juror complained that "the judge should have let more come out, or at least have found out for himself before he sentenced the boys."

A concerned citizen, Dr. Harold A. Knapp, submitted a one-hundred-and-thirty-page report. Knapp received a Christmas card in 1962 from John Giles, thanking him for writing a letter to a newspaper deploring the death sentence. Touched, Knapp wrote Giles and later began a search of the girl's background and that of Foster, her escort. Included in Knapp's exhibit was a recent press clipping reporting the fact that a young gentleman farmer of southern Maryland had been sentenced to six months in jail and fined $625 for manslaughter. In a drunken rage at a charity ball he had beaten a fifty-one-year-old Negro barmaid with a cane causing her death.

Knapp's report showed that Foster compiled a record of eleven offenses in a two-year period, ranging from drinking and fighting to petty larceny and reckless driving. One of the major points made by the State at the trial of the Giles brothers was that Foster could not have provoked the altercation with the defendants, the Giles brothers, as they claimed by calling them some vicious name, because no person in his right mind in the dark, where there were three other persons, would do a thing like that. However, the report shows that Foster had a reputation of being a notorious brawler and that he would walk into a barroom where there were six Negroes and dare them to fight.

The report revealed much new evidence on the girl that was either unknown or not disclosed at the trials. The testimony of John Giles that the girl had told him she had had sexual relations with sixteen or seventeen boys that week and that three more wouldn't make any difference, may well have seemed unbelievable to the jury. However, the report showed that police records indicated that the girl was lying on the witness stand and that she had a history of almost incredible promiscuity.

When questioned by the police, she admitted numerous acts of sexual intercourse with so many men "she couldn't begin to tell how many." She also admitted engaging in oral sexual acts and in sexual intercourse with groups of six or eight males at a time. After the alleged rape by Giles and Johnson, she claimed she had been raped by two other men. The complaint was later marked "unfounded" by the police.

John Giles testified she told him she was on probation but she denied this in the courtroom. Yet three months before the alleged rape by the trio she was charged in Juvenile Court with being beyond control of her parents and according to the defense petition she was in effect on probation. Furthermore, prior to the trial she was charged with being a "delinquent child" and committed to the Montrose School for Delinquent Girls. After the Giles brothers' trial but before the Johnson Trial, she was apprehended at a teen-age "rumble" with a .25 caliber automatic pistol in her pocketbook.

Emphasizing that none of this information reached the jury in either of the trials, a defense attorney argued that it renders the entire foundation of the case insecure.

On October 24, 1963, the Governor commuted the death sentences to life imprisonment, but declined to further review the case, noting, "The accused were represented by able counsel, they were tried in accordance with due process of the law and their convictions have been upheld by the Maryland Court of Appeals. For these reasons I do not review here the question of guilt or innocence for, in my considered opinion, the guilt of these three persons has been established through the judicial process."

The *Evening Star* (Washington, D.C.) October 25, 1963, expressed concern for the whole fabric of the criminal process.

> The two Giles brothers and Joseph Johnson would be dead today but for the efforts of several private citizens. Had the Giles's mother not been employed by Mrs. Howard Ross, there would have been no Giles-Johnson Defense Committee. Had Harold Knapp not written a letter about the case to a weekly newspaper, and had John Giles not answered it from prison, Mr. Knapp would not have embarked upon the months of patient detective work that won the three young men's commutation. On this fragile concatenation of coincidence hung three men's lives. It is not a history to strengthen a citizen's enthusiasm for the practice of capital punishment.
>
> The missing evidence was pivotal; five of the Giles's jurors have said as much, as well as State's Attorney Kardy, the prosecutor in both trials. The public is left to

ponder the dangerous disparity between the massive investigative resources commanded by the State and those available to an indigent defendant. The sheer scale of modern police organization makes the adversary trial, in its present form, a far less certain avenue to truth than it once seemed. Can a court-appointed lawyer be expected to go to the lengths to which Mr. Knapp went? If not, then who had the responsibility to bring those essential records into court?

The Governor could have commuted the death sentence to less than a life term in jail and was criticized for making the most meager possible gesture toward justice. An appeal to the United States Supreme Court for a new trial was unsuccessfully opposed by the Attorney General of Maryland. This appeal (which contended that the State had suppressed evidence particularly concerning the character of the girl and her credibility as a witness) was argued in October 1966 before the Supreme Court which gave its decision in February 1967, almost six years after the crime.

The Supreme Court noted that evidence allegedly suppressed by the prosecution included the fact that in a juvenile court proceeding a caseworker had recommended probation for the girl because she was beyond parental control. Also allegedly suppressed were the facts concerning a party five weeks after the alleged rape, and over three months before the trial. The girl had sexual relations with two men at the party, and later that night took an overdose of pills and was hospitalized in a psychiatric ward for nine days as an attempted suicide.

She told a friend who visited her at the hospital that the two men had raped her. The friend told her parents and later the girl's father filed a formal charge of rape against the two men. A police officer interviewed the girl who refused to say that she had been raped. She told the officer she had previously had relations with one of the men and also that in the previous two years she had had sexual relations with numerous boys and men, some of whom she did not know.

The Supreme Court reviewed evidence which had not been reviewed by the Court of Appeals. The evidence consisted of two police reports not part of the record but considered by the trial judge in imposing sentence. The reports were on police interviews with the girl and Foster conducted on the morning after the alleged rape. The report quotes both as stating they were engaged in sexual intercourse shortly prior to the appearance of Johnson. They testified at the trial, however, that they were merely "sitting" in the back seat of the car from the time their companions left until the appearance of the Negroes.

Furthermore, Foster on cross-examination answered no to the question whether he "didn't take her out there to have sexual relations with her yourself . . . ?" Finally, neither of the police officers mentioned in their summaries at the trial of what each person involved in the incident had told them, the fact that the girl and Foster had stated they were engaged in sexual relations when they heard the three men.

The Supreme Court opinion notes that the testimony of the girl and Foster is open to the construction that these key witnesses deliberately concealed from the judge, jury and defense counsel evidence of the girl's promiscuity. The Supreme Court also notes with regard to conflicting testimony about the number of Negroes who had intercourse with her that evening, that the contents of the (police) report go not only to the credibility of the State's witnesses, but also to the issue at trial whether John Giles had raped the girl. Serious question was also raised as to the accuracy of one police officer's testimony at the original trial.

In a dissenting opinion Mr. Justice Harlan pointed out that disposition of this case was the product of three opinions, none of which commanded the votes of a majority of the court. "On the basis of the trial record, it would be difficult to imagine charges more convincingly proved than were those against these three youths for raping this teen-age girl. Following conviction, evidence came to light which seriously reflected on the sexual habits of the girl and on the stability of her character . . . the unarticulated basis of today's disposition . . . is quite evidently nothing more than the Court's uneasiness with these convictions engendered by posttrial indications of the promiscuity of this unfortunate girl.

"Unable to discover a constitutional infirmity and unwilling to affirm the convictions, the Court simply returns the case to the Maryland Court of Appeals in hopes that despite the plurality's repeated disclaimers, that court will share the Court's discomfort and discover a formula under which these convictions can be reversed. The Court is unable even to agree upon a state law basis with which to explain its remand. I cannot join such a disposition. We on this bench are not free to disturb a state conviction simply for reasons that might be permissible were we sitting on the state court of last resort. Nor are we free to interject our individual sympathies into the administration of state criminal justice."

On May 15, 1967, the convictions of the Giles brothers were set aside as unconstitutionally obtained in a postconviction proceeding in the Circuit Court for Montgomery County. On October 30, 1967, the case of the Giles brothers was called for retrial in the Circuit Court for Baltimore County, and thereupon the charges against them were dropped. The Giles brothers are now at liberty, free of all criminal charges.

The third Negro, Johnson, did not fare so well. In January 1968 the Circuit Court denied his petition for postconviction relief; however, he was pardoned by the Governor of Maryland in February 1968 and released after spending over six years in prison.

Chapter 13

JUDICIAL REVIEW OF A RAPE CONVICTION

"Justice is that virtue of the soul which
is distributive according to desert."
— Aristotle, *Metaphysics*

A TWENTY-ONE-YEAR-OLD man was convicted of first degree rape on a fourteen-year-old girl and was sentenced to fifteen years' imprisonment in the Oklahoma State Penitentiary. In his appeal to the Criminal Court of Appeals of Oklahoma the man claimed that the evidence was insufficient to support a verdict of guilty of first degree rape.

> According to the law, at the time of the trial, rape committed by a male over eighteen years of age and accomplished with any female by means of force overcoming her resistance, or by means of threats of immediate and great bodily harm accompanied by apparent power of execution, preventing such resistance, is first degree rape. Where female is 14 but under 18 years of age, and she consents to intercourse or offers no resistance, intercourse constitutes second degree rape.

The Criminal Court of Appeals reported its consideration of the four hundred pages of testimony in the trial court.*

The evidence discloses that the defendant, William R., was brought up by his mother, the parents having been divorced when the defendant was quite young. His mother worked and defendant performed labor for contractors, and others, and a younger brother washed dishes in a restaurant. Defendant had an old 1937 model pickup Ford truck that he used in his work. He had finished high school. He moved with his mother to Oklahoma City when he was about twelve years of age. Defendant admitted on cross-examination that in January 1951 he plead guilty in Arapaho, Oklahoma, to the crime of larceny of an automobile, and received a three-year suspended sentence. This evidence was admitted as bearing on defendant's credibility as a witness. He was a tall, red-headed young man and weighed around two hundred pounds. He was in the habit of visiting DeCoursey's Dairy Bar on Northeast Twenty-third Street, Oklahoma City, in the evenings, visiting with former schoolmates and talking with the carhops.

Carolyn was born May 20, 1940, in Tillman County. Her father died a few months after her birth and several years later her mother married and moved to Oklahoma City. Carolyn remained in Tillman County at Tipton to live

---

*The opinion of the Criminal Court of Appeals is reprinted from *Pacific Reporter*, 2nd Series, Volume 290 (Okl.Cr. 290, P. 2d 775) with the permission of the West Publishing Company. Surnames have been deleted.

with her stepfather's parents and attended the Tipton school. She spent the
summers with her mother, who was very strict about her dating boys. She
wore her hair shoulder length, wore heavy rouge on her lips and weighed 130
pounds. She and her mother gave her age as seventeen when she obtained the
job at DeCoursey's as a carhop on June 1, 1954, and Carolyn had no trouble
in passing for that age. She worked until June 7, 1954.

The evidence discloses that the prosecutrix was known at DeCoursey's as
Carolyn. She was so carried on the payroll. When she commenced working
on June 1, she wore gray slacks and a white blouse, but for several days,
including June 7, she wore the same blouse — an aqua one. It had the second
button off, and the top button was left unbuttoned. One of the girls who
worked with Carolyn offered her a pin, but she refused, saying that she
might want someone "to see something." Her girl associates testified that
Carolyn wore heavy makeup and could have passed for twenty-one. They
said that at trial she had cut her hair and dressed modestly, and looked five
or six years younger, and that they hardly recognized her. They said that
Carolyn was quite proud of her body, that her ambition was to be a
striptease dancer; that a stripteaser known as The Cat Girl was her ideal; that
she felt that she had as good a figure as The Cat Girl or Marilyn Monroe. One
of the girls said that Carolyn fit her slacks like she had been poured in.

The evidence disclosed that on the evening of June 2, 1954, the defendant
drove up to DeCoursey's in an old Ford pickup, got out to go inside and saw
some boys standing in front talking to the prosecutrix. He has gone to school
with one or two of the boys and spoke to them; Charles C. went in with
defendant and later introduced him to prosecutrix. That he left in his pickup
but later on returned and sat in a car with C. and two boys by the name of
B. and Carolyn waited on them and then went back and talked to them.

A night or so later defendant returned to the Dairy Bar and went in and
Carolyn waited on him. That her blouse was open and defendant reached
over and buttoned the top button, and defendant said, "Do you want me to
get you a safety pin?" And she unbuttoned the top button. The second
button was gone. She acted proud of a large bosom. She was conceded by
her acquaintances to be a very pretty girl. Prosecutrix cursed defendant and
also cursed Jimmie B. calling him "A God-damn son-of-a-bitching bastard."
She used bad language easily. The boys were in and out of the Dairy Bar, and
prosecutrix, despite her apparent anger, followed them around to talk to
them. Also she gave the defendant her address and telephone number, and
for two mornings straight defendant telephoned Carolyn, and each time she
told him that she was just getting out of bed. Defendant testified that she
said, "Well, let me go get some clothes on," and that one morning she said,
"I can't find anything except a bra and a pair of panties. My mother has
gone next door and I cannot find anything but a bra and a pair of panties."
He said that he waited a little while and she came back and said, "Aw, hell,

my mother is not here and I cannot find them." At one time she told him that she was "standing in the raw."

Defendant testified that he asked Carolyn what she was going to do and she said that she was going to a show at the Will Rogers Theatre in the afternoon. She asked defendant why he did not come over. He met her at the show, but told her that he would have to leave pretty soon, as he had an appointment downtown; that they held hands, and sat there a little while and that she said to him, "Don't you have something else to do?" and later said, "I wish you would leave me," and that he went across the aisle and sat down and prosecutrix went over and sat down with two or three other boys, and defendant left.

The night following the picture show date, defendant and Carolyn and the B. brothers were again at the Dairy Bar, and prosecutrix told them that she was going to be a "stripper" and could make Marilyn Monroe look sick and invited them to pat her on the seat, which all of them did; that she invited them back of the Dairy Bar building, saying that she had something to show them, and each took turns at hugging and kissing her. The next morning, June 7, defendant again telephoned the prosecutrix, and as on his prior call, she told him that she did not have on any clothes and left the telephone to get her clothes, and then detailed what clothing she had found, and while she was talking, was putting on her clothes and detailing the procedure. He made a date with her to take her to the show, but told her that he had to be at work at 2 P.M. She wanted to go about 12:30 or 1:00.

Adverting further to the short acquaintance between the prosecuting witness and the defendant, and further to the background, Louise W. testified that she worked at DeCoursey's Dairy Bar from 4 to 10 in the evenings; that Carolyn, the prosecutrix, had worked there from June 1 to 7, 1954. Witness said that: "She (Carolyn) had been saying things about her body, and things like that, for quite a while, and one evening one of the boys dared another boy to offer her his ring — and he said, 'Here is my key'; and he turned around and walked off, and I turned around and looked at her and she said, 'What is the matter? Haven't you ever slept all night with a man?' And I said, 'No, I'm afraid not.' " Witness further testified: "She (Carolyn) talked about sex constantly. Every time she would say anything — about her body — 'Don't you think I have sexy eyes?' and she said she had her clothes especially made to bring out her good points."

Nelda M., a fellow car-hop employed with Carolyn at DeCoursey's Diary Bar, testified:

Q. Now referring to Sunday, June 6, 1954, did you see her out there on that day and talk to her?

A. Yes, sir; she was in the dining room — dressing room — and I went back to the dressing room to see what she was doing, and she came out and asked me if I knew what she was doing, and I said no; and she said she had been playing, and, I told her she had cars out front that needed to be waited on.

She said this was about 9:30 or 10 P.M. At another time witness said, "Well, she asked me, in the dressing room, if I didn't think she had a pretty navel, and, at that time I told her she had cars outside and I left the dressing room and shortly afterwards she came out."

Carolyn, in testifying for the State, said that she first saw the defendant on the fourth day of June, 1954, at DeCoursey's; that she had a conversation with him that night, told him her name was Carolyn. He was riding in a Ford pickup. She saw him the next day, June 5, when he drove up to DeCoursey's accompanied by a man named Jack S. who was driving a Cadillac. She talked with the parties. She told about seeing the defendant at the Will Rogers Theatre the next day, about telephone calls and said that on one occasion at DeCoursey's defendant got out of his car, pulled her back of it and "kinda fooled with me, kinda pulled me around to the back and he forcibly kissed me twice." That was the last time she saw him until the next day, about one o'clock in the afternoon, at her home. That he called her about 10 A.M. and wanted to know where she was going and wanted to know if he could see her, and she told him that she was going to her girl friend's (next door) and if he wanted to see her, he could come over there. He came there and she told him that she was going to the show and defendant asked her if she would mind for him to come back and take her; that he and another man, a chauffeur, were in the Cadillac; that he returned in about fifteen minutes in his Ford pickup. She told about driving to a swimming pool, which was closed, showing her an oil well near Pennsylvania Avenue where he had worked, and then parking in a clearing off that street. After that she detailed what happened as follows:

> A. Well, he pulled me over to him and kissed me once or twice; and I must have bit him on the lip, and, anyway, he got mad because he turned me over his knee and kind of spanked me; and so I pulled away from him; and so I looked, and I noticed the third button on my blouse was ripped off; and so he grabbed me again and kissed me again once real hard, and then another time, and so I tried to push away from him; and so finally I got away from him and I told him I wanted to go clean up my hair, and something that way.
>
> And so he said, "Okey"; and so I scooted over to the door and started to open the door and the door would not open; and so he grabbed me again and started out kissing me again, and I pushed away from him somehow, and I looked down and I noticed the fourth button — the very last button on my blouse — was ripped off; and so I started to button up my blouse and he grabbed me again and started out kissing me; and so finally he got his hand in underneath my blouse and unsnapped my brassiere and started out playing with my breasts; and, anyway, he pulled up my brassiere and looked at my breasts, and I screamed and started out to cry, and he told me to shut up or he would — he told me to shut up or he would knock my teeth out.
>
> Q. All right. What did he say?
>
> A. Well, he was holding me in his lap and so he said, "I will take you home in a little while." But he said, "You keep quiet," or — that is when he said he would

knock my teeth out — and so then he asked me if I had a bathing suit, and I said yes; and so he told me to buy me a really pretty one and I just ignored him.

She said that they then talked about religion, and what churches they belonged to, etc. She was asked:

Q. Was he sitting under the driver's wheel all this time, Carolyn?

A. Yes, he kissed me twice and I could not get my breath, and I must have caught on something because there was a little drop of blood right here on his face; and so he let me alone just for a minute until I could get my breath back, and I noticed my skirt was up above my knees and so (witness cries) and so I tried to motion towards my skirt and he looked at it and kind of laughed, and then he ran his hand underneath my skirt — (witness cries) — and put his fingers inside my pants and so I screamed and he told me to shut up or he would fix me up so nobody would ever want me again. And so I was crying and trying to get away from him, and he asked me if I wanted to get out of the car; and I did not answer him at first, and then I thought to myself I might have a chance to get away from him; and so we got out of the car and he taken hold of my arm, and I fought him, and kicked him, and tried to get away from him, and he kept a hold of my arm all of the time and I tried to get away; and he forced my legs apart — (witness cries) — and he started — (witness crying).

Q. Where were you at that time, Carolyn?

A. I was just in the car seat with my head towards the door on my side. With my head beside the door. And when I raised up I was tangled up in the door handle; and I could not get the door open; it would not come open; and then my skirt — he told me to shut up — (witness crying).

Q. Did he hold you on the seat, Carolyn?

A. Yes.

Q. And did he insert his private parts in yours? Is that right?

A. Yes.

Q. Then what was said? What happened?

A. Well, it hurt me quite a bit and I was crying and so he said for me to get out of the car and get in the back seat then; and I did not say anything, and than I said, "Okey"; and so he got out first, and he grabbed a hold of my arm, and I kicked him, and fought him, and he pushed me up against the back of the seat.

She further testified:

A. And so he pushed me up in the back of the seat — back of the pickup, and there was a tarpaulin — he had two tarpaulins — in the back and he reached down for one and his grip kinda loosened on my arm, and so I was able to get away from him; and so I jumped out of the pickup; and before I could get to my feet and start off he grabbed ahold of me and he kinda pushed and pulled me around on the other side of the pickup and he pulled down the tarpaulin and told me to get down and I didn't get down, and so he knocked me down — pushed me down — and then he pulled up my dress and forced my legs apart, and then I was crying all this time — and he inserted his private parts in mine — (witness crying).

Q. And you got back in the car. Then what happened?

A. Well, we had started back towards Pennsylvania Avenue. And he said, "You don't have to worry about anything — you won't get pregnant". And so I did not say anything; and he said, "Are you going to tell your mother?" and I did not say anything at first; and then he asked me again, and I said, "I don't know" — I said I didn't know — I really wasn't. I was scared to tell him that I was; and then he said, "You aren't going to make something out of this, are you?" And I said, "I don't know." And finally he said, "Are you going to the police about it?" And I

said, "I don't know"; and so we got back on Northwest Highway, and so he said,
"You want me to return to work tonight and see you?" and so I said, "I don't
want to see you, I hate your guts, and I don't want to see you again." And he
said, "Oh, damn."

Q. All right. What happened next?

A. And so then we drove on in silence until we got within a half block of my
house; then he said, "You want me to get out and to go inside and tell your
mother?" And I said no. And then when he got to my house, he said, "Do you
want me to go inside and tell your mother?" again, and I said no; and I tried to
get out the door on that side and I could not get it open, and so finally he opened
it up for me. And then I went . . .

Prosecutrix testified that on arriving back home she went to the front
door, rang the bell, that nobody answered, so she went to the back door and
that her mother was in the kitchen and saw her. Witness went in her
bedroom and was crying and the mother went in and questioned her and the
stepfather went in and telephoned Dr. C. and the police. In the meantime
witness took a bath, put on clean clothes and her parents took her to the
doctor's office, where she was examined by Dr. C.

The mother, Verda, said that her daughter left the house at approximately
five minutes after one and returned at 2:45; that when she returned she was
crying; that her blouse buttons were torn, the collar was torn, the back of
her blouse was dirty; her skirt was very wrinkled, her panties and slip were
bloody; that she washed the panties and in twenty or thirty minutes they
drove to Dr. C.'s office and then to the police station.

On cross-examination witness said that her daughter could pass for
seventeen years of age.

Three police officers testified to talking with defendant after his arrest.
They did not warn him of his constitutional rights with reference to any
statements that he might make. One officer said that defendant finally
admitted having sexual intercourse with the prosecutrix but said that it was
with her consent. Two other police officers said he admitted that she did not
consent, but that he went ahead anyway.

John A. C., M.D. testified that on June 7, 1954, he had occasion to see
Carolyn at about 3:30 P.M. at his office; that her parents brought her; that
he first made a routine examination of her body for trauma, or bruises; that
he found nothing at all on the general body; that is, no bruises or evidence of
trauma; that he then made a pelvic examination of her vulva and vagina, or
private parts; that he found fresh blood at the inlet of the vagina and also
two small tears into the hymen; that the hymen is a small membrane,
skinlike membrane at the entrance to the vagina. The interior of the vagina
was clean. Smears were taken which revealed no sperm germ cells present.
No gonococci were present, and a Wassermann test was negative. The girl
would not answer many of his questions. The doctor testified to many
possible ways the injury could have happened, the effect of masturbation,

etc. By reason of the absence of sperm cells the doctor could not give an opinion as to what caused the two small tears in the hymen. He thought it was some object as large or larger than three fingers.

The defendant in defense produced Charles Van S., a commercial photographer who identified a picture of a clearing off Pennsylvania Avenue, later identified by the defendant as the place where he parked his pickup during the time testified to by prosecutrix; and a second picture showed the cars on Pennsylvania Avenue clearly visible as they would pass.

Ted M. H., testified that he lived at 2225 Northwest Thirty-fifth Street, and had lived there for twenty-five years; that he employed the defendant to accept delivery of ready-mixed cement, which was to be delivered at his place by the Murphy-Perkin Company at 2:30 P.M. on June 7, 1954. Witness identified the delivery ticket, defendant's "Exhibit C" from the cement mixing company, showing two yards of cement loaded at 2:01 for Ted H., 2225 N.W. Thirty-fifth Street. Witness stated that later on in the afternoon on June 7 he arrived home and helped the defendant finish laying a cement floor in one of the rooms of the garage apartment at his home. Witness further said that at about 3 P.M. of the day in question the defendant telephoned him at the Elfenix Cafe, where witness was installing air-conditioning, for directions as to what to do with some surplus cement.

Dewey P., driver for the Murphy-Perkin Company, testified to delivering the ready-mixed cement at 2225 N.W. Thirty-fifth Street the afternoon of June 7, 1954, at approximately 2:30 and that the cement was received by the defendant R.

The defendant testified about agreeing with Ted M. H., to be at his place by 2:30 P.M., June 7, 1954, to receive and lay cement for him. He claimed that he had gone in the S. Cadillic, driven by a chauffeur, to a grocery store where the chauffeur was to get some groceries, that he purchased some cookies, etc. himself and returned to Carolyn's home in his pickup and knocked on the door but that Carolyn came from the house next door and got in his pickup with him. He detailed their movements thereafter substantially as Carolyn had until he parked in the clearing about two hundred feet off Pennsylvania Avenue. He said he then kissed Carolyn several times and then got the tarpaulin from the truck, spread it on the ground and suggested that they get a lunch which he had theretofore purchased and consisting of cheese, crackers and cookies, out of the car. Defendant denied that he had intercourse with the prosecutrix as detailed by her. He said that he did not have much time to spend with her on account of his employment to receive and lay the cement for Mr. H.

Several witnesses, associates of Carolyn at the DeCoursey Dairy Bar, and young men customers who patronized the Bar at the time defendant was there, testified concerning the acts and conduct of prosecutrix with defendant and others, several nights just prior to the alleged rape. They all testified that the aqua blouse introduced by the State and said to have been worn by the prosecutrix at the time the offense was committed, was torn and had one or two buttons missing.

Carolyn testified in rebuttal, but she only said that she was not menstruating on June 7, 1954, the last time being the latter part of May. She also said that she had never had sexual intercourse before. She was not asked and did not deny the specific conduct of inviting the defendant and three other boys to pat her seat, or the obscene language attributed to her, or the remarks and conduct by her described by her fellow carhops.

This completed the case.

The testimony of the prosecutrix that she had intercourse with the defendant as claimed is corroborated by all the evidence. The fact that Dr. C. in an examination of prosecutrix a short time after the act alleged was unable through a microscopic examination of specimen from the vagina of prosecutrix to discern any sperm cells or traces of male semen, could be accounted for by the bath Carolyn took just prior to going to the doctor, or the defendant may have used a condom, as she stated that he told her after the act that she need have no fear of becoming pregnant.

Having reached the above conclusion without difficulty, we now come to the real problem presented by the record, that being whether the evidence was sufficient to support a verdict of guilty of first degree rape. Was there sufficient evidence produced by the State to show that there was real resistance in good faith to the advances of the defendant, and not a passive or feigned resistance, or pretence amounting to a sham? To constitute resistance in good faith it must have been commenced at the inception of the advances and continued until the offense was consummated. Resistance by mere words is not sufficient, but such resistance must be by acts, and must be reasonably proportionate to the strength and opportunities of the woman. If there was lack of resistance, then force would not have been used. The evidence must be evaluated in relation to these principles in order to determine if there was sufficient evidence to support the verdict of the jury.

We must interpret the testimony of the prosecutrix as to the details of her alleged ravishment with reference to her testimony of her entire relationship with the defendant and in relation to the unrefuted testimony of other witnesses as to such relationships, and the general conduct of prosecutrix, where unrefuted, as told by Louise W. and Nelda M., her co-workers at the DeCoursey Dairy Bar.

Our task, of course, is not to weigh the evidence — that was for the jury and does not fall within the exception involved in the recent case of *De Armond v. State,* Okl.Cr., 285 P.2d 236. We must determine if the undisputed evidence was sufficient to support the judgment rendered. And while we must accept at face value that portion of the evidence of the two girl associates of prosecutrix, where unrefuted, still we recognize the possible motivation of jealousy as influencing part of the testimony of these witnesses. And it is our thought that possibly it is not abnormal for a girl of the age of prosecutrix, apparently an underprivileged girl, regardless of her physical development, to have a tendency to boast and pretend to her girl associates that she was far more experienced and "vampish" and popular with boys than she actually was.

Prosecutrix testified about her four days' acquaintance with the defendant and their whirlwind courtship. She said that on Sunday night, June 6, 1954, the defendant got out of his car and "kind of fooled with me and drug me around — (interrupted).

Q. What did he do then?

A. Well, he kinda pulled me around to the back and he forcibly kissed me twice . . ."

This was the time that witness C. and the B. brothers and the defendant testified that prosecutrix had invited them to pat her seat and that she had "necked" with each one of them, which included the defendant. But in spite of this she gave defendant a date at noon the next day. When she testified in rebuttal she did not deny defendant's testimony that at the time they made the date by telephone she told him that she was "standing in the raw" and then detailed her dressing, telling him when she was putting on her panties, her bra, etc. And although on cross-examination following her direct examination for the State in proof of its case she had denied bragging to her co-workers Louise W. and Nelda M. about her body, no attempt was made on rebuttal to deny much of their testimony making her out as a sexy girl, interested in men.

In view of the testimony of prosecutrix as to defendant's violent caresses on Sunday night, June 6, would she not have known what to expect the next day when he wanted a date, and particularly when she recounted about her panties, her bra, etc., which could be expected to arouse him sexually?

There was a house within about two hundred feet of the rendezvous off Pennsylvania Avenue occupied by Negroes, and there was a clear view of the avenue where motorists were continually passing. Prosecutrix said that she sat in defendant's lap. She did not detail any struggle to get away. There were no black marks or bruises on her body. She was a robust girl who weighed 130 pounds and capable of putting up formidable resistance. From defendant's conversation and conduct he had done nothing or said nothing to demonstrate that he would injure her, except that he told her once that he would knock her teeth out; but the normal language of the parties seems to have been rough. Prosecutrix, according to the testimony of other witnesses, was in the habit of using foul language, and had "cussed out" the defendant the first night they met, but moments later was back at the car talking with defendant and his friends, and even got in the car to sit with them. This was never denied by her.

Prosecutrix said that defendant assured her that she would not get pregnant. No male sperm cells were found by the doctor who examined her, indicating that defendant had time to use a condom. Defendant offered to go with prosecutrix to see her mother. She had by her own testimony asked him how long it would take when he was on the tarpaulin with her. She admitted that after defendant tried and had penetrated her in the front seat of the pickup that she had agreed to get out of the car, but she said it was with the idea of getting away. The only offer to strike her was by pushing her down on the tarpaulin. The force was not enough to leave any marks on her person.

The physician testified that it would have required an object as large or larger than three fingers to produce the two small tears in the hymen of prosecutrix. From a study of medical testimony given in a great number of rape cases, we find that it is difficult to get more than one finger in a virgin, unless the hymen has been ruptured, and two fingers after rupture, so that prosecutrix may have gotten more than she contemplated as she was teasing with the defendant. But however that may be, she was not of the age of consent (eighteen years) and while the contention is made that defendant did not know that the prosecutrix was under the age of sixteen years, such, if true, would not condone his act of having sexual relations with the prosecutrix, but such fact may be considered by the court in connection with the amount of punishment which defendant should suffer. (*Law v. State,* 92 Okl.Cr. 444, 224 P.2d 278).

We are convinced that there was not sufficient evidence of resistance on the part of the prosecutrix of the advances of the defendant to sustain the conviction of rape in the first degree, but that the evidence is ample to sustain a conviction of the included offense of rape in the second degree.

The verdict and judgment as so modified is affirmed, with punishment fixed at ten years imprisonment in the state penitentiary.

Chapter 14

CRIMINAL INVESTIGATION

"It seems . . . to be one of those simple cases which are
so extremely difficult."
— Conan Doyle, *The Adventures of Sherlock Holmes*

THE crime of rape poses a serious challenge to law enforcement officers. Clues are often slender, and almost 40 per cent of forcible rapes in the United States are not cleared by arrest. Indeed the clearance rates by arrest and by conviction are lower for forcible rape than for the other Crime Index offenses against the person — aggravated assault, murder and nonnegligent manslaughter. Investigation of claims of rape which later prove to be false adds to the burden of police departments, especially those handicapped by lack of staff.

The objectives of the criminal investigation are to determine whether the crime of forcible rape has occurred and, if so, to obtain evidence which will lead to the identification, arrest and conviction of the offender. The problem of determining whether a rape has occurred at all is often difficult and time consuming, especially when the persons involved have known each other for some time.

THE PATROLMAN

Occasionally police discover a rape in progress in an alley or parking lot; sometimes they are called to the scene by witnesses. Curiously victims do not always appreciate the appearance of the police. A patrol car responded to a call from an apartment house manager who reported that one of his tenants was screaming for help. Furniture had been overturned in her room and the woman had obviously been struggling with the man who was in her apartment. She was lying on her bed sobbing, her clothing was disarrayed and her panties and hose were on the floor beside her bed. Despite her obvious distress, she refused to file charges against the man, who claimed to be a friend.

Usually police are notified by the victim after the crime has been committed. The suspect is seldom immediately available for interview. A drunken offender may, however, fall asleep after the rape and remain at the scene of the crime until awakened by the police. The suspect should be advised of his rights to remain silent, to talk to a lawyer before and during

269

questioning and to have an attorney appointed if he cannot afford one. If after all these warnings he is willing to talk to police officers, he should be questioned at length.

The suspect who admits sexual intercourse may claim at his trial that he thought sexual intercourse referred to kissing. A medical examination with his informed consent should be performed without delay to detect injuries and the presence of blood and semen on his person. His clothing and fingernail scrapings may provide important evidence. Bruises or scratches inflicted on the suspect should be photographed.

The initial investigation is usually performed by the patrolmen who are sent to interview the victim. Although these officers may lack experience in the investigation of sex crimes, their contribution is vital. A distraught victim, an excited witness and an intoxicated or remorseful suspect may reveal information which might not be disclosed later. A thorough investigation and report provides a sound basis for subsequent inquiry. The perfunctory investigation and brief report enable suspect, witness or victim at later interviews to omit significant information or to make false or misleading statements.

The victim should be asked to describe the duration of her acquaintance with the offender, the circumstances of their first meeting and the extent of their previous relationship, including any prior sexual relationship with the offender. She should be allowed to describe the rape in privacy without interruption. When she has finished, it will be necessary to clarify her statements by direct inquiry.

Victims often omit embarrassing details such as perverse sexual acts by the suspect. They are more likely to do so when the officers are embarrassed or ill at ease. Experienced sex detail detectives are able to talk to victims in a detached yet not insensitive manner. The inexperienced officer should cultivate this approach and should ask himself whether he is restricting his inquiry due to awkwardness or as a consequence of either great sympathy for or prejudice against the victim. He should be neither too credulous nor too skeptical. What the victim will tell about the assault on herself will depend on whether the officer seems interested and concerned or unfriendly and impatient.

The officers should keep in mind the three important legal issues — lack of consent, force and penetration. Their report should be in plain language. The description of the offense itself cannot be confined to the use of terms such as rape and sexual intercourse. In order to make it clear that penetration occurred with a penis and not with a finger, the victim should not be permitted to give such a vague description that it is not clear what actually occurred at the time of the assault.

Force includes not only physical violence but also threats, which are usually on the life of the victim or her child. Lack of consent shows itself in resistance, appeals for help and attempts to escape. The woman's fear of physical injury or death may be so great as to lead to quick submission. Submission, however, does not necessarily mean consent. Torn clothing, bruises and other physical injuries strongly suggest the use of force and lack of consent; however, women have been known to tear their clothing and inflict injuries on themselves to bolster false claims of rape.

A complete account of the rape and surrounding events will show whether the victim seized any available opportunity to summon help or to escape. The girl who has been wakened from sleep to find a pillow over her face may not have a clear glimpse of her attacker. Every effort should be made to obtain a description of the suspect. Even fragmentary details may be invaluable. Bad breath, body odors, discolored teeth, a recent cut on a finger, a facial tic, unusual expressions of speech or mannerisms should be noted. One suspect, on dressing after the rape, placed a rubber band around the top of his socks. This observation by the victim contributed significantly to his later identification and conviction.

As the victim tells the story of the rape and any prior relationship with the suspect she will also tell a great deal about herself. Her mood and general emotional reaction, her choice of words and her comments on unrelated matters will aid in the evaluation of her complaint. Is she more concerned over the theft of her purse and a few dollars than she is about the sexual assault? Does she speak quietly but with obvious concern about her ordeal? A host of observations by an alert officer will contribute to his impression of her character and reliability as a witness.

Arrangements should be made as quickly as possible for medical examination of the victim, preferably at the city general hospital, where the medical staff are familiar with the medicolegal requirements of such an examination. If the victim insists on seeing her private physician, he should be made aware of the need for careful records on the nature and extent of bruises and other injuries, vaginal examination, as well as examination for sperm and venereal infection. Foreign materials and fingernail scrapings should be preserved for laboratory examination. Parental consent has to be obtained for the examination of children.

If the victim's clothing is torn or stained, it may be necessary to drive her to her home so that she will have something to replace the torn clothing, which should be kept for laboratory examination and use as evidence. The officers should search the scene of the crime and collect other evidence such as stained sheets or cushions, weapons and so on. It is their duty to call on experts to aid in the search for fingerprints, and to take laboratory specimens as well as casts and photographs of tire and shoe impressions when indicated. Color photographs should be taken of injuries to the victim. Persons living near the scene of the crime should be interviewed.

Inexperienced police officers sometimes fail to obtain important evidence such as the victim's underclothing. When detectives later request it, they may find that it has been washed and hence useless as evidence. The necessity for thorough collection and identification of evidence cannot be over-emphasized.

When the name of the suspect is known, it may be difficult to find him if he no longer lives at the address which is listed on his automobile license application. The title to his car should be obtained, as this will list the bank or loan company which has financed purchase of the car. They keep careful check on any change of address of their customers. Agencies which make credit checks for department stores are also able to provide the address of any person who has applied for a loan or for a charge account.

THE DETECTIVE

Later investigation by detectives will involve further interviews with the victim and others. At this time it is helpful to ask the victim to write out a description of the rape. As the victim's character may be the subject of cross-examination when she appears on the witness stand, tactful questioning in this area may be indicated. She should be asked the date of her last sexual intercourse, since intercourse prior to the rape may account for the presence of sperm in her vagina. She should also be asked the date of her last menstrual period and whether she is using birth control pills.

Questioning about prior sexual assaults may be revealing. Repeated claims of rape are seldom legitimate. Police records of victims should be checked. In Amir's study 19 per cent of the victims had an arrest record; the highest proportion of these arrests was for sexual misconduct.

She should review photographs of known sex offenders if she is unable to identify her assailant. Her response as she looks at these photographs is of psychological interest. "I'll probably see some men I dated." "No, he's not cute enough." "He could have been the one that attacked me (sigh), just think he could have been." The occasional victim will select not just one or two photographs of men who resemble her assailant, but six or seven pictures of persons of widely differing facial appearance and body build, ranging in height from five feet six inches to over six feet. Beards may be removed immediately after the rape as in the case of one offender who was arrested late one night as he was shaving off his beard in his home.

In a doubtful case of rape or in a genuine case in which the victim gives some information which appears to be untruthful, it is helpful to arrange for a polygraph examination. In a doubtful case the suspect may demand a polygraph examination, while the victim finds one excuse after another for not taking the test. Although the results cannot be used in court, the test may lead to a spontaneous admission that some or all of the information previously given to police officers was not true.

The police artist's drawing of the suspect, derived from the memory of the victim, may aid in detection of the rapist. Identification kits are produced commercially which enable a victim to provide a picture of the suspect without the aid of an artist. She selects from the kit various features which are placed together to form a composite picture.

There may be insufficient information to lead to the identification of the offender, yet this information when added to that obtained from other victims of the same offender may lead to his arrest. Rapists tend to use the same technique or *modus operandi* from one crime to the next.

MODUS OPERANDI

> *The criminal judges the value of his methods solely on the basis of successful accomplishment. Having achieved a few minor successes, he is loathe to alter his operational procedure, his reluctance stemming from superstition, lack of imagination and inertia.*
> — Charles E. O'Hara, *Fundamentals of Criminal Investigation*

Rapists resemble other criminals in their tendency to use the same method of operation, or *modus operandi,* from one assault to the next. Thus some offenders commit rapes only in public parks or lover's lanes; others in homes or laundromats. One man will approach all his victims in a street with the question "Where is Bannock Street?" or "Have you seen a small black dog?"

One man will attack only elderly women; another always chooses very young girls, while a third may confine himself to assaulting prostitutes. The personal touch may not be the choice of victims, selection of the rape scene or the mode of initial approach to the victim, but rather a stereotyped sequence and pattern of events during and following the rape. Careful review of the following reports of rape by three victims shows many striking similarities in the *modus operandi.*

Case 1. I walked in the house and he came from the kitchen holding a gun and a lead pipe and asked me if I had any money in the house and I mentioned I had five dollars. Then he said, "Don't move," and he asked if I had any weapons in the house, a gun or any sort of weapon. He then ordered me to come with him and said he would let me go at around five blocks. I went out to his car and he mentioned that he had some friends waiting for him. He made me sit on the floor and he drove around, saying that he was looking for his friends. He made a big point of this.

Eventually he drove to a deserted area near the Platte River. He made me get out of the car and he told me to take off my clothes. I refused and he threatened me with his gun. So he took off my clothes and he made me get back in the car. I kept closing my legs and he kept threatening me and then with his fingers he assaulted me. I kept asking him to stop, that I didn't enjoy this sort of thing and we kept talking and talking. He made me change positions and it didn't work. He made me change position again — sit on him, lie on my back, on my stomach.

The entire time I was pleading with him and crying. Finally he entered me. He got off me and he said he was sorry. He gave me my clothes and he said, "I'm really sorry but you're going to have to get down on the floor, I hate to make you do this," and he seemed rather remorseful. He drove off then, he stopped on the side of the road and he said that he really was sorry. "You don't believe me, please believe me, I'm very sorry." I told him that he had to quit this and he said he guessed I was right. He mentioned his wife and said that there were two people he was sorry for, it was his wife and me.

He said this was going to be hard on me to forget even in later life and he said, "When you love someone, don't let this enter into it, I hope this hasn't ruined you, I really believe you are one fine woman, one of the finest I have met." He inquired about where I lived and he asked me my name, and for fear of lying I told him my name and he wrote it down on a pad and put it in the glove compartment, also he put his gun in the glove compartment. He drove me home and left me in an alley a block to walk home.

He warned me before I got out that if the "pigs" found out about him, and if he were apprehended that he had friends and my life would be in danger. He said that he was not playing around, like I'd be in the morgue. He said, "If I get caught by the pigs, you'll be erased by my friends." He didn't harm me in any way except for once when I wouldn't comply with his wishes and he gave me a little hit in the ribs with the lead pipe. He said he would hate to see those lips all bruised up and the face all puffy.

Case 2. He walked in the back door and asked me my name. I told him and he put a gun to my head and said to go with him. He took my coin purse and kept the bills. We went out the back door to his car and he made me lay on the floor with my head down so I couldn't see where he was taking me. He said that he was a professional in that line and not to try anything, say anything or move. He said he didn't like what he was doing and had to be drunk everytime he did something like that, which he was at the time.

He talked about Negroes and whites and how he and all colored got such a rough deal. He said he had three years of college but couldn't get a decent job, that's why he was in this kind of work. He said he was happily married and had two children. His mother was a Negro but she died when he was born and his father remarried to a white woman. He said he loved her, but most every other white woman was out to give him a bad deal. He talked a lot about his not being able to get a decent job because of the whites, that the Negro had two knocks against him from the time he was born. He said, "Don't hold what I'm doing to you against all black people."

He stopped by a house somewhere and honked the horn for the person that he was to pick up. He said if the person was there he would have to gag and blindfold me, but no one was there. He got very angry over that and said that he had been watching me for two weeks and was supposed to get four hundred dollars when I was delivered. He held an ice pick thing to me in the car when he put the gun down and made his point not to try anything. He said he was going to get something out of it and took off with me.

I asked him what he was going to do. He said, "You know what I'm going to do, take your clothes off. If I have to make you, you won't like it." I undressed on the floor. He stopped by some railroad tracks. Then he took the gun out again and told me to give him any weapons I had. I told him I had none and he checked my clothes to be sure. He made me get in the back seat. He still had the gun on me and said I'd better be cool and give him no trouble or else.

He told me to lay on my back. He fondled me and kissed me, then told me to lay on my stomach. He raped me, then he put his finger in me very roughly. He said I was a real sweet girl and that he wouldn't have had to do it if the guy he was to leave me with wouldn't have given him a bad deal. He then laid down on the seat but could not be comfortable that way and he couldn't get in me so he did it the other way again.

He then told me to get dressed but that he was going to keep my panties. He said he had the wall of his room full of panties from other girls. He then took me home. He left me off in the alley, and he said if I got any ideas about reporting this, if he got caught he had some friends that would do to me what he would if he got the chance. [The victim had scratches about her shoulders and neck.]

Case 3. As I tried to put my key in the door, I saw a shadow out of the corner of my eye. I turned and saw a black person slowly running toward me with his arm stretched out with a gun pointed at my head. I banged on the door, he pulled my arm away with the gun in my ribs. He told me to get in his car. He pointed the gun toward me and said to get on the floor. He drove off. He asked me how much money I had. I looked, I only had five dollars. He said, "I need more than that, I have to have it tonight to save a buddy." He kept talking about his buddy who had saved his life twice.

He talked for about an hour about black and white people in society then he said, "Well, I've kidnapped you and broke my bottle of whiskey over you and I'm not benefiting so . . . " then he pointed his gun at me and said, "Take your clothes off." I started crying and said, "You can't do this." And he said, "Oh, yes, I can and I am, get out of the car. Yeah, and don't worry about getting pregnant, I am sterile."

I got out, he got out. He said, "Now stand back because I don't want you to try anything." He was pointing his gun at me. He said, "You could know karate or judo and knock this gun out of my hand. Now take your clothes off." I said, "Please don't, you might screw me up mentally." He said, "You have a bad habit of stalling — now get moving."

He reached in the front seat and took an ice pick and poked it in my face. "Now if you try to scream and kick or go for the gun, I'll have to use this." Then he stabbed it into the upholstery of the back seat. He said, "Lay down," and he started to molest me. He raped me; then he said, "Put your back to me," and he proceeded again. He talked about his wife and kid. Then I said, "Can I get dressed?" and he picked up this steel bar, laid it on my leg and said, "You know what this is for, just one wrong move and bam over the head and you'll never get up again."

I said I was tired and he said, "You're really beautiful, I wish I met you before, but you wouldn't of let me get anywhere with you." He handed me my clothes. He talked about why he would rape me and insist on taking me home; he talked about friendship, compassion for people, how all people are brothers and the car he stole. After a while he said, "Let me see your wallet." He took my name and address. "This is just in case you try to squeal, I can get my friends and they would kill you or your husband." He drove me home (a short distance away) and said, "I guess I'll need your money after all." [As he drove away, the victim obtained the license number of the car which resulted in the arrest of the offender.]

Distinctive Features of These Three Rapes

All three victims described their assailant as a young Negro with brown eyes. His height was variously estimated as five feet five, six and seven inches; his age as in the twenties, twenty-one and twenty-five; and his weight as 135 and 140 pounds and of slim build. All three victims gave the same general description of the car, although they varied in the extent of their observations of the interior of the car. Quite apart from these observations there is a striking similarity in the *modus operandi.* Common features included the following:

1. All abductions took place in or outside the victim's homes, which were all in the same Denver suburb.
2. A hand gun was shown at the outset and later a metal object was used to threaten the victims.
3. Verbal threats of physical injury.
4. Inquiry regarding possession of weapons by two of the victims and knowledge of karate or judo by the other victim. He appeared to be quite fearful of counterattack in all rapes.
5. Mention of accomplices who never appeared in two rapes.
6. Initial driving around the area of abduction, then a drive to a deserted area.
7. Victim required to undress outside the car.
8. Repeated sexual intercourse in different positions.
9. Expression of remorse after the rape.
10. Prolonged conversations with the victims, including discussion of racial problems and discrimination.
11. Mention of his wife.
12. Mention of his need for alcohol on occasions of rape. (Note items 10 to 12 were spontaneously reported by two victims and confirmed by the third victim on later inquiry).
13. Demand for the victim's name.
14. Threats of harm if police informed.

Although some of the above items, for example threats of harm and warnings that the police should not be contacted, are frequent accompaniments of rape; other items such as inquiry about possession of a weapon or knowledge of karate or judo are not common features of rape. The overall similarity of the *modus operandi* in these three rapes needs no emphasis.

Some police departments use computers to collect data on rape offenses and the offenders. A *modus operandi* form is completed whenever there is sufficient information available to justify use of the computer system. Information can be obtained from the computer files by listing on the *modus operandi* form the known characteristics of the offender and his technique, and the computer will list all criminals and or crimes that match the description. One of the most successful computer-based *modus operandi* systems in the country is maintained by the Detroit Police Department. A copy of their *Sex Crime Modus Operandi* form is provided in Appendix One.

THE RAPIST WHO RETURNS AGAIN

When there is good reason to suspect that the rapist may attack the same victim again or when the rapist has again raped the same victim, it is helpful to arrange for the telephone company to install a buzzer on the headboard of the victim's bed. If she hears the man returning, she presses the buzzer which alerts the desk officer at her neighborhood police station. Fluorescent powder, which can be seen under ultra-violet light, should be sprinkled on window ledges, door latches and other places where the suspect is likely to gain entrance.

If the offender leaves before attacking the victim or before the police arrive, the presence of the powder on the hands or clothes of a person arrested in the neighborhood of the victim's house is a valuable factor in securing his conviction in court.

FALSE ACCUSATIONS OF RAPE

> *"O, what a tangled web we weave*
> *When first we practice to deceive."*
> – Sir Walter Scott, *Marmion*

False accusations of rape add to the investigative problem and great care should be taken to avoid the arrest and detention of innocent persons. The decision to arrest the person accused by the victim should not be made hastily without careful consideration. Each case should be considered individually. The advantages of a prompt search of the suspect, his car and his home have to be weighed against the risk of detaining a person who has not committed a crime. Factors to be considered include the nature of the crime, the extent of the victim's injuries, her character and prior criminal record, as well as the record of the suspect and the evidence of witnesses.

It should be remembered that a woman's injuries may have been self-inflicted or may have been the result of a fight with someone other than the alleged rapist, either prior to or after the alleged rape. A young girl who was evicted from a tavern because she was under twenty-one, later returned and became involved in an altercation in the women's restroom. A male employee of the tavern in his attempts to restrain her choked her and she later supported her claim of rape by another man by drawing the attention of police officers to the marks on her neck.

A distinction should be made between the woman who deliberately concocts a false story of rape and the woman who, in relatively good faith, claims that she was the victim of rape or attempted rape when in fact she was the victim of seduction or attempted seduction. (Many women would frown upon the use of the term "victim" in the context of seduction or attempted seduction.) It is not unusual for a woman who has responded to the amorous approaches of a boyfriend, to panic when the boyfriend succeeds in making more headway than her conscience, if not her instincts, permit. The term "unfounded" which is used by the police, covers both deliberately concocted false claims of rape and the latter situation which involves a woman's misapprehensions on the legal definition of rape.

The frequency of unfounded claims of rape emphasizes the need for careful consideration of a claim of rape before deciding upon the arrest of the man accused. In 1968 as a national average, 18 per cent of all forcible rapes were determined by police investigation to be unfounded. Twenty-five per cent of rapes reported to the police in this study were unfounded. A further 20 per cent of the complaints of rape were open to considerable question; for example, a woman claimed that she was followed from a restaurant late at night by a young man, attacked, dragged into an alley and raped. The suspect claimed that she agreed to have sexual relations. Restaurant employees report that the suspect sat next to her in the restaurant, that she paid for his coffee and they left together. There were no bruises on the victim who, in contrast to the suspect, was unwilling to take a polygraph examination. District attorneys are unwilling to prosecute dubious cases such as this one.

An experienced detective can often predict with accuracy that a complaint lacks basis simply from careful scrutiny of the patrolman's report. No decision should be made until the victim, witnesses and, whenever possible, the suspect have been interviewed. Failure to call for help and failure to attempt escape when the opportunity presents itself demand explanation. The many reasons for false accusations of rape have been described in Chapter 11. There are several factors which arouse suspicion of a false or unjustified complaint of rape.

Improbable Circumstances

> *"If a man is sufficiently unimaginative to produce*
> *evidence in support of a lie, he might as well*
> *speak the truth at once."*
> — Oscar Wilde, *The Decay of Lying*

Unlikely or improbable events speak for themselves. Truth may be stranger than fiction, but the claim of a robust young woman that she was raped by an unarmed middle-aged man in a wheelchair will test the credulity of even the most gullible police officer. A girl who described her assailant as having blue eyes, blond hair short on top, five feet ten inches in height and weighing two hundred pounds refused to look through photographs of known sex offenders, as she was positive she could not identify him. Another girl said she could not describe the offender, yet she spent six hours with him.

A woman reported to police that she had been raped in her home five days earlier. She complained that she telephoned the police after the rape but no officers responded to the call. The transcript of calls made to the radio room at the police department on the night of the alleged rape showed she had reported to the dispatcher that there was a black car with several occupants parked in her driveway. A patrol car did not find any car in the driveway. Another call was made to the dispatcher the day after the alleged rape and she told the officer who went to her home that she had been troubled by prowlers. No mention was made of a rape.

A victim reports that she was beaten, kicked and raped despite her fierce resistance, yet her clothing is not torn and she has no bruises. Some accounts of kidnapping and rape do not withstand even superficial inquiry. A girl complained that she had been held captive for eleven days and that in the first five days she was raped by fifty-five men. She said that she lost count after this, as many men came back for "seconds." Inquiry quickly established that she was a psychiatric hospital patient. Some stories, though bizarre, have a basis in fact, and it is important to check out all complaints.

A twenty-four-year-old obese secretary was found lying on the floor of her apartment with no clothes on and with her hands and feet tied with adhesive tape. A broken coke bottle was found alongside her. She said that she had been hit on the head and knocked out as she was collecting her mail in her apartment house by a man with a smell of alcohol on his breath. She complained of vaginal pain and medical examination showed small pieces of glass in her vagina. She also had scratch marks on her breasts.

Detectives who called at the home of her employer were about to leave when the employer's wife came into the living room and said, "Aren't you going to talk to me?" The detectives said that they did not wish to talk to her, whereupon she turned to her husband and said, "That's what you said this morning." Her husband paled visibly and said, "No, darling, they're through, they know what they are doing." When the detectives telephoned her later, she said that her husband blamed her for the rape and inferred that she had hired someone to attack the victim. She added that her husband had been having an affair with his secretary.

The woman lived in a third floor apartment and it would have been difficult for a man to have carried her up three floors. She was confronted with the problems involved in carrying an unconscious heavy woman up three floors and the peculiar circumstances of pieces of glass placed inside her vagina without causing injury. She became enraged and refused to take a polygraph examination. Possibly she had lost the affection of her employer and was endeavoring to arouse his sympathy for her and to reawaken his interest in her.

False Statements

False statements to police officers raise doubt as to the genuineness of a complaint of rape. A woman who claimed that she had been raped gave the officers who responded to her complaint her home address and place of employment. Detectives who tried to contact her the following day found that her place of employment was a private home and she was not known to the occupants. There was no such street as the one she gave for her home address. Another woman who claimed that she was dragged into a home and raped said that after the rape she ran a half block and caught a taxi. Records of all the taxi companies showed no record of a customer being driven from that area.

Police officers called to the scene of an alleged rape were told that the assailant was a white man. The following day the woman was asked to write an account of the rape. She described the assailant as a Negro. Another woman told detectives that she was driven into the mountains and raped. When informed that she would have to report the rape to the police department in the county in which she was raped, she said, "Can't we lie, say it was right by the airport in Denver?" She may in fact have been raped, but her testimony would be regarded with skepticism by a jury.

> Police officers who were called one afternoon to a street fight between two Negroes were informed by a woman standing nearby that one of the men, a Mr. Jones, was her boyfriend and that the other man, a Mr. Smith, had raped her in the early hours of the morning. Mr. Smith was taken to police headquarters, where he admitted having had sexual relations with the woman but said that it was with her consent. He added that after the intercourse he accompanied the woman to police headquarters where she reported the theft on the previous evening of her purse containing money and her car keys.
>
> Police records showed that Mr. Smith had been with the woman at the police department after the time of the alleged rape. While reporting the theft she made no reference to a rape. It became clear that the woman's boyfriend had learned that she had been out with Mr. Smith. The boyfriend had attacked Mr. Smith in the street and when police appeared, the woman accused Smith of rape in order to prevent her boyfriend's arrest on a charge of assault.

A woman complained to police that she had received a number of letters threatening her life. Later she reported that a man broke into her house, ripped off her nightgown and started to assualt her sexually, at which time she passed out. When she regained consciousness, the suspect was gone. Her husband, who was concerned over the threats, had been watching his home from a neighbor's house. No one had entered his home that day.

A chronic alcoholic lady told officers that the man who raped her had a red mask over his face. Later she said the mask could have been a product of her imagination. The jury might well conclude that this was not the only product of her imagination.

> A twenty-six-year-old married woman telephoned a police department to report that she had been assaulted by a man who attempted to rape her at a party in a motel sponsored by a large sales company for which her husband worked. She said that it was hot indoors and she went outside for fresh air. A man joined her as she was sitting alongside the motel swimming pool and invited her to sit with

him in his car. She refused and he forced her to accompany him to his car, where he started kissing her and telling her that her husband did not satisfy her. He told her that he wanted to have sexual relations and when she refused he choked her.

At this time the wife of another guest appeared and told the woman her husband was looking for her. She left the car and told her husband she had been assaulted. She had bruises on her neck and arm. The man accused of the rape told police "I brought her a drink. She asked for a couple more. She suggested we go outside for fresh air and we went to my car. She wanted to go to my apartment, but I told her that her husband would be looking for her. She then said that her husband didn't interest her. We were necking when a lady came out and told her that her husband was looking for her, and she got out and left."

The day after the report of the attempted rape which at first sight appeared to be genuine, another guest at the party rang the police and gave the name of a witness. The witness, when contacted by the police, was reluctant to become involved but was eventually persuaded to come to the police department. He reported, "As I was outside I saw Mr. A. come out with a redheaded female. She was sort of pulling him by the arm.

"He stopped and tried to introduce her but he had forgotten her name, at which time she introduced herself as 'Mrs. X. when I'm sober.' To me she did not look drunk. After this introduction she mumbled something about 'Let's go to your car.' The exact words I do not recollect. She appeared to be 'in heat' for as they sat in the car she started making a violent attempt to seduce him. This happened so fast I didn't have time to get over my astonishment, I didn't want to watch any further and I went inside."

Contradictory Accounts of the Rape

The victim who tells a story to detectives which differs from that given to the patrolmen immediately after the rape, or who contradicts herself when talking to either the patrolmen or the detectives, or who tells a story which differs greatly from information provided by witnesses who have seen her in the company of the alleged assailant or who have knowledge of incidents related to the rape may not be a truthful informant. Thus the woman who claims that she was forced into a car in the parking lot of a tavern may have been seen drinking with, then leaving the tavern in the company of her alleged assailant.

A wife claimed that a man had cut the screen of her bedroom window, climbed in and raped her. Yet her husband who was sleeping on a couch in the adjacent living room heard no outcry. A police dog in a room next to that of the woman did not bark during the evening. The husband later reported that the screen had been cut and damaged a year previously. It did not appear to be any different from what it had been prior to the alleged rape.

Confrontation

Confrontation of the victim with the account of the alleged rape provided by the suspect may lead to a quick admission that the claim of rape was not true. A woman who said that she was raped by a casual acquaintance was confronted with the suspect's statement that the woman's parents were asleep in an adjoining room at the time of the alleged assault. She responded, "I want to drop the whole thing."

Failure to Cooperate

The woman who refuses to cooperate with the police may fear that inquiry will reveal that her claim is false or unfounded. Failure to cooperate may also occur in genuine cases of rape because of the victim's wish to avoid the embarrassment of appearance in court, her unwillingness to have the offender sentenced to a penitentiary or her antagonism toward police officers ("You fucking cops think you're tough").

A girl who leads a man on, then cries rape after voluntary sexual intercourse may refuse to come to the detective bureau because she is "too upset," "has other things to do," "has nothing further to add to the investigation" or does not want to look at photographs of sex offenders, as "I might identify the wrong man." She says she knows only the man's first name but will not allow detectives to interview the friend who introduced the man to her. Thus identification of the suspect becomes impossible.

Some women initially are cooperative and eager to proceed with criminal charges. However, when the interview brings to light discrepancies in the account of the rape or unusual circumstances which raise doubt as to the truth of the complaint or the role of the victim, there may be a sudden lack of cooperation or loss of interest in further police action against the accused.

Requests for a polygraph examination are refused. "If I don't prosecute, will I have to take a lie detector test?" The victim may agree to take the test, subject to the approval of her attorney, but she does not consult her attorney. After weeks of indecision she finally makes an appointment for the test but fails to keep it. She talks about her civic duty to prosecute but is too busy to write out an account of the alleged rape.

"Blackouts"

Loss of consciousness or a "blackout" in the course of a rape in the absence of significant physical injury is more often than not associated with false complaints of rape. Compare the following two reports of "blackouts," the first report was genuine and the second false.

> Case 1. The victim was found naked in her apartment, covered with blood and in a state of shock. Both eyes were swollen shut, there were cuts on her mouth and bruises on her thighs. An electric cord was attached to one wrist and there were marks of the cord on the skin on both wrists and on her neck. While she was lying in bed, the cord was placed around her throat and she was choked. She was

unable to describe the man who had assaulted her. All she could remember was two eyes staring down at her. The only person's face she could later recall was that of one of the ambulance attendants who took her to a hospital. She said it was like a dream and she could remember nothing more of the attack.

Case 2. The woman claimed that she was attacked in her home by an unknown man with a mask on his face who attempted to rape her. She ran from her home after the attack and did not report the assault till an hour and a half later. She could not explain her delay in calling the police and dismissed this lapse of time by saying she "blacked out."

Delay in Reporting the Rape

The sensitive victim who fears the publicity of a court trial or who is reluctant to reveal her shame may well wait several days before reporting the rape. Onset of pregnancy may overcome her resistance to making a report. Pregnancy may also prompt false claims of rape. A review of many false claims of rape showed that a delay, whether of several hours or days, was encountered more often than might be expected by chance.

Other Factors

> *"The best liar is he who makes the smallest*
> *amount of lying go the longest way."*
> – Samuel Butler, *The Way of all Flesh*

Accounts of being forced to drink an unknown liquid or being forced to swallow drugs appear more often in false than in genuine reports of rape. Black cars feature prominently in false reports, which may contain many of the features already mentioned. Thus a woman with a casual, lighthearted attitude about the rape describes being dragged along two city blocks in daylight during rush hour traffic to a black car. She was only able to catch a glimpse of the first letter of the license plate. In the car she was forced to drink some wine.

Another woman with a belligerent attitude did not notify police of the rape till the following day, as she had a low opinion of all police officers. She did not scream at the time of the rape, since she did not wish to wake the other tenants. Although she said her clothing was ripped off her, inspection showed no damage to her clothes. She claimed that she fought the assailant by pushing him away from her, yet when questioned further she said she was attacked from behind and therefore could not resist.

The complaint of rape may appear genuine, yet some slight slip by the complainant provides a clue for the alert detective. Thus a woman reported that as she was walking down the street the driver of a car pulled up alongside her and pointed a gun at her out of the car. He ordered her to get in the car, then drove her to an alley and raped her. On inquiry she said that it was a street with two-way traffic and the driver pointed the gun at her out of the window on the driver's side of the car. It would have been impossible for the driver to point the gun at her in the manner she described. She admitted that she had made up the story of rape.

"In a case of belated allegation such a colorful tale was told that the police already had their suspicions that the story was fabricated before making further inquiries. The girl, who produced a blood-stained slip, undoubtedly had a freshly torn hymen: but the pear-shaped stain on the slip was in two complementary parts through which a tear had (clearly subsequently) taken place. In a struggle to get possession of a girl the clothing would first be torn, if at all, the bleeding following as some forceful penetration is made. This complementary piece of staining proved, as was suspected, to be a deliberate act, effected to bring some pressure to bear on her fiance, who would not marry her. She had herself damaged the hymen, stained her slip and subsequently torn it" (Simpson).

THE DANGEROUS FALSE ACCUSATION

False accusations of rape carry with them the danger that an innocent man will not only be arrested but also convicted of rape. A twenty-six-year-old woman claimed that a man with a prominent birthmark on his face called her over to his car as she was leaving a tavern one evening. She said that he had an automatic pistol in his hand and that he drove her out into the country, where he raped her.

Police investigation quickly resulted in the identification of the man with the prominent birthmark. Fortunately for this man his car was different from that described by the woman and reliable informants were with him at the time of the alleged rape. The woman later admitted that she invented the rape to explain her late return home to her husband. She had seen the man with the birthmark in the tavern.

THE SKILLFUL DETECTIVE

Systematic application of routine investigative procedures should be combined with an imaginative approach responsive to the special features of the individual case. There is a need for flexibility, a readiness to shift one's focus, to discard a hunch that finds no support or to return to a hunch too quickly discarded. The peril of the preconceived opinion which excludes consideration of alternative explanations is no less dangerous than an unwillingness to speculate until the routine investigation is far advanced.

You will recall the police officer who sought the advice of Sherlock Holmes: The detective drew the officer's attention to the curious incident of the dog in the night. When the officer remonstrated that the dog did nothing in the night, Holmes remarked that this was the curious incident. The failure of the family dog to bark during a recent nighttime rape led to the arrest of a member of the household, who had disguised his voice and blindfolded the victim.

The combination of sensitivity to discordant circumstances and unrestrained curiosity is perhaps the most important quality of the able detective. Perseverance is essential. An alert mind, retentive memory and keen powers of observation contribute to his skill. Above all, he must know the minds of men, yet this knowledge surely stems from his lively curiosity and his active search for answers. The investigation of rape is a challenge indeed for the detective who would master the art and science of his profession.

THE DETECTIVE AND THE PHYSICIAN

At first sight there might appear to be little in common between the detective and the physician. The former is concerned with the detection and punishment of the criminal, the latter with the diagnosis and treatment of the sick. Yet both seek to discover something which is hidden or obscure. Despite the aid of modern scientific devices, both require keen powers of observation, a knowledge of men and an alert, discerning mind. When Conan Doyle, a physician as well as an author, created Sherlock Holmes, he endowed him with the quick perception and remarkable deductive reasoning of Joseph Bell, one of his medical-school teachers.

Bell, a former President of the Royal College of Surgeons of Edinburgh, "excelled as a teacher and taught the students much else besides surgery, as he was wont to diagnose not only the disease or injury, but also the occupation and personal characteristics of each patient. Seated in his chair, his fingertips pressed together, he would study closely the gait, expression and mentality of each patient and would surprise both patients and students by the accuracy of his deductions. It might have been Holmes addressing Watson, when Bell taught his students the importance of the observation of trifles . . . A study of hands and fingernails revealed to Bell the nature of a man's craft; the color of the mud on his boots indicated a certain district of the city; wood shavings or metal filings in folds of clothing, dialect or manner of speech, each had its tale to tell" (Guthrie).

One of the many anecdotes attesting to Bell's wizardry in diagnosis has been recorded by Harnagel. A civilian outpatient, a total stranger, was brought to Bell's clinic. After studying him for a moment, Dr. Bell spoke, "Well, my man, you've served in the army." "Aye, sir." "Not long discharged?" "No, sir." "A highland regiment?" "Aye, sir." "Stationed in Barbados?" "Aye, sir." Turning to his students, Dr. Bell explained, "You see, gentlemen, the man was a respectful man, but he did not remove his hat.

They do not do so in the army, but he would have learned civilian ways had he been long discharged. He had an air of authority and was obviously Scottish. As to Barbados, his complaint is elephantiasis, which is West Indian and not British." Bell employed such displays of deductive skill to emphasize to students the importance of careful observation in the detection of disease.

The logical reasoning of Sherlock Holmes and his comments on criminal investigation are equally applicable to clinical diagnosis: "It has long been an axiom of mine that the little things are infinitely the most important." "It is a capital mistake to theorize before one has the data." "Singularity is almost invariably a clue." Holmes emphasizes the importance of looking for things — "However did you see that?" said the Police Inspector, as Holmes pointed to a hole in the window sash. "Because I looked for it" was the reply. How often in clinical medicine is the correct diagnosis made because the physician is actively looking for certain clinical signs and symptoms. Myxedema, for example, often passes unrecognized because it is not sought.

The reports of public health physicians who track down the origins of a typhoid epidemic read like a detective story. However, the closest relationship between detective and physician occurs in the practice of psychiatry. The detective seeks confession of crime; the psychiatrist seeks confession of forbidden thoughts, impulses or actions. Nietzsche has stated that the psychotherapist must possess the persuasiveness that adjusts itself to every individual, a diplomat's suave way of negotiating and the adroitness of a detective in understanding the secrets of a soul without betraying it.

Janet, a great French psychiatrist, considered psychoanalysis a criminal investigation which aims at the discovery of a culprit in the unearthing of a past happening. Freud himself drew attention to the similarity of the investigations of the law and psychiatry. In an address to law students he stated that the task of the therapist is the same as that of the examining magistrate. "We have to uncover the hidden psychical material, and in order to do this we have invented a number of detective devices, some of which it seems that you gentlemen of the law are now about to copy from us."

Modern textbooks of criminal interrogation in some respects read like a monograph on the psychiatric interview. The interviewer is advised to be tolerant, understanding, courteous and respectful in his attitude toward the suspected offender. The need for privacy and a quiet room is emphasized. Attention is drawn to the possible significance of nonverbal communication, sudden change in posture, swinging one leg over another, covering up of the mouth, averted gaze and so on. The celebrated German criminologist Gross described the case of the man suspected of murder, who said he lived very peaceably with his neighbor and at the same time clenched his fist. The latter meant ill will toward the neighbor which the words did not.

Gross also quotes the case of a girl who was suspected of murdering her newborn child. "The girl told that she had given birth to the child all alone, and then laid it on the bed beside herself. She had also observed how a corner of the coverlet had fallen on the child's face, and thought it might interfere with the child's breathing; but at this point she swooned, was unable to help the child and it was choked. While sobbing and weeping as she was telling this story, she spread the fingers of her left hand and pressed it on her thigh, as perhaps she might have done if she had first put something soft, the corner of a coverlet possibly, over the child's nose and mouth and then pressed on it. This action was so clearly significant that it inevitably led to the question whether she hadn't choked the child in that way. She assented sobbing."

Chapter 15

PUNISHMENT

*"They have sown the wind and they shall
reap the whirlwind."*
— Hosea

THE indignation aroused by rape is reflected in the severe punishments for this crime. The first rape recorded in the Bible — that of Dinah, the daughter of Jacob, by Shechem, son of a Hivite prince — was followed by the treacherous massacre of all the Hivite men. Shechem wished to marry Dinah, and the Israelites agreed on condition that the Hivite men submitted to circumcision. On the third day, when all the men were in great pain, Jacob's sons boldly entered the city and killed them. When Jacob complained, his sons answered, "Is our sister to be treated as a common whore?"

The mass rape of a girl in Gibeah by some men of the tribe of Benjamin almost resulted in the complete destruction of this tribe by the other Israelite tribes. Twenty-five thousand armed men of Benjamin were killed and only six hundred men survived the battle. All the women were massacred and this posed a problem, as the other tribes had made a solemn oath that none of their daughters would ever marry a member of the tribe of Benjamin. The Israelites did not want this one tribe to be lost to Israel. The problem was resolved by sending twelve thousand armed men to plunder the town of Jabesh-Gilead, which had failed to contribute soldiers to the battle against the Benjaminites. All the inhabitants with the exception of the virgins were put to the sword.

The virgins were handed over to the men of the tribe of Benjamin. As there were six hundred men and as only four hundred virgins were captured in Jabesh-Gilead, further action was required. The men of Benjamin were instructed to go to Shiloh at the time of the annual festival of dancing in the vineyards and to seize the daughters of Shiloh when they came out to dance. Thus the group rape of a young girl and her later death ended with a battle, a slaughter and a double rape — of the virgins of Jabesh-Gilead and of the daughters of Shiloh (Cole).

All this slaughter resulted from the complaint of a Levite, a traveler who was staying overnight in Gibeah with his concubine, the victim of the rape. Some of the worst scoundrels in the town, as the *New English Bible* describes the assailants, requested that the Levite come out of the house and have intercourse with them. Despite their homosexual inclinations, these men raped the concubine whom the Levite thrust outside as a substitute victim. He found her at daybreak dead on his doorstep and later cut up her body into twelve pieces which he sent throughout Israel. Curiously, the Levites' ungentlemanly behavior is not questioned in the Biblical account, which illustrates the years of lawlessness when Israel was without a king.

In Deuteronomy the law on illicit sexual intercourse is defined. When a virgin, pledged in marriage, has sexual intercourse with another man in a town, both are stoned to death; the girl because, although in the town, she did not cry for help, and the man because he dishonored another man's wife. If the man rapes a girl in the country, then the man alone dies because the girl cried for help and there was no one to rescue her. When the girl is not pledged in marriage and the man rapes her, then the man shall give the girl's father fifty pieces of silver and he shall marry her and is not free to divorce her.

Cole comments that the rape itself was not so serious. It was the violation of another man's rights which was of concern. The rape of a betrothed woman was tantamount to adultery and therefore merited death. But the rape of an unbetrothed girl could be expiated by marriage, though the husband had forfeited his right to divorce. Once more, as Cole points out, the rights of the male asserted themselves.

THE DEATH PENALTY

> *"As I live, saith the Lord God, I have no pleasure in the*
> *death of the wicked; but that the wicked turn from*
> *his way and live."*
> — Ezekiel 33:11

Blinding castration and death were among the penalties for rape in early times. Castration and death still face the rapist in many jurisdictions, although the former is now referred to as treatment, a distinction which is not always clear to the offender. Castration will be considered in Chapter 16. Despite the failure of those in favor of the death penalty to show that it has a deterrent effect and despite the campaign against this barbaric form of punishment, courts continue to sentence rapists to death.

Capital punishment is cruel and unusual because it involves deliberate destruction of human life. The facts that punishment has been ordered by a judge and jury in accordance with the law and that punishment is carried out by an executioner in accordance with the law do not make it any less cruel and unusual. One does not have to attend an execution to be aware of the cruelty of this sentence, yet the personal experience brings home the cruelty of the occasion.

Seeing a condemned man bending down to put on his shorts and slippers, his funeral garments, moments before his final walk to the gas chamber; seeing a man thus participating in his own destruction, these sights made me more aware of the meaning of capital punishment. George Orwell was similarly affected by the execution of a nameless Indian coolie. On his way to the gallows, the man about to be hanged stepped aside to avoid a puddle.

"It is curious, but till that moment I had never realized what it means to destroy a healthy, conscious man. When I saw the prisoner step aside to avoid the puddle I saw the mystery, the unspeakable wrongness, of cutting a life short when it is in full tide. He and we were a party of men walking together, seeing, hearing, feeling, understanding the same world, and in two minutes, with a sudden snap, one of us would be gone – one mind less, one world less."

Although Orwell writes of the wrongfulness of the death penalty, his words portray the cruelty of the occasion. Death by execution is a cruel punishment. There are other cruel and unusual aspects of the death penalty: the punishment of innocent relatives of the condemned man who must bear throughout their lives this painful stigma and the degrading effect of the occasion on all those who participate in this ultimate indignity to man. Yet, these and other cruel and unusual aspects of capital punishment are insignificant compared with the cruelty to the man who pays his penalty in the gas chamber. Capital punishment lowers rather than increases respect for the value of human life.

The argument that it is kinder to execute a man than to imprison him for life probably has few supporters among those best qualified to judge – the inhabitants of death row.

During the period 1930 to 1968, 455 men (11.8%) of the 3,334 persons executed in the United States were executed for rape. These 455 men included 405 Negroes (89%), 48 whites (10.5%) and two men of other races (0.4%). On December 31, 1968, there were 479 prisoners reported as being under sentence of death. Sixty prisoners (12.5%) had been sentenced to death for rape *(National Prisoner Statistics,* Number 45, August 1969).

Two Negro men, Edgar Labat and Clifton Poret, were sentenced to death in 1953 for the 1950 rape of a twenty-four-year-old white woman in New Orleans. These two men spent over sixteen years on death row. The conviction of the two Negroes went to the United States Supreme Court four times. In 1967 the Supreme Court reversed their convictions on the ground that Negroes had been systematically excluded from the jury system in New Orleans. The high court ordered the men freed unless the state gave them a new trial.

The victim signed this statement. "I don't relish the idea of going through a new trial. I am now married and have a family and most earnestly desire to forget the terrible events of Sunday, November 12, 1950. I feel they have been justly punished for their deed." The two men then pleaded guilty in

1969 to the lesser charge of attempted aggravated rape and were sentenced to sixteen years two months and two days, the exact time they had been on death row. They were given credit for the time served and released.

Labat was the center of an international squabble in 1960 when the state prison halted his three-year correspondence with Mrs. Solveig Johanssen, a housewife in Stockholm, Sweden. A prison official explained that Negroes could not have such correspondence with whites. State officials said later the prison official was mistaken.

IMPRISONMENT

In those states which do not provide the death penalty for rape, the maximum sentence is usually life imprisonment. Assault with intent to commit rape has a less severe maximum penalty but in some states may lead to the death penalty or life imprisonment. The man convicted of rape is likely to be sentenced to a long term of imprisonment. The average time served by Federal and state prisoners released during 1960 was longer for rapists than for men convicted of manslaughter, robbery, aggravated assault or indeed any offense other than murder.

In Fort Worth, Texas, in 1969 Samuel Hemphill, aged nineteen, convicted of raping an eighteen-year-old high school girl, was sentenced to eight hundred years in prison! Hemphill's sentence was the longest ever given in the memory of Fort Worth prosecutors. Despite the sentence, Hemphill will still be eligible for parole in twenty years. If he is a model prisoner, he could be eligible for parole within ten years. The state had qualified the jury on the death penalty.

THE EFFECT OF INCREASED PENALTIES FOR RAPE

At three o'clock one Sunday morning in April 1966 three Negro men broke into a Philadelphia home occupied by an eighty-year-old widow, her forty-four-year-old daughter and fourteen-year-old granddaughter. Both women and the child were beaten and raped. The upstairs and downstairs were spattered with blood; and the grandmother, who was found unconscious by the police, later died from her wounds. This Palm Sunday rape became a *cause célèbre* throughout Pennsylvania, and legislators began to speak of doubling the penalties for rape.

In May 1966 the Pennsylvania Penal Code of 1939 was amended to provide more severe punishment for rape. The maximum sentence for rape with bodily injury was increased from fifteen years to life imprisonment. The *minimum sentence* for this offense was set at fifteen years' imprisonment. The maximum penalty for attempted rape with bodily injury was increased from five to fifteen years' imprisonment. For those convicted at least twice of attempted rape without bodily injury, the maximum sentence was increased from five years to life imprisonment.

Schwartz, in his evaluation of the effectiveness of these increased penalties for rape, notes that one of the three sponsors of the bill, a state senator, declared that "the passage of this bill is a major breakthrough in the fight on crime throughout the state, and especially in Philadelphia, and will bring about a definite deterrent on future rapists." However, both the Governor and the Senate Majority Leader had earlier accused the Democrats of exploiting the rape crisis for political gain.

The rationale underlying the investigation by Schwartz was that the deterrent effect of the new penalties should affect the rate of rape and attempted rape most forcefully in the very community in which the celebrated Palm Sunday offense occurred. Schwartz found that there was no reduction in the total number of rapes and attempted rapes following the imposition of harsher penalties.

APPEALS TO HIGHER COURTS

In England an appeal against conviction and sentence carries the risk of imposition of an even longer sentence if the appeal fails. Thus a man convicted of rape and sentenced to seven years' imprisonment may find that the court of appeal will double his sentence.

In Paris two men convicted of the rape of a barmaid, were fined one thousand dollars in damages and sentenced to three years in prison. When the verdict was appealed, the judge asked the victim how many times she was assaulted. She replied, "If I told you, you wouldn't believe me." Finally she said that in an hour she had been assaulted eighteen times. One of the defendants exclaimed that he was not a bull; and his attorney, a twenty-seven-year-old woman, said, "Permit me to be skeptical, eighteen assaults in one hour, even perpetrated by two men in relay, seem to me to be pure myth. It would have made Francois I, Henry IV and Louis XV jealous, and they were Kings of France. After all, where is the woman who after eighteen assaults would have the effrontery to complain?" The judge increased the victim's damages to three thousand dollars but suspended the defendants' sentences (*Time,* February 23, 1970).

RACE AND PUNISHMENT

Negroes are more often executed for rape than whites. Eighty-nine per cent of the 455 men executed for rape in the United States during the period 1930 to 1968 were Negroes. In July 1949 four young Negroes were accused of raping a seventeen-year-old white girl in Groveland, Florida. Shortly after the crime one of the accused was killed by a posse. Another, a sixteen-year-old was sentenced to life imprisonment.

The other two offenders were sentenced to death. The United States Supreme Court later ordered a new trial and on November 6, 1951, when the two prisoners were being transferred from the county jail to the place of the new trial, they were shot by the sheriff while handcuffed together. One was killed outright; the other was gravely wounded. The sheriff claimed self-defense and was exonerated by a coroner's jury.

In South Africa no white man has ever been executed for the rape of a nonwhite woman. Since 1960 two whites have been executed for rape; in both cases the victims were whites. Whites convicted of raping nonwhite women generally receive sentences of imprisonment which rarely exceed five years.

Execution of a nonwhite for the rape of a white woman is, however, the general rule in South Africa. In 1955 the Minister of Justice, Mr. C. R. Swart, announced that during his term of office not a single nonwhite who had been sentenced to death for raping a European woman had escaped the death penalty. Between 1947 and 1956 forty-seven nonwhites were executed for rape.

As Welsh notes, judges are not isolated from the sanction of public opinion within the white group; sentencing a white to death for the rape of a nonwhite would undoubtedly raise a far greater sense of shock than in the converse racial situation, where the death penalty is widely held by most whites to be the only fitting punishment.

In an attempt to discover the validity of charges that Negroes are treated differently than whites in sentencing, Bullock conducted a study of 3,644 inmates in a Texas state prison. Careful comparisons of data were made, after controlling the influence of nonracial factors, to determine the effect of race on the length of sentence. Negro prisoners received sentences significantly different from those given white prisoners; however, the bias was not invariably against the Negro.

Negro offenders are apparently underpenalized for one type of offense and overpenalized for another; racial discrimination appears to be motivated more by the desire to protect the order of the white community than to effect the reformation of the offender. Thus Negro prisoners committed for intraracial rape get short sentences more often than whites committed for this offense, even when prisoners of the two racial groups are alike in terms of plea and area from which they were committed. If the Negro rapist crosses racial lines and rapes a white woman, his penalty is heavier than that given whites who appear in court under the same circumstances.

LYNCHING

The execution of a suspected criminal by a mob acting without legal authority is not peculiar to the United States, although the term is derived from Colonel Charles Lynch, a Virginia farmer, who, during the War for Independence, headed an irregular organization formed to punish thieves and outlaws. In the Western States the victims of lynching were largely white men suspected of murder or crimes against property, especially horse stealing. In the South the victims were usually Negroes suspected of murder or rape.

Between 1872 and 1951, 1,198 persons suspected of rape or attempted rape were lynched in the United States. Some of these victims were mutilated or otherwise tortured prior to their execution. Needless to say, the majority of the victims of lynching were Negroes. Raymond Gunn is an example. In 1925 he was convicted of attempted rape and sentenced to four years in the state penitentiary. After his release, he made two further attempts at assault on college girls, who refused to prosecute because of their wish to avoid publicity.

In 1930 he was arrested for the murder of a nineteen-year-old white schoolteacher. He still had on the bloody clothes worn when he committed the crime which he confessed. He admitted that he had been in the neighborhood of the school when the idea occurred to rape the school-teacher. The following day he returned to the schoolhouse and lay in hiding until the pupils had gone home. He struck her over the head with a club, fracturing her skull. At this point he heard a noise and, becoming frightened, he left without performing the intended rape.

A mob formed but found a unit of the Missouri National Guard on duty with a machine gun truck barring entrance to the jail. When the date was set for his trial, the mob unofficially announced that he would be lynched on that date. The governor offered assistance, but the sheriff refused to call out the National Guard, insisting that there was not going to be any trouble. The sheriff went through the crowds on the day of the trial to secure the Negro. When his car stopped outside the courthouse, the Negro was seized by the crowd.

An unknown man announced that they would take him to the scene of the crime and burn him in the schoolhouse. The mob yelled its approval, and no action was taken by the sheriff. After the Negro repeated his confession, he was told, "Well, nigger, we're going to burn you." He was chained to the roof, gasoline was thrown inside the schoolhouse and a lighted paper was tossed through a window. The sheriff later said that he was unwilling to turn the guardsmen "loose in that crowd with their automatic pistols; somebody would have been killed or badly injured, and probably it would have been the guardsmen."

STATUTORY RAPE

In statutory rape the punishment usually depends on the age of the girl who has consented to sexual intercourse; the older the victim, the less severe the penalty. Thus in Washington state the maximum penalty varies according to the age of the victim as follows: under ten, life imprisonment; ten and under fifteen years of age, twenty years imprisonment; fifteen and under eighteen years of age, fifteen years imprisonment.

In several states if the girl is under twelve, the maximum penalty is death. Sexual intercourse with the consent of a girl under fourteen in Maryland, Oklahoma and Virginia may cost a man his life. One month of difference in the age of a girl may make many years of difference in the maximum sentence. In England sexual intercourse with the consent of a girl just under thirteen years of age can lead to a sentence of life imprisonment. If she has just reached thirteen, the maximum sentence is two years.

The age of the offender may also influence the duration of the maximum sentence. Thus if the defendant is under eighteen (or under sixteen in some states), he may escape the death penalty or be subject to a shorter term of imprisonment than that applicable to older offenders. In some states the sentence for statutory rape is very similar to that for forcible rape. In consequence the district attorney may charge statutory rather than forcible rape to avoid the burden of proving the use of force. Alternatively he may accept the offer of the defendant to plead guilty to statutory rape. This arrangement benefits the district attorney, who avoids the tedium of a trial, and the defendant, who avoids a criminal record of forcible rape.

Newman cites the following example of a change in criminal charges at the request of the defendant to avoid the repugnant label of "rapist."

> A defendant in Wisconsin entered a small store and at knife point ordered the lone female proprietor into the basement, where he forcibly disrobed her and attempted sexual assault. Failing to complete the crime of rape, he left the store taking some money and goods. He was originally charged with attempted rape but, unwilling to be branded with this label, he bargained to plead guilty to the crime of armed robbery, which carried a longer maximum sentence.

INCEST

There is a wide variation among the states in the maximum penalties for incest, ranging from three years' imprisonment to a mandatory life sentence. In some states the penalties vary according to the degree of blood relationship. Louisiana prescribes fifteen-year prison sentences for incest between ancestor and descendant or brother and sister, but five-year sentences where it is between uncle and niece, or aunt and nephew. Illinois distinguishes in severity between father-daughter incest and all other forms (including mother-son!). The Model Penal Code draws no such distinctions but indicates doubts about whether uncle-niece, aunt-nephew relationships should be included at all.

SELF-PUNISHMENT

"There is no greater punishment for wickedness
than that it is dissatisfied with itself and
its deeds."
− Seneca

"There is no refuge from confession but suicide,
and suicide is confession."
− Daniel Webster, in *Commonwealth v. Knapp*

One of the offenders in the Denver study, a twenty-four-year-old man who rented an apartment from his victim, came to her door one day on the pretense of wanting to talk to her husband. On entering the house he pulled out a revolver and forced the woman into her bedroom where he raped her. He left the house by the back door when the victim's small son rang the front door bell. She left to obtain help and returned with two police officers. They heard a shot in the man's apartment; the police, on forcing the door open, found the man lying dead on the floor with a bullet wound in his chest. Earlier he had told his victim that he knew he "couldn't get away with it" and would have to kill himself.

Rapists seldom commit suicide after their offense, but suicidal attempts are not rare. A young man who returned home late one night confessed to his wife that he had killed a woman. A woman had been seriously injured during an apparent sexual assault that evening but the man later told his wife that he had not attacked her but had been told about the attack by two strangers. In the following months his wife asked him several times if he had assaulted the woman, but he denied it. However, his sleep was disturbed by frightening dreams and periodically he would be quiet and subdued as if something was bothering him. He attempted suicide by cutting his wrist following an argument with his wife, but later he could not recall what the argument was about.

He was arrested five months after the crime and entered a plea of guilty. "I probably feel as low as you can get. I really feel sorry for her. I pray to God that everything works out for her." At this time he admitted prior rapes and attempts at rape. He also described an earlier attempt at suicide. "I tried to think why. I thought if I did have a problem and didn't get help I might easily do something real bad. Finally I did." Other rape offenders who attempted suicide denied that their suicidal acts were related to feelings of guilt over their sexual assaults, but in each case there was both direct and indirect evidence of considerable feelings of remorse and guilt.

Many writers have pointed out that crime carries within itself the seeds of retribution and it has been suggested that clues are the traces of guilt which the offender leaves behind. These clues may be so obvious as to suggest the most incredible stupidity. Indeed, as Gross observes, many detectives are put off the scent because they say to themselves, "No, the culprit could not have been as stupid as all that." Gross goes on to say, "I once even asked myself whether the essence of a criminal did not consist precisely in his inability to avoid making blunders."

PUNISHMENT IN OTHER CULTURES

In some cultures ridicule and shame are employed to discourage the rapist. Hoebel reports that among the Comanche Indians sex relations were so free that there seems to have been little cause for rape. Rape was an act beyond the pale of normal conduct, and he describes the following case of attempted rape by Blow It Away, which was reported to him by Holding Her Sunshade.

> Blow It Away was a chronic offender. He was not favored by the women and was generally avoided by them. He made up for this by attempting surreptitious night unions with women in their teepees. He would sneak in and try to arouse them to desire. He never had much success. Then, too, he would attempt to rape such women as he found alone away from the camp. These attacks he would make in the daytime and in these he was usually successful. No one ever caught him attacking a married woman, so he was never called to account by a husband. But one night he tried his night-stealing on a large married woman and she broke him.
>
> The woman awoke to find Blow It Away feeling her. She struggled with him, then she got him down. Holding him to the ground, she ripped his breech clout from his loins and grabbed his penis. She was starting to drag him from the teepee when her son awoke and saw them. Her boy begged her not to do that to the man, but the mother was going to teach that nuisance a lesson. Holding him as she had him, she dragged Blow It Away through the door out into the open spaces between the teepees where all the people could see him.
>
> This was the first time anyone took action against him. It was the last time he tried to force himself on a woman.

Hoebel comments that this is shaming par excellence, plus a painful conditioning. A similar attitude toward rape is reported among the Navaho Indians by Dyk. "Rape is hardly a recognizable offense. It is believed that women are well able to take care of themselves. They do so by grabbing a man's penis. If out herding sheep where most advances take place, they may threaten to drag the man to their home, until pain and fear of public exposure make him capitulate. He buys himself off with a gift of a blanket, beads or other property of similar worth."

"On occasion women have been seduced with drink, and then attacked throughout the night by gangs of men. Such sport is likely to take place during the performance of a chant, when a large number of people are present and drink flows freely. There is little stigma attached to such bouts and a woman has very little redress. Her only hope of revenge and compensation is taking away some pieces of property from the men who enjoy her.

"The man who attacked her with impunity stands helpless before this act of deprivation. Society condones one act, and approves the other. A woman always has the right to demand and to take some material reward for past, present and even future favors offered, granted or stolen."

In 1869 Forbes reported that among the Aymara Indians of Bolivia and Peru the doctrines of Christianity may become grafted into Aymara belief and the so-called "Indio-Christiano" of the Puna of La Paz believes that on one day in the year, which is Good Friday, he may commit any crime short of murder with impunity. On this day instances are known where they have even raped their own daughters in the presence of their mothers. This was regarded as being no sin, as on that day God was dead and consequently could not possibly on the next day remember anything which happened the day before. As Forbes comments — rather a strange application of a Christian dogma!

In Tibet the punishment used to depend on the rank of the victim. Rape on the person of a married woman of high degree was punishable by emasculation and fines. If the woman belonged to the middle or lower classes, the culprit paid the husband a fine and gave the woman a suit of clothes. Incest was frequently practiced and even if detected, the offenders received light punishment but were more or less socially ostracized.

In those cultures with very permissive sexual standards there may be no punishment for rape. Hunt, writing on the Micronesians of Yap, states that there is no concept of "rape" in Yap. "The idea that a woman would have to be overpowered to submit to sexual relations was amusing to informants; it amused them that the men would resort to such a stupid tactic when it could be done more efficiently in other ways. Properly conducted preliminaries, the supplement of magic, and a little patience were infallible ways of obtaining the women's consent to intercourse. They might not win her love, but neither would rape. Such a conception is clearly based on the expectation that women by nature are inclined to be willing, not unwilling."

Virginity does not exist and has no representative value in the eyes of the Taureg. Indeed, Lhote claims that the women are more or less easy. Some give themselves to the first comer; others grant their favors to only a small group of friends. To grant them only to a single person, however, would be judged in very bad taste and a sign of perversion.

In the northern Gilbert Islands the incest participants were tied to a log of wood and set adrift in a small canoe without sails and given a few coconuts as provisions. Death was inevitable. They believed that the sun would depart from the tribe if the participants went unpunished. The Mohaves ostracized the offenders and considered incest an omen of the inevitable extinction of the family with the children predestined to die (Weinberg). The Tikopians forced the male participant in incest to commit suicide or to be expelled. Other cultures also punish incest with death or social ostracism.

Chapter 16

TREATMENT AND PREVENTION

"He falls low that cannot rise again."
— George Meriton, 1683

THE young lover who misinterprets his girl friend's resistance to sexual intercourse as no more than a conventional protest to protect her virtuous image rather than her virginity may find himself charged with the same offense as the rapist who brutally assaults a succession of women in their homes or on the streets. The former is unlikely to repeat his error, the latter might benefit from psychiatric treatment. Sexual psychopath laws provide for such treatment.

In their favor it may be said that the sexual psychopath laws represent an advance in legislative outlook by their provision for psychiatric examination and treatment of the sexual offender. Here, as Overholser points out, is a recognition by the law that there are persons who stand between the shade of insanity and the sunlight of sanity, that there is a middle ground which calls for special handling and for an indeterminate period of segregation, during which treatment can be attempted, or who, treatment failing, may be continued in confinement.

In some states, the sex offender who is committed to a mental hospital under a sexual psychopath law is required to stand trial on the original criminal charge upon his release from the hospital. The period of commitment in a few states is counted as time served on the prison sentence. Several statutes state that no person committed as a sexual psychopath may thereafter be tried or sentenced upon the original criminal charge. This seems to be a more logical and much fairer procedure.

Sexual psychopath laws have been subjected to considerable criticism. Certain essential procedural safeguards of individual liberty have been relaxed or completely abandoned. The laws have been used unjustly to confine persons for a longer period than would be possible under the usual criminal statutes. In some jurisdictions, the offender can be confined from one day to life in either a hospital or a penitentiary. Treatment facilities are not always available even though the court may order psychiatric treatment. Custodial care in overcrowded, understaffed mental hospitals is often the limit of psychiatric care, and there is an urgent need for specialized institutions and research centers. It is not surprising that some rape offenders prefer a fixed prison sentence to an indefinite term in a hospital.

299

PSYCHOTHERAPY

*"The most important difference between a good
and an indifferent clinician lies in the amount
of attention paid to the story of the patient."*
– Sir Farquhar Buzzard

Psychotherapy is both an art and a science. The therapist's training however extensive, cannot compensate for a lack of sensitivity and concern for the welfare of his patient. Therapy is based upon a thorough knowledge of the patient, his psychological conflicts and his life experiences. The nondirective psychiatric interview with its emphasis on the value of the spontaneous comments of the patient, in general, is likely to be more revealing than the question-answer type of interview. Effective evaluation also requires some direct questioning. Liebling expresses this point well. "I had a distaste for asking direct questions, a practice I considered ill bred. This handicapped me not as much as you might think. Direct questions tighten a man up, and even if he answers, he will not tell you anything you have not asked him. What you want is to get him to tell his story. After he has you can ask clarifying questions such as 'How did you come to have the axe in your hand?' "

Physicians unfamiliar with sex offenders do not always explore the full range of abnormal sexual behavior. One needs to know the patient's early sexual experiences. Subjects for review include sex relations with animals, incestuous impulses and acts, fetishism, indecent exposure, window peeping, theft of women's underclothing, touching or grabbing women's breasts or genitals, the use of a camera to photograph nude women or women who have been bound with ropes, purchase of pornographic pictures and magazines, threatening letters or telephone calls to women, masturbation, firesetting, cruelty to animals or other behavior which leads to sexual gratification and all manner of homosexual and heterosexual fantasies and acts, including anal intercourse.

As a child, was the patient required to wear dresses and learn embroidery as well as other activities more suited to a girl? What were the sleeping arrangements? Did mother comfort him in her bed when he was upset? Did she bathe him until a late age? Did he ever see his mother or sisters naked? Did he witness or overhear sexual intercourse? The range of topics includes, among other subjects, dressing and undressing in the home, use of the bathroom, infidelity, discussion of sexuality and instruction on sex, parental attitudes on dating, choice of a girl friend and marriage. Did the parents attend the patient's wedding? What, if any, were their wedding gifts? Were there any other adults in the home?

Inquiry on these and related subjects should not be limited to one occasion. During treatment the recall of forgotten memories is not always reported to the therapist. Furthermore as the patient gains confidence in his physician he may be more willing to reveal facts previously withheld. As he reviews his early childhood he may select as a scapegoat one parent and make only relatively positive comments about the other parent. When, as is so often the case in rapists, one parent stands out as having inflicted all manner of psychological traumata on the child, it is easy to overlook the role of the other parent in contributing to the patient's psychopathology.

Clues to significant information not readily available from the patient may be obtained from interviews with other members of the family. It is instructive to interview family members together as well as individually. The most vocal relative may not be the best informant. Frowning, a shift in position or other nonverbal communications of silent members of the family indicate the need for further inquiry, either in the joint interview or in a later private interview.

School, armed forces and hospital records should be obtained. Police records may reveal information which differs from the patient's account of the rape. A young man charged with forcible rape described at length the compliant behavior of his victim. When confronted by the discrepancies between his version and the victim's, he became very upset and spontaneously revealed for the first time sadistic fantasies of raping and torturing women.

The therapist should not be discouraged by the reluctance of the patient to reveal himself. Slight apparent motivation for treatment and refusal to acknowledge illness are too often regarded as portents of therapeutic failure rather than as a therapeutic challenge. The patient, whether he seeks help or has it imposed on him by the court, will not find it easy to look at himself and at those childhood experiences which contributed to his abnormal behavior. The recall of forgotten memories may be a painful process, yet the outcome of treatment will depend upon the sacrifices he makes to overcome his impulses to take women by force rather than by love. The internal struggle involved has been well described by the patient discussed in Chapter six who spent three long years in a penitentiary before he sought and obtained the treatment he needed so desperately.

Psychiatric treatment of these men involves more than emotional support and guidance in a time of crisis. Cure cannot be left to nature and the healing process of time. It is the task of the therapist to make known the unknown, to restore confidence and self-esteem and to aid the patient in his efforts to master his abnormal impulses. The psychotherapist helps the patient to realize that his behavior is influenced not only by conscious reasoning but also by psychological processes within himself beyond his awareness. The patient becomes aware of the never-ending struggle involved in the integration of instinctual drives, the prohibitions of conscience and the conflicting demands of the world around him.

Exploration of the origins of the abnormal sexual behavior cannot be accomplished quickly. Nor does intellectual insight necessarily confer control over behavior. The patient needs to gain mastery over his impulses as he copes with day-to-day stresses in his life. He may have to make considerable changes in his manner of relating to others; changes which cannot be made simply by an exercise of willpower. He has to recognize the ways in which he provokes other people to react negatively toward him. His wife may also be in need of psychotherapy, especially when her behavior either provokes her husband's acts of rape or hinders his efforts to reach a more mature level of social adjustment.

Family therapy involving parents and the wife may help resolve long-standing conflicts which continue to handicap the patient. One rapist who had committed many rapes was completely dominated by his mother, who controlled him to an almost unbelievable extent. He was quite unable to relate effectively either to her or to his girl friends, who differed from his mother in age but not in their attitude toward him. His rapes followed incidents with his mother or a girl friend which aroused great anger which was not expressed. He would submit to their demands without protest, then drive around in search of a (substitute) victim. In his rapes he controlled his victims as he would have liked to control the women in his life. Although he was of husky build and despite the aid of a gun, he would tie up his victims securely with rope before assaulting them.

In some hospitals for criminal offenders, the sexual offender has no opportunity to work alongside women or to socialize with them. Many rapists are fearful of women, do not understand them and do not know how to approach them. The rapist cannot be expected to improve his mode of relating to women if his contact with them is confined to visits by relatives. As he improves he should be transferred to a ward for both male and female patients. Institutions which have no female patients should include women employees among the staff who work with patients and should arrange for volunteers and relatives to attend dances and other social functions. The more the institution resembles the world outside its walls, the easier will be the transition for the patient on his discharge.

GROUP PSYCHOTHERAPY

The rapist, deeply ashamed of his behavior, finds comfort in the presence of other men who have committed the same crime. The setting makes it easier for him to talk about his behavior. Realization that other members of the group have similar morbid ideas helps relieve guilt and further facilitates frank discussion. It is easier to recognize psychological problems and unhealthy responses in others than in oneself. Group discussion of such problems leads, however, to greater self-awareness. The group constitutes the norm from which individual members deviate, and it is both easier to accept and also more difficult to reject criticism from the group than from the psychotherapist.

New members of the group are helped by those who have been in the group longer to recognize their defensive tactics in blaming the courts, their wives and others for their own shortcomings. At the same time, they receive much support and encouragement from those who have progressed further in treatment. It becomes possible to explore not only current conflicts which precipitated the act of rape, but also deeper more important factors which contributed to the crime.

THE PRISON AS A THERAPEUTIC COMMUNITY

> *"The first prison I ever saw had inscribed on it, 'Cease To Do Evil: Learn To Do Well'; but as the inscription was on the outside, the prisoners could not read it. It should have been addressed to the self-righteous free spectator in the street and should have run, 'All Have Sinned and Fallen Short of the Glory of God.'"*
> — George Bernard Shaw, *The Crime of Punishment.*

Many of our prisons give the appearance of having been expressly designed to reinforce the prisoner's grudge against society rather than to serve the purpose of rehabilitation. A study of life within a penitentiary often shows a combination of idleness, boredom and regimented uselessness. Any other closed community, such as an army or monastery, regards its discipline and discomfort as a means to an end, but penitentiary institutional life is sometimes an end in itself — a dead end.

Regimentation and removal of all responsibility have their dangers. Men can learn to accept responsibility only when they are given an opportunity to exercise it. In the restrictive mental atmosphere of the conventional prison the inmate becomes progressively less well equipped to return to a useful life within society. Efforts to improve our prisons meet with slight public support. Yet even the longest penitentiary sentences come to an end, and if prisoners emerge no better than when they went in, it will be the public which pays the price.

In recent years an effort has been made in some states to improve the rehabilitation of prisoners by the introduction of group therapy. In California the therapeutic community approach, which was first introduced in psychiatric hospitals by Maxwell Jones, has been utilized in prisons, prison camps, community correctional centers and in both adult and youth institutions.

The experience of Maxwell Jones has shown the value of the hospital community as a therapeutic force supplementing individual psychotherapy. Emphasis on the development of the potential therapeutic influence of both patients and staff has resulted in the creation of a social structure within the hospital which differs considerably from that of the conventional mental hospital. He describes the usefulness of this approach in helping antisocial psychopaths, who are so likely to be encountered in prisons. "Authority is distributed in the community, and in this way the antisocial behavior of patients becomes the concern of everyone. Most of the patients have never belonged to a family or any other group before, and in our community they for the first time begin to feel a sense of belonging, and to realize what their behavior means to the rest of the group. They accept the authority of people like themselves more readily than that of a single authoritarian figure. By doing so they come to understand that by identification with the group and a willingness to impose self-discipline they can achieve new and more socially acceptable patterns of gratification.

"A community such as this encourages personality growth. In it the patient has unusually favorable opportunities to associate with nonpunitive figures, including the social therapists or other patients. He can test the possibilities of sharing his troubles verbally instead of showing them by rebelliousness or other forms of acting out. If he finds that he can get more satisfaction through frank and sympathetic communication (friendship and understanding), than by anti-social ways, he may come to adopt this more mature pattern of behavior. In time he may come to identify himself with the unit and refer to it as "our unit" – a further step in the development of a social conscience. Such a community can come to have great tolerance for the behavior of its members, but calls for forbearance and understanding on the part of the staff which can only be achieved with the help of special training."

Wilmer, former psychiatric consultant to the group-living program at San Quentin Prison, describes six fundamental principles of therapeutic communities.

1. The social system is organized to facilitate treatment.
2. Open communication is the hallmark of a therapeutic community.
3. The group fosters individual responsibility for words, beliefs and behavior.
4. Decisions are made openly with considerations for the entire group.
5. The dynamics of group therapy must be understood by the staff.
6. The uniqueness of the individual is not subjugated to the group, both go hand in hand.

HORMONES

Female sex hormones (estrogens) have been used to reduce or suppress the rape offender's sexual drive. The dose may be adjusted to reduce sexual fantasies and impulses to rape women, yet at the same time to permit occasional sexual intercourse, an important requirement for married men. Undesirable side effects of the drug include enlargement and tenderness of the breasts. This treatment depends on the willingness of the sex offender to continue taking the drug regularly. Unfortunately these men cannot always be relied upon to cooperate in therapy.

Scott believes that the treatment is brilliantly successful in those rather rare hypersexual individuals who engage in all sorts of normal and abnormal sexual acts at any time of the day or night, whose main preoccupation in life is sexual activity. The gratitude of these patients for the relief which Stilbestrol® brings is only exceeded by that of their wives.

A thirty-three-year-old man who was afraid that he would give in to his strong compulsion to rape women and children did not work and isolated himself from others. He locked himself in a room of his parents' house for fifteen years and he had barricaded the door of his room for two years. He used a ladder, which he built, to enter and leave his room through a window. All his food was put into a basket, which he pulled up through his window with the help of a rope. Twice when his mother reproved him, he hit her violently.

He had been in a mental hospital for a week but had run away. Psychoanalytic therapy was not successful. Group psychotherapy was out of the question, as female company aroused his compulsive ideas of rape with feelings of tension too strong for him to endure. After treatment with Stilbestrol his feelings of tension in the company of girls and his compulsion to rape them disappeared. It then became possible to attempt resocialization through therapeutic social clubs (Bierer and van Someren).

CASTRATION

> *"One should not underestimate the importance of the fact that such a compulsory operation is at variance with the prevailing principles of medical treatment. Neither should one make light of the danger of the community losing its soul when it uses such inhuman — or at least according to what is generally termed inhuman — means."*
>
> — Louis LeMaire

Voluntary castration of sex offenders is permitted by law in Denmark, Norway, Sweden, Switzerland and Germany. The inducement for the offender to undergo the operation is a reduction in sentence. Thus in Norway if the operation is performed before conviction the prosecutor may waive prosecution. If the offender is convicted, he may receive a shorter sentence. If the operation is performed while the offender is serving a sentence of imprisonment, it can lead to his early release. Although the offender must give his consent to the operation, if he is confined in a hospital or prison for an indeterminate length of time, indirect pressure can be used to obtain his consent.

The main effect of castration on men with serious sexual difficulties is that their capacity to respond to sexual stimuli is diminished, as is their sexual fantasy life and their sexual interests in general (Sturup). Castration does not always abolish the capacity for sexual intercourse. Juvenal long ago reported sexual activity in Roman slaves who had been castrated. Bremer reported persistence of sexual potency from one to sixteen years in thirteen of 157 cases of castration. Sturup, in his review of eighteen rapists castrated in the Herstedvester (Denmark) Institute for Abnormal Criminals, reported that two of them were able to have sexual relations three to four times a month following the operation.

One man, several years after his discharge from the Institute, went to a private physician and obtained testosterone, a sex hormone, by saying that he was impotent. This reawakened his sexual activity. After being reproached for this, he stopped. Twenty-six years after his castration, while on substantial doses of testosterone, he was charged with committing an indecency against a seven-year-old girl.

A schizophrenic offender attempted six months after castration to attack a woman visitor to the Institute and later hid a knife and then aggressively attacked a young girl who was the dentist's assistant. One man was dangerously aggressive following castration and after eight years was transferred to the security section of a mental hospital. Another man was confined indefinitely in a mental hospital because of his aggressive behavior. It was noted that in one case psychotic episodes were much more severe after the operation.

Although Sturup claims that the majority of men after castration show less anxiety and seldom have stable depressive reactions or psychosomatic symptoms, one wonders about loss of self-esteem and resentment toward the physicians. The information provided sex offenders at Herstedvester concerning the effects and results of the operations is given in Appendix Two. A survey of nine hundred men castrated in Denmark between 1929 and 1959 showed that ten, or just over 1 per cent, committed sex crimes after the operation. Recidivism rates as high as 7 per cent following castration have been reported from Norway and Switzerland. Sturup's own experience with eighteen castrated rapists is difficult to evaluate because of the absence of a follow-up study of a comparable group of rapists who have not been castrated.

Castration is an irreversible operation which is abhorrent to many physicians. It may reduce the sexual drive, but it may fail to eliminate the offender's impulses to attack women. There is always the possibility that the offender may obtain sex hormones illegally to restore his sexual drive. Symptoms of psychosis may be precipitated or intensified by the operation. Among the 284 persons castrated at Herstedvester between 1935 and 1967, five committed suicide (less than 2 per cent) during their stay in Herstedvester or in the period of parole of usually four years or more. Sturup does not consider that castration was a decisive factor in these suicides and points out that suicide rates among criminal groups are higher than in the population at large.

RELEASE FROM CUSTODY

Procedures for release of sex offenders vary widely. Under sex psychopath laws a common requirement is a medical opinion that the patient has recovered and that commission of further sex offenses is unlikely. When a person has been found not guilty of a sex offense by reason of insanity, the hospital is usually required to show that he is not likely to be a danger to himself or to others in the reasonably forseeable future. Difficulty may be experienced in predicting whether an offender is likely to commit a serious sexual crime if set at liberty.

Statistics suggest that recidivism rates are low among those offenders who commit serious sexual crimes. Clinical experience, however, suggests otherwise. Statistics record merely arrests and convictions, and as sex crimes are often not reported, the official records may be misleading. In any event, statistics are of doubtful value in the consideration of the individual case. The persistent sex offender and the offender who uses force or violence deserve very careful study. Sadistic behavior or sadistic fantasies should also arouse concern. It is a good practice to have a complete review of the man's history, his criminal record and his response to treatment.

Hospital records may be incomplete and it is important to obtain information which should previously have been made available to the treatment team. One should never rely on the offender for an account of his illegal behavior. The following case illustrates this point.

> A twenty-two-year-old married man charged with the rape of two women was found to be legally insane and committed to a security hospital. According to the records of that hospital "he had intercourse with both women and he stated they both consented willingly. However, following intercourse with the older one, he stated he thought she was his wife and without provocation he hit her with a rootbeer mug. Presumably it was the latter attack that precipitated the charges of rape." These records also showed a prior conviction for statutory rape. "He was caught with a girl under the age of eighteen and apparently her parents pressed charges." The patient was considered to be a reliable informant by the hospital physician. Presumably this was the reason no effort was made to check the

accuracy of his statements.

When the security hospital recommended that this patient should be released from the hospital and restored to sanity, the author was instructed by the court to examine him. He gave much the same story as that reported above. The records of the trial, which were readily available, included the following account of the rape of a twenty-six-year-old woman and a sixteen-year-old girl who were alone in their house with young children including a baby. Details of the actual rapes and some perverse sexual acts forced on the victims have been deleted. "There was a knock on the door, I got up out of bed to answer the door, he put his hand on my mouth and told me to keep quiet or he would hurt me. He hit me in the mouth with his fist.

"He picked up a rootbeer glass, then he hit me. I went black for a second. He told us if we didn't do as he said he'd kill my kids and us. I remember him hitting Betty two or three times. He asked for a hammer. He got a butcher knife and threatened to use it on both of us. All this time he kept hitting me with the rootbeer glass until it broke, then he continued hitting me with his fist about the face and head. He also pounded me in the stomach.

"He also rammed his fingers up inside of me trying to pull my insides out, he then forced me to lick his hand off. He rammed his hand up inside me again . . . All of this time we were both scared half out of our minds. I was afraid to go for help because if he caught me I knew he would kill me and the kids. But I knew I had to try or he would end up killing all of us anyway."

The older victim escaped while he was assaulting her sixteen-year-old girl friend. On admission to hospital she was treated for two lacerations of her scalp. One was three inches and the other six inches in length and both were to the periosteum. Her face was badly bruised and she had a hematoma of her left ear. The vagina was tender and bloody.

The records on the previous charge of statutory rape showed that he had originally been charged with forcible rape, but the charge was reduced when he entered a plea of guilty. On this occasion, a few weeks after his marriage, he raped three times a babysitter in a friend's home after threatening to kill her and choking her. Photographs showed evidence of his attempts to choke her. Further inquiry revealed other charges of rape and assault to rape. The fourth rape victim reported that he had threatened to kill her and her baby.

Kozol *et al.* state that "a psychotic person with molestive sexual interests may harbor an extremely dangerous potential even if he is consistently docile in the institutional setting. The danger is compounded if such a person, while acutely psychotic, experiences hallucinatory disparagement . . . The appearance of assaultive and particularly pedophilic sex offenses in a psychotic should be looked upon with gravest caution. In general extreme protestations of shame, remorse, guilt and self-hatred should be regarded as ominous signs of a dangerous potential and not as hopeful signs of an emerging acceptance of conventional moral standards."

Excellent behavior in an institution does not guarantee similar behavior on release. Patients should not be released directly from a maximum security ward into the community. There should be a gradual increase in privileges and responsibilities. At the Colorado State Hospital sex offenders committed by the criminal courts as legally insane are transferred from the maximum security unit to a locked ward and eventually to an unlocked general psychiatric ward for members of both sexes. Many of these men while still patients at the hospital obtain full-time employment in the city of Pueblo.

This gradual transition back into the community prepares the patient for the stresses outside the hospital and provides a better opportunity for the staff to evaluate his readiness for discharge from the hospital. The selection of adolescent girls as companions on the ward, hostile or threatening attitudes and frank sexual remarks or advances toward female patients, and the use of alcohol or drugs show that the patient needs further treatment. Home visits may bring to light conflicts with mother or wife which can be concealed during brief family visits within the hospital.

PREVENTION OF RAPE

"Society has the criminals it deserves."

The forcible-rape rate can and should be reduced. The high crime rates in the United States show the urgent need for remedial action. Primary prevention can be accomplished by programs for promotion of mental health in the community. Such programs, hopefully, would lower the incidence of men with serious sexual psychopathology. Early recognition and treatment of the rapist should also be of value. Educational programs directed toward women and children provide guidance on measures to avoid rape.

PRIMARY PREVENTION

Primary prevention programs are designed to lower the incidence of mental disorder in the community. Attention is directed toward conditions in the home or in society which produce mental illness. Visotsky notes that a primary prevention program will necessarily involve significant members of the community and engage those institutions of our society which, by virtue of their role, have a crucial impact on the bulk of our citizenry. More specifically, with respect to the individual, the principles of primary prevention are implemented by social agencies, schools and churches, physicians and health professionals, local government leaders and, most important, the individual's family and other significant people in his life.

The family physician and the pediatrician should be alert to the danger signals which suggest that the parents are fostering unhealthy sexual attitudes in their children. The mother who expresses undue concern about her child's sexual development seems preoccupied about sex, is seductive in her behavior toward the child or is overprotective may be in need of counseling. Johnson and Robinson make the following suggestions. "There should be a few simple but pointed routine queries by the physician. Who sleeps with whom in the family? Which ones bathe together, and do they bathe themselves? What are the family habits regarding bathroom privacy? Are dressing and undressing communal functions? Is there a healthy degree of modesty in the home? What are the children's chief interests at play and habits in dress? Too often, such interrogation reveals unmistakable signs of an unhealthy atmosphere. When encountered, such tendencies should be met with an uncompromising counsel of prohibition.

"If the parents are unhappily married and their hostile sexual impulses strain for an outlet, a physician's simple education of the parents, admonition to proper behavior or direct prohibition of the seductive behavior may be of no avail. In such cases, combined psychiatric treatment of parents and child is indispensable. However, instances amenable to a forthright, relatively simple management are sufficiently numerous to warrant a rather general effort by pediatricians and family physicians. Such a program holds genuine promise for prophylaxis, for sparing many children a miserable life outlook, for strengthening the fiber of the public character and for preserving society from an unhappy quota of hurt and violence."

Children may confide in their teachers about difficulties within the home, and may hint at or reveal incestuous approaches by the father. Although instruction regarding sex is the responsibility of the parents, this duty is often neglected and school programs on sex education serve a necessary and useful purpose. School counselors and psychologists may be the first to recognize that all is not well within the home and are in a position to arrange for remedial action. Physicians in emergency rooms should remember that injuries to the genitals of a young girl, attributed by the father to a fall from a bicycle, may not have been caused by a fall from a bicycle.

EARLY DIAGNOSIS

Secondary prevention is the early identification of the potential or actual rapist. Many rapists come to the attention of the police before they are arrested and charged with rape. They may be arrested for such crimes as burglary, theft of women's underclothing, indecent assaults, voyeurism or exhibitionism.

It is commonly stated by such authorities as Guttmacher, Bowman, Tappan and others that the sex offender does not progress from minor to major sex crimes. Yet some offenders commit both minor and major sex crimes, and while it may be true that persons convicted of voyeurism and indecent exposure seldom commit violence or murder, nevertheless, the writer has seen several persons charged with rape or murder who gave a history of indecent exposure or voyeurism. In all these cases, the sexual perversion occurred in the setting of severe sociopathic personality disorder.

Generalizations derived from statistical studies of large numbers of cases should always be considered in the light of the total clinical findings in the individual case.

PREVENTIVE MEASURES BY POTENTIAL VICTIMS

The woman who accepts a ride home from a stranger, picks up a hitchhiker, sunbathes alone or works in the garden in a two-piece bathing suit which exposes rather than conceals her anatomy invites rape. The woman who by immodest dress, suggestive remarks or behavior flaunts her sexuality should not be surprised if she is attacked sexually. These ladies are referred to as "rape bait" by police officers. The woman who walks along dark streets or alleys late at night, drinks to excess at taverns or strikes up conversation with strangers may pay a heavy price for her lack of caution.

Since many rapes take place in homes or apartments, preventive measures are essential. Special care should be taken not to allow strangers to gain access. A locked screen door provides some security because the moment the man tries to force it open, the woman can close and lock the door. The screen door should be locked at all times. A peep hole or glass frame in an apartment door makes it possible to check whether a stranger or friend seeks admission. The door should not be opened if there is no screen door. Chain door locks provide a false feeling of security as a quick forceful push of a partially opened door snaps the chain from the door. It is a simple matter to call the apartment house manager before opening the door. Once the door is open, the woman may be helpless to protect herself. The wife of the manager of an apartment house would be wise to await the return of her husband before showing vacant apartments to men who seek accommodation.

Before leaving an apartment or home, one should shut and lock windows as well as doors and leave a light and a radio on. Children should be taught to take similar care. It is not sufficient to shut windows, they should also be locked. Keys should not be left under the doormat, in the mailbox, flower pot or other obvious hiding places. Women should keep the front door and garage door locked while they are outside hanging up clothes on the clothes line, unless someone is at home to protect them.

At night drapes, curtains and blinds should be drawn. Window peepers may also be rapists. Venetian blinds, unless adjusted properly, allow the voyeur to peep between the slats. Thoughtful rapists sometimes warn their victims to be more careful in the future.

Women should beware of the man who wants to check their telephone, furnace or lighting system and ask to see his identification. If a man comes to the door and says that his car has broken down and he wants to use the telephone, he should be asked to wait outside while someone calls a service station for him. A young man who claimed that a gang was chasing him asked to use the telephone to call his family. Once inside the home he called his brother who said he would be over in an hour. The woman then asked him to leave, but he forced her to the floor and attempted to rape her. A wife should beware of the man who telephones and asks if her husband is at home. She should not say that he is away for the weekend but should ask who is calling and say that he is expected shortly or that he is asleep and does not wish to be disturbed. She should also ask for the caller's telephone number.

Before renting an apartment or purchasing a home, one should find out the reputation of the neighborhood. Certain areas of large cities have high crime rates and should be avoided. Before accepting employment, a woman should make sure that she does not have to walk through dangerous areas to reach her office or factory. Nurses on night duty at hospitals should make sure that the hospital parking lots are well lighted and are patrolled by security officers at night. If a woman's handbag is stolen, she should remember that it contains her identification and keys and should have her door lock changed.

Girls who live in apartment houses should write only their names and initials on the apartment house register or mailbox and not "Mrs." or "Miss," otherwise they may have unwelcome visitors. Women should beware of the man who follows them into the apartment house. He may gain entrance through the locked apartment house door by keeping close behind her then following her to her apartment and force entrance.

Elevators in apartment houses and other buildings are a place of danger. Women should be prepared to press the elevator emergency button, which will bring help. If in doubt a woman should not enter the elevator with a man whom she suspects. Subway trains at night can be dangerous. The car with many passengers or a train guard would be safer. Women should always keep all the doors locked when they are riding in a car or taxi.

One rapist pointed a gun through the open car window at the woman driver. The resourceful victim quickly wound up the window and the man dropped his gun inside the car as he was withdrawing his arm.

> A woman was returning to her hotel in a taxi in the early hours of the morning when a man jumped in the taxi while it was stopped for a red light at an intersection. The man robbed the driver and his passenger at knife point, and then forced the driver to drive to a neighboring city. On the way he forced the woman to commit an unnatural act. Later she fell out of the taxi while it was moving at a high speed. The man then forced the driver to drive the wrong way back on the divided interstate highway to pick up the injured woman. After locking the driver in the trunk he assaulted her.

The presence of a male companion in the car should not give rise to a false feeling of security. Lovers' lanes attract rapists who assault the man or hold him up at gun point and then rape the woman.

Caryl Chessman, who was executed for kidnapping in San Quentin after spending almost twelve years on death row, used to pull up beside a car on a lovers' lane and abduct the girl. He had a flashing red light on the top of his car and was known as the "red-light bandit." Hitchhikers are a source of danger as in the following case.

> My boyfriend, Dick, and I had dinner at home. We went out for a drive. At a stoplight a guy hollered. We looked back and saw this Negro standing in the street. He walked over to the car and said he was out of gas and would pay us to take him to a gas station. I told my boyfriend, "Dick, don't do it." My boyfriend said he can't do any harm and told him to get in. I had my hand on my boyfriend's knee. The man said, "Get your hand off his knee and don't make any fast moves, I've got a gun on you."
>
> I felt a gun in my side. He said, "Drive on and don't let anyone know what is going on. Make a right turn then a left turn. You don't need both hands to drive with; give me all your money." We came to an alley; he told Dick to turn in. He grabbed the keys to the ignition, ran around the car and pulled my boyfriend out and told him to walk down the alley. I was blindfolded. He drove around for about twenty minutes and then pulled into an alley. He held the gun to my head and told me to take my clothes off. I didn't want to get hurt. He raped me and afterwards drove me to Welton street and let me out.

A woman should lock her car when she leaves it to go shopping, otherwise a rapist may hide behind the front seat and surprise her when she returns.

> A woman parked her car while she went to a beauty shop. She returned to her car and started driving home. When she looked in the rear view mirror she was shocked to see the face of a stranger who was sitting in the back seat. She stopped her car and ran. The man caught her and began ripping off her clothes, tearing the buttons off her blouse and the zipper off her skirt. He ran away when a man came to her aid.

When returning home, before leaving her car, a woman should make sure that no stranger is nearby. If someone follows her, she should drive to the nearest police station and not rely on her driving skill to lose the man. If she has a puncture or if her car breaks down, it is sometimes wiser for her to ask would-be helpers to notify the police or nearest gasoline station than to accept immediate help from a stranger.

Girl hitchhikers may get more than a ride. They should beware of men who claim to be police officers yet do not wear a police uniform or are wearing security guard uniforms and should insist on seeing their identification and study it carefully. They should never get into a car that has no police car insignia unless they are confident of the officer's identity.

> We were waiting for a bus in front of a drugstore on Colfax. We had been there about five minutes when a man drove up and showed us a badge. He was holding it in his hand. He asked us to step over to the car. We were standing on the curb, he said we were out after curfew. He asked why. We told him we had been to a movie. He told us it was pretty late and he had better take us home.
>
> We got in the front seat, I was in the middle. He started to drive out over a viaduct somewhere and turned down a dirt road. He stopped the car, took a

handful of Roberta's hair and pulled her head toward my shoulder. He said he had a knife and if we cooperated neither of us would get hurt. He told me to undress and then he molested me. Later he brought us back into town and let us out.

*   *   *

As I stepped from my car a man pulled up in a late model Ford and showed me his badge, at which time he asked me for my car registration. I informed him that I didn't have it with me and it was at home. The man told me that it would be necessary that I accompany him to police headquarters until it was checked out. I then asked him to wait a minute until I gave a friend who was waiting for me my keys. When I returned, he was still waiting, so I got in his car. He asked me my name and took my driver's license.

He'd gone only a few blocks before I realized he wasn't going in the direction of the police headquarters. I questioned him why and he said that he wanted to talk to me first. At this time I knew something definitely was wrong. Eventually he parked in a dark alley and he told me he'd give me a break if I had a quick intercourse with him. I panicked and insisted that he take me directly to the police station or let me go. He continued to try to persuade me to be nice to him. I began to cry because I was extremely nervous. He told me he should beat me up with his billy club, but I was making him nervous with all that crying and he was going to let me out and make me walk home. [The man was not a police officer.]

A mother should use caution in the selection of babysitters; a babysitter might bring with her a boyfriend who would molest the child. Babysitters should be aware of the risks of rape. The alcoholic man who drives the babysitter home may assault her on the way. The babysitter who advertises her services will often allow a complete stranger to call for her in his car. He may not have any children at all, and once the girl is in his car he drives to a suitable location and rapes her. Alternatively he may break into an unoccupied home, then telephone a babysitting agency and request that a babysitter be sent to the home. Not a few babysitters have paid with their lives for their lack of caution.

Children should be warned not to accept candy or rides from strangers or to run errands for them.

SELF-DEFENSE

Newspaper advertisements warn women that the only answer to a rapist is a tear gas gun, but guns are awkward objects to carry around and if buried in a handbag, are not readily available in an emergency. Hat pins, knitting needles and knives are alternative weapons of defense, but once again, women who walk around carrying knitting needles or knives do look rather odd. When the victim has prior warning of an impending attack, for example if she notices a man following her at night, she will have time to remove her weapon of defense from her handbag.

The boy scout motto, *be prepared,* should be kept in mind by women in danger of rape; and what woman is not in danger of rape? Rape is not confined to beautiful young girls; it may come to the old as well as to the young, to the ugly as well as to the comely. The best opportunity for escape is often at the onset of the attack, yet it is at this time that victims are paralyzed by fear. Immediate counterattack, loud screams and an attempt to run away may end the matter. A sharp backward jab of the elbow for the assailant from behind may take him off guard.

Ida Younger, a Denver woman deputy sheriff, suggests grabbing and twisting a man's most vulnerable part, his genitals. While he is recovering from this unexpected assault the woman makes her escape. She can also stamp on his instep with the heel of her shoe. If he attacks from in front, a knee to the groin or fingers in his eyes may be very effective. Not every woman is capable of such action. As an alternative she suggests that the victim give the appearance of fainting.

"The attacker expects you to struggle. Instead you go absolutely limp as you would if you really fainted. Suddenly he's holding one hundred or more pounds of inert female. He's got to do something with that deadweight. He may try to hold you up or try to put you down, but either way he relaxes his grip on you. That's your chance to kick, gouge or scream and run ... You may freeze for incredibly long seconds. But do not stop thinking – and think only of getting away."

Resisting the rapist who is armed with a gun or knife may have fatal consequences. Nevertheless, many women succeed in talking armed men out of rape. They may do so by claiming that they are menstruating, pregnant or have had a recent operation. Claims of venereal and other infectious diseases or cancer may also deter the rapist. Upon occasion tearful reference to virginity or impending marriage may be sufficient.

A quick-witted girl who was abducted by a rapist in a car as she was walking along a street struggled with her assailant. She eventually succeeded in persuading him that he could visit her at her home. "I told him I lived on the seven hundred block of Madison. When we reached Madison, the first house that I saw had lights on, I told him I lived there. I got out and told him to drive around the back alley and I would let him in. When I got to the door, a girl answered. I told her there was a man out there and asked to use the phone. She saw lights coming down the alley and got scared and let me in."

It is not possible to suggest the ideal response to the man intent on rape. The woman should exercise some judgment based upon her evaluation of her assailant, in deciding upon what action to pursue. Preservation of her life may be more important than protection of her virtue. Some victims show much more determination than others. A seventy-year-old woman attacked in the street threatened to break the glasses of her assailant. A much younger woman made no effort to resist when a youth, without any threats, started to remove her underclothes in an alley. Rape involves both the offender and his victim.

APPENDICES

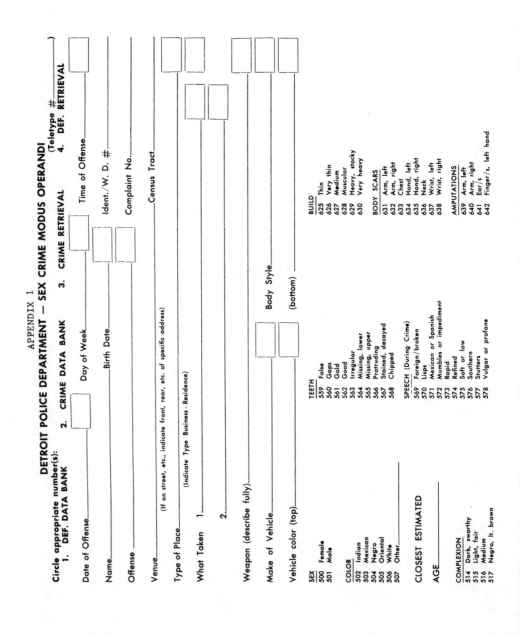

APPENDIX 1

DETROIT POLICE DEPARTMENT — SEX CRIME MODUS OPERANDI

Circle appropriate number(s):

1. DEF. DATA BANK   2. CRIME DATA BANK   3. CRIME RETRIEVAL   4. DEF. RETRIEVAL (Teletype #)

Date of Offense _____   Day of Week _____   Time of Offense _____

Name _____   Birth Date _____   Ident./W. D. # _____

Offense _____   Complaint No. _____

Venue _____   Census Tract _____
(If on street, etc., indicate front, rear, etc., of specific address)

Type of Place _____
(Indicate Type Business - Residence)

What Taken 1. _____
2. _____

Weapon (describe fully) _____

Make of Vehicle _____   Body Style _____

Vehicle color (top) _____   (bottom) _____

SEX
500 Female
501 Male

COLOR
502 Indian
503 Mexican
504 Negro
505 Oriental
506 White
507 Other

CLOSEST ESTIMATED

AGE

COMPLEXION
514 Dark, swarthy
515 Light, fair
516 Medium
517 Negro, lt. brown

TEETH
559 False
560 Gaps
561 Gold
562 Good
563 Irregular
564 Missing, lower
565 Missing, upper
566 Protruding
567 Stained, decayed
568 Chipped

SPEECH (During Crime)
569 Foreign/broken
570 Lisps
571 Mexican or Spanish
572 Mumbles or impediment
573 Rapid
574 Refined
575 Soft or low
576 Southern
577 Stutters
578 Vulgar or profane

BUILD
625 Thin
626 Very thin
627 Medium
628 Muscular
629 Heavy, stocky
630 Very heavy

BODY SCARS
631 Arm, left
632 Arm, right
633 Chest
634 Hand, left
635 Hand, right
636 Neck
637 Wrist, left
638 Wrist, right

AMPUTATIONS
639 Arm, left
640 Arm, right
641 Ear/s
642 Finger/s, left hand

318

Appendix 1 *(continued)*

518 Negro, med. brown
519 Negro, dk. brown
520 Ruddy
521 Sallow

EYE COLOR
522 Black
523 Blue
524 Brown
525 Gray
526 Hazel
527 Green

EYE DEFECTS
528 Bulging
529 Cast, left eye
530 Cast, right eye
531 Cataracts
532 Crossed
533 Different colors
534 Eye missing
535 Squints or blinks
536 Slanted

HAIR COLOR
537 Black
538 Blonde
539 Brown
540 Brown, light
541 Dyed
542 Gray
543 Gray, partially
544 Red
545 White
546 Auburn

HAIR TYPE
547 Bald
548 Bald, partially
549 Bushy
550 Crew cut, very short
551 Curly
552 Fad, Quo-vadis, etc.
553 Kinky
554 Processed
555 Straight
556 Thin or receding
557 Wavy
558 Long

D.P.D. 202
Form C of D-1-OP-E (8-66)

MOUSTACHE, BEARD, ETC.
579 Beard
580 Eyebrows, heavy/bushy
581 Goatee
582 Moustache, heavy
583 Moustache, medium
584 Moustache, thin or light
585 Moustache, Chinese
586 Sideburns
587 Unshaven

FACIAL SCARS
588 Cheek, left
589 Cheek, right
590 Chin
591 Ear, left
592 Ear, right
593 Eyebrow, or left eye area
594 Eyebrow, or right eye area
595 Forehead
596 Hare-lip
597 Lip, lower
598 Lip, upper
599 Nose
600 Pierced earlobes

FACIAL ODDITIES
601 Birthmark/s
602 Chin, protruding
603 Chin, receding
604 Freckles
605 Lips, thick
606 Lips, thin
607 Moles
608 Pimples
609 Pockmarks
610 Hollow cheeked

NOSE
611 Broken, crooked
612 Broad
613 Flat
614 Hooked
615 Large
616 Long
617 Small
618 Thin
619 Upturned

HEIGHT
620 Very short
621 Short
622 Medium
623 Tall
624 Very tall

CLOSEST ESTIMATED
HEIGHT

Under 5/2
5/2 - 5/6
5/7 - 5/9
5/10 - 6/1
6/2 - Over

643 Finger/s, right hand
644 Foot, left
645 Foot, right
646 Hand, left
647 Hand, right
648 Leg, left
649 Leg, right

DEFORMITIES
650 Bow-legged
651 Cauliflower ears
652 Crippled arm, left
653 Crippled arm, right
654 Crippled finger/s
655 Crippled hand/s
656 Crippled leg, left, limps
657 Crippled leg, right, limps

TATOOS
658 Arm, left
659 Arm, right
660 Chest or neck
661 Fingers, left
662 Fingers, right
663 Hand, left
664 Hand, right
665 Pachuco

TYPE OF TATTOO
666 Initials
667 Names
668 Words/Phrases
669 Pictures
670 Designs

EARS (Shape)
671 Protruding
672 Large
673 Small
674 Close to head

FACE (Shape)
676 Thin
677 Round
678 Long
679 High cheek bones
680 Broad
681 Caucasian features

MISCELLANEOUS
Add any additional physical characteristic in this space

TIME OF ASSAULT
700 Sunrise-Sunset (Daylight)
701 Sunset—Midnight (Evening)
702 Midnight—Sunrise (Early A.M.)
703 Unknown

WEARS
710 Cloth, hankie over face
711 Earrings
712 Faddish, flashy clothes
713 Glasses, regular
714 Glasses, sun
715 Gloves
716 Hood
717 Head cloth or rag
718 Hand held over face
719 Mask
720 No shoes
721 Rings
722 Silk stocking over face
723 Sloppy dressed
724 Well dressed
725 Work uniform
726 If any disguise used, circle

APPROACH
740 Asks victim to help find dog, books, etc.
741 Admitted to victim's home as salesman, etc.
742 Answers ads
743 Asks for information, directions, etc.
744 B & E
745 Claims to be Police Officer, etc.
746 Claims to be sent by parents
747 Enters victim's home after knocking
748 Follows victim into lobby, elevator
749 Follows—sneaks up from behind
750 From concealment—bushes, etc.
751 Loiters in area
752 Meets victim at party, bar
753 Offers job
754 Offers gifts/or money
755 Offers assistance
756 Pretext medical treatment

CHARACTERISTICS OF ASSAILANT
800 Abnormal genitals
801 Female attire, wears, possession
802 Grins, stares, leers—makes no comment
803 Hands, long slender
804 Hands, short broad
805 Hands, stained, greasy
806 Fingers, long nails
807 Fingers, nails bitten close
808 Handsome
809 Has accomplice
810 Jostles women
811 Left handed
812 Laughs at victim
813 Mentally disturbed or retarded
814 Narcotic user
815 Obscene pictures, shows, possession
816 Removes all clothing (own)
817 Ransack house
818 Rips/cuts/disconnects telephone
819 Smells (body odor, greasy, etc.)
820 Voice deep
821 Voice high pitched
822 Voice raspy
823 Removes or drops pants
824 Is exposed (during approach)
825 Uses weapon and/or objects found at scene, i.e., knife, rope, etc.
826 Fingerprint conscious

CONVERSATION OF ASSAILANT
840 Apologizes
841 Asks victim to meet again
842 Abusive language to victim
843 Demands money
844 Demands jewelry
845 Has been in prison
846 Has raped, murdered, etc. before
847 Obscene language during crime
848 Polite
849 Reveals racial hostility
850 States will return/returns
851 Talkative
852 Threatens to harm victim's children, etc.
853 Silent—makes no comment

SEX ACTS (ALSO ATTEMPTS)
920 Bites
921 Beastiality
922 Forces victim to masturbate thug
923 Forces victim to disrobe thug
924 Fondles, sucks breast
925
926 Intercourse—canine position
927 Inserts finger in vagina
928 Inserts object in vagina
929 Inserts foreign objects into rectum
930 Kisses
931 Lifts or raises women's clothing
932 Licks victim
933 Masturbates
934 Oral perversion on victim
935 Places victim on lap
936 Plays with victim's privates
937 Places privates between victim's legs
938 Rapes
939 Rubs privates against victim
940 Requests help to accomplish sex act
941 Shows—uses contraceptive
942 Sodomy
943 Uses lubricant on victim
944 Victim forced to commit oral perversion
945 Unable achieve erection
946 Cries during offense
947 Lies on top of victim

VICTIM
970 White
971 Negro
972 Male — under 10
973 Female

AGE
974 Infant
975 Immature
976 Mature
977 Elderly

757 Pretext utility, tradesman, etc.
758 Ringing bell
759 Requests assistance
760 Sits near (bus, theater)
761 Victim lured to thug's home, business, concealment
762 Window peeping
763 Robbery
764 Asks for cigarette, light
765 Pretext of looking for work

VEHICLE INVOLVED
780 After victim puts car in garage or parking
781 Demands transportation after crime
782 Forces victim into car
783 Forces victim to lie (sit) floor/seat of car
784 Forces victim to accompany in vehicle
785 Follows victim's car
786 Hides in victim's car
787 Hitch-hikes (thug)
788 Jumps into victim's car
789 Lures victim into car (offers ride, etc.)
790 Parks car and follows on foot
791 Throws victim's car keys away

TREATMENT OF VICTIM
875 A & B Breast
876 A & B Buttocks
877 A & B Sex
878 Cuts clothing of victim
879 Covers victim's head with blanket, etc.
880 Forces victim into concealment
881 Grabs with hand over mouth
882 Grabs/drags to other area
883 Rips, tears clothing of victim
884 Removes all of victim's clothes
885 Sadist—beats victim after subdued
886 Tortures—any form
887 Victim/s beaten with fists
888 Victim/s beaten with weapon
889 Victim/s blindfolded
890 Victim/s choked
891 Victim/s gagged
892 Victim/s shot
893 Victim/s tied/bound
894 Victim/s grabbed around neck
895 Victim/s thrown to ground/or floor
896 Victim/s kidnapped
897 Victim/s stabbed
898 Victim/s taped

MISCELLANEOUS
Additional Data:

_____
_____
_____
_____
_____
_____

Submitted by_____ NAME _____ PCT./BUR.

Checked by_____ NAME _____ PCT./BUR.

Date _____

Keypunched by_____

Verified by_____

D.P.D. 202
Form C of D—1-OP-E (8-66)

ADVICE TO PATIENTS
CONCERNING CASTRATION*

IN Herstedvester, Denmark, this instruction is used to advise the doctor concerning what to cover during the interview and is not supposed to be read aloud to the patient. In Germany Professor Lange-luddeke (1963) has advised that similar instructions be given in writing to the patient.

Castration is a surgical intervention which calls for careful consideration. Statistical analysis of a considerable number of cases has shown that a first-time sexual offender has a low rate of relapse. But for the small group who do relapse into new sexual crime (usually of the same type as the first one committed), the relapse rate is much higher and for the selected group of people we usually get in Herstedvester the rate of relapse into new sexual crime for the nonoperated group is about 40 per cent.

Castration means the removal of the testes. It is important in discussing this to use the colloquial terms for testes so that there can be no doubt that the patient realized what the operation means. Usually a prosthesis is used (formerly these were made of glass, now they are made of plastic) which means that the scrotum does not look empty after the operation. Castration is different from sterilization which is only cutting of the vas deferens. After castration there is a definite diminution of hormonal secretion. After sterilization no changes in hormonal secretion are usually seen.

The human sexual life, direction of the sexual drive and strength of the drive, is partly dependent on the hormonal production of the testes, although some persons produce sexual hormones from other glands.

After castration the direction of the sexual drive will usually not be changed but the intensity of the drive will be definitely weaker, making it easier for the castrate to control unwanted, unlawful sexual activity. In many cases castration results in complete elimination of the interest in obtaining sexual relations as well as of the possibility to perform such relations.

Studies done in many different countries show that the number of relapses to new sexual offenses is very small after the operation (about 2%). Usually the castrated group relapses to other types of offenses to a lesser degree than the nonoperated group of sexual offenders.

*Reprinted from "Treatment of Sexual Offenders in Herstedvester, Denmark" by Georg K. Sturup. *Acta Psychiatrica Scandinavica,* Supplement 204, Volume 44, 1968.

The change in the sexual libido does not occur immediately after the operation, and therefore we usually wait up to about six months before we advocate parole. The operation as such does not guarantee parole, but practice shows that there is a great possibility that the expected changes in sexual interest occur to such a degree that discharge on parole will be possible within a reasonable time after the operation. In some cases moderate side effects may be observed. About one third of those operated on suffer from inconveniences of the same type as experienced by some women during menopause; fits of sweating, blushing and pallor. These inconveniences usually disappear after a reasonable period of time. They may be diminished by some form of treatment but this is not effective in all cases. In many cases these inconveniences do not occur at all.

Physical Changes. The beard growth will usually be weaker as well as the hairiness of the body; but the head hair will usually be stronger, and castrates usually do not become bald. For some men, usually if they tend to be fat, a weight gain may occur, especially around the breasts and hips but such type of fatness is common in other fat men. Slim men may sometimes lose weight. The skin will in most cases become thinner and softer. Muscular power is usually not diminished.

The psychological changes are usually small. In some cases we have seen some diminution of activity but in some of these this has made social adaptation easier. This is the same sort of change which is normally seen in men getting older and more sedate. Many castrates have continued with great energy in responsible jobs or built up new careers for themselves. Dullness is not observed and neither are other psychological side effects.

Special care must be taken when schizophrenic symptoms are observed and the family warned that the psychosis may continue and that the result of the operation in such cases is more doubtful.

A married man must be warned that he will probably not be able to have sexual relations and the situation discussed with the wife if the marriage is supposed to continue. Later marriage is not excluded, and several castrated inmates have married and both parties in the marriage seem to have a satisfactory life together. This, of course, depends on the expectation the wife has concerning sexual life.

After castration some men demonstrate a sort of inferiority complex for which there is no basis. A decision aiming at developing a new basis for social life ought to be recognized and esteemed to a very high degree, and follow-up through several decades of several thousand castrates has demonstrated that the majority are satisfied and many are especially happy because their former troubles have disappeared. These have stated, after many years, that they would not act differently if they had to repeat their decision.

Only a few have regretted that they applied for castration. Usually these have been men whose sexual life had been their main enjoyment in life. If the person has not felt his sexual life a heavy strain or if the decision has been based only on the hope for early parole, it is possible that he will feel that he got too little result from the operation.

REFERENCES

Allen, C.: A Textbook of Psychosexual Disorders. London, Oxford U. P., 1969.

Amir, M.: Alcohol and forcible rape. Brit J Addict, 62:219, 1967.

Amir, M.: Forcible rape. Fed Probation, 31:51, 1967.

Amir, M.: Patterns in Forcible Rape: With Special Reference to Philadelphia, Pennsylvania, 1958 and 1960. Unpublished thesis. Ann Arbor, Michigan, University Microfilms Inc, 1965.

Amir, M.: Patterns of forcible rape. In Clinard, M.B., and Quinney, R. (Eds.): Criminal Behavior Systems. New York, Holt, 1967.

Amir, M.: Victim precipitated forcible rape. J Crim Law, 58:493, 1967.

Anonymous: A Woman in Berlin. New York, Harcourt, 1954.

Anthony, F.W.: Rape. Boston Med Surg J, 132:29, 1895.

Anttila, I., et al.: Kriminologinen Tutkimuslaitos, Helsinki, 1968.

Asuni, T.: Personal communication, 1969.

Barnes, J.: Rape and other sexual offenses. Brit Med J, 1:293, 1967.

Barry, M.J.: Incest. In Slovenko, R., op. cit.: Sexual Behavior and the Law, Springfield, Thomas, 1965.

Barry, M.J., and Johnson, A.M.: The incest barrier. Psychoanal Quart, 27:485, 1958.

Bartholomew, A.A.: A long-acting phenothiazine as a possible agent to control deviant sexual behavior. Amer J Psychiat, 124:917, 1968.

Bender, L., and Blau, A.: The reaction of children to sexual relations with adults. Amer J Orthopsychiat, 7:500, 1937.

Bender, L., and Grugett, A.E.: A follow-up report on children who had atypical sexual experience. Amer J Orthopsychiat, 22:825, 1952.

Bierer, J., and Someren, G.A.: Stilboestrol in out-patient treatment of sexual offenders. Brit Med J, 1:935, 1950.

Bierman, J.: Necrophilia in a thirteen-year-old boy. Psychoanal Quart, 31:329, 1962.

Blanchard, W.H.: The group process in gang rape. J Soc Psychol, 49:259, 1959.

Bloch, H.A., and Niederhoffer, A.: The Gang. New York, Philosophical Library, 1958.

Bonger, W.A.: Criminality and Economic Conditions. Boston, Little, 1916.

Borchard, E.M.: Convicting the Innocent. New Haven, Yale, 1932.

Bourdiol, L., and Pettenati, G.: Reflexions a propos de 40 expertises medico-legales en matiere d'attentats aux moeurs. Ann Med Leg (Paris), vol. 41, 1961.

Bowlby, J.: Forty-four juvenile thieves. Int J Psychoanal, 25:19, 1944.

Bremer, J.: Asexualization. New York, Macmillan, 1959.

Brill, A.: Necrophilia. Criminal Psychopathology, 2:433, 1941.

Bromberg, W.: Crime and the Mind. New York, Macmillan, 1965.

Bronson, F.R.: False accusations of rape. Amer J Urol, 14:539, 1918.

Brown, J.S.: A comparative study of deviations from sexual mores. Amer Sociol Rev, 17:135, 1952.

Bryce, C.A.: A boy of seven raped by a nymphomaniac, and infected with syphilis. Southern Clin, 4:159, 1881.

Bullock, H.A.: Significance of the racial factor in the length of prison sentences. J Crim Law, 52:411, 1961.

Burton, L.: Vulnerable Children. London, Routledge and Kegan Paul, 1968.

Cavallin, H.: Incestuous fathers: a clinical report. Amer J Psychiat, 122:1132, 1966.

Clark, and Marshall: A Treatise on the Law of Crimes, revised by M.F. Wingersky. Chicago, Callagan, 1952.

Cleaver, E.: Interview. Playboy, December, 1968.

Cleaver, E.: Soul on Ice. New York, McGraw-Hill, 1968.

Cohen, R.: Sexual molestations in hospitals. Clin Pediat (Phila.), 3:689, 1964.

Cole, W.G.: Sex and Love in the Bible. New York, Assn. Pr., 1959.

Colin, M., and Bourjade: Les attentants aux moeurs dans les bandes d'adolescents. Ann Med Leg (Paris), vol. 41, 1961. (cited by Burton, L.)

Cormier, B.M. *et al.:* Psychodynamics of father-daughter incest. Canad Psychiat Ass J, 7:203, 1962.

Cormier, B.M. *et al.:* The problem of the dangerous sexual offender. Canad Psychiat Ass J, 14:329, 1969.

Cowan, H.: Case of rape during sleep. Edinburg Med J, 8:570, 1862.

Dalmau, C.J.: Post-oedipal psychodynamics. Psychoanal Rev, 44:1, 1957.

Das, S.C.: Journey to Lhasu and Central Tibet. London, Murray, 1902.

Davidson, H.A.: Appraisal of the witness. Amer J Psychiat, 110:481, 1954.

Davis, K.C.: Discretionary Justice, Baton Rouge, Louisiana State U. Press, 1969.

Dewhurst, C.: Gynaecological Disorders of Infants and Children. London, Cassell, 1961.

Doshay, L.J.: The Boy Sex Offender and His Later Career. New York, Grune, 1943.

Dubois, J.A.: Hindu Manners, Customs and Ceremonies. Oxford, Clavendon, 1906.

Dyk, W.: A Navaho Autobiography. New York, Viking Fund, 1947.

Dyk, W.: Son of Old Man Hat. New York, Harcourt, 1938.

Easson, W.M., and Steinhilber, R.M.: Murderous aggression by children and adolescents. Arch Gen Pyschiat (Chicago), 4:27, 1961.

East, W.N.: Forensic Psychiatry in the Criminal Courts. London, Churchill, 1927.

East, W.N.: Society and the Criminal. Springfield, Thomas, 1950.

Eaton, A.P.: The sexually-molested child. Clin Ped (Phila.), 8:438, 1969.

Editorial: Sexual assaults on children. Brit Med J, 2:1623, 1961.

Ellis, H.: Studies in the Psychology of Sex. Philadelphia, F.A. Davis, 1927.

Ellis, H.: The Criminal. New York, Scribner & Welford, 1890.

Erlanson, O.: The scene of a sex offense as related to the residence of the offender. J Crim Law, 31:339, 1940-41.

Euripides: Hippolytus. Transl. by K. Cavander. San Francisco, Chandler, 1962.

Falk, G.J.: The influence of the seasons on the crime rate. J Crim Law, 43:199, 1952.

Federal Bureau of Investigation: Uniform Crime Reports 1960-1969. Washington, U.S. Government Printing Office, 1961-1970.

Ferdinand, T.N.: The criminal patterns of Boston since 1849. Amer J Sociol, 73:84, 1967.

Ferenczi, S.: Further Contributions to the Theory and Technique of Psychoanalysis. London, Hogarth, 1926.

Forbes, D.: On the Aymara Indians. J Enthnolog Soc London, 2:232, 1870.

Frank, G.: The Boston Strangler. New York, New American Library, 1966.

Frank, J., and Frank, B.: Not Guilty. Toronto, Doubleday, 1957.

Frazer, J.G.: The Golden Bough. London, Macmillan, 1950.

Freud, S.: The Complete Psychological Works, vol. 9. London, Hogarth, 1959.

Gebhard, P., *et al.:* Sex Offenders. New York, Harper Row and Paul Hoeber, 1965.

Gibbens, T.C.N.: Sane and insane homicide. J Crim Law, 49:110, 1958.

Gibbens, T., and Prince, J.: Child Victims of Sex Offenses. London, ISTD, 1963.

Gigeroff, A.K.: Sexual Deviations in the Criminal Law. Toronto, U. of Toronto, 1968.

Glueck, B.C.: Final Report Research Project for the Study and Treatment of Persons Convicted of Crimes Involving Sexual Aberrations. New York, State Department of Hygiene, 1956.

Goldhirsh, M.I.: Manifest content of dreams of convicted sex offenders. J Abnorm Soc Pyschol, 63:643, 1961.

Grassberger, R.: Die Unzucht Mit Tieren. Kriminologische Abhandlungen, Neue Folge 8, Wien, Springer Verlag, 1968.

Gross, H.: Criminal Psychology. Boston, Little, 1915.

Grunhut, M., *et al.:* Sexual Crime Today. Martinus Nijhoff, The Hague, 1960.

Guthrie, D.: Janus in the Doorway. London, Pittman, 1963.

Guttmacher, M.S.: Sex Offenses: The Problem, Causes and Prevention. New York, Norton, 1951.

Halleck, S.L.: Psychiatry and the Dilemmas of Crime. New York, Harper, 1967.

Halleck, S.L.: The physician's role in management of victims of sex offenders. JAMA, 180:273, 1962.

Harnagel, E.E.: Doctors afield; Joseph Bell, M.D. – the real Sherlock Holmes. New Eng J Med, 258:1158, 1958.

Hayman, C.R., *et al.:* A public health program for sexually assaulted females. Public Health Rep, 82:497, 1967.

Hayman, C.R., *et al.:* Sexual assault on women and girls in the District of Columbia. Southern Med J, 62:1227, 1969.

Helfer, C.: Book review. Brit J Crimin, 9:199, 1969.

Hentig, Hans von: Crime, Causes and Conditions. New York, McGraw-Hill, 1947.

Hentig, Hans von: The criminality of the Negro. J Crim Law, 30:662, 1940.

Hentig, Hans von: The sex ratio. Soc Forces, 30:443, 1952.

Hentig, Hans von: The suspect. J Crim Law, 39:19, 1948.

Herodotus: Historiae, II.

Hill, D., and Pond, D.A.: Reflections on 100 capital cases submitted to EES. J Ment Sci, 98:23, 1952.

Hoebel, E.A.: The political organization and law – ways of the Commanche Indians. Suppl Amer Anthrop, 42-3:2, 1960.

Hooton, E.A.: Crime and the Man. Cambridge, Harvard, 1939.

Hooton, E.A.: The American Criminal. Cambridge, Harvard, 1939.

Huffman, J.W.: The Gynecology of Childhood and Adolescence. Philadelphia, Saunders, 1968.

Hunt, E.E., *et al.:* The Micronesians of Yap and their Depopulation. Cambridge, Peabody Museum Harvard University.

Johnson, A.M., and Robinson, D.B.: The sexual deviant (sexual psychopath) – causes, treatment, and prevention. JAMA, 164:1559, 1957.

Johnson, A.M., and Szurek, S.A.: Etiology of antisocial behavior in delinquents and psychopaths. JAMA, 154:814, 1954.

Jones, H.: Crime and the Penal System. London, University Tutorial, 1956.

Jones, M.: Delinquency and Crime. Lancet, 2:1277, 1954.

Karpman, B.: The Sexual Offender and His Offenses. New York, Julian, 1954.

Kaufman, I., *et al.:* The family constellation and overt incestuous relations between father and daughter. Amer J Orthopsychiat, 24:266, 1954.

Kozol, H.L., *et al.:* The criminally dangerous sex offender. New Eng J Med, 275:79, 1966.

Krafft-Ebing, R.: Psychopathia Sexualis. Chicago, W.T. Keener, 1900.

Lafon, R., *et al.:* Victimologie et criminologie des attentats sexuels sur les enfants et les adolescents. Ann Med Leg (Paris), vol. 41, 1961. (cited by Burton, L.)

Lambert, H.E.: Kikuyu Social and Political Institutions. London, Oxford U. P., 1956.

Landes, R.: The Ojibwa Woman. New York, Columbia, 1938.

Landis, J.: Experiences of 500 children with adult sexual deviation. Psychiat Quart [Suppl] 30:91, 1956.

Lang, D.: Incident on Hill 162. London, Pan Books, 1970.

Le Maire, L.: Legal Kastration I Strafferetlig Belysning. Copenhagen, 1946.

Leppmann, F.: Essential differences between sex offenders. J Crim Law, 32:366, 1941.

LeVine, R.A.: Gusii sex offenses: a study in social control. Amer Anthrop, 61:965, 1959.

Lhote, H.: The Hoggar Taureg. Paris, Payot, 1944.

Liebling, A.J.: New Yorker, April 12, 1959.

Lipton, G.L., and Roth, E.I.: Rape: a complex management problem in the pediatric emergency room. J Pediat, 75:859, 1969.

Litin, E.M., et al.: Parental influence in unusual sexual behavior in children. Psychoanal Quart, 25:37, 1956.

Lombroso, C.: Crime, Its Causes and Remedies. Boston, Little, 1918.

Lustig, N., et al.: Incest. Arch Gen Psychiat (Chicago), 14:31, 1966.

MacDonald, G.: The Land of the Lama. London, Seeley, 1929.

Macdonald, J.M.: Homicidal Threats. Springfield, Thomas, 1968.

Macdonald, J.M.: Psychiatry and the Criminal. Springfield, Thomas, 1969.

Macdonald, J.M.: The Murderer and His Victim. Springfield, Thomas, 1961.

Malinowski, B.: The Sexual Life of Savages in Northwestern Melanesia. New York, Eugenics, 1929.

Mannheim, H.: Comparative Criminology, vol 1. London, Routledge and Kegan Paul, 1965.

Masters, F.W., and Greaves, D.C.: The quasimodo complex. Brit J Plast Surg, 20:204, 1967.

Masters, W.H., and Johnson, V.E.: Human Sexual Inadequacy. Boston, Little, 1970.

Mayer, L.: Das Verbrechen in Hyhnose. Munich-Berlin, 1937.

McCaldon, R.J.: Rape. Canad J Corr, 9:37, 1967.

McGeorge, J.: Sexual assaults on children. Med Sci Law, 4:245, 1964.

Medlicott, R.W.: Erotic professional indiscretions, actual or assumed, and alleged. Aust New Zeal J Psychiat, 2:17, 1968.

Medlicott, R.W.: Lot and his daughters — parent-child incest in the Bible and mythology. Aust New Zeal J Psychiat, 1:134, 1967.

Medlicott, R.W.: Parent-child incest. Aust New Zeal J Psychiat, 1:180, 1967.

Medlicott, R.W.: Truth in medicine. New Zeal Med J, 56:168, 1957.

Messer, A.A.: The "Pheadra complex." Arch Gen Psychiat, (Chicago), 21:213, 1969.

Michael, J., and Wechsler, H.: Criminal Law and its Administration. New York, Foundation Press, 1940.

Middleton, R.: Brother-sister and father-daughter marriage in ancient Egypt. Amer Sociol Rev, 27:603, 1962.

Milner, A.: African Penal Systems. New York, Praeger, 1969.

Mohr, J.W.: Rape and Attempted Rape. Mimeographed, Toronto Hospital, 1965.

Moses, J.: Psychische Auswinkurgen sexueller Angriffe bei jungen Madchen. Z Kinderforsch, vol 40, 1932. (cited by Burton, L.)

Mueller, G.O.: Legal Regulation of Sexual Conduct. New York, Oceana, 1961.

Negro Year Book, 1952.

Newman, D.J.: Conviction. Boston, Little, 1966.

Orwell, G.: Shooting an Elephant. New York, Harcourt, 1950.

Packer, H.L.: The Limits of the Criminal Sanction. Stanford, 1968.

Palm, R., and Abrahamsen, D.: A Rorschach study of the wives of sex offenders. J Nerv Ment Dis, 119:167, 1954.

Parke, J.R.: Human Sexuality. Philadelphia, Professional, 1908.

Patai, R.: Sex and Family in the Bible and the Middle East. Garden City, Doubleday, 1959.

Perkins, R.M.: Criminal Law. New York, Foundation Press, 1969.

Perr, I.N.: Statutory rape of an insane person. J Forensic Sci, 13:433, 1968.

Ploscowe, M.: Sex and the Law. New York, Prentice-Hall, 1951.

Popella, E.: Uber die forensisch-psychiatrische beurteilung falscher gestandnisse und selbstbezichtigungen. Psychiat Neurol (Basel), 18:391, 1965.

Pospisil, L.: Kapauku Papuan Economy. New Haven, Yale, 1963.

President's Commission on Law Enforcement and Administration of Justice: The Challenge of Crime in a Free Society. Washington, U.S. Government Printing Office, 1967.

Radzinowicz, L.: Sexual Offenses. London, Macmillan, 1957.

Raphling, D.L., et al.: Incest. Arch Gen Psychiat (Chicago), 16:505, 1967.

Rapoport, J.: A case of necrophilia. J Crim Psychopath, 4:277, 1942.

Rasmussen, A.: Die bedeutung sexueller attentate auf kinder unter 14 fahren fur die entwickelung von geisteskrankheiten und charakteranomalien. Acta Psychiat Neurol, 9:351, 1934.

Reichel-Dolmatoff, G.: The Kogi. Bogata, 1949.

Reifen, D.: Protection of children involved in sexual offenses: a new method of investigation in Isreal. J Crim Law, 49:22, 1958.

Reik, T.: The Compulsion to Confess. New York, Farrar, Straus, 1959.

Reinhardt, J.M.: Sex Perversions and Sex Crimes. Springfield, Thomas, 1957.

Riemer, S.: A research note on incest. Amer J Sociol, 45:566, 1939.

Rothchild, E.: Anatomy is destiny. Pediatrics 39:532, 1967.

Rupp, J.C.: Sperm survival and prostatic acid phosphatase activity in victims of sexual assault. J Forensic Sci, 14:177, 1969.

Salisbury, H.E.: The Shook-up Generation. New York, Harper, 1958.

Schafer, S.: The Victim and His Criminal. New York, Random House, 1968.

Schauffler, G.C.: Pediatric Gynecology. Chicago, Year Book, 1958.

Schiff, A.F.: Statistical features of rape. J Forensic Sci, 14:102, 1969.

Schwartz, B.: The effect in Philadelphia of Pennsylvania's increased penalties for rape and attempted rape. J Crim Law, 59:509, 1968.

Scott, P.D.: Definition, classification, prognosis and treatment. In Rosen, I.: The Pathology and Treatment of Sexual Deviation. London, Oxford U. P., 1964.

Segal, H.: A necrophilic phantasy. Int J Psychoanal, 34:98, 1953.

Sellin, T.: The Negro criminal: a statistical note. Ann Amer Acad Polit Soc Sci, 140:52, 1928.

Sharpe, N.: The significance of spermatozoa in victims of sexual offenses. Canad Med Ass J, 89:513, 1963.

Shay, F.: Judge Lynch, His First Hundred Years. New York, Ives Washburn, 1969.

Shupe, L.M.: Alcohol and crime. J Crim Law, 44:661, 1954.

Simpson, K.: A Doctor's Guide to Court. London, Butterworths, 1962.

Simpson, K.: Forensic Medicine. London, Edward Arnold, 1955.

Sloane, P., and Karpinski, E.: Effects of incest on the participants. Amer J Orthopsychiat, 12:666, 1942.

Slovenko, R.: Sexual Behavior and the Law. Springfield, Thomas, 1965.

Smith, S.: Alleged rape. Brit Med J, 2:1454, 1951.

Stekel, W.: Sadism and Masochism, Vol II. New York, Liveright, 1953.

Sturup, G.K.: Treatment of sexual offenders in Hestedvester, Denmark. Acta Psychiat Scand, Suppl. 204, 1968.

Sutherland, D.F.: Medical evidence of rape. Canad Med Ass J, 81:407, 1959.

Sutherland, S., and Scherl, D.J.: Patterns of response among victims of rape. Amer J Orthopsychiat, 40:503, 1970. Copyright, the American Orthopsychiatric Association. Reproduced by permission.

Svalastoga, K.: Rape and social structure. Pacif Sociol Rev, 5:48, 1962.

Svensson, A., *et al.:* Techniques of Crime Scene Investigation. New York, Am. Elsevier, 1965.

Szurek, S.A.: Concerning the sexual disorders of parents and their children. J Nerv Ment Dis, 120:369, 1954.

Thoinot, L., and Weysse, A.M.: Medicolegal Aspects of Moral Offenses. Philadelphia, Davis, 1921.

Thrasher, F.M.: The Gang. Chicago, U. of Chicago, 1936.

Tormes, Y.M.: Child Victims of Incest. Denver, American Humane Ass, no date.

Visotsky, H.M.: In Freedman, A.M., and Kaplan, H.I.: Comprehensive Textbook of Psychiatry. Baltimore, Williams and Wilkins, 1967.

Wagner, M.S.: The Monster of Dusseldorf: The Life and Trial of Peter Kurten. London, Faber and Faber, 1932.

Wahl, C.W.: The psychodynamics of consummated maternal incest. Arch Gen Psychiat (Chicago), 3:188, 1960.

Walker, J.: Reports, with comments, of twenty-one cases of indecent assault and rape upon children. Arch Pediat, 3:269, 1886.

Watsa, M.C.: Rape. Indian J Med Sci, 16:366, 1962.

Weinberg, S.K.: Incest Behavior. New York, Citadel, 1955.

Weiner, I.B.: Father-daughter incest: a clinical report. Psychiat Quart, 36:607, 1962.

Weiner, I.B.: On incest: a survey. Excerpta Criminol, 4:137, 1964.

Wells, N.H.: Sexual offenses as seen by a woman police surgeon. Brit Med J, 2:1404, 1958.

Weiss, J., Rogers, E., Darwin, M.R., Dutton, C.E.: A study of girl sex victims. Psychiat Quart, 29:1, 1955.

Williams, A.H.: Rape-murder. In Slovenko, R. (Ed): Sexual Behavior and the Law. Springfield, Thomas, 1965.

Williams, G.: Rape in children and in young girls. Int Clin, 2:245, 1913.

Wilmer, H.A.: Good guys and bad guys. Federal Probation, vol. 30, September, 1966.

Wolfgang, M.E.: Patterns in Criminal Homicide. Philadelphia, U. of P., 1958.

Wolfgang, M.E.: Race and crime. In Klare, H.J. (Ed.): Changing Concepts of Crime and its Treatment. London, Pergamon, 1966.

Wong, C.L.: Personal communication, 1969.

Wortis, J.: Sex taboos, sex offenders and the law. Amer J Orthopsychiat, 9:554, 1939.

Yablonsky, L.: The Violent Gang. New York, Macmillan, 1962.

Younger, I.: Denver Post, November 16, 1969.

INDEX

331